ISBN 978-1-5278-9108-1
PIBN 10926079

1 MONTH OF
FREE
READING

at

www.ForgottenBooks.com

By purchasing this book you are eligible for one month membership to ForgottenBooks.com, giving you unlimited access to our entire collection of over 1,000,000 titles via our web site and mobile apps.

To claim your free month visit:

www.forgottenbooks.com/free926079

English
Français
Deutsche
Italiano
Español
Português

www.forgottenbooks.com

Mythology Photography **Fiction**
Fishing Christianity **Art** Cooking
Essays Buddhism Freemasonry
Medicine **Biology** Music **Ancient
Egypt** Evolution Carpentry Physics
Dance Geology **Mathematics** Fitness
Shakespeare **Folklore** Yoga Marketing
Confidence Immortality Biographies
Poetry **Psychology** Witchcraft
Electronics Chemistry History **Law**
Accounting **Philosophy** Anthropology
Alchemy Drama Quantum Mechanics
Atheism Sexual Health **Ancient History**
Entrepreneurship Languages Sport
Paleontology Needlework Islam
Metaphysics Investment Archaeology
Parenting Statistics Criminology
Motivational

THE

'FIRST PART

OF

JACOBS AND DÖRING'S

LATIN READER:'

ADAPTED TO

ANDREWS AND STODDARD'S

LATIN GRAMMAR,

AND TO

ANDREWS' FIRST LATIN BOOK

BY

E. A. ANDREWS, LL. D.

SEVENTY-FIRST EDITION.

BOSTON:

PUBLISHED BY CROCKER AND BREWSTER,
NEW YORK: A. S. BARNES & CO.

1868.

10221

PREFACE. *1868 MAIN*

THE Latin Reader, a new edition of which is here presented to the public, was originally prepared by its present editor, as the first of a series of elementary works adapted to the Grammar of Andrews and Stoddard. This series now comprises, in addition to the Grammar above mentioned, Questions on the Grammar, Latin Lessons, The Latin Reader, Latin Exercises, A Key to Latin Exercises, Viri Romæ, Cæsar's Commentaries on the Gallic War, Sallust, and Selections from Ovid. In the present edition, the adaptation of this work to the Grammar, and to its place in the series above enumerated, remains unaltered; but, in addition to its original design, the Reader is now intended to constitute the second part of a less extended series, comprising the editor's First Latin Book, the Latin Reader, and the Viri Romæ. The latter series is designed especially for those who commence the study of Latin at a very early age, and also for such as intend to pursue the same study to a limited extent only, or merely as a part of general education.

The references at the foot of the pages relate to the sections and subordinate divisions of Andrews and Stoddard's Latin Grammar. The references to Andrews' First Latin Book may be found at the close of the volume. The marks of reference in the text refer both to the notes at the foot of the page and to those at the end of the book. In the latter series, indeed, other notes are occasionally added, and their place is denoted by quoting the words of the text to which such notes relate.

The following extracts from the preface to the first edition will sufficiently explain the manner in which the Reader was originally prepared by its present editor.

Three things were found to claim particular attention, in preparing a new edition of this work. The first was the arrangement of the Introductory Lessons, so as best to illustrate the principles of the Grammar, to which they were to be adapted. The second was to furnish such grammatical notes and references as should be necessary, in order to explain the more difficult forms and constructions occurring in the work. The third was the preparation of a vocabulary more perfectly adapted, than those usually found in introductory works, to the purpose for which it was intended.

To accomplish the first purpose, it was found necessary to make a few additions to the original work, with the intention of illustrating more fully the principal rules of Latin construction. That the object of the Introductory Lessons may be better understood, and the place which each lesson occupies in syntax more fully apprehended, each section is prefaced by a series of questions relating to those parts of the Grammar intended to be illustrated.

In the notes appended to this edition, the editor has carried into effect a design, which he had long since formed, of explaining the idioms of the language, in introductory works, by references to the Grammar, rather than by remarks couched in different language from that with which the student is already, in some degree, familiar. He has hoped, by this means, to aid the student in forming a clear, connected, and consistent view of the idiomatic peculiarities of the language, and a habit of referring every difficulty, whether in form or construction, to its appropriate place in the Grammar. It is a matter of common observation, that, to most students, the philological notes usually found in elementary works are in a great degree lost, in consequence of their connection with the grammar not being sufficiently evident. This evil cannot, indeed, be avoided, while the grammar with which the student is furnished does not fully explain the idioms of the language. While referring to the Grammar, the editor has endeavored to keep in view the fundamental principle of education, that the only efficient help which the student can receive, is that which leads him ultimately to exercise his own faculties. While, therefore, the less prominent difficulties are usually explained upon their first occurrence, the student is afterwards, in most cases, left to perceive the additional instances in which the same principle is to be applied. In cases of greater difficulty, however, reference is repeatedly made to the same principle; and this is more particularly the case in regard to idioms which are either imperfectly exhibited, or altogether overlooked, in the grammars heretofore in common use. It is not improbable that, to some teachers, the references may appear too numerous, while, to others, the unexplained difficulties may still seem too formidable for a majority of those for whose use the work is intended. No plan of assistance can be equally well adapted to all students; but the hope is entertained, that a system which sends them back to their Grammar for information, will be liable to as few objections and abuses as any which can be devised.

The preparation of the vocabulary has occasioned more labor than any other part of the Reader; and, in its present form, I trust that it will be found better adapted to its purpose than such vocabularies usually are. The meanings assigned to the words have been selected with careful reference to all the places where those words occur in the Reader. In this part, more than in any other, the former editions of this work were defective, and that in a degree that would scarcely be suspected by one who had not examined them in reference to this subject.

1 *

The participles occurring in the Reader may generally be found in the vocabulary; but in some cases, and especially when regularly formed from verbs of the first conjugation, they have been intentionally omitted, since their formation is as easy as that of any other part of the verb. The definitions of the participles have, in general, been omitted, except in cases in which their meaning cannot be easily inferred from that of their verbs. The formation of the passive voice is seldom given, since its omission can occasion no embarrassment to one who is moderately acquainted with the paradigms of the Grammar. On the other hand, the oblique cases of nouns and pronouns, and the perfect tenses of verbs, when peculiarly irregular, are inserted in their alphabetical order, with a reference to the words from which they are derived. The derivation of words, except when they immediately follow their primitives, is, in general, given in the vocabulary. The quantity of the penult, in all words of more than two syllables, when not determined by general rules, is marked throughout this volume, as well as in the Grammar to which it refers, in the hope that early habits of incorrect pronunciation may, by this means, be in a great measure prevented.

The references, at the foot of the pages, relate to the sections and subdivisions of Andrews and Stoddard's Lat n Grammar.

E. A. ANDREWS.

New Britain, *Sept.*, 1849.

INTRODUCTORY EXERCISES.

SIMPLE SENTENCES.

SUBJECT—NOMINATIVE AND VERB.

WHAT is the rule for the agreement of a verb? Gram. § 209, (b.) Of what does a sentence consist? § 200, 5. What is a simple sentence? § 201, 10. Of what does a proposition consist? § 201, 1. What is the subject of a proposition? § 201, 2. What is the predicate? § 201, 3. What is the grammatical subject? § 202, 2. What is the grammatical predicate? § 203, 2. Define moods. § 143. Define the indicative mood. § 143, 1. Define the active voice. § 141, 1. 1. Give the personal terminations of the active voice. § 147, 3. What is the connecting vowel of a verb? § 150, 5. How does the present tense represent an action? § 145, I. What are the terminations of the active voice, indicative mood, present tense, in each conjugation? § 152.

Ego amo. Tu mones. Rex* regit. Nos audīmus. Vos vidētis. Puĕri* ludunt.

Why are the nominatives *ego, tu, nos,* and *vos,* usually omitted? § 209, R. 1.

Audio. Amas. Aves* volant. Scribĭmus. Vocātis. Reges* regunt.

Voco. Jubes. Musa* canit. Rusticus* arat. Audītis. Puĕri legunt. Crescit arbor.

---

a §§ 28 and 78, 2. *b* §§ 28 and 46. *c* §§ 62 and 74. *d* § 29, 1.

Sperāmus. Praeceptor[a] docet. Labor[b] vincit. Fata[c] vocant. Manus[d] tangunt. Sol lucet.

Tempus[e] fugit. Venit hiems.[f] Mors[f] venit. Latrant canes.[g] Fugiunt nubes.[h]

How does the imperfect tense represent an action? § 145, II What are the terminations of the active voice, indicative mood, imperfect tense, in each conjugation? § 152.

Eram.[i] Ambulābas. Silva[j] stabat. Monebāmus. Dormiebātis. Fulgēbant stellæ.[j]

What does the future tense denote? § 145, III. What are the terminations of the active voice, indicative mood, future tense, in each conjugation? § 152.

Vidēbo. Audies. Deus dabit. Uret ignis.[k] Crescent arbōres.[l] Tempŏra venient.

How does the perfect tense represent an action? § 145, IV. What are the terminations of the active voice, indicative mood, perfect tense? § 152.

Veni, vidi, vici. Fuisti.[i] Fortūna dedit. Cecĭnit avis. Cepĭmus. Audivistis.[m] Hostes[g] fugērunt.

How does the pluperfect tense represent an action? § 145, V. What are the terminations of the active voice, indicative mood, pluperfect tense? § 152.

Fugĕrat umbra. Dixĕras. Hannĭbal juravĕrat.[m] Ceperātis. Puĕri legĕrant.

What does the future perfect tense denote? § 145, VI. What are the terminations of the active voice, indicative mood, future perfect tense? § 152.

---

[a] §§ 28 and 70. [c] §§ 66 and 76, 1. [h] §§ 62 and 73, 1. [k] §§ 63 and 74.
[b] §§ 58 and 70. [f] §§ 62 and 77, 2. [i] § 153. [l] §§ 61 and 70.
[e] § 46. [g] §§ 30 and 74. [j] § 41. [m] § 150, 3.
[d] §§ 87 and 88, 1.

Risĕro. Vidĕris. Venĕrit hora. Pomum cecidĕnt. Ambulaverĭmus. Caneş cucurrĕrint.

Define the subjunctive mood. § 143, 2. What are the terminations of the active voice, subjunctive mood, present tense, in each conjugation? § 152.

Labōret manus. Faveat Fortūna. Sol* fulgeat. Veniat tempus. Canāmus. Capiātis. Arbŏres cadant.

What are the terminations of the active voice, subjunctive mood, imperfect tense, in each conjugation? § 152.

Philomēla cantāret. Pomum pendēret. Luna micāret. Essētis. Vellēmus.* Troja* staret.

What are the terminations of the active voice, subjunctive mood, perfect tense? § 152.

Amavĕrim. Docuĕris. Ocŭlus* vidĕrit. Latravĕrint canes. Arbŏres crevĕrint.

What are the terminations of the active voice, subjunctive mood, pluperfect tense? § 152.

Fuissem.* Potuisses.* Miles pugnavisset. Lepŏres cucurrissent. Canes momordissent.

Define the imperative mood. § 143, 3.

Surge.* Legīto.* Studēte. Disce. Dicīte. Equus currito. Facitōte.* Puĕri scribunto.*

Define the passive voice. § 141, I. 2. What is frequently omitted or left indefinite in the active voice? What in the passive voice? § 141, R. 2. What are the terminations of the passive voice, indicative mood, present tense, in each conjugation? § 152.

---

* §§ 66, E and 70.   * § 29, 2.   * § 153.   * § 267.
* § 178, 1.   * § 46.   * § 154, R. 7.

Amor. Monēris. Vox[a] audītur. Laudāmur. Au-
dimīni. Tempŏra mutantur.

Docēris. Vincĭtur hostis. Flos[b] carpĭtur. Fabŭla[c]
narrātur. Carmina[d] leguntur.

What are the terminations of the passive voice, indicative mood
imperfect tense, in each conjugation ? § 152.

Aqua[e] fundebātur. Oppĭdum[e] defendebātur. Pande-
bantur portæ. Saxa[e] volvebantur. Bella parabantur.

What are the terminations of the passive voice, indicative mood,
future tense, in each conjugation ? § 152.

Domus[f] ædificabĭtur. Narrabuntur fabŭlæ. Epistŏla[e]
mittētur. Culpabimĭni.

What are the terminations of the passive voice, indicative mood,
perfect tense ? — pluperfect tense ? — future perfect tense ? § 152.

Audītus es. Naves mersæ sunt. Datæ sunt leges.[a]
Sparsa erant folia.[e] Hostes victi erant. Missi erĭmus.

What are the terminations of the passive voice, subjunctive
mood, present tense ? — imperfect tense ? — perfect tense ? — pluperfect tense ? § 152.

Præmia dentur. Panis emātur. Premerētur caseus.
Vehĕrer. Tegerētur caput. Victus sit miles. Hostes
capti essent.

What are the terminations of the passive voice, imperative
mood ? § 152.

Laudātor[e] industria. Puniuntor fures.

Oves non ubĭque tondentur. Alĭter psittăcus loquĭtur,
alĭter homo.[h] Ocŭli sæpe mentiuntur.

---

[a] §§ 62 and 78.   [d] §§ 66 and 71.   [g] § 267.
[b] §§ 58 and 75.   [e] § 46.   [h] §§ 31, 1, and 69, E. 2
   § 41.   [f] §§ 88 and 89.

Predicate–Nominative.

What is the rule for the predicate-nominative? § 210.

Eurōpa est *peninsŭla*.
Ossa[a] ejus[b] *lapis* fiunt
Ego *poēta*[c] salūtor.
Inertia est *vitium*.
Homo sum.
Ebriĕtas[d] est *insania*.
Dux[e] electus est Q. Fabius.

Agreement of Adjectives.

What is the rule for the agreement of adjectives? § 205.
What is the logical subject of a proposition? § 202, 3. What is
the logical predicate? § 203, 3.

Fugāces[f] labuntur anni.
Fugit irreparabĭle tempus.
Venit glaciālis hiems.[g]
Silva vetus[h] stabat.
Culpa tua[i] est.
Dira parantur bella.
Nulla[j] mora est.
Brevis est voluptas.[g]
Parvæ res crescunt.
Brevis est via.
Terra est rotunda.
Vera amicitia est sempiterna.

---

[a] §§ 61, and 75, E. 1.   [e] §§ 30 and 78.   [i] § 139.
[b] § 211.   [f] §§ 112 and 78.   [j] § 107.
[c] § 28.   [g] §§ 62 and 77, 2.
[d] §§ 62 and 72.   [h] § 113, 3.

Fames et sitis sunt° molestæ.°

Plurĭmæ° stellæ sunt soles.

Ebriĕtas est vitanda.°

Nemo semper° felix est.

Non° omnes milĭtes° sunt fortes.

Maxĭmum° anĭmal° terrestre est elĕphas.°

Fortes° laudabuntur, ignāvi° vituperabuntur.

Ursi interdum bipĕdes° ingrediuntur.

Aquĭlæ semper solæ prædantur.

Bonus° laudātur, imprŏbus vituperātur.

Omnes moriēmur,° alii° citiùs,° alii seriùs.°

Avārus nunquam erit contentus.

The Accusative after Active Verbs.

What is the rule for the object of an active verb ? § 229

Diem° perdĭdi.

Terra parit *flores.*

Crocodīlus° *ova*° parit.

Elephantus° odit° *murem*° et *suem.*°

Camēli diu *sitim*° tolĕrant.

Accipĭtres° non edunt *corda*° avium.

Lanæ nigræ *nullum*° colōrem bibunt.

Senes° minĭmè° sentiunt *morbos contagiōsos.*

Cervi *cornua sua*° quotannis amittunt.

° § 209, R. 12.	° § 205, R. 7, (1.)	° §§ 67, E. 4, and 76, E. 3
° § 205, R. 2	° § 210. R. 3, (2.)	° §§ 30, and 76, E. 3.
° § 125, 5.	° § 209, R. 1.	° § 79, 2.
° § 274, R. 8.	° § 107.	° §§ 58 and 71, E. 1.
° § 277, I.	° § 194, 2.	° §§ 61 and 71, E. 2.
° § 73.	° § 90, E.	° § 78, 2, (2.)
° §§ 66 and 70.	° § 46.	° § 208.
° §§ 62, E. 1, and 72, E. 2.	° § 183, 3, N. 3.	

Ceres*a* *frumentum* invēnit; Bacchus *vinum;*[b] Mercurius *littĕras.*[b]

Canes soli[c] *domĭnos suos*[d] benĕ[e] novēre,[f] soli *nomĭna*[g]
sua[d] agnoscunt.

Hystrix *acŭleos* longè[e] jaculātur.

Sturni[h] et psittāci *humānas voces*[i] imitantur.

Miltiādes *Athēnas*[j] totamque *Grœciam* liberāvit.

APPOSITION.

What is the rule for words in apposition? § 204.

Plurĭmi[k] Scythæ, *bellicosissĭmi*[l] *homĭnes*, lacte[m] vescuntur.

Delphīnus, *anĭmal*[n] homĭni[o] *amīcum*, cantu[p] gaudet.

Carthāgo[q] atque Corinthus,[q] *opulentissĭmœ*[r] *urbes*,[r] eōdem anno[s] a Romānis[t] eversæ sunt.

Quàm brevi[u] tempŏre[s] popŭli Romāni, omnium gentium[n] *victōris*, libertas fracta est!

Mithridātem, Ponti *regem*, Tigrānes, *rex Armenius*,
excēpit.

GENITIVE AFTER NOUNS.

What is the rule for the genitive after nouns? § 211.

Crescit amor *nummi*.

Honos est præmium[w] *virtūtis*.

---

a § 73, E. 2.	*i* §§ 62 and 78.	*t* § 29, 2.
b § 229, R. 3, 1.	*j* § 96.	*r* §§ 62 and 77.
c § 107.	*k* § 125, 5.	*s* § 253.
d § 205.	*l* § 124.	*t* § 248, 1.
e § 192, II. 1.	*m* § 245, 1.	*u* § 113, 1.
f § 183, 3, N. 3.	*n* §§ 66 and 70.	*v* § 83, II. 3.
g §§ 66 and 71.	*o* § 222, 3.	*w* § 210.
h § 46.	*p* § 247, 1, (2.)	

2

Sol est lux *mundi*.

Semirāmis erat *Nini* uxor.

Infinīta est multitūdo* *morbōrum*.

Litterārum usus est antiquissĭmus.

Asia et Afrĭca greges *ferōrum asinōrum* alit.*

Magna est *linguārum* inter* homĭnes variĕtas.

Canis vestigia *ferārum* diligentissĭmè scrutātur.

Nemo non* benignus est *sui* judex.

Leōnum anĭmi index* cauda.*

GENITIVE AFTER ADJECTIVES.

What is the rule for the genitive after adjectives? § 211. after partitives? § 212.

Semper *fragilitātis humānæ* sis* memor.

Elephanti *frigōris* impatientes sunt.

Stultissĭma* *animalium* sunt lanāta.

Velocissĭmum* *omnium animalium* est delphīnus.

Neque *stultōrum* quisquam* beātus, neque *sapientium* non beātus.

Gallōrum omnium fortissĭmi sunt Belgæ.

DATIVE.

What is the rule for the dative after verbs? § 223. — aftei adjectives? § 222, 3.

Arma* fecit Vulcānus *Achilli*.

Reddĭtur *terræ* corpus.

Oves nobis suam* lanam præbent.

---

a §§ 59, 2, and 69, E. 1.   e § 209, R. 4.   i § 205, R. 12.

b § 209, R. 12, (2.)   f § 260, R. 6.   j § 96.

c § 277, R. 4.   g §§ 66 and 76.   k § 208.

d § 210.   h § 83, II. 1.   l § 235.

Tristitiam et metum*a* tradam *ventis.*

Natūra *animalĭbus* varia tegumenta*b* tribuit, testas, coria, spinas, villos, setas, pennas, squamam.

Homĭni soli*c* avaritia et ambitio*d* data est.*e*

Inter omnes bestias*f* simia *homĭni* simillĭma*g* est.

Leōni*h* vis*i* summa est in pectŏre.

*Antiquissĭmis*j *homĭnĭbus*k specus erant pro domĭbus.*k*

Gallinacei *leonĭbus*l *terrōri*l sunt.

Homo furiōsus ne*m* *libĕris* quidem*m* *suis* parcit.

Grata*n* *mihi* tua epistŏla fuit.

ACCUSATIVE AFTER PREPOSITIONS.

What is a preposition? § 195. What is the rule for the accusative after prepositions? § 235.

Ad *finem* propĕro.

Apud *Romānos* mortui*o* plerùmque cremabantur.

Culĭces*p* acīda*q* petunt; ad *dulcia* non advŏlant.

Nulla habēmus arma contra *mortem.*

Vir*r* generōsus mitis est erga *victos.*o

Germāni habĭtant trans *Rhenum.*

Nulla est firma amicitia inter *malos.*

Camēlus naturāle odium adversùs *equos* gerit.

Pictæ vestes jam apud *Homērum* commemorantur.

Comētæ ob *raritātem* et *speciem* sunt mirabĭles.*n*

Navigatio*d* juxta *litus* sæpe est periculōsa.

---

a § 278.	*f* § 125, 2.	*m* § 279, 3, (*a.*) & (*d.*)
b § 102, III. 4.	*h* § 226.	*n* § 205, N. 1.
c § 107.	*i* § 85.	*o* § 205, R. 7, (1.)
d §§ 59, 1, and 69.	*j* § 124.	*p* § 78, 2, (2.)
e § 209, R. 12, (2.)	*k* § 241.	*q* § 205, R. 7, (2.)
f § 212, R. 2, N. 4.	*l* § 227.	*r* § 48, 2.

Apud *Æthiŏpes* maxīmi elephanti in silvis[a] vagantur.
Hippopotămus segĕtes[b] circa *Nilum* depascĭtur.[c]

IN AND SUB.

What is the rule for *in* and *sub* ? § 235, (2.)

Aquilæ nidificant[c] in *rupĭbus* et *arborĭbus*.[d]

Coccyx semper parit in *aliēnis nidis*.

In *senectūte*[c] hebescunt[f] sensus; visus, audītus debili
tātur.[c]

In *Indiâ* gignuntur maxĭma animalia.

Hyænæ plurĭmæ in *Africâ* gignuntur.

In *Africâ*, nec[g] cervi, nec apri, nec ursi reperiuntur.

In *Syriâ* nigri leōnes reperiuntur.

Circa Cyllēnen,[h] montem in *Arcadiâ*, merŭlæ candĭdæ
nascuntur.

Serus in *cœlum* redeas.[i]

Victi Persæ in *naves* confugērunt.

Numa Pompilius annum in *duodēcim menses* distribuit.

Pontius Thelesinus Romānos sub *jugum* misit.

Gallia sub *septentrionĭbus* posita est.

ABLATIVE AFTER PREPOSITIONS.

What is the rule for the ablative after prepositions ? § 241.

Littēræ a *Phœnicĭbus*[j] inventæ sunt.

Carthāgo, Corinthus, Numantia, et multæ aliæ urbes,
a *Romānis*[j] eversæ sunt.

---

[a] § 235, (2.)	[e] §§ 67, 2, and 76, E. 2.	[i] § 260, R. 6.
[b] §§ 61, 1, and 73.	[f] § 187, II. 2.	[j] § 248, I.
[c] § 145, I. 1.	[g] § 278, R. 7.	
[d] § 278.	[h] § 44.	

Quidam[a] homĭnes nati sunt cum *dentĭbus*.[b]

Xerxes cum *paucissĭmis militĭbus*[c] ex *Græciā* a ıfūgıt.[d]

Metellus primus[e] elephantos ex *primo Punĭco bello* duxit in *triumpho*.

Cantābit vacuus coram *latrōne* viātor.

Sidĕra ab *ortu* ad *occāsum* commeant.

Britannia a *Phœnicĭbus* inventa est.

Apes sĭne *rege* esse[f] non possunt.

Infans[g] nihil[h] sine *aliēnā ope* potest.

Dulce est pro *patriā* mori.[i]

Venēnum aliquando pro *remedio* fuit.

Aqua Trebiæ flumĭnis erat *pectorĭbus* tenus.

• **ABLATIVE WITHOUT A PREPOSITION.**

What is the rule for nouns denoting the *cause, manner,* &c. ? § 247. What is the rule for *utor,* &c.? § 245, I.—for *nitor innitor,* &c.? § 245, II.—for verbs signifying to *abound,* &c.? § 250, 2, (2.)—for a noun denoting the *time* at or within which any thing is said to be or to be done ? § 253.—for a limiting noun denoting a *property, character,* or *quality?* § 211, R. 6.—for the *price* of a thing? § 252.

Apri in morbis sibi[j] medentur *hedĕrā*.

Pyrrhus rex[k] *tactu* pollĭcis in dextro pede[l] lienōsis[j] medebātur.

Oleo insecta exanimantur.

Feræ domantur *fame* atque *verberĭbus*.[m]

Anacreon poēta[k] *acino* uvæ passæ exstinctus est.

---

a § 207, R. 33.   f § 271.   j § 223, R. 2.
b § 64, 1.   g §§ 30 and 77, 2.   k § 279, 9.
c § 249, III.   h § 232, (2.)   l §§ 58, and 73, E. 1.
d § 196, I. 1.   i § 269.   m § 60, 2.
e § 205, R. 15.

Crocodīlus *pelle durissimâ*ᵃ contra omnes ictus n unītur.

In Africâᵇ elephantiᶜ capiuntur *foveis*.

Elephanti spirant, bibunt, odorantur *proboscīde*.

Popūli quidamᵈ *locustis* vescuntur.

Dentes *usu*ᵉ atteruntur, sed *igne*ᶠ non cremantur.

Mures Alpīni *binis pedĭbus* gradiuntur, *prioribus*que ut *manĭbus* utuntur.

Leænæ *jubâ* carent.

Elephanti maxĭmè *amnĭbus* gaudent.ᵍ

Apes *tinnītu* æris gaudent *eō*que convocantur.

Quibusdam in locisᵇ ansĕres bis *anno* velluntur.

Color lusciniārum *autumno* mutātur.

Hiĕme ursi in antris dormiunt.

Nemo mortaliumʰ *omnĭbus horis* sapit.

Primōres dentes *septĭmo mense* gignuntur; *septĭmo* iīdem decīduntⁱ *anno*.

Antipāter Sidonius, poëta, quotannis, *die natāli suo*, *febre* corripiebātur.

Æstāte dies sunt longiōres quàm *hiĕme*.

Reperiuntur interdum cervi *candīdo colōre*.ʲ

Isocrātes orātor unam oratiōnem *viginti talentis* ven-dīdit.

Luscinia candīda, *sex sestertiis* Romæ venit.

Leōnes facīlè per triduum *cibo* carent.

INFINITIVE.

Upon what may the infinitive depend? § 270. After what classes of verbs is the infinitive used without a subject? § 271.

ᵃ § 124.	ᵈ § 207, R. 33.	ᵍ § 142, 2.	ⁱ § 163, E. 1.
ᵇ § 254, R. 3.	ᵉ § 87.	ʰ § 212.	ʲ § 211, R. 6.
ᶜ § 99	ᶠ § 63, 1		

Whose action must an infinitive denote when used after a verb without a subject? § 271, R. 3.

Te cupio *vidēre*.

Volui *dormīre*.

Aude *contemnĕre* opes.

Carmina[a] possŭmus *donāre*.

Potĕram[b] *contingĕre* ramos.

Nihil[c] amplius *scribĕre* possum.

Ego cupio ad te *venīre*.

Intelligĕre non possum.

Cessātor *esse* noli.

Cur timet flavum Tibĕrim *tangĕre?*

Philippus volēbat[d] *amāri*.

Alexander *metui* volēbat.

Tecum[e] *vivĕre* amo.

Natūram *mutāre* pecunia nescit.

Benè *ferre* disce magnam fortūnam.

Angustam pauperiem *pati* puer discat.[f]

Dici beātus[g] ante obĭtum nemo debet.

Æquam memento[h] rebus in arduis *servāre* mentem.

Aurum vestĭbus[i] *intexĕre* invēnit rex Attălus.

Non omnes homĭnes æquo amōre[j] *complecti* possŭmus.

Illecĕbras voluptātis *vitāre* debēmus.

Romæ elephantes per funes *incedĕre* docebantur.[d]

What is the rule for the infinitive *as a subject?* § 269.

Errāre est[k] humānum.[l]

Turpe[l] est[k] beneficium *repetĕre*.

---

[a] §§ 66 and 71.	[e] § 133, 4.	[i] § 224.
[b] § 154, R. 7.	[f] § 260, R. 6.	[j] § 247.
[c] § 94.	[g] § 210, R. 1.	[k] § 209, R. 3, (5.)
[d] § 145, II.	[h] § 183, 3.	[l] § 205, R. 8.

Beneficiis[a] gratiam non *referre* etiam turpius est.

Parentes suos[b] non *amāre* est impium.

GERUNDS AND GERUNDIVES.

By what cases are gerunds followed? § 275, I. What is the rule for the genitive of gerunds and gerundives? § 275, III. R. 1.

Plurīmæ sunt illecĕbræ *peccandi.*

Artem *scribendi* Phœnices, artem acu[e] *pingendi* Phryges[d] invenērunt.

Cupidītas *vivendi* nunquam immensa esse debet.

Honestissīma[e] est contentio beneficiis[e] beneficia *vincendi.*

Homo natūrâ[f] est cupĭdus nova semper *videndi* et *audiendi.*

Libri sunt inutīles ignāro[g] *legendi.*

Inĭtum[h] est consilium urbis *delendæ,*[i] civium *trucidandōrum,* nomĭnis Romāni *exstinguendi.*

What is the rule for the *dative* of gerunds and gerundives? § 275, III. R. 2.

Olim calămus adhibebātur[j] *scribendo.*

Aqua marīna inutĭlis est *bibendo.*

Culex habet telum et[k] *fodiendo* et[k] *sorbendo* idoneum.

What is the rule for the accusative of gerunds and gerundives? § 275, III. R. 3.

Non omnes æqualĭter[l] ad *discendum* proni sumus.

---

[a] § 223.	[e] § 205, N. 1.	[i] § 275, II.
[b] §§ 208 and 269, R. 1.	[f] § 249, II.	[j] § 145, II. 1.
[c] § 247.	[g] § 222, 3.	[k] § 278, R. 7.
[d] § 78.	[h] § 182, R. 3.	[l] § 192 II. 2

Omnes Græciæ civitātes pecuniam ad *ædificandam*[a] classem dedērunt.

What is the rule for the *ablative* of gerunds and gerundives? § 275, III. R. 4.

Funem abrumpes nimiùm[b] *tendendo*.
Docendo discimus.
Mens·alītur *discendo* et *cogitando*.
Lacedæmonii exercēbant[c] juvĕnes, *venando, currendo, esuriendo, sitiendo, algendo, æstuando.*
Simiæ catŭlos sæpe * *complectendo* necant.
Amīcus amīcum semper alīquâ re juvābit, aut re, aut consilio, aut *consolando* certè.*

COMPOUND SENTENCES.

What is a compound sentence? § 201, 12. How may the members of a compound sentence be connected? § 203, III. 3.

CONJUNCTIONS.

What is the rule for copulative and disjunctive conjunctions? § 278.

Sol ruit *et* montes umbrantur.
Vir[d] bonus *et* prudens dici delector ego.
Immensa est, finem*que*[e] potentia Dei non habet.
Accipĕre præstat[f] *quàm* facĕre injuriam.
Rapĕre *atque* abīre semper assuēvit lupus.
Semper honos, nomen*que* tuum, laudes*que* manēbunt.

---

* What does this adverb modify?

[a] § 275 II.   [c] § 145, II. 1.   [e] § 198, II. 1.
[b] § 192 II. 4, *(b.)*   [d] § 210.   [f] § 209, R. 3, (5.)

Sapientem *neque*[a] paupertas, *neque*[a] mors, *neque*[a] vincŭla terrent.

Juno erat Jovis *et* soror *et* conjux.

Nox[b] erat *et* fulgēbat luna.

In prælio cita mors venit, *aut* victoria læta.

Marius *et* Sylla civīle bellum gessērunt.[c]

Leti vis rapuit, rapiet*que* gentes.

Non fonnōsus erat, *sed*[d] erat facundus Ulysses.

Si[e] divitiæ felicitātem præstant, avaritia prima virtus est.

ADVERBS.

Quoties litĕras tuas lego, omnem mihi[f] præteritōrum tempŏrum memoriam in mentem revŏco.

Magna debēmus suscipĕre, *dum* vires suppĕtunt.

Cervi, *quamdiu* cornĭbus carent, noctu ad pabŭla procēdunt.

Quidam crocodīlum,[g] *quamdiu* vivat,[h] crescĕre[i] existĭmant, vivit autem[j] multos annos.[k]

Gloria virtūtem, *tanquam* umbra, sequĭtur.

COMPARISON.

What are the two ways of expressing a comparison by means of the comparative degree? § 256, 1, & 2.

Canes Indĭci[l] grandiōres sunt *quàm* cetĕri.[m]

Nullum malum est vehementius[n] et importunius[n] *quàm* nvidia.[m]

---

[a] § 278, R. 7.	[f] § 211, R. 5, (1.)	[k] § 236.
[b] §§ 62, and 78, 2, & 4.	[g] § 239.	[l] § 128, 1. 2.
[c] § 209, R. 12.	[h] § 266, 1.	[m] § 278.
[d] § 198, 9.	[i] § 272.	[n] § 124.
[e] § 198, 5.	[j] § 279, 3, & (c.)	

Interdum ferārum animos mitiōres^a invenīinus *quàm* hominum.^b

Latro feræ est similior *quàm* homĭni.^c

Major est anĭmi voluptas *quàm* corpŏris.^b

In montĭbus aër^d purior est et tenuior *quàm* in vallĭbus.

What is the rule for the *ablative* after comparatives? § 256.

Nihil est *clementiâ* divinius.

Aurum gravius est *argento*

Adămas durior est *ferro* ; ferrum^e durius ceteris *metallis*

Luna terræ propior est *sole.*

Quid magis est durum *saxo*, quid mol"ius *aquâ?*

RELATIVE PRONOUNS.

What is the rule for the construction of relatives? § 206.

Non omnis ager, *qui* serĭtur, fert^f fruges.^g

Psittăcus, *quem* India mittit, reddit verba, *quæ* accēpit.

Achilles, *cujus* res gestas Homēri carmĭna celĕbrant, ad Hellespontum sepultus est.

Myrmecīdes quidam quadrīgam fecit ex ebŏre,^h *quam* musca alisⁱ integēbat.

Qui bonis^j non rectè utĭtur, ei^k bona mala fiunt.^l

Beneficium reddit, *qui* ejus^m benè memor est.

Gruesⁿ in itinerĭbus ducem, *quem* sequantur,^o elĭgunt

Copias suas Cæsar in proxĭmum collem subduxit, equitatumque, *qui* sustinēret^o hostium impĕtum, misit.

---

^a § 124.	^f § 179.	^b § 206, (3,) (*a.*)
^b § 211, R. 7.	^g § 94.	^l § 180.
^c § 278.	^h § 71, E. 3.	^m § 213.
^d § 5	ⁱ § 247.	ⁿ §§ 67, E. 4, and 76, E. 3.
^e § 209, R. 4.	^j § 245, 1.	^o § 264, 5.

SUBJUNCTIVE MOOD.

What mood does *cùm* take? § 263, 5. What is the rule for *cùm* in narration? § 263, 5, R. 2.

Platea, *cùm* devorātis se *implēvit* conchis,[a] testas evŏmit.

Ceres frumenta[b] invēnit, *cùm* antea homīnes glandĭbus[c] *vescerentur.*

Nave[d] primus[e] in Græciam Danăus advēnit, *cùm* antea ratĭbus[f] *navigarētur.*[g]

Alexander, rex[h] Macedoniæ, *cùm* Thebas *cepisset,* Pindări vatis[h] familiæ[i] pepercit.

What is the general rule for the subjunctive after particles? § 262.

Tanta est in Indiâ ubertas soli, *ut*[j] sub unâ ficu[k] turmæ equĭtum[l] *condantur.*

Ursi per hiĕmem[m] tam gravi somno[a] premuntur, *ut*[j] ne[n] vulnerĭbus quidem[n] *excitentur.*

Delphīni tantâ interdum vi e mari[o] exsiliunt, *ut*[j] vela[p] navium *transvŏlent.*

In Indiâ serpentes ad tantam magnitudĭnem adolescunt, *ut* intĕgros *hauriant* cervos taurosque.

Fac,[q] *ut* homīnes anĭmum tuum pluris[r] *faciant,* quàm omnia, quæ illis[s] *tribuĕre possis.*[t]

---

[a] § 249, I.	[h] § 204.	[o] § 82, E. 1.
[b] § 102, 4.	[i] § 223, R. 2.	[p] § 233.
[c] § 245, I.	[j] § 262, R. 1.	[q] § 162, 4.
[d] §§ 62 and 74.	[k] § 235, (2.)	[r] § 214.
[e] § 205, R. 15.	[l] § 31.	[s] § 223.
[f] § 247.	[m] § 236, R. 5.	[t] § 266, 1.
[g] § 209, R. 3, (2.)	[n] § 279, 3.	

Alexander edixit, *ne* quis ipsum*ᵃ* præter Apellem *pingĕret.ᵇ*

Pythagorēis interdictum fuit, *ne* fabis*ᶜ vescerentur.*

Ocŭli palpĕbris*ᵈ* sunt munīti, *ne* quid *incĭdat.ᵉ*

Nihil ferè*ᶠ* tam recondĭtum est, *quinᵍ* quærendoʰ inveniri *possit.ᵉ*

Nunquam tam manè egredior, neque tam vespĕri domumʲ revertor, *quinᵍ* te in fundo *conspĭcerⁱ* fodĕre,ᵏ aut arāre,ᵏ aut alĭquid facĕre.ᵏ

Xerxes non dubitābat, *quinᵍ* copiis suis Græcos facīlè *superatūrus esset.ˡ*

In what mood is the verb put in dependent clauses containing an indirect question? § 265.

Quæritur, unus *ne sit*ⁱ mundus, an plures.ᵐ

Disputābant vetēres philosŏphi, casu *ne factus sit* mundus, an mente divīnâ.

Augustus cum amīcis suis consultābat, *utrùm* imperium *servāret, an deponĕret.*

Perpĕram quæritur, *num* in amīci gratiam jus violāri *possit.ⁱ*

Ciconiæ *quonam* e loco *veniant,* aut in *quas* se regiōnes *confĕrant,* incompertum est.ⁿ

Quis numerāre potest, *quoties* per totam vitam lacrȳmas *fudĕrit?*

What is the rule for the infinitive with the accusative? § 272.

Aristotēles *tradit,* in Latmo, Cariæ monte, *hospĭtes* a scorpionĭbus° non *lædi, indigĕnas interīmi.*

ᵃ § 207, R. 28.	ᶠ § 277, R. 1.	ᵏ § 272, R. 5.
ᵇ § 258, 2, (2.)	ᵍ § 262, R. 10, 2.	ˡ § 258, 2, (1.)
ᶜ § 245, I.	ʰ § 275, III. R. 4.	ᵐ § 110.
ᵈ §§ 13 and 15.	ⁱ § 258, 1, (1.)	ⁿ § 209, R. 3, (5.)
ᵉ § 258, 1, (2.)	ʲ § 237, R. 4.	° § 248, 1.

3

M. Varro narrat, a cunicŭlis *suffossum*[b] in H.spaniâ *oppĭdum*,[c] a talpis in Thessaliâ ; ab ranis *incŏlas* urbis in Galliâ *pulsos*,[b] ab locustis in Africâ ; ex Gyăro insūlâ *incŏlas* a murĭbus *fugātos*,[b] in Italiâ *Amȳclas*[c] a serpentĭbus *delētas esse*.

Observātum est,[d] *pestilentiam* semper a meridiānis partĭbus ad occidentem *ire*.

Homērus *Pygmæos*, popŭlum ad oceănum, a gruĭbus *infestāri* prodĭdit ; Aristotĕles *eosdem* in cavernis *vivĕre* narrat.

Postĕri aliquando querentur nostrâ culpâ *mores eversos esse*.

Virgilius per testamentum[e] jussĕrat *carmĭna sua cremāri ; id*[f] Augustus *fĭeri* vetuit.

Sertorius cervam alēbat candĭdam, *quam*[c] Hispaniæ gentes *fatidĭcam esse* credēbant.

Illustre est inter philosŏphos nomen Anaxagŏræ,[f] *quem* vetĕres nunquam in vitâ *risisse* ferunt.

PARTICIPLES.

What is the rule for the agreement of participles ? § 205. By what cases are participles followed ? § 274, 1. What is said of the time of the present, perfect, and future active participles ? § 274, 2.

Exempla fortūnæ *variantis* sunt innumĕra.

Galli diem *venientem* cantu[h] nuntiant.

Cecrops urbem[i] a se[a] *condĭtam* appellābat Cecropiam.[f]

---

[a] § 248, I.	[d] § 209, R. 3, (5.)	[g] § 44.
[b] § 270, R. 3.	[e] § 247, R. 4.	[h] § 247.
[c] § 239.	[f] § 206, (13.)	[i] § 230.

Augustus primus[a] Romæ[b] tigrin[c] ostendit *mansue-factam.*

Gymnosophistæ in Indiâ toto die[d] *ferventĭbus* arēnis insistunt, Solem[f] *intuentes.*

Epimenĭdes puer,[e] æstu[h] et itinēre fessus, septem et quinquaginta annos[d] in specu dormivisse dicĭtur.

Julius Cæsar simul dictāre,[i] et *legentem*[j] audīre solēbat Leo *prostrātis*[k] parcit.

Aves aduncos ungues *habentes* carne[l] vescuntur, nec unquam congregantur.

Canis venatĭcus venatōrem *comitantem* loro[h] ad ferārum lustra trahit.

Beneficium non in eo[m] consistit, quod datur, sed in ipso *dantis*[j] anĭmo.

Struthiocamēli Afrĭci altitudĭnem equĭtis equo[e] *insidentis* excēdunt.

Interdum[n] delphīni conspecti sunt, *defunctum* delphīnum *portantes*, et quasi[n] funus *agentes.*

Multa, quæ de infantĭbus ferārum lacte *nutrītis* produntur, fabulōsa videntur.

Homo quidam, lapĭde *ictus*, oblītus est litĕras;[o] alius, ex præalto tecto *lapsus*, matris et affinium nomīna dicĕre non potuit.

L. Siccius Dentātus, centies vicies *præliātus*, quadraginta quinque cicatrīces adverso corpŏre[p] habēbat, nullam in tergo.[p]

---

[a] § 205, R. 15.
[b] § 221. I.
[c] § 80, I., E. 2.
[d] § 236
[e] § 224
§ 229.

[f] § 204.
[h] § 247.
[i] § 271.
[j] § 205, R. 7, (1.)
[k] § 223, R. 2.

[l] § 245, I.
[m] § 205, R. 7, (2.)
[n] § 277.
[o] § 216.
[p] § 254, R. 3.

Leōnes *satiāti* innoxii sunt.

Elephantes nemini [a] nocent, nisi *lacessīti*.

Elephantes amnem [b] *transitūri* [c] minūnos præmittui t.

Pavo *laudātus* [c] *gemmātam* pandit caudam.

Gallus, ab adversario [d] *victus,* [c] occultātur [*] *silens*, et servitium patītur.

Leo *vulnerātus* [c] percussōrem intellīgit, et in quantâlībet multitudīne appĕtit.

Olōres iter *facientes* colla impōnunt *præcedentĭbus;* [c] fessos duces ad terga recipiunt.

Testudĭnes in mari [f] *degentes* conchyliis [g] vivunt; in terram *egressæ*, herbis. [g]

Sarmātæ, longinqua itinĕra *factūri*, inediâ pridie præpărant equos, potum exiguum *impertientes;* atque ita longissĭmam viam continuo cursu conficiunt.

Elephanti, equitātu *circumventi*, infirmos aut fessos *vulnerătos*que in medium agmen recipiunt.

Multos *morientes* cura sepultūræ angit.

Danāus, ex Ægypto in Græciam *advectus*, rex [h] Argivōrum factus est.

Alexander, Bucephălo equo *defv cto*, duxit exequias, urbemque Bucephălon *appellātam* ejus tumŭlo [c] circumdĕdit.

P. Catiēnus Plotīnus patrov im a eò dilexit, ut, heres omnĭbus ejus bonis [j] *institūtus* in roģ am ejus se conjicĕret [k] et concremarētur. [l]

---

[*] *occultātur*, instead of *se c xultat,*' ides himself. § 248, I. R. 1, (2.)

[a] § 223, R. 2.	§ 224	[i] § 224, R. 1.
[b] § 233.	[f] § 87, E. 1.	[j] § 211, R. 5.
[c] § 274, 3.	[g] § 45, II. 4.	[k] § 262.
[d] § 248, I.	[h] § 210.	[l] § 278.

Erinacei *volutāti* super poma, humi*ᵃ* *acentia*, illa spinis*ᵇ* *affixa* in cavas arbōres portant.

Indĭcum mare testudĭnes tantæ magnitudĭnis*ᶜ* alit, ut singŭlæ tugurio *tegendo*ᵈ sufficiant.*ᵉ*

Leōnes, senes *facti*, appĕtunt homĭnes, quoniam ad *persequendas*ᶠ feras vires non suppĕtunt.

Struthiocamēlis*ᵍ* ungŭlæ sunt cervīnis simĭles, *comprehendendis*ᵈ lapidĭbus utĭles, quos in fugâ contra *sequentes*ʰ jaculantur.

ABLATIVE ABSOLUTE.

What is the rule for the ablative absolute ? § 257.

Senescente Lunâ,＊ ostrea tabescĕre dicuntur, *crescente câdem,* gliscunt. Cepe contrà, *Lunâ deficiente,* revirescĕre, *adolescente,* inarescĕre dicĭtur.

Geryŏne＊ *interempto,* Hercŭles in Italiam*ⁱ* venit.

Sabīnis＊ *debellātis,* Tarquinius triumphans Romam*ʲ* rediit.

Jasŏne＊ *Lycio interfecto,* canis, quem habēbat, cibum capĕre noluit, inediâque confectus est.

Regis Lysimăchi canis, *domĭno* accensæ pyræ*ᵇ* *imposĭto,* in flammas se conjēcit.

Nicomēde rege *interfecto,* equus ejus vitam finīvit inediâ.

Chilo, unus e septem sapientĭbus,*ᵏ* *filio victōre*ˡ Olympiæ,*ᵐ* præ gaudio exspirāvit.

＊ What is denoted in this case by the ablative absolute ?

ᵃ § 221, 1, R. 3.	*ᶠ* § 275, II., & III. R. 3.	*ʲ* § 237.
ᵇ § 224.	*ᵍ* § 226.	*ᵏ* § 212, R. 2, N. 4
ᶜ § 211, R. 6.	*ʰ* § 205, R. 7, (1.)	*ˡ* § 257, R. 7, (a.)
ᵈ § 275, II., and III. R. 2.	*ⁱ* § 237, R. 5.	*ᵐ* § 221, 1.
ᵉ § 262		

3＊

Apes, *aculeo amisso*, statim emŏri existimantur. Eæ dem, *rege interfecto* aut morbo *consumpto*, fame [a] luctūque moriuntur.

Pavo, *caudâ amissâ*, pudibundus ac mœrens quærit latĕbram.

Erinacei, ubi sensêre venantem, *contracto ore pedibus-*que, convolvuntur [*] in formam pilæ, ne quid [b] comprehendi possit [c] præter aculeos.

---

[*] *convolvuntur*, for *se convolvunt*, roll themselves. § 248, I. R. 1, (2.)

[a] § 247.　　　[b] § 138.　　　[c] § 262.

FABLES FROM ÆSOP.

---

1. Accipiter et Columbæ.

Columbæ milvii metu * accipItrem rogavērunt, ut eas defenderet.^a Ille annuit. At in ^b columbāre receptus, uno die ^c majōrem stragem edīdit, quàm milvius longo tempŏre ^e potuisset ^d edĕre.

Fabŭla docet, malōrum ^e patrocinium ^f vitandum ^g esse.^h

2. Mus et Milvius.

Milvius laqueis ⁱ irretītus muscŭlum ^j exorāvit, ut eum, corrōsis plagis,^k liberāret.^a Quo ^k facto, milvius liberātus murem arripuit et ^l devorāvit.

Hæc fabŭla ostendit,^m quam gratiam mali ^e pro beneficiis reddĕre ⁿ soleant.^o

3. Hœdus et Lupus.

Hœdus, stans in ^b tecto domûs, lupo ^p prætereunti ^q

---

* Supply *ductæ*. § 247, R. 2, (*b*.)

^a § 262.	ⁱ § 274, R. 8.	^m § 229, R. 5.
^b § 235, (2.)	^h § 272	ⁿ § 271.
^c § 253.	ⁱ § 247.	^o § 265.
^d §§ 154, R. 7, and 260, II.	^j § 231, and R. 3, (*b*.)	^p § 225.
§ 205, R. 7, (1.)	^k § 257, and R. 1.	^q § 182, and R. 3.
^f § 239.	^l § 278.	

maledixit. Cui* lupus, *Non tu*, inquit,[b] *sed tectum mihi maledicit.*[c]

Sæpe locus et tempus homĭnes timĭdos audāces reddit.[d]

4. GRUS ET PAVO.

Pavo, coram grue pennas suas[e] explĭcans, *Quanta est*,[a] inquit,[b] *formosĭtas mea et tua deformĭtas!* At grus evŏlans, *Et quanta est*, inquit, *levĭtas mea et tua tardĭtas!*

Monet hæc fabŭla, ne ob alĭquod bonum, quod[f] nobis[a] natūra tribuit, alios[e] contemnāmus,[h] quibus natūra alia[i] et[j] fortasse majōra dedit.

5. PAVO.

Pavo gravĭter[k] conquerebātur[l] apud Junōnem, domĭnam[m] suam, quòd vocis suavĭtas sibi negāta esset,[n] dum luscinia, avis tam parum decōra, cantu excellat.[o] Cui Juno, *Et merĭtò*, inquit; *non enim*[o] *omnia bona*[i] *in unum conferri oportuit.*[p]

6. ANSĔRES ET GRUES.

In[f] eōdem quondam prato pascebantur[l] ansĕres et grues. Adveniente domĭno[r] prati, grues facīlè avolābant; sed ansĕres, impedīti corpŏris gravitāte,[s] deprehensi et[j] mactāti sunt.

Sic sæpe paupĕres, cum potentioribus in eōdem crimĭne deprehensi, soli dant[t] pœnam, dum illi salvi evādunt.

---

[a] § 223.	[h] § 273, 2.	[o] § 279, 3, (a.) & (c.)
[b] § 279, 6.	[i] § 205, R. 7, (2.)	[p] § 273, 4.
[c] § 209, R. 12, (7.) & (a.)	[j] § 278.	[q] § 235, (2.)
[d] § 209, R. 12, (2.)	[k] § 192, II. 2.	[r] § 257.
[e] § 208.	[l] § 145, II. 1.	[s] § 247.
[f] § 206.	[m] § 204.	[t] § 145, I. 1.
[g] § 205, R. 7, 1.)	[n] § 266, 3.	

7. CAPRA ET LUPUS.

Lupus capram* in altâ rupe stantem conspicātus, *Cur non*, inquit, *relinquis nuda illa et sterilia loca, et huc descendis in herbĭdos campos, qui tibi lætum pabŭlum offĕrunt?* Cui respondit capra: *Mihi* [b] *non est in anĭmo, dulcia* [c] *tutis* [c] *præponĕre.* [d]

8. VENTER ET MEMBRA.

Membra quondam dicēbant ventri: *Nosne* [e] *te semper* [f] *ministerio* [e] *nostro alēmus,* [h] *dum ipse summo otio* [i] *fruēris? Non faciēmus.** Dum igitur ventri [j] cibum subdūcunt, corpus debilitātur, et membra [k] serò invidiæ [l] suæ pœnituit.

9. CANIS ET BOVES.

Canis jacēbat [m] in præsēpi [n] bovesque latrando [o] a pabŭ-lo arcēbat. Cui unus boum,[p] *Quanta ista* [q], inquit, *invidia est, quòd non patĕris, ut eo cibo* [r] *vescāmur,* [s] *quem tu ipse capĕre nec velis* [t] *nec possis!* Hæc fabŭla invidiæ indŏlem declārat.

10. VULPES ET LEO.

Vulpes, quæ nunquam leōnem vidĕrat, quum ei [u] fortè occurrisset,* ita est perterrĭta, ut [w] pæne morerētur [v] formid-

---

* Supply *hoc.*

[a] § 274, 1.
[b] § 226.
[c] § 205, R. 7, (2.)
[d] § 269.
[e] § 279, 3, (a.) & (c.)
[f] § 279, 15, (a.)
[g] § 247.
[h] § 209, R. 1, (a.) & (b.)

[i] § 245, I.
[j] § 224, R. 2.
[k] § 229, R. 6.
[l] § 215, (1.)
[m] § 145, II. 1.
[n] § 82, E. 1.
[o] § 275, II. R. 4.
[p] § 212.

[q] § 207, R. 25.
[r] § 245, I.
[s] § 262.
[t] § 266, 1.
[u] § 224.
[v] § 263, R. 2.
[w] § 262, R. 1.

īne.ᵃ Eundem conspicātaᵇ itĕrum, timuit quidem,ᶜ seᴅ
nequāquam,ᵈ ut antea.* Tertiò illiᵉ obviàm facta, ausaᶠ
est etiam propiùs† accedĕre, eumqueᵍ allōqui.

11. CANCRI.

Cancer dicēbatʰ filio: *Miⁱ fili,ʲ neᵏ sic oblīquis semper
gressĭbusᵐ incēde, sed rectâ viâᵃ perge.* Cui ille, *Mi
pater,* respondit, *libenter tuis præceptisˡ obsĕquar, si te
priùs idem facientem vidĕro.*ᵐ

Docet hæc fabŭla, adolescentiamⁿ nullâ reᵒ magìs,
quàm exemplis°, instrui.ᵖ

12. BOVES.

In eōdem prato pascebanturʰ tres boves in maxĭmâᵠ
concordiâ, et sic ab omniʳ ferārum incursione tuti erant.
Sed dissidio° inter illos orto, singŭli a ferisˢ petīti et laniāti
sunt.

Fabŭla docet, quantum boniᵘ sit° in concordiâ.

13. ASĬNUS.

Asĭnus, pelleᵛ leōnis indūtus, territābat homĭnes et
bestias, tanquam leo esset.ˣ Sed fortè, dum se celeriùsʷ

---

* What do *nequáquam* and *antea* modify?
† What is understood after *propiùs?*

ᵃ § 247.	ʲ § 52.	ʳ § 279, 7, (a.)
ᵇ § 274, 1.	ᵏ § 267, R. 1.	ˢ § 257.
ᶜ § 279, 3, (a.) & (d.)	ˡ § 223, R. 2.	ᵗ § 248, I.
ᵈ § 277.	ᵐ § 145, VI.	ᵘ § 212, R. 3.
ᵉ § 228.	ⁿ § 239.	ᵛ § 265.
ᶠ § 142, 2.	ᵒ § 278.	ʷ § 249, I.
ᵍ § 233.	ᵖ § 272.	ˣ § 263, 2.
ʰ § 145, II. 1.	ᵠ § 125, 5.	ʸ § 256, R. 9, (a.)
ⁱ § 139.		

movet, aures eminēbant; unde agnĭtus in pistrīnum abductus est, ubi pœnas petulantiæ dedit.

Hæc fabŭla stolīdos⁰ notat, qui immerĭtis honorĭbus⁰ superbiunt.

14. Mulier et Gallīna.

Mulier quædam habēbat gallīnam, quæ ei quotidie ovum pariēbat aureum. Hinc suspicāri⁰ cœpit, illam auri massam intus celāre,⁴ et gallīnam occīdit. Sed nihil in eâ repĕrit, nisi quod⁰ in aliis gallīnis reperīri⁰ solet. Itāque dum majorĭbus divitiis⁴ inhiăbat, etiam minōres * perdĭdit.

15. Viatōres et Asĭnus.

Duo⁰ qui unâ iter faciēbant, asĭnum oberrantem in solitudĭne conspicāti, accurrunt læti, et uterque eum sibi vindicāre cœpit, quòd eum prior⁰ conspexisset.ʰ Dum verò contendunt et rixantur, nec⁴ a⁴ verberĭbus abstĭnent, asĭnus aufūgit, et neuter eoᵏ potītur.

16. Corvus et Lupi.

Corvus partem prædæ petēbat a lupis,ˡ quod eos totum diemᵐ comitātus esset.ʰ Cui illi, *Non tu nos,* inquiunt, *sed prædam sectātus es, idque eo anĭmo,⁰ ut ne nostris quidemⁿ corporĭbus⁰ parcĕres,ᵖ si exanimarentur.ᵖ*

---

* With what noun does *minōrcs* agree?

ᵃ § 205, R. 7, (1.)	ᵍ § 205, R. 15.	ˡ § 231, R. 2
ᵇ § 247.	ʰ § 266, 3.	ᵐ § 236.
ᶜ § 271.	ⁱ § 198, II. 1, & (c.)	ⁿ § 279, 3.
ᵈ § 272.	ʲ § 242, and R. 1.	ᵒ § 223, R. 2.
ᵉ § 206, (4.)	ᵏ § 245, 1.	ᵖ § 261, 1.
ᶠ § 224.		

Meritò in actiònĭbus non spectātur, quid fiat,[a] sed quo animo fiat.[a]

17. Pastōres et Lupus.

Pastōres cæsâ ove[b] convivium celebrābant. Quod[c] quum lupus cernēret,[d] *Ego,* inquit, *si agnum rapuissem,[e] quantus tumultus fĭeret !*[e] *At isti[f] impūne ovem comĕdunt !* Tum unus illōrum,[g] *Nos enim,*[h] inquit, *nostrâ, non aliēnâ ove[i] epulāmur*

18. Carbonarius et Fullo.

Carbonarius, qui spatiōsam habēbat domum, invitāvit fullōnem, ut ad se commigrāret.[j]   Ille respondit : *Quænam inter nos esse possit[k] socĭĕtas ? quum tu vestes, quas ego nitĭdas reddidissem,[l] fuligĭne et maculis inquinatūrus esses.*[m]

Hæc fabŭla docet dissimilia[n] non debēre[o] conjungi.[p]

19. Tubīcen.

Tubĭcen ab hostĭbus[q] captus, *Ne[r] me,* inquit, *interficĭte ; nam inermis sum, neque[s] quidquam habeo præter hanc tubam.*   At hostes, *Propter hoc ipsum,* inquiunt,[t] *te interimēmus, quòd, quum ipse pugnandi[u] sis[v] imperītus, alios ad pugnam incitāre soles.*

Fabŭla docet, non solùm malefĭcos[w] esse puniendos,[x] ꞏd etiam eos,[x] qui alios ad malè faciendum[y] irrītent.[l]

---

[a] § 265.	[j] § 273, 2.	[r] § 267, R. I.
[b] § 257.	[k] § 260, II. R. 5.	[s] § 198, 1, & (a.)
[c] § 206, (13.)	[l] § 266, 1.	[t] § 279, 6.
[·] § 263, 5.	[m] § 260, II. R. 7, (2.)	[u] § 275, III. R. 1.
[·] § 261, 1.	[n] § 205, R. 7, (2.)	[v] § 205, R. 7, (1.)
[·] § 207, R. 25.	[o] § 272.	[w] § 274, R. 8.
[·] § 212.	[p] § 271.	[x] § 278.
[·] § 198, 7, & (a.)	[q] § 248, 1.	[y] § 275, III., R. 3.
[·] § 245, II. 4.		

20. Accipĭtres et Columbæ.

Accïpĭtres quondam acerrĭmè inter se belligerābant Hos columbæ in gratiam reducēre[a] conātæ effecērunt,[b] ut lli pacem inter se[c] facĕrent. Quâ[d] firmātâ, accipĭtres vim suam in ipsas columbas convertērunt.

Hæc fabŭla docet, potentiōrum discordias[e] imbecilliorĭbus[f] sæpe prodesse.

21. Mulier et Gallīna.

Mulier vidua gallīnam habēbat, quæ ei quotidie unum ovum pariēbat. Illa existimābat,* si gallīnam diligentiùs sagināret,[g] fore,[h] ut illa bina[i] aut terna ova quotidie parĕret. Quum autem cibo superfluo gallīna pinguis esset[j] facta, planè ova parĕre[a] desiit.[k]

Hæc fabŭla docet, avaritiam sæpe damnōsam[k] esse.

22. Vulpes et Uva.

Vulpes uvam in vite conspicāta ad illam subsiliit omnium virium suārum contentiōne,[l] si eam fortè attingĕre posset.[k] Tandem defatigāta ināni labōre discēdens dixit: *At nunc etiam acerbæ sunt, nec[m] eas in viâ repertas[n] tollĕrem.[o]*

Hæc fabŭla docet, multos ea contemnĕre, quæ se[p] assĕqui posse despērent.

---

* What is the object of *existimābat?* § 229, R. 5.

[a] § 271. [g] § 260. [m] § 278, R. 4.
[b] § 273, 1, (b.) [h] § 268, R. 4, (b.) [n] § 274, 3, (a.)
[c] § 208. [i] § 119, III [o] § 261.
[d] § 257. [j] § 263, 5, & R. 2. [p] § 271, R. 3.
[e] § 239 [k] § 205, N. 1, & 2. [q] § 162, 7.
  § 224. [l] § 247.

4

23. Vulpes et Leæna.

Vulpes leænæ exprobrābat, quòd nonnīsi unum catŭlum parĕret.[a] Huic dicitur respondisse, *Unum, sed leōnem.*

Hæc fabŭla, non copiam sed bonitātem rerum æstiman dam[b] esse, docet.

24. Mures.

Mures aliquando habuērunt consilium, quomŏdo sibi[c] a fele cavērent.[d] Multis aliis[e] positis, omnĭbus[f] placuit, ut ei[g] tintinnabŭlum annecterētur; sic enim ipsos[h] sonĭtu admonĭtos eam fugĕre posse.[i] Sed quum jam inter mures quærerētur,[j] qui feli[k] tintinnabŭlum annectĕret,[d] nemo repertus est.

Fabŭla docet, in suadendo[k] plurĭmos esse audāces,[l] sed in ipso pericŭlo timĭdos.[m]

25. Canis mordax.

Cani[f] mordāci paterfamilias jussit tintinnabŭlum ex ære appendi,[n] ut omnes eum cavēre possent.[o] Ille verò æris tinnītu[p] gaudēbat, et, quasi[q] virtūtis suæ præmium[r] esset,[*] alios canes præ se contemnĕre cœpit. Cui unus senior, *O te*[s] *stolĭdum,* inquit, *qui ignorāre* [t] *vidēris, isto tinnītu pravitātem morum tuōrum indicāri!* [u]

---

[*] What is the subject-nominative of *esset?*

[a] § 266, 3.	[h] § 208, (4.)	[o] § 262.
[b] § 274, R. 8.	[i] § 270, R. 2.	[p] § 247, 1, (2.)
[c] § 223.	[j] § 263, 5, R. 2.	[q] § 263, 2.
[d] § 265.	[k] § 275, III. R. 4.	[r] § 210.
[e] § 205, R. 7, (2.)	[l] § 205, N. 1.	[s] § 238, 2.
[f] § 223, R. 2.	[m] § 278.	[t] § 271.
[g] § 224.	[n] § 273, 2.	[u] § 272.

Hæc fabŭla scripta est in[a] eos, qui sibi[b] insignibus flagi
tiōrum suōrum placent.

26. CANIS ET LUPUS.

Lupus canem videns benè saginātum,. *Quanta est,*
inquit, *fèlicĭtas tua! Tu, ut vidētur, lautè vivis, at ego
fame enĕcor.* Tum canis, *Licet,* inquit, *mecum[c] in urbem
venias,[d] et eâdem felicitāt̬e[e] fruāris.* Lupus conditiōnem
accēpit. Dum unà eunt, animadvertit lupus in collo canis
attritos[f] pilos. *Quid hoc est?*[*] inquit.[†] *Num jugum
sustĭnes? cervix enim tua tota est glabra.* Nihil est,
canis respondit. *Sed interdiu me alligant, ut noctu sim
vigilantior; atque hæc sunt vestigia collāris, quod cervici[g]
circumdāri solet.* Tum lupus, *Vale,* inquit, *amĭce![h]
nihil[i] moror felicitātem servitūte emptam!*

Hæc fabŭla docet, libĕris[j] nullum commŏdum tanti[k]
esse, quod servitūtis calamitātem compensāre possit.[l]

27. LUPUS ET GRUS.

In faucĭbus lupi os inhæsĕrat. Mercēde igĭtur condūcit
gruem, qui illud extrăhat.[m] Hoc[n] grus longitudĭne colli
facĭlè effēcit. Quum autem mercēdem postulāret, subrīdens lupus et dentĭbus infrendens, *Num tibi,* inquit, *parva
merces[o] vidētur,[‡] quòd caput incolŭme ex lupi faucĭbus
extraxisti?*

---

[*] What is the predicate-nominative of *est?*
[†] What is the object of *inquit?*
[‡] What is the subject of *vidētur?* § 202, III. R. 3.

[a] § 235, (2.)	[f] § 270, R. 3.	[k] § 214.
[b] § 223, R. 2.	[g] § 224, R. 1.	[l] § 264, 1.
[c] § 133, 4.	[h] § 240.	[m] § 264, 5.
[d] § 262, R. 4.	[i] § 214, R. 2, N. 2.	[n] § 206, (13.) (a.)
[e] § 245, I.	[j] § 211, R. 5.	[o] § 210.

28. Agricŏla et Anguis.

Agricŏla anguem repĕrit frigŏre pæne extinctum.   Misericordiâ* motus eum fovit sinu,[b] et subter alas[c] recondĭdit.
Mox anguis recreātus vires[d] recēpit, `et agricŏlæ[e] pro
benefĭcio letāle vulnus inflixit.

Hæc fabŭla docet, qualem mercēdem mali pro beneficiis
reddĕre soleant.[f] .

29. Asĭnus et Equus.

Asĭnus equum beātum[g] prædicābat, qui tam copiōsè
pascerētur,[h] quum sibi post molestissĭmos labōres ne
paleæ quidem satis præberentur.[i]   Fortè autem bello[k]
exorto equus in prœlium agĭtur, et circumventus[l] ab
hostĭbus, post incredibĭles labōres tandem, multis vulnerĭbus confossus, collabĭtur.   Hæc omnia asĭnus conspicātus,
O me stolĭdum, inquit, *qui beatitudĭnem ex[m] præsentis
tempŏris fortūnâ æstimavĕrim!*[k]

30. Agricŏla et Filii.

Agricŏla senex, quum mortem sibi[k] appropinquāre
sentīret, filios convocāvit, quos, ut fiĕri solet,[n] interdum
discordāre[o] novĕrat, et fascem virgulārum afferri[o] jubet.
Quibus* allātis, filios hortātur, ut hunc fascem frangĕreut.[p]
Quod[q] quum facĕre non possent, distribuit singŭlas virgas,

---

* What is here denoted by the ablative absolute? § 257.

[a] § 247, R. 2, (*b.*)	[g] § 230	[m] § 195, R. 2.
[b] § 254, R. 2.	[h] § 264, 8, (1.)	[n] § 209, R. 3, (6.)
[c] § 235, (4.)	[i] § 279, 3.	[o] § 272.
[d] § 85.	[j] § 263, 5.	[p] § 273, 2
[e] § 224.	[k] § 257.	[q] § 206, (13.)
[f] § 265.	[l] §§ 248, 1., and 274, 1.	

iisque celerĭter fractis, docuit * illos, quàm firma res † esset concordia, quàmque imbecillis discordia.

31. Equus et Asĭnus.

Asĭnus onustus sarcĭnis equum rogāvit, ut aliquâ parte[a] onĕris se[c] levāret,[d] si se[c] vivum vidēre vellet.[e] Sed ille asĭni preces repudiāvit. Paulò pòst igĭtur asĭnus labōre consumptus in viâ corruit, et efflāvit anĭmam. Tum agitātor omnes sarcĭnas, quas asĭnus portavĕrat, atque insŭper etiam pellem asĭno[f] detractam in equum imposuit. Ibi ille serò priōrem superbiam deplōrans, *O me[g] misĕrum,* inquit, *qui parvŭlum onus in me recipĕre noluĕrim,[h] quum nunc cogar tantas sarcĭnas ferre, unà cum pelle comĭtis mei, cujus preces tam superbè contempsĕram.*

32. Mulier et Ancillæ.

Mulier vidua, quæ texendo[i] vitam sustentābat, solēbat ancillas suas de nocte excitāre ad opus, quum primùm galli cantum audivisset. At illæ diuturno labōre fatigātæ statuērunt gallum interficĕre.[j] ˙Quo[k] facto, deteriōre condĭtiōne[l] quàm priùs‡ esse coepērunt. Nam domĭna, de horâ noctis incerta,[m] nunc famŭlas sæpe jam primâ nocte excitābat.

---

* What is the accusative of the "thing" after *docuit?* § 231, R. 3, (b.)
† What is the subject-nominative of *esset ?*
‡ Supply *fuĕrant*

[a] § 251	[f] § 224, R. 2.	[j] § 271, and R. 3.
[b] § 265.	[g] § 238, 2.	[k] § 206, (13.) (a.)
[c] § 208, (1.)	[h] § 264, 8, (1.)	[l] § 211, R. 6, (3.)
[d] § 273, 2.	[i] § 275, III. R. 4.	[m] § 213, R. 4, and (4.)
[e] § 265, 1.		

33. Testūdo et Aquīla.

Testudo aquĭlam magnopĕre orābat, ut sese[a] volāre docēret.[b] Aquĭla ei ostendēbat quidem, eam[c] rem[d] petĕre natūræ[e] suæ contrariam; sed illa nihĭlo[f] minùs instābat, et obsecrābat aquĭlam,[g] ut se[h] volŭcrem facĕre vellet.[i] Ităque ungŭlis arreptam[*] aquĭla sustŭlit in sublīme, et demīsit illam, ut per aërem ferrētur. Tum in saxa incĭdens comminūta interiit.

Hæc fabŭla docet, multos cupiditatĭbus suis[j] occœcātos consilia prudentiōrum respuĕre, et in exitium ruĕre stultitiâ[k] suâ.

34. Luscinia et Accipĭter.

Accipĭter esuriens rapuit lusciniam. Quæ, quum intelligĕret sibi[l] mortem[c] impendēre, ad preces conversa orat accipĭtrem,[g] *ne se perdat sine causâ. Se enim*[m] *avidissimum ventrem illĭus non posse*[n] *explēre, et suadēre adeò, ut grandiōres alĭquas volŭcres venētur.*[i] Cui accipĭter, *Insanĭrem,*[o] inquit, *si partam prædam amittĕre, et incerta*[p] *pro certis*[p] *sectāri vellem.*[o]

35. Senex et Mors.

Senex in silvâ ligna cecidĕrat,[q] iisque[r] sublātis domum

---

[*] With what does *arreptam* agree?

[a] §§ 133, R. 2, and 208, (1.)	[h] § 208, (1.)	[n] § 270, R. 2, (b.)
[b] § 209, R. 2, (1,) (b.)	[i] § 273, 2.	[o] § 261, 1.
[c] § 239.	[j] § 208.	[p] § 205, R. 7, (2.)
[d] § 229.	[k] § 247.	[q] § 145, V.
[e] § 222, 3.	[l] § 224.	[r] § 257.
[f] § 256, R. 16.	[m] § 198, 7.	[s] § 237, R. 4.
[g] § 231. R. 3, (b.)		

redīre cœpit. Quum aliquantum*a* viæ*b* progressus esset, et*c* onĕre et viâ defatigātus fascem deposuit, et secum*d* ætātis et inopiæ mala*e* contemplātus Mortem clarâ voce invocāvit, quæ ipsum ab omnĭbus his malis*f* libeı āret.*g* Tum Mors senis precĭbus audītis*h* subĭtò adstĭtit,* et, quid vellet,*i* percunctātur.*j* At Senex, quem*j* jam votōrum*k* suōrum pœnitēbat,*l* *Nihil,*† inquit, *sed requīro, qui*ᵐ *onus paulŭlùm allēvet,*ᵉ *dum ego rursus subeo.* ‡

36. Inimīci.

In eâdem navi vehebantur duo,* qui inter se*o* capitalia odia exercēbant. Unus eōrum*p* in prorâ, alter in puppi residēbat. Ortâ tempestāte ingenti, quum omnes de vitâ desperārent, interrŏgat ‖ is, qui in puppi sedēbat, gubernatōrem, *Utram partem navis*ᵖ *priùs submersum iri existimā-ret.*ⁱ Cui gubernātor, *Proram,*¶ respondit. Tum ille, *Jam mors mihi non molesta est, quum inimĭci mei n.ortem adspectūrus sim.*ʳ

37. Hinnuleus et Cervus.

Hinnuleus quondam patrem suum his verbis interro gâsse*ᵉ* dicĭtur: *Mi*ᵗ *pater, quum multo*ᵘ *sis major canĭbus*ᵛ

---

* Supply *seni.*   † Supply *volo.*   ‡ Supply *id.*

‖ What is the accusative of the " thing " after *interrŏgat?* § 231, R. 3

¶ To what does *prora* correspond ? § 204, R. 11.

a § 236.	*i* § 265.	*p* § 212.
b § 212, R. 3.	*j* § 229, R. 6.	*q* § 258, R. 1, (*a.*)
c § 278, R. 7.	*k* § 215, (1.)	*r* § 260, R. 7, (2.)
d § 133, R. 4	*l* § 209, R. 3, (4.)	*s* § 162, 7.
e § 274, 1.	*m* § 206, (4.)	*t* § 139.
f § 251, R. 1	*n* § 205, R. 7, (1.)	*u* § 256, R. 16.
g § 264, 5.	*o* § 235, R. 2.	*v* § 256.
h § 257.		

et tam ardua cornua habeas,[a] *quibus a te vim ꝓropulsāre possis,*[b] *quî fit,*[*] *ut canes tantopĕre metuas?* Ibi cervus ridens, *Mi nate,* inquit, *vera memŏras; mihi*[c] *tamen, nescio quo pacto, semper accĭdit,*[*] *ut audītâ canum*[d] *voce, in fugam statim convertar.*

Hæc fabŭla docet, natūrâ[e] formidolōsos nullis rationĭbus fortes[f] reddi posse.

38. Hœdus et Lupus.

Quum hœdus evasisset lupum, et confugisset in caulam ovium,[g] *Quid*[h] *tu, stulte,* inquit ille,† *hìc te salvum futū rum*[i] *speras, ubi quotidie pecŭdes rapi et diis mactārı videas?*[j]   *Non curo,* inquit hœdus; *nam si moriendum*[k] *sit, quanto*[l] *præclarius*[m] *mihi*[n] *erit, meo cruōre aspergi aras*[o] *deōrum immortalium, quàm irrigāri siccas lupi fauces.*

Hæc fabŭla docet, bonos mortem, quæ[p] omnĭbus[q] i.omĭnet, non timēre,[r] si cum honestāte et laude conjuncta sit.[s]

39. Corvus et Vulpes.

Corvus alicunde caseum rapuĕrat, et cum illo in altam arbŏrem subvolârat.[t] Vulpecŭla illum caseum appĕtens corvum blandis verbis adorĭtur; quumque primùm fonnam

---

[a] § 278.	[h] § 231, R. 5, (a.)	[o] § 239.
[b] § 266, 1.	[i] § 270, R. 3.	[p] § 206.
[c] § 223.	[j] § 266, 1.	[q] § 224.
[d] § 83, II. 2, E.	[k] § 225, III., R. 1.	[r] § 272.
[e] § 249, II.	[l] § 256, R. 16.	[s] § 260.
[f] § 210, R. 1.	[m] § 205, R. 8.	[t] § 162, 7.
[g] § 83, II. 2.	[n] § 222, 3.	

ejus[a] pennarumque nitōrem laudâsset, *Poi*, inquit, *te avium*[b] *regem esse dicĕrem,*[c] *si cantus pulchritudĭni*[d] *tuæ respondĕret.*[e] Tum ille laudĭbus vulpis inflātus etiam cantu se valēre demonstrāre voluit. Ita verò[e] e rostro aperto caseus delapsus est, quem vulpes arreptum devorāvit.

Hæc fabŭla docet, vitandas[f] esse adulatōrum voces, qui blanditiis suis nobis[g] insidiantur.

40. Leo.

Societātem junxĕrant leo, juvenca, capra, ovis. Prædâ[h] autem, quam cepĕrant, in quatuor partes æquāles divīsâ, leo, *Prima*, ait, *mea est;* debētur* enim hæc præstantiæ meæ. Tollam et secundam, quam merētur robur meum. Tertiam vindĭcat sibi*[i] *egregius labor meus. Quartam qui sibi arrogāre voluĕrit,*[j] *is*[k] *sciat,*[l] *se habitūrum*[m] *me inimīcum sibi.*[n] Quid facĕrent[o] imbecilles bestiæ, aut quæ † sibi leōnem infestum habēre vellet?[o]

41. Mus et Rustĭcus.

Mus a rustĭco[p] in[q] caricārum acervo deprehensus tam acri morsu ejus digĭtos vulnerāvit, ut[r] ille eum dimittĕret, dicens: *Nihil, mehercŭle, tam pusillum est, quod de salūte desperāre debeat,*[s] *modò*[t] *se defendĕre et vim depulsāre velit.*

* What is the subject of this verb?
† Supply *bestia*.

[a] § 208, (6.) (*a.*)
[b] § 83, II. 2.
[c] § 261, 1.
[d] § 223.
[e] § 279, 3, (*a.*) & (*c.*)
[f] § 274, R. 8.
[g] § 224
[h] § 257.
[i] § 208.
[j] § 266, 1.
[k] § 206, (3,) (*a.*)
[l] § 260, R. 6.
[m] § 270, R. 3.
[n] § 222, 3.
[o] § 260.
[p] § 248, I.
[q] § 279, 10.
[r] § 262, R. 1
[s] § 264, 1.
[t] § 263, 2.

42. Vultur et Avicŭlæ.

Vultur aliquando avicŭlas invitāvit[a] ad convivium, q. od illis datūrus esset[b] die[c] natāli suo. Quæ quum ad tempus adessent, eas carpĕre et occidĕre, epulasque sibi de invitātis instruĕre cœpit.

43. Ranæ.

Ranæ lætabantur, quum nuntiātum esset Solem uxōrem duxisse.[d] Sed una cetēris[e] prudentior, *O vos[f] stolĭdos*, inquit; *nonne meministis,[g] quantopĕre nos sæpe unīus Solis æstus excruciet?[h] Quid igĭtur fiet, quum libĕros etiam procreavĕrit?[i]*

44. Ranæ et Jupĭter.

Ranæ aliquando regem sibi a Jove[j] petivisse dicuntur. Quarum ille precĭbus exorātus trabem ingentem in lacum dejēcit. Ranæ sonĭtu perterrĭtæ primùm refugĕre,[k] deinde verò trabem in aquâ natantem conspicātæ magno cum contemptu[l] in eâ consedērunt, aliumque sibi novis clamorĭbus regem expetivērunt. Tum Jupĭter eārum stultitiam punitūrus[m] hydrum illis misit, a quo[n] quum plurĭmæ captæ perirent, serò eas stolidārum precum pœnituit.

45. Lupi et Pastōres.

Quum Philippus, rex Macedoniæ, cum Atheniensibus fœdus initūrus esset eâ conditiōne,[o] ut oratōres suos

---

[a] § 145, IV.	[f] § 238, 2.	[k] § 209, R. 5.
[b] § 266, 3.	[g] § 183, 3, N 3.	[l] § 247, 2.
[c] § 253.	[h] § 265.	[m] § 274, R. 6.
[d] § 272.	[i] § 145, VI.	[n] § 248, I.
[e] § 256.	[j] § 85.	[o] § 249 II.

ipsi[a] traderent, Demosthenes populo narravit fabulam, quâ iis[b] callidum regis consilium ante oculos poneret.[c] Dixit enim lupos quondam cum pastoribus pactos esse,[d] se nunquam in posterum[e] greges esse impugnaturos, si canes ipsis dederentur. Placuisse stultis pastoribus conditionem; sed quum lupi caulas excubiis[f] nudatas vidissent, eos[g] impetu facto[h] omnem gregem dilaniâsse.

46. PUER MENDAX.

Puer oves pascens crebrò per lusum magnis clamoribus opem rusticorum imploraverat, lupos gregem suum aggressos esse fingens. Sæpe autem frustratus eos, qui auxilium[i] laturi[j] advenerant, tandem lupo reverâ irruente, multis cum lacrymis[k] vicinos orare coepit, *ut sibi*[l] *et gregi*[m] *subvenirent.* At illi eum pariter ut antea ludere[n] existimantes[o] preces ejus et lacrymas neglexerunt, ita ut lupus liberè in oves grassaretur, plurimasque earum[p] dilaniaret.

47. CORVUS.

Corvus, qui caseum fortè[q] repererat, gaudium altâ voce[r] significavit. Quo[s] sono[t] allecti plures corvi famelici advolaverunt,* impetûque in illum facto, opimam ei[t] dapem eripuerunt.

---

* Supply *ad eum.*

[a] § 223.	[h] § 257.	[o] § 274, 2.
[b] § 211, R. 5, (1.)	[i] § 274, 1.	[p] § 212.
[c] § 264, 5.	[j] § 274, 6.	[q] § 192, l. 3.
[d] § 272	[k] § 247, 2.	[r] § 247.
[e] § 205, R. 7, (1.)	[l] § 208, (1.)	[s] § 206, (17.)
[f] § 251.	[m] § 224.	[t] § 224, R. 2.
[g] § 278.	[n] § 268.	

48. CORNIX ET COLUMBA.

Cornix Columbæ gratulabātur^a fœcunditātem, quòd
isngūlis mensĭbus pullos excludĕret.^b   At illa, *Ne mei*,
inquit, *dolōris causam commemŏres.*^c   *Nam quos^d pullos
edūco, eos domĭnus raptos aut ipse comĕdit, aut aliis
comedendos^e vendit.   Ita mihi mea fœcundĭtas novum
semper luctum parit.*

49. LEO, ASĬNUS, ET VULPES.

Vulpes, asĭnus, et leo venātum^f ivĕrant.^g   Amplâ
prædâ factâ, leo asĭnum illam partīri jubet.^h   Qui quum
sĭngūlis singŭlas partes ponĕret æquāles, leo eum correptum
dilaniāvit, et vulpecŭlæ partiendiⁱ negotium tribuit.   Illa
astutior leōni^j partem maxĭmam apposuit, sibi vix minĭ-
mam reservans particŭlam.   Tum leo subrīdens ejus
prudentiam laudāre, et unde hoc didicĕrit^k interrogāre,
cœpit.   Et vulpes, *Hujus me,* inquit, *calamĭtas docuit,*[*]
quid minōres potentiorĭbus debeant.^l

50. MUSCÆ.

Effūsa mellis copia est : Muscæ advŏlant : †
Pascuntur.   At mox impedītis crurĭbus
Revolāre^l nequeunt.^m   *Heu misĕram,* inquiunt, *vĭcem !*ⁿ

---

* What is the accusative of the " thing " after *docuit ?*
† Supply *ad mel.*

^a § 223, and (1.)	^f § 276, II.	^k § 265.
^b § 266, 3.	^g § 209, R. 12.	^l § 271.
^c § 260, R. 6.	^h § 273, 2.	^m § 182,R.3,N
^d § 206, (3.)	ⁱ § 275, III., R. 1.	ⁿ § 238, 2.
^e § 274, R. 7, (a.)	^j § 224.	

Cibus iste blandus, qui pellexit suavĭter,
Nunc fraudulentus quàm crudelĭter necat!
Perſida voluptas fabŭlâ hac depingĭtur.

51. Cancer.

Mare cancer olĭm deseruit, in litŏre
Pascendi* cupĭdus.   Vulpes hunc simul adspĭcit
Jejūna, simul accurrit,* et prædam capit.
Næ, dixit ille, *jure plector, qui, salo*[b]
Quum fuĕrim natus, voluĕrim[c] solo ingrĕdi!
    Suus unicuique[d] præfinĭtus est locus,
Quem præterire sine perĭclo non licet.[e]

52. Culex et Taurus.

In cornu tauri parvŭlus quondam culex
Consēdit; seque[f] dixit, mole sĭ suâ
Eum[g] gravāret, avolatūrum[h] illīco.
At ille:[i] *Nec te considentem sensĕram.*

53. De Vitiis Homĭnum.

Peras imposuit Jupĭter nobis duas:
Propriis replētam † vitiis post tergum dedit,
Aliēnis ante pectus suspendit gravem.†
    Hac re vidēre nostra mala non possŭmus;
Alii simul delinquunt, censōres sumus.

---

* Supply *ad eum*.   † Supply *peram*.

* § 275, III., R. 1.   [d] § 279, 14.   [f] § 208, (6,) (*a*.)
[b] § 254, R. 3.   [c] § 273, 4, (*a*.)   [h] § 270, R. 3.
[e] § 264 5, (1.)   [f] § 272   [i] § 229, R. 3.

MYTHOLOGY.

1. CADMUS, Agenŏris filius,[a] quòd dracōnem, Martis filium, fontis cujusdam in Bœotiâ custōdem,[b] occidĕrat, omnem suam prolem interemptam vidit, et ipse cum Harmoniâ,[b] uxōre suâ, in Illyriam fugit, ubi ambo[c] in dracōnes conversi sunt.

2. Amÿcus, Neptūni filius, rex Bebryciæ, omnes, qui in ejus regna venissent,[c] cogēbat cæstĭbus secum contendĕre, et victos occidēbat. Hic quum Argonautas ad certāmen provocâsset,[d] Pollux cum eo contendit, et eum interfēcit.

3. Otos et Ephialtes, Aloëi filii,[e] mirâ magnitudĭne[f] fuisse[g] dicuntur. Nam singŭlis mensĭbus[h] novem digĭtis[i] crescēbant. Itāque quum essent[g] annōrum novem,[f] in cœlum ascendĕre sunt conāti. Huc sibi adĭtum sic faciēbant,[j] ut montem Ossam super Pelion ponĕrent, aliosque præterea montes exstruĕrent. Sed Apollīnis sagĭttis inter empti sunt.

4. Dædălus, Euphēmi filius, artĭfex peritissĭmus, ob

---

[a] § 204.	[e] § 204, R. 5.	[i] § 236.
[b] § 249, III.	[f] § 211, R. 6.	[j] § 145, II.
[c] § 264, 12.	[g] § 211, R. 8, (2.)	[k] § 205, R. 2, (1.)
[d] § 263, 5, R. 2.	[h] § 253.	

cædem Athēnis[a] commissam in Cretam[b] abiit ad regem
Minōëm. Ibi labyrinthum exstruxit. A Minōë[c] aliquando
in custodiam conjectus, sibi et Icāro filio alas cerâ[d] aptāvit,
et cum eo[e] avolāvit. Dum Icărus altiùs[f] evolābat, cerâ
solis calōre calefactâ, in mare decīdit, quod ex eo Icarium
pelăgus[g] est appellātum. Dædălus autem in Siciliam
pervēnit.

5. Æsculapius, Apollĭnis filius, medĭcus præstantissĭ-
mus, Hippolȳto, Thesei filio, vitam reddidisse dicitur. Ob
id facĭnus Jupĭter eum fulmĭne percussit. Tum Apollo,
quòd filii mortem in Jove ulcisci non potěrat, Cyclōpes,
qui fulmĭna fecěrant, interēmit. Ob hoc factum, Apollĭnem Jupĭter Admēto, regi Thessaliæ, in servitūtem
dedit.

6. Alcestim,[h] Peliæ filiam, quum multi in matrimonium
petěrent, Pelias promisit, se[i] filiam ei esse datūrum, qui
feras currui junxisset.[j] Admētus, qui eam perditè amā-
bat, Apollĭnem rogāvit, ut se in hoc negotio adjuvăret.
Is quum ab Admēto, dum ei[k] serviěbat, liberalĭter esset
tractātus, aprum ei et leōnem currui junxit,[l] quibus ille
Alcestim avexit. Idem gravi morbo implicĭtus, munus ab
Apolline accēpit, ut præsens pericŭlum effugěret, si quis
sponte pro eo morerētur.[m] Jam quum neque pater, neque
mater Admēti pro eo mori voluissent,[n] uxor se Alcestis
morti obtŭlit, quam Hercŭles fortè adveniens Orci manĭbus[o] eripuit et Admēto reddīdit.

7. Cassiŏpe filiæ suæ Andromēdæ formam Nereïdum

---

[a] § 254.	[f] § 256, R. 9, & (a.)	[k] § 223, R. 2.
[b] § 237, R. 5.	[g] § 210.	[l] § 227.
[c] § 248, I.	[h] § 80, 1., E. 2.	[m] § 260, II.
[d] § 247.	[i] § 266. 2.	[n] § 209, R. 12.
[e] § 249, III.	[j] § 266, 2, R. 4.	[o] § 224, R. 2.

formæ anteposuit.* Ob hoc crimen illæ a Neptūno*
postulavērunt,* ut Andromĕda ceto immāni, qui oras
populabātur, objicerētur.* Quæ quum ad saxum alligāta
esset, Perseus ex Libyâ, ubi Medūsam occidĕrat, advolāvit,
et, belluâ* devictâ et interemptâ, Andromĕdam liberāvit.

8. Quam quum abducĕre vellet victor, Agēnor, cui
antea desponsāta fuĕrat, Perseo insidias struxit, ut eum
interficĕret, sponsamque eripĕret. Ille, re* cognītâ, caput
Medūsæ insidiantĭbus ostendit, quo viso,† omnes in saxa
mutāti sunt. Perseus autem cum Andromĕdâ* in patriam
rediit.

9. Ceyx, Hespĕri filius, quum in naufragio periisset,
Alcyŏne, conjŭgis morte audītâ, se in mare præcipitāvit.
Tum deōrum misericordiâ ambo in aves sunt mutāti, quæ
Alcyŏnes appellantur. Hæ aves pariunt hiberno tempŏre.
Per illos dies* mare tranquillum esse dicītur; unde nautæ
tranquillos et serēnos dies Alcyonēos appellāre solent.

10. Tantălus, Jovis filius, tam carus fuit diis,* ut
Jupiter ei consilia sua concredĕret,* eumque ad epūlas
deōrum admittĕret. At ille, quæ* apud Jovem audivĕrat,
cum mortalĭbus communicābat. Ob id crimen dicītur*
apud infĕros in aquâ collocātus esse, semperque sitīre.
Nam, quoties haustum aquæ sumptūrus* est, aqua recēdit.
Tum etiam poma ei* super caput pendent; sed, quoties
ea decerpĕre conātur, rami vento moti recēdunt. Alii

---

* What is the accusative of the "thing"? § 231, R 3, (b.)

† What does this ablative absolute denote? § 257.

* § 224.   f § 249, III.   j § 206, (4.)
b § 231, R. 2.   g § 236, R. 5.   k § 271, R. 2.
c § 273, 2·   h § 53.   l § 274, R. 6.
d § 257.   i §·145, I:. 1.   m § 211, R. 5, (1.)
e § 257, R. 5.

saxum ejus capīti° ünpendēre dicunt, cujus rùinam timens perpetuo metu cruciātur.

11. In nuptiis Pelei et Thetĭdis omnes dii invitāti erant præter Discordiam. Hæc irâ commōta malum misit in medium, cui° inscripta erant verba: *Pulcherrïma me habēto.* Tum Juno, Venus et Minerva illud simul appetēbant; magnâque inter eas discordiâ exortâ, Jupĭter Mercurio° impĕrat, ut deas ad Parĭdem, Priǎmi filium, ducĕret,° qui in monte Idâ greges pascēbat; hunc eārum litem diremptūrum esse.° Huic° Juno, si se pulcherrĭmam judicâsset,° omnium terrārum regnum est pollicita; Minerva ei splendĭdam inter homĭnes famam promīsit; Venus autem° Helĕnam,° Ledæ et Jovis filiam, se° ei in conjugium dare° spopondit. Paris, hoc dono° priorĭbus° anteposĭto, Venĕrem pulcherrĭmam esse judicāvit. Postea Venĕris hortātu Lacedæmŏnem° profectus, Helĕnam conjŭgi° suo° Menelāo eripuit. Hinc bellum Trojānum origĭnem cepit, ad quod tota ferè Græcia, duce° Agamemnŏne, Menelāi fratre, profecta est.

12. Thetis, Pelei conjux, quum sciret Achillem filium suum citò peritūrum esse, si Græcōrum exercĭtum ad Trojam sequerētur,° eum misit in insŭlam Scyron, regĭque Lycomēdi commendāvit. Ille eum muliĕbri habĭtu° inter filias suas servābat. Græci autem quum audivissent eum ïbi occultāri,° unus eōrum° Ulysses, rex Ithācæ, in regio° vestibŭlo munĕra femĭnea° in calathiscis posuit, simulque

---

° § 224.	° § 229.	° § 257, R. 7.
° § 223, R. 2.	° § 239.	° § 247.
° § 273, 2.	° § 272.	° § 268.
° § 270, R. 2, (*a.*) & (*b.*)	° § 257.	° § 212.
° § 223.	° § 237.	° § 211, R. 4, (*a.*)
° § 266, 2, R. 4.	° § 224, R. 2.	° § 260. II.
° § 279, 3, (*a.*) & (*c.*)	° § 208, (7.)	

5 *

clypeum et hastam, mulieresque advocāri jussit.[a] Quæ dum omnia contemplabantur, subĭtò tubĭcen cecĭnit; quo sono audīto, Achilles arma arripuit. Unde eum[b] virum[c] esse intellectum est.

13. Quum totus[c] Græcōrum exercĭtus Aulĭde[c] convenisset, adversa tempestas eos ob iram Diānæ retinēbat. Agamemnon enim,[f] dux illĭus expeditiōnis, cervam deæ[c] sacram[d] vulneravĕrat, superbiùsque[b] in Diānam locūtus erat. Is quum haruspĭces convocâsset, respondērunt,[i] iram[j] deæ expiāri[k] non posse, nisi filiam suam Iphigeniam ei immolâsset. Hanc ob causam Ulysses Argos profectus mentītur Agamemnōnem filiam Achilli in matrimonium promisisse. Sic eam Aulĭdem[l] abduxit. Ubi quum pater eam immolāre vellet, Diāna virgĭnem miserāta cervam ei[m] supposuit. Iphigenĭam ipsam per nubes in terram Taurĭcam detŭlit, ibĭque templi sui sacerdōtem[n] fecit.

14. Trojâ eversâ, quum Græci domum[c] redīre vellent, ex Achillis tumŭlo vox dicītur fuisse audīta, quæ Græcos monēbat, ne fortissĭmum virum sine honōre relinquērent.[p] Quare Græci Polyxĕnam, Priămi filiam, quæ virgo fuit formosissĭma, ad sepulcrum ejus immolavērunt.

15. Promētheus, Iapĕti filius, primus[q] homĭnes ex luto finxit, iisque[m] ignem e cœlo in ferŭlâ attŭlit, monstravitque quomŏdo cinĕre obrŭtum servārent.[r] Ob hanc rem Vulcānus eum in monte Caucăso Jovĭs jussu clavis ferreis

---

[a] § 273, 2.	[f] § 222, 3.	[m] § 224.
[b] § 269.	[h] § 256, R. 9, & (a.)	[n] § 230.
[c] § 210.	[i] § 209, R. 2, (1,) (b.) .	[o] § 237, R. 4.
[d] § 279, 7, (a.)	[j] § 266, 2.	[p] § 262.
[e] § 254.	[k] § 271.	[q] § 205, R. 15.
[f] § 279, 3 (a.) & (o.)	[l] § 237.	[r] § 265.

alligāvit ad saxum, et aquĭlam ei* appŏsuit, quæ cor
exedĕret.[b] Quantum verò interdiu exedĕrat, tantum nocte
crescēbat. Hanc aquĭlam insequenti tempŏre Hercŭles
transfixit sagittis, Prometheumque liberāvit.

16. Pluto, inferōrum deus, a Jove fratre petēbat,[c] ut
sibi Proserpĭnam, Jovis et Cerĕris filiam, in matrimonium
daret. Jupĭter negāvit quidem Cerĕrem[d] passūram esse,
ut filia in tenĕbris Tartări morarētur;[e] sed fratri permisit,
ut eam, si posset, rupĕret.[f] Quare Proserpĭnam, in nemŏre
Ennæ in Siciliâ flores legentem, Pluto quadrigis ex terræ
biātu provēniens rapuit.

17. Ceres quum nesciret ubi filia esset,[g] eam per
totum orbem terrārum quæsivit. In quo itinĕre ad
Celeum venit, regem Eleusiniōrum, cujus uxor Metanīra
puĕrum Triptolēmum peperĕrat, rogavitque ut se tanquam
nutrīcem in domum recipĕrent.[f] Quo facto, quum Ceres
alumnum suum immortālem reddĕre vellet, eum interdiu
lacte · divīno alēbat, noctu clam igne obruēbat. Ităque
mirum in modum crescēbat. Quod quum mirarentur
parentes, eam observavērunt. Qui quum vidērent Cerĕrem puĕrum in ignem mittĕre,[h] pater exclamāvit. Tum
dea Celeum exanimāvit; Triptolēmo autem currum dra-
conĭbus[i] junctum tribuit, frugesque mandāvit, quas per
orbem terrārum vectus dissemināret.[b]

18. Althæa, Thestii filia, ex Œneo pepĕrit Meleāgrum.
Ei Parcæ ardentem titiōnem dedērunt, præfantes[j] Meleāgrum tam diu victūrum,[k] quàm diu is titio foret[l] incolŭmis

---

[a] § 224.	[c] § 273, 4.	[g] § 223.
[b] § 264, 5.	[f] § 265.	[j] § 274, 2.
[d] § 145, II, 1.	[e] § 273, 2.	[h] § 270, R. 3.
[c] § 239.	[k] § 272. R. 5.	[l] § 266, 2.

Hunc* ităque Althæa diligenter in arcâ clausum servāvit. Intĕrim Diāna Œneo*ᵃ irāta quia ei sacra annua non fecĕrat, aprum mirâ magnitudĭne *ᵇ misit, qui agrum Calydonium vastāret.*ᶜ Quem Meleăger cum juvenĭbus *ᵈ ex omni Græciâ delectis interfĕcit, pellemque ejus Atalantæ donāvit. Cui*ᵉ quum Althææ fratres eam eripĕre vellent, illa Meleăgri auxilium implorāvit, qui avuncŭlos occĭdit. Tum Althæa, gravi irâ*ᶠ in filium commōta, titiōnem illum*ᵍ fatālem in ignem conjēcit. Sic Meleăger periit. At sorōres ejus, dum fratrem insolabilĭter lugent, in aves mutātæ sunt.

19. Eurōpam, Agenŏris filiam, Sidoniam, Jupĭter in taurum mutātus Sidōne*ʰ Cretam transvexit, et ex eâ procreāvit Minōëm, Sarpedŏnem, et Rhadamanthum. Hanc ut reducĕrent Agēnor filios suos misit, conditiōne addĭtâ, ut nec ipsi redīrent,† nisi sorōrem invenissent.*ⁱ Horum unus, Cadmus nomĭne,*ʲ quum errāret, Delphos*ᵏ venit, ibĭque responsum accēpit, bovem præcedentem sequerētur ;*ˡ ubi ille decubuisset,*ⁱ ibi urbem condĕret. ‡ Quod quum facĕret,*ᵐ in Bœotiam venit. Ibi aquam*ⁿ quærens ad fontem Castalium dracōnem invēnit, Martis filium, qui aquam custodiēbat.*ᵐ Hunc Cadmus interfēcit, dentesque ejus sparsit et arāvit. Unde Sparti enāti sunt. Pugnâ inter illos exortâ, quinque superfuērunt, ex quibus quinque nobĭles Thebanōrum stirpes origĭnem duxērunt.

---

* Supply *titiōnem.*

† On what proposition does this subjunctive depend ?   § 257, R. 1.

‡ Connected to *sequerētur* by *et* understood.   § 278, R. 6.

ᵃ § 222, 3.	ᶠ § 247, R. 2.	ᵏ § 237.
ᵇ § 211, R. 6.	ᵍ § 207, R. 24.	ˡ § 262, R. 4.
ᶜ § 264, 5.	ʰ § 255.	ᵐ § 145, II.
ᵈ § 249, III.	ⁱ § 266, 1.	ⁿ § 274, 1.
ᵉ § 224, R. 2.	ʲ § 250.	

20. Quum Bacchus, Jovis ex Semĕle filius, exercĭtum in Indiam ducĕret, Silēnus ab agmīnę aberrāvit. Quem*
Mĭdas, rex Mygdoniæ, hospitio[b] liberalĭter accēpit, eīque ducem dedĭt, qui eum ad Bacchum reducĕret.* Ob hoc beneficium Bacchus Midæ optiōnem dedit, ut quicquid vellet[c] a se petĕret.* Ille petiit, ut quidquid tetigisset[c] aurum fiĕret.[d] Quod quum impetrâsset,* quidquid tetigĕrat aurum fiēbat. Primò gavīsus est hâc virtūte[e] suâ; mox intellexit nihil[f] ipsi hoc munēre[g] perniciosius esse. Nam etiam cibus et potio in aurum mutabātur.[h] Quum jam fame cruciarētur, petit a Baccho, ut donum suum revocāret.[i] Quem[j] Bacchus jussit in flumīne Pactōlo se abluĕre, quumque aquam tetigisset, facta[k] est colōre[l] aureo.

21. Schœneus Atalantam filiam formosissĭmam dicĭtur habuisse, quæ cursu viros superāl·at.[m] Hæc quum a plurĭbus[n] in conjugium peterētur, pater ejus conditiōnem proposuit, ut, qui eam ducĕre vellet,[e] priùs cursu cum eâ contendĕret;[d] si victus esset,[e] occiderētur.[d] Multos quum superâsset et interfecisset, tandem ab Hippomĕne victa est. Hic enim a Venĕre tria mala aurea accepĕrat. Dum currēbant, horum unum post altĕrum projēcit, iisque[b] Atalantæ cursum tardāvit. Nam dum mala collĭgit, Hippomēnes ad metam pervēnit. Huic ităque Schœneus filiam uxōrem dedit. Quam quum in patriam ducĕret, oblītus Venĕris beneficio se vicisse,[o] grates ei non egit. Hanc

---

* Why is this verb in the subjunctive?

<table>
<tr><td>[a] § 206, (17.)</td><td>[f] § 272.</td><td>[k] § 209, R. 2, (1,) (b.)</td></tr>
<tr><td>[b] § 247.</td><td>[g] § 256, 2.</td><td>[l] § 211, R. 6.</td></tr>
<tr><td>[c] § 266, 1.</td><td>[h] § 209, R. 12, (2.)</td><td>[m] § 145, II. 1.</td></tr>
<tr><td>[d] § 262.</td><td>[i] § 258, I. 2, R. 1.</td><td>[n] § 248, I.</td></tr>
<tr><td>[e] § 247, 1, (2.)</td><td>[j] § 273, 2.</td><td>[o] § 268, 2.</td></tr>
</table>

ob[a] causam Hippomĕnes mutātus est in leōnem, Atalanta in leænam.

22. Nisus, rex Megarensium, in capĭte crinem purpureum habuisse dicītur, eīque prædictum[b] fuit, tam diu eum regnatūrum,[c] quàm diu eum crinem custodisset.[d] Hunc Minos, rex Cretensium, bello[e] aggressus est. Qui quum urbem Megăram oppugnāret, Scylla, Nisi filia, amōre ejus correpta est, et, ut ei victoriam parāret,[f] patri[g] dormienti fatālem crinem præcidit. Ita Nisus a Minōë victus et occīsus est. Quum autem Minos in Cretam redīret,[h] Scylla eum rogāvit, ut eam secum avehĕret.[i] Sed ille negāvit Cretam tantum scelus[*] esse receptūram. Tum illa se in mare præcipĭtat, navemque persequĭtur. Nisus in aquĭlam marīnam conversus est, Scylla in piscem, quem Cirim vocant.[j] Hodiēque, siquando illa avis hunc piscem conspexĕrit,[j] mittit se in aquam, raptumque unguĭbus dilaniat.

23. Amphĭon, Jovis et Antiŏpes filius, qui Thebas muris cinxit, Niŏben, Tantăli filiam, in matrimonium duxit. Ex quâ procreāvit filios septem totidemque filias. Quem partum Niŏbe Latōnæ libĕris anteposuit, superbiùsque[k] locūta est in Apollĭnem et Diānam. Ob id Apollo filios ejus venantes sagittis interfēcit, Diāna autem filias.[l] Niŏbe libĕris[m] orbāta in saxum mutāta esse dicĭtur, ejusque lacrÿmæ hodiēque manāre narrantur Amphĭon autem, quum templum Apollĭnis expugnāre vellet, ab Apollĭne sagittis est interfectus.

---

* The crime for the criminal. § 324, 2.

[a] § 279, 10, (a.)	[f] § 258, 2.	[j] § 260.
[b] § 205, R. 8, (a.)	[g] § 224.	[k] § 256, R. 9, & (a.)
[c] § 270, R. 3.	[h] § 145, II. 4.	[l] § 229, R. 3, 1.
[d] § 266, 1.	[i] § 230.	[m] § 251.
[e] § 247.		

24. Phineus,ᵃ Agenŏris filius, ab Apollĭne futurārumᵇ rerum scientiam accepĕrat. Quum verò hominĭbus deōrum consilia enuntiāret,* Jupĭter eum excæcāvit, et immisit eiᶜ Harpyias,ᵈ quæ Jovis canes esse dicuntur, ut cibum ab ore eiᶜ auferrent. Ad quem quum Argonautæ venissent, ut eum iterᶠ rogārent,ᵍ dixit seʰ illis iter demonstratūrum esse,ⁱ si eum pœnâʲ liberārent. Tum Zetes et Calaïs, Aquilōnis filii, qui pennas in capĭte et in pedĭbus habuisseⁱ dicuntur, Harpyias fugavērunt in insŭlas Strophădas, et Phineum pœnâʲ liberârunt.

---

* What does this imperfect tense denote?

ᵃ § 293, N.	ᵉ § 224, R. 2.	ʰ § 266, 2.
ᵇ § 162, 19.	ᶠ § 231.	ⁱ § 268, 2.
ᶜ § 224.	ᵍ § 258, 2, and (3.)	ʲ § 251.
ᵈ § 9, 1.		

ANECDOTES OF EMINENT PERSONS

1. THALES interrogātus* an facta homĭnum deos° latē 'rent,ᵇ respondit, neᶜ cogitāta † quidem.

2. Solon, qui Atheniensĭbus leges scripsit, dicēbat nemĭnem,ᵈ dum vivĕret,ᵉ beātum habēri posse, quòd omnes ad ultĭmum usque diem ancipĭti fortūnæ obnoxii essent.ⁱ

3. Pythagŏræ philosŏphi tanta fuit apud discipŭlos suos auctorĭtas, ut, quæ ab eo audivissent,ᶠ ea in dubitatiōnem adducĕre non audērent. Rogāti autemᵉ ut causam reddĕrentᵉ eōrum, quæ dixissent,ᶠ respondēbant, *Ipsum dixisse.*ʰ *Ipse* autem erat *Pythagŏras.*

4. Bias unus ex septem Sapientĭbus,ⁱ quum patriam Priēnen ab hostĭbus expugnātam et eversam fugĕret, . interrogātus, cur nihil ex bonisⁱ suis secum ferret,ᵇ *Ego verò,*ᶜ respondit, *bona mea mecum porto omnia.*

5. Democrĭtus, cui pater ingentes divitias reliquĕrat, omne ferè patrimoniumʲ suum civĭbus donāvit, neʰ

---

* What is the accusative after *interrogātus?* § 234, 1.
† Supply *latent.*

ᵃ § 232, (2.)   ᵉ § 266, 2.   ⁱ § 212, R. 2, N. 4.
ᵇ § 265.   ᶠ § 266, 1.   ʲ § 100, 6.
ᶜ § 279, 3, & (d.)   ᵍ § 273, 2.   ʰ § 262.
ᵈ § 239.   ʰ § 268, 2.   ⁱ § 266, 3.

domesticārum rerum curâ a philosophiæ studio avoca-rētur.

6. Etiam Crates Thebānus bona sua inter Thebānos divīsit, nihil sibi servans præter peram et bacŭlum. Hæc enim Cynicōrum instrumenta erant. A quo consilio quum amīci et propinqui eum avocāre studērent, eos correpto bacŭlo° fugāvit, nihil pulchrius esse arbitrātus, quàm ab omnĭbus curis° vacuum * uni philosophiæ opĕram dare.°

7. Anaxagŏras, quum a longinquâ peregrinatiōne scientiæ° augendæ causâ susceptâ in patriam rediisset, agros-que suos neglectos et desertos vidēret, *Non essem,*° inquit, , *salvus, nisi ista° periissent.*°

8. Carneādes usque ad extrēmam senectam nunquam cessāvit a philosophiæ studio. Sæpe ei accīdit,† ut, quum cibi° capiendi causâ accubuisset, cogitationĭbus° inhærens manum ad cibos appositos porrigĕre obliviscerētur.°

9. Idem adversùs Zenōnem Stoĭcum scriptūrus caput hellebŏro purgābat,° ne corrupti humōres sollertiam et acū-men mentis impedīrent.°

10. Anaxagŏras philosŏphus, morte° filii audītâ, vultu nihil ° immutāto dixit : *Sciēbam me mortālem genuisse.*

11. Archȳtas Tarentīnus, quum ab itinĕre reversus agros suos villīci socordiâ neglectos vidēret, *Gravĭter te castigārem,*° inquit, *nisi irātus essem.*°

12. Plato quoque, quum in servum vehementiùs ‡ exar-

---

* Supply *homĭnem* or *se.* § 269, R. 1.
† What is the subject of *accīdit?*
‡ What peculiar meaning has this comparative ? § 256, R. 9, (*a.*)

° § 257.	° § 261, 1.	° § 145, II. 1.
° § 213, R. 4, (4)	° § 207, R. 25.	° § 262.
° § 278·	° § 224.	° § 234. II.
° § 275, III., R. I.	° § 262, R. 3.	

6

sisset, verĭtus ne* vindictæ modum excedĕret, Speus ppu*
adstantı mandāvit, ut de illlus pœnâ statuĕret.*

13. Idem discendi* cupiditāte* ductus Ægyptum pera-
grāvit, et a sacerdotĭbus illlus regiōnis geometriam et as-
tronomiam didīcit. Idem in Italiam trajēcit, ut ibi Py-
thagōræ philosophiam et institūta discĕret.

14. Athenienses Socrătem damnavērunt, quòd novos
deos introducĕre videbātur. Protagŏram quoque* philosŏphum, qui ausus* fuĕrat scribĕre, se ignorāre an dii essent,*
Athenienses ex urbe pepulērunt.

15. Xanthippe, Socrătis uxor, morōsa admŏdùm fuisse
fertur. Quam ejus indŏlem quum perspexisset Alcibiādes,
Socrătem interrogāvit, quid esset,* quòd muliĕrem tam
acerbam et jurgiōsam non exigĕret* domo.* Tum ille,
Quoniam, inquit, *dum illam domi* perpetior, insuesco, ut
ceterōrum quoque foris petulantiam et injurias faciliùs
feram.*

16. Xenocrătes philosŏphus, quum maledicōrum quorundam sermōni* interesset, neque quidquam ipse loque-
rētur,* interrogātus, cur solus tacēret,* respondit: *Quia
dixisse* me* aliquando pœnituit, tacuisse* nunquam.*

17. Hegesias philosŏphus in disputationĭbus suis mala
et cruciātus vitæ tam vivĭdis colorĭbus repræsentābat, ut
multi, qui eum audivĕrant,* sponte se occidĕrent. Quare
a Ptolemæo* rege ulterius his de rebus disserĕre est prohibĭtus.

---

* § 262, R. 7.   ƒ § 142, 2.   ᵐ § 278.
ᵇ § 223, R. 2.   ʰ § 265.   ⁿ § 215, and R
* § 273, 2.   ⁱ § 264, 7, N. 3.   ° § 229, R. 6.
ᵈ § 275, III., R. 1.   ʲ § 255, R. 1.   ᵖ § 145, V.
* § 247, R. 2, (*b.*)   ᵏ § 221, R. 3.   ⁱ § 248. I.
ƒ § 279, 3, & (*d.*)   ˡ § 224.

18. Gorgiæ Leontīno,[a] qui eloquentiâ[b] et eruditiǐne omnes[c] suæ ætātis homīnes superāre existimabātur, universa Græcia in templo Apollīnis Delphǐci statuam auream collocāvit.

19. Idem, quum annum centesǐmum septǐmum agěret, interrogātus, quapropter tam diu vellet[d] in vitâ remanēre, respondit: *Quia nihil habeo, quod senectūtem meam accūsem.*[e]

20. Illustrissǐmi sæpe viri humǐli loco[f] nati fuērunt. Socrātes, quem oracǔlum Apollīnis sapientissǐmum omnium homīnum[g] judicāvit, obstetrǐcis filius fuit. Euripīdes, poëta tragǐcus, matrem habuit, quæ olěra venditābat; et Demosthěnis, oratōris eloquentissǐmi,·patrem cultellos ven didisse[h] narrant.

21. Homērus, princeps poëtārum Græcōrum, dolōre absumptus esse credǐtur, quòd quæstiōnem a piscatorǐbus ipsi propositam solvěre non posset.[i]

22. Simonīdes, poëta præstantissǐmus, gloriātur in quodam poëmǎte, se[j] octoginta annos[k] natum in certāmen musǐcum descendisse et vǐctoriam inde retulisse. Idem aliquandiu vixit apud Hǐpparchum, Pisistrāti filium, Athenārum tyrannum. Inde Syracūsas se contǔlit ad Hierōnem regem, cum quo familiarǐter vixisse dicǐtur. Primus[l] carmǐna statūto pretio[m] scripsit; quare eum Musam venālem reddidisse dicunt.

23. Quum Æschȳlus Atheniensis, qui parens[n] tragœdiæ dicǐtur, in Siciliâ versarētur, ibǐque in loco aprǐco

[a] § 223	[f] § 246.	[k] § 236.
[b] § 250.	[g] § 212.	[l] § 205, R. 15.
[c] § 279, 7, (a.)	[h] § 279, 11.	[m] § 252.
[d] § 265	[i] § 266, 3.	[n] § 210.
[e] § 264 7, N. 3.	[j] § 272.	

sedēret, aquīla testudīnem glabro ejus capīti" immīsit quod pro saxo habuit. Quo ictu ille exstinctus est.

24. Euripīdes, qui et ipse magnum inter poëtas tragicos nomen habet, a cœnâ domum rediens a canībus lacerātus est.

25 Athenienses quondam ab Euripīde postulābant, ut ex tragœdiâ sententiam quandam [b] tollēret. Ille autem in scenam progressus dixit, se fabūlas componēre solēre, ut popūlum docēret, non ut a popūlo discēret.

26. Philippīdes, comœdiārum scriptor, quum in poëtārum certamīne præter spem vicisset, [c] et illâ victoriâ impensè gaudēret, eo ipso gaudio repentè exstinctus est.

27. Pindārus, poëta Thebānus, Apollīni gratissīmus fuisse dicītur. Quare sæpe a sacerdotībus in templum Delphīcum ad cœnam vocabātur, parsque ei tribuebātur donōrum, [d] quæ sacrificantes [e] deo obtulērant. Ferunt etiam Pana [f] Pindāri hymnis [g] tantopēre fuisse lætātum, ut eos in montībus et silvis canēret. Quum Alexander, rex Macedoniæ, Thebas diripēret, unīus Pindāri domo [h] et familiæ pepercit.

28. Diogēnes Cynīcus Myndum profectus, quum vidēret magnifīcas portas et urbem exiguam, Myndios monuit, ut portas claudērent, [i] ne urbs egrederētur.

29. Demosthēnes Atheniensis incredibīli studio et labōre eò pervēnit, ut, quum [j] multi eum ingenio [k] parum valēre existimārent, omnes ætātis suæ oratōres superāret eloquentiâ. Nunquam tamen ex tempōre dicēbat, neque in conciōne volēbat assurgēre, nisi rem, de quâ agerētur, [l]

---

[a] § 224.

[b] § 207, R. 33, (a.)

[c] § 263, 5.

[d] § 212.

[e] § 205, R. 7, (1.)

[f] § 80, I.

[g] § 247, 1, (2.)

[h] § 223, R. 2

[i] § 218, R. 2.

[j] § 263, 5, R. 1.

[k] § 250.

[l] § 261, 1.

accurātè antea meditātus esset.[a] Unde plerique eum
timĭdum esse existimābant. Sed in hac re Perĭclis con-
suetudĭnem imitabātur, qui non facĭlè de quâque re dicĕre,
nec existimatiōnem suam fortūnæ committĕre solēbat.

30. Perĭcles in conciōnem itūrus, quum animo perpen-
dĕret, quantum pericŭli[b] inconsiderātè dicta[c] hominĭbus
afferrent, solēbat precāri a diis,[d] ne quod ipsi[e] verbum
imprudenti excidĕret, quod reipublĭcæ officĕre posset.[f]

31. Minos, Cretensium rex, sæpe se in speluncam
quandam conferēbat, ibĭque se cum Jove collŏqui legesque
ab eo accipĕre dicēbat. Etiam Lycurgus Lacedæmoniis[e]
persuāsit, se leges suas ab Apolline didicisse.

32. Quum Lycurgus, Lacedæmoniōrum legislātor, Del-
phis[h] in templum Apollĭnis intrâsset, ut a deo[d] oracŭlum
petĕret, Pythia eum his verbis allocūta est: *Nescio utrùm*[i]
deus an homo appellandus sis ; sed deus[j] *potiùs vidēris esse.*

33. Leonĭdas, rex Lacedæmoniōrum, quum Persæ dice-
rentur sagittārum multitudĭne solem obscuratūri, respondisse
fertur: *Meliùs ităque in umbrâ pugnabĭmus.*

34. Cyrus omnium suōrum milĭtum nomĭna memoriâ
tenēbat. Mithridātes autem, rex Ponti, duārum et viginti
gentium, quæ sub regno ejus erant, linguas ita didicĕrat,
ut cum omnĭbus, quibus imperābat, sine interprĕte loqui
posset.

35. Themistŏcles interroganti,[k] utrùm[l] Achilles esse
mallet, an Homērus,[j] respondit: *Tu verò mallesne te in*
Olympĭco certamĭne victōrem renuntiāri,[l] *an præco esse,*
qui victōrum nomĭna proclāmat?

---

[a] § 260, II.
[b] § 212, R. 3.
[c] § 205, R. 7, (2.)
[d] § 231, R. 2, & 3, (b.)
[e] § 224, R. 1.
[f] § 266, 1.
[g] § 223, R. 2.
[h] § 254.
[i] § 265, R. 2.
[j] § 210.
[k] § 205, R. 7, (1.)
[l] § 271.

36. Epaminondas, Thebanōrum imperātor, in bello adversùs Lacedæmonios, anīmos suōrum religiōne excitandos* ratus, arma in templis affixa nocte detraxit, persuasitque militĭbus, quum illa abesse[b] vidērent, deos iter suum sequi,[b] ut ipsis[c] prœliantĭbus adessent.

37. Idem in pugnâ ad Mantinĕam gravĭter vulnerātus est. Quum anĭmam recepisset, interrogāvit circumstantes amĭcos, an clypeus salvus esset;[d] deinde, an hostes fusi essent. Illi utrumque affirmavērunt. Tum demum hastam e corpŏre edūci jussit. Quo facto* statim exspirāvit.

38. Epaminondas tantâ fuit abstinentiâ[f] et integritāte, ut post plurĭma bella, quibus Thebanōrum potentiam incredibilĭter[g] auxĕrat, nihil in supellectĭli habēret præter ahēnum et veru.

39. Lysander, dux Lacedæmoniōrum, milĭtem quendam viâ[h] egressum castigābat. Cui dicenti, ad nulĭus rei rapīnam se ab agmĭne recessisse, respondit: *Ne[i] speciem quidem raptūri[j] præbeas[k] volo.*

40. Iphicrātes, dux Atheniensium, quum præsidio tenēret Corinthum, et sub adventum hostium ipse vigĭlias circum īret, vigĭlem, quem dormientem invenĕrat, hastâ transfixit Quod factum[l] quibusdam* ei[m] ut sævum exprobrantĭbus, *Qualem[n] invēni,* inquit, *talem relĭqui.*

41. Quum quidam Thrasybūlo, qui civitātem Atheniensium a tyrannōrum dominatiōne liberāvit, dixisset. *Quantas tibi gratias Athēnæ debent!* ille respondit: *Dii*

---

* § 270, R. 3.	[f] § 211, R. 6.	[k] § 273, 4, (a.)
[b] § 272.	[g] § 192, II. 2.	[l] § 274, 1.
[c] § 224.	[h] § 242.	[m] §§ 223 and 274.
[d] § 265.	[i] § 279, 3.	[n] § 206, (16.)
[e] § 257.	[j] § 205, R. 7, (1.)	

faciant," *ut quantas*[b] *ipse patriæ debeo gratias, tantas ei videar*[c] *retulisse.*

42. Philippus, rex Macedŏnum, monentĭbus eum quibusdam, ut Pythiam quendam cavēret,[d] fortem militem, sed ipsi[e] alienātum, quòd tres filias ægrè alēret,[f] nec a rege adjuvarētur, dixisse fertur: *Quid?*[g] *si partem corpŏris habērem*[h] *ægram, abscindĕrem potiùs, an curārem?* Deinde Pythiam ad se vocātum, acceptâ difficultāte rei domestĭcæ, pecuniâ[i] instruxit. Quo facto nullum rex milĭtem Pythiâ[j] fideliōrem habuit.

43. Mulier quædam ab eōdem Philippo, quum a convivio temulentus[k] recedĕret, damnāta, *A Philippo,* inquit, *temulento ad Philippum sobrium provŏco.*

44. Philippus, rex Macedoniæ, prædicāre[l] solēbat, se oratorĭbus Atheniensium maximam gratiam habēre.[m] *Nam*[n] *conviciis suis,* inquit, *efficiunt, ut quotidie melior*[o] *evādam, dum eos dictis*[p] *factisque mendacii*[q] *arguĕre conor.*

45. Ejusdem regis epistŏla fertur scripta ad Aristotĕlem philosŏphum, quâ filium sibi[r] natum esse nuntiāvit. Erat illa epistŏla verbis concepta ferè his: *Filium mihi*[s] *genĭtum esse scito.*[t] *Quod*[u] *equĭdem diis habeo gratiam: non tam quòd natus est, quàm quòd ei contigit nasci temporĭbus vitæ tuæ. Spero enim fore,*[?] *ut a te educātus et erudītus dignus evādat et nobis*[w] *et rebus, quas ipsi relictūri sumus.*

[a] § 260, II. R. 6.	[h] § 261, 1.	[o] § 247.
[b] § 206, (16.)	[i] § 249.	[p] § 217.
[c] § 273, 1.	[j] § 256, 2.	[q] § 223.
[d] § 273, 2.	[k] § 128, 4.	[r] § 162, 4.
[e] § 224, R. 2.	[l] § 271.	[s] § 206, (14.)
[f] § 266, 3.	[m] § 272.	[t] § 268, R. 4, (b.)
[g] § 229, R. 3, 2.	[n] § 210, R. 1.	[u] § 244.

46. Alexander Macĕdo, Philippi filius, quum puer a præceptōre suo audivisset innumerabīles mundos esse, *Heu me*[a] *misĕrum*, inquit, *qui ne uno*[b] *quidem adhuc potītus sum!*

47. Quum Alexander quondam Macedōnum quorundam benevolentiam largitionībus sibi conciliāre conātus esset, Philippus eum his verbis increpuit: *Sperasne eos tibi*[c] *fidēles esse futūros, quos pecuniâ tibi conciliavĕris?*[c] *Scito amōrem non auro emi sed virtutĭbus.*

48. Alexandro[e] Macedōni, Asiâ[f] debellātâ, Corinthii per legātos[g] gratulāti sunt, regemque civitāte[h] suâ donavērunt. Quod officii genus quum Alexander risisset, unus ex legātis, *Nulli unquam*, inquit, *civitātem dedĭmus alii quàm tibi*[i] *et Hercŭli.* Quo audīto, Alexander honōrem sibi delātum lubentissĭmè accēpit.

49. Quum Alexander Græciæ popŭlis[g] imperâssét, ut divīnos ipsi honōres decernĕrent,[j] Lacedæmonii his verbis utebantur: *Quoniam Alexander deus esse voluit, esto*[k] *deus;* Laconīcâ brevitāte regis notantes vecordiam.

50. Lysimāchus, rex Thraciæ, Theodōrum Cyrenæum, virum libertātis[l] amantissĭmum et regiæ dominatiōni[c] infestum, cruci affīgi jussit. Cui ille, *Hujus modi minis*, inquit, *purpurātos tuos terreas.*[m] *Meâ*[n] *quidem nihil*[o] *intĕrest, humīne*[p] *an sublīmè putrescam.*

51. Mausōlus, rex Cariæ, Artemisiam habuit conjŭgem. Hæc, Mausōlo defuncto, ossa cineremque marīti

---

[a] § 238, 2.	[g] § 247, R. 4.	[l] § 213.
[b] § 245, I.	[h] § 249, I.	[m] § 260, R. 6.
[c] § 222, 3.	[i] § 278.	[n] § 19, R. 1.
[d] § 266, 2.	[j] § 273, 2.	[o] § 19, R. 5.
[e] § 223, R. 2.	[k] § 267.	[p] § 221, 1., R. 3
[f] § 257.		

contūsa et odorĭbus* mixta cum aquâ potābat. Extruxit quoque, ad conservandam ejus memoriam, sepulcrum illud nobilissĭmum, ab ejus nomĭne appellātum, quod inter septem orbis terrāruin miracŭla numerātur. Quod quum Mausōli manĭbus dicāret, certāmen instituit, præmiis amplissĭmis ei proposĭtis, qui defunctum regem optĭmè. laudâsset.[b]

52. Dionysius, qui a patre Syracusārum et pæne totīus Siciliæ tyrannĭdem accepĕrat, senex patriâ[c] pulsus Corinthi[d] puĕros littĕras docuit.[e]

53. Mithridātes, rex Ponti, sæpe venēnum hausĕrat, ut sibi a clandestīnis cavēret insidiis. Hinc factum est, ut quum a Pompeio superātus mortem sibi consciscĕre vellet, ne velocissĭma quidem venēna ei nocērent.[f]

54. Quum Gyges, rex Lydiæ ditissĭmus, oracŭlum Apollĭnis interrogāret, an quisquam mortalium[g] se esset* felicior, deus, Aglaüm quendam Psophidium feliciōrem, prædicāvit. Is autem erat Arcădum pauperrĭmus, parvŭli agelli possessor, cujus termĭnos quàmvis senex nunquam excessĕrat, fructĭbus[h] et voluptatĭbus angusti ruris contentus.

55. Pyrrhus, rex Epīri, quum in Italiâ esset, audīvit, Tarentīnos quosdam juvĕnes in convivio parŭm honorifĭcè de se locūtos esse. Eos igitur ad se arcessītos percunc tātus est, an dixissent* ea, quæ ad aures suas pervēnissent.[i] Tum unus ex his,[j] *Nisi*, inquit, *vinum nobis defecisset, multo[k] etiam plura et graviōra in te locutūri erāmus.*[l] Hæc crimĭnis excusatio iram regis in risum convertit.

---

* Why is this verb in the subjunctive ?

[a] § 245, II. 2.	[e] § 231.	[i] § 266, 1
[b] § 266, 3.	[f] § 262, R. 3.	[j] § 212, N. 4.
[c] § 251.	[g] § 212.	[k] § 256, R. 16.
[d] § 221, 1	[h] § 244.	[l] § 274, R. 6.

56. Marsyas, frater Antigŏni, regis Macedoniæ, quum causam habēret cum privāto quodam, fratrem rogā·it, ut de eâ domi cognoscēret. At ille, *In foro potiùs,** inquit. *Nam si culpâ* vacas, innocentia tua ibi meliùs apparēbit; sin damnandus es, nostra justitia.**

. 57. Clara sunt apud Catanenses nomina fratrum Anāpi[b] et Amphinŏmi,[b] qui patrem et matrem humĕris per medios[c] ignes Ætnæ portârunt, eosque cum vitæ suæ periculo e flammis eripuērunt.

58. Spartānus quidam quum riderētur, quòd claudus in pugnam iret,[d] *At mihi,[e]* inquit, *pugnāre,[f] non fugĕre est propositum.*

59. Spartānus quidam in magistrātûs petitiŏne ab æmūlis victus, maximæ sibi lætitiæ esse,[g] dixit, quòd patria sua[h] se[i] meliōres cives habēret.[d]

60. Quum homo quidam, qui diu in uno pede stare didicĕrat, Lacedæmonio cuidam dixisset, se non arbitrāri Lacedæmoniōrum[j] quemquam tamdiu idem facĕre posse, ille respondit: *At anseres te** diutiùs.*

61. Diagŏras Rhodius, quum tres ejus filii in ludis Olympīcis victōres renuntiāti essent, tanto affectus est gaudio,[k] ut in ipso stadio, inspectante popŭlo, in filiōrum manĭbus anĭmam reddĕret.

62. Scipio Africānus nunquam ad negotia publīca accedēbat, antĕquàm in templo Jovis precātus esset.[l]

63. Scipio dicĕre solēbat, hosti non solùm dandam[m]

---

* What is to be supplied?

[a] § 250.	[f] § 269.	[j] § 212.
[b] § 204, R. 10.	[g] § 227.	[k] § 249, I.
[c] § 205, R. 17.	[h] § 208, (1.)	[l] § 263, 3.
[d] § 266, 3.	[i] § 256, 2.	[m] § 274, R. 3.
[e] § 224.		

esse viam fugiendi, sed etiam muniendam. Similiter Pyrrhus, rex Epīri, fugienti hosti *a* pertinacīter instandum esse*b* negābat; non solùm, ne fortiùs ex necessitāte resistēret,* sed ut postea quoque faciliùs acie*c* cedēret, ratus victōres fugientībus non usque ad perniciem instatūros esse.

64. Metellus Pius, in Hispaniâ bellum gerens interrogātus, quid postēro die factūrus esset?* *Tunicam meam,* inquit, *si id elŏqui posset,d comburerem.d*

65. L. Mummius, qui, Corintho captâ, totam Italiam tabŭlis*e* statuisque exornāvit, ex tantis manubiis*f* nihil in suum usum convertit, ita ut, eo defuncto, non esset* unde ejus filia dotem accipēret.*g* Quare senātus ei ex publico dotem decrēvit.

66. Scipio Africānus major Ennii poëtæ imaginem in sepulcro gentis Corneliæ collocāri jussit, quòd† Scipiōnum res gestas carminībus suis illustravērat.

67. M. Cato, Catōnis Censorii filius, in acie cadente equo prolapsus, quum se recollegisset,* animadvertissetque gladium excidisse*h* vagīnâ,*i* rediit*j* in hostem: acceptisque aliquot vulnerībus, recuperāto demum gladio ad suos reversus est.

68. Q. Metellus Macedonĭcus in Hispaniâ quinque cohortes, quæ hostībus*k* cessērant, testamentum facĕre jussas ad locum*l* recuperandum misit; minātus eos nonnĭsi post victoriam receptum iri.

---

* Why is this verb in the subjunctive ?
† Is the writer answerable for the validity of this reason ? § 266, 3
a § 224. *c* § 249, I. § 242.
b § 239, R. 3. *f* § 212, N. 4. *j* § 182, R. 3'
e § 255, R. 3, (a.) & (b.) *g* § 264, 6, & R. 3. *k* § 223
d § 261, 1. *h* § 268, 2. *l* § 275, III. R. 3.

69. Publius Decius consul,[a] quum in bello contra Latinos Romanōrum aciem cedentem vidēret, capīte pro reipublicæ salūte devōto, in medium hostium agmen irruit, et magnâ strage edītâ plurimis telis obrūtus cecīdit. Hæc ejus mors Romanōrum aciem restituit, iisque victoriam parāvit.

70. L. Junius Brutus, qui Romam a regībus liberāvit, filios suos, qui Tarquinium regem expulsum restituēre conāti erant, ipse capītis[b] damnāvit, eosque virgis cæsos secūri[c] percūti jussit.[d]

71. Q. Marcius Rex consul, quum filium unīcum, juvē-nem summæ pietātis[e] et magnæ spei, morte amisisset, dolōrem suum ita coёrcuit, ut a rogo adolescentis protēnus curiam petēret, ibíque munēris sui negotia strenuè obīret.

72. In bello Romanōrum cum Perseo, ultīmo Mace-doniæ rege, accīdit,[f] ut serēnâ nocte subītò luna deficēret. Hæc res ingentem apud milītes terrōrem excitāvit, qui existimābant hoc omīne futūram cladem portendi.* Tum verò Sulpicius Gallus, qui erat in eo exercītu, in conciōne milītum causam hujus rei tam disertè exposuit, ut postēro die omnes intrepīdo anīmo pugnam committērent.

73. L. Siccius Dentātus ob insignem fortitudīnem appellātus est Achilles Romānus. Pugnâsse is dicitur centum et viginti prœliis;[g] cicatrīcem aversam nullam, adversas quinque et quadraginta tulisse; corōnis[h] esse donātus aureis duodeviginti, obsidionāli unâ, muralībus tribus, civīcis quatuordēcim, torquībus tribus et octoginta, armillis plùs centum sexaginta, hastis duodeviginti. Phal-

* What time is denoted by this verb ? § 268.
[a] § 279, 9, (a.)   [d] § 273, 2.   [g] § 254, R. 3.
[b] § 217, R. 3, (a.)   [e] § 211, R. 6.   [h] § 249, I.
[c] § 79, 2, and 82, E. 2. [f] § 262, R 3.

ĕris idem donātus est quinquies viciesque. Triumphāvit cum imperatorĭbus suis triumphos[a] novem.

74. Hannibălem in Italiam proficiscentem tria millia[b] Carpetanōrum reliquērunt. Quorum exemplum ne cetĕri quoque barbări sequerentur, edixit eos a se esse dimissos, et insŭper in fidem ejus rei alios etiam, quorum fides ipsi[c] suspecta erat, domum remīsit.

75. Hannĭbal quum elephantos compellĕre non posset, ut præaltum flumen transīrent, neque rates habēret, quibus eos trajicĕret,[d] jussit ferocissĭmum elephantōrum sub aure vulnerāri, et eum, qui vulnerâsset,[e] se in flumen conjicĕre illudque tranāre. Tum elephantus exasperātus ad perse-quendum dolōris sui auctōrem tranāvit amnem,[f] et relīqui quoque eum secūti sunt.

---

[a] § 232, (1.)   [c] § 222, 3.   [e] § 266, 2.
[b] § 118, 6, & (a.)   [d] § 264, 5.   [f] § 233.

7

AN EPITOME OF ROMAN HISTORY

FROM THE EARLIEST TIMES TO THE EMPERORS.

LIBER PRIMUS.

1. Antiquissĭmis temporĭbus Saturnus in Italiam venisse dicĭtur. Ibi haud procul a Janicŭlo arcem condĭdit, eamque Saturniam appellāvit. Hic Itălos pri·mus*ᵃ agricultūram docuit.*ᵇ

2. Postea Latīnus in illis regionĭbus imperāvit. Sub hoc rege Troja in Asiâ eversa est. Hinc Ænēas, Anchī·sæ filius, cum multis Trojānis,*ᶜ quibus*ᵈ ferrum Græcōrum pepercĕrat, aufūgit, et in Italiam pervēnit. Ibi Latīnus rex ei benignè recepto filiam Laviniam in matrimonium dedit. Ænēas urbem condĭdit, quam in honōrem conjŭgis Lavinium*ᵉ appellāvit.

3. Post Æneæ mortem Ascanius, Æneæ filius, reg·num accēpit. Hic sedem regni in alium locum transtŭlit, urbemque condĭdit in monte Albāno, eamque Albam*ᵉ Longam nuncupāvit. Eum secūtus est Silvius, qui post Æneæ mortem a Laviniâ genĭtus erat. Ejus

---

ᵃ § 205, R. 15.   ᶜ § 249, III.   § 230.
ᵇ § 231.   ᵈ § 223, R. 2.

postĕri omnes usque ad Romam condĭtam^a Albæ^b regna-
vērunt.

4. Unus horum regum, Romŭlus Silvius, se Jove^c
majōrem esse dicēbat,^d et, quum tonāret, militĭbus imperāvit, ut clypeos hastis percutērent, dicebatque hunc
~onum multò clariōrem esse quàm tonĭtru.   Fulmĭne
ctus,^e et in Albānum lacum præcipitātus est.

5. Silvius Procas, rex Albanōrum, duos filios relīquit
Numitōrem^f et Amulium.^f   Horum minor^g natu,^h Amulius, fratri optiōnem dědit, utrùm regnum habēre vellet,ⁱ
an bona, quæ pater reliquisset.^j   Numĭtor paterna bona
prætŭlit ; Amulius regnum obtinuit.

6. Amulius, ut regnum firmissĭmè possidēret, Numitō-
ris filium per insidias interēmit, et filiam fratris Rheam
Silviam Vestālem virgĭnem fecit.   Nam his Vestæ sacerdotĭbus non licet viro^k nubĕre.   Sed hæc a Marte geminos
filios Romŭlum et Remum pepĕrit.   Hoc^l quum Amulius comperisset, matrem in vincŭla conjēcit, puĕros autem
in Tibĕrim abjĭci jussit.

7. Fortè Tibĕris aqua ultra ripam se effudĕrat, et, quum
puĕri in vado essent posĭti, aqua refluens eos in sicco*
relĭquit.   Ad eōrum vagītum lupa accurrit, eosque uberĭ-
bus suis aluit.   Quod^l videns Faustŭlus quidam, pastor
illīus regiōnis, puĕros sustŭlit, et uxōri Accæ Laurentiæ
nutriendos^m dedit.

8. Sic Romŭlus et Remus pueritiam inter pastōres

---

* Supply *loco.*

^a § 274, R. 5.   ^f § 204, R. 10.   ^j § 266, 1.

^b § 221.   ^g § 212.   ^k § 223, R. 2.

^c § 256, 2.   ^h § 250, 1.   ^l § 206, (13.)

^d § 145, II. 1.   ⁱ § 265.   ^m § 274, 2, R 7.

^e § 209, R. 4.

transegērunt. Quum adolevissent, et fortè comperissent, quis ipsōrum avus, quæ mater fuisset,[a] Amulium inter

Ante fecērunt, et Numitōri avo regnum restituērunt.
Christum Tum urbem condidērunt in monte Aventīno,
754. quam Romŭlus a suo nomĭne Romam vocāvit.
Hæc quum mœnĭbus circumdarētur, Remus occīsus est, dum fratrem irrīdens mœnia[b] transiliēbat.

9. Romŭlus, ut civium numĕrum augēret, asȳlum patefēcit, ad quod multi ex civitatĭbus suis pulsi accurrērunt. Sed novæ urbis civĭbus[c] conjŭges deērant. Festum ităque Neptūni et ludos instituit. Ad hos quum multi ex finitĭmis popŭlis cum mulierĭbus et libĕris venissent,[d] Romāni inter ipsos ludos spectantes virgĭnes rapuērunt.

10. Popŭli illi, quorum virgĭnes raptæ erant, bellum adversùs raptōres suscepērunt. Quum Romæ appropinquārent, fortè in Tarpēiam virgĭnem incidērunt, quæ in arce sacra procurābat. Hanc rogābant, ut viam in arcem monstrāret,[e] eique permisērunt, ut munus sibi poscĕret.[f] Illa petiit, ut sibi[g] darent,[e] quod in sinistris manĭbus gerĕrent,[h] annŭlos aureos et armillas significans. At hostes in arcem[i] ab eâ perducti scutis Tarpēiam obruērunt; nam et ea in sinistris manĭbus gerēbant.

11. Tum Romŭlus cum hoste, qui montem Tarpēium tenēbat, pugnam conseruit in eo loco, ubi nunc forum Romānum est. In mediâ[j] cæde raptæ* processērunt, et hinc patres hinc conjŭges et socĕros complectebantur, et rogābant, ut cædis finem facĕrent. Utrique his precĭbus

---

* Supply *mulĭĕres.*

[a] § 265.	[e] § 273, 2.	[h] § 266, 1.
[b] § 233.	[f] § 273, 4.	[i] § 225, IV.
[c] § 224, R. 1.	[g] § 208, (1.)	[j] § 205, R. 17.
[d] § 258, 2, (2.)		

commōti sunt. Romŭlus fœdus icit, et Sabīnos in urbem recēpit.

12. Postea civitātem descripsit. Centum senatōres legit, eosque cùm[a] ob ætātem tum ob reverentiam iis[b] debītam patres appellāvit. Plebem in triginta curias distribuit, easque raptārum nominibus nuncupāvit. Anno regni tricesĭmo septĭmo, quum exercĭtum lustrāret, inter tempestātem ortam[c] repentè ocŭlis[d] homĭnum subductus est. Hinc alii eum a senatorĭbus interfectum, alii ad deòs sublātum esse existimavērunt.

A. U. C. 37.

13. Post Romŭli mortem unīus anni interregnum fuit. Quo elapso, Numa Pompilius Curĭbus,[e] urbe in agro Sabinōrum, natus rex creātus est. Hic vir bellum quidem[f] nullum gessit ; nec minùs tamen civitāti profuit. Nam et leges dedit, et sacra plurĭma instituit, ut popŭli barbāri et bellicōsi mores mollīret. Omnia autem, quæ faciēbat,[f] se nymphæ Egeriæ, conjŭgis suæ, jussu facĕre dicēbat.[e] Morbo decessit, quadragesĭmo tertio imperii anno.

14. Numæ[d] successit Tullus Hostilius, cujus avus se in bello adversùs Sabīnos fortem et strenuum virum[h] præstitĕrat. Rex creātus bellum Albānis indīxit, idque trigeminōrum Horatiōrum et Curiatiō rum certamĭne finīvit. Albam propter perfidiam Metii Suffetii diruit. Quum triginta duōbus annis regnâsset, fulmĭne ictus cum domo[i] suâ arsit.

A. U 81.

15. Post hunc Ancus Marcius, Numæ ex filiâ nepos, suscēpit imperium. Hic vir æquitāte[j] et religiōne avo[k] simĭlis, Latīnos bello domuit, urbem

A. U 114.

[a] § 278, R. 7.	[e] § 254.	[i] § 249, III.
[b] § 274, 1.	[f] § 279, 3, (a.) & (d.)	[j] § 250.
[c] § 274, 3, (a.)	[g] § 145, II. 1.	[k] § 222, 3.
[d] § 224.	[h] § 230, R. 2.	

7 *

ampliāvit, et nova ei mœnia circumdēdit. Carcěre n prī
mus ædificāvit. Ad Tibēris ostia urbem condĭdit, Ostĭ-
amque vocāvit. Vicesĭmo quarto anno imperii morbo
obiit.

A. U.
137.
16. Deinde regnum Lucius Tarquinius Priscus
accēpit, Demarāti filius, qui tyrannos patriæ Corinthi fugiens in Etruriam venĕrat. Ipse Tarquinius, qui nomen ab urbe Tarquiniis accēpit, aliquando
Romam profectus erat. Advenienti * aquĭla pileum ab-
stŭlit,* et, postquam altē evolavĕrat, reposuit. Hinc
Tanăquil conjux, mulier auguriōrum* perĭta, regnum ei
portendi intellexit.

17. Quum Romæ commorarētur, Anci regis familiari-
tātem consecūtus est, qui eum filiōrum suōrum tutōrem
reliquit. Sed is pupillis* regnum intercēpit. Senatorĭbus,
quos Romulus creavĕrat, centum alios addidit, qui minōrum
gentium* sunt appellāti.† Plura bella felicĭter gessit, nec
paucos agros hostĭbus* ademptos urbis territorio adjunxit.
Primus triumphans urbem intrāvit. Cloācas fecit; Capitolium inchoāvit. Tricesĭmo octāvo imperii anno per Anci
filios,* quibus* regnum eripuĕrat, occīsus est.

A. U.
176.
18. Post hunc Servius Tullius suscēpit imperium, genĭtus ex nobĭli feminā,* captivā tamen et
famŭlā. Quum in domo Tarquinii Prisci educa-
rētur, flamma in ejus capĭte visa est. Hoc prodigio Tanăquil ei summam dignitātem portendi intellexit, et conjūgi *
persuāsit, ut eum sicūti libēros suos educāret. Quum
adolevisset, rex ei filiam in matrimonium dedit.

---

* Supply et.   † Supply Senatōres.

ᵃ § 224, R. 2.   ᵈ § 211, R. 6.   ᶠ § 246, R. 2.
ᵇ § 213.   ᵉ § 247. R. 4.   ᵍ § 223, R. 2.
ᶜ § 224.

19. Quum Priscus Tarquinius occīsus osset, Tanāquil de superiōre parte domûs popŭlum° allocūta est, dicens ; *regem grave quidem sed non letāle vulnus accepisse ; eum petĕre, ut popŭlus, dum convaluisset,*[b] Servio Tullio obedī-*ret.* Sic Servius regnāre cœpit, sed benè imperium ad-ministrāvit. Montes tres urbi adjunxit. Primus omnium censum ordināvit. Sub eo Roma habuit capĭtum octo-ginta tria millia civium Romanōrum cum his, qui in agris erant.

20. Hic rex interfectus est scelĕre filiæ Tulliæ et Tarquinii Superbi, filii ejus regis, cui° Servius successĕrat. Nam ab ipso Tarquinio de gradĭbus

A. U. 220.

curiæ dejectus, quum domum[d] fugĕret, interfectus est. Tullia in forum properāvit, et prima conjŭgem regem° salu-tāvit. Quum domum redīret, aurīgam super patris corpus in viâ jacens carpentum agĕre jussit.

21. Tarquinius Superbus cognōmen morĭbus meruit. Bello tamen strenuus plures finitimōrum populōrum[f] vicit. Templum Jovis in Capitolio ædificāvit. Postea, dum Ardeam oppugnābat, urbem Latii, imperium perdĭdit. Nam quum filius ejus Lucretiæ, nobilissīmæ femīnæ, conjŭgi Tarquinii Collatīni, vim fecisset, hæc se ipsam[g] occĭdit in conspectu marīti, patris, et amicōrum, postquam eos obtestāta fuĕrat, ut hanc injuriam ulciscerentur.

22. Hanc ob causam L. Brutus, Collatīnus, aliīque nonnulli in exitium[h] regis conjurārunt, popu-lōque[i] persuasērunt, ut ei portas urbis claudĕret.

A. U. 243.

Exercĭtus quoque, qui civitātem Ardeam cum rege oppug-nābat, eum reliquit. Fugit ităque cum uxōre et libĕris

---

° § 233. [d] § 237, R. 4. [f] § 135, R. 1.

[b] § 263, 4. (1.) ° § 230, R. 2. [h] § 235, (2.)

° § 224. [f] § 212. [i] § 223, R. 2.

suis. Ita 'Romæ' regnātum' est per septem reges annos ducentos quadraginta tres.

23. Hinc consŭles cœpere pro uno rege duo creāi, ut, si unus malus esset,' alter eum coërcēret. Annuum iis imperium tribūtum est, ne per diuturnitātem potestātis insolentiōres redderentur. Fuērunt igĭtur anno primo, expulsis regĭbus,ᵈ consŭles L. Junius Brutus, acerrĭmus libertātis vindex, et Tarquinius Collatīnus, marītus Lucretiæ. Sed Collatīnoᵉ paulò pòst dignĭtas sublāta est. Placuĕrat enim, ne quis ex Tarquiniōrum familiâ Romæ manēret.ᶠ Ergo cum omni patrimonio suo ex urbe migrāvit, et in ejus locum Valerius Publicŏla consul factus est.

24. Commōvit bellum urbi rex Tarquinius. In primâ pugnâ Brutus consul, et Aruns, Tarquinii filius, sese invīcem occidērunt. Romāni tamen ex eâ pugnâ victōres recessērunt. Brutum Romānæ matrōnæ quasi commūnem patrem per annum luxērunt. Valerius Publicŏla Sp Lucretium, Lucretiæ patrem, collēgam sibi fecit; qui quum morbo exstinctus esset, Horatium Pulvillum sibi collēgam sumpsit. Ita primus annus quinque cònsŭles habuit.

25. Secundo quoque anno itĕrum Tarquinius bellum Romānis intŭlit, Porsĕnâ,ᵈ rege Etruscōrum, auxilium ei ferente. In illo bello Horatius Cocles solus pontem ligneum defendit, et hostes cohibuit, donec pons a tergo ruptus esset.ᵉ Tum se cum armis in Tibĕrim conjēcit, et ad suos transnāvit.

A. U. 245.

26. Dum Porsĕna urbem obsidēbat, Qu. Mucius Scævŏla, juvĕnis fortis anĭmi,ʰ in castraⁱ hostis se contŭlit eo

---

ᵃ § 221, I. ᵈ § 257. ᶠ § 263, 4.
ᵇ § 209, R. 3, (2.) ᵉ § 224, R. 2. ʰ § 211, R. 6.
ᶜ § 260. ᶠ § 262. § 225, IV.

consilio,* ut regem occidĕret. At ibi scribam˙regis pro ipso rege interfĕcit. Tum a regiis* satellitĭbus comprehensus et ad regem deductus, quum Porsĕna eum ignĭbus allātis terrēret, dextram* aræ* accensæ imposuit, donec .flammis consumpta esset.* Hoc facĭnus rex mirātus juvĕnem dimīsit incolŭmem. Tum hic quasi beneficium refērens ait, trecentos alios juvĕnes in eum conjurâsse.* Hac re terrītus Porsĕna pacem cum Romānis fecit, Tarquinius autem Tuscŭlum se contŭlit, ibīque privātus cum uxōre consenuit.

27. Sexto decĭmo anno post reges exactos,* popŭlus Romæ* seditiōnem fecit, questus quòd tribūtis et militiâ a senātu exhaurirētur.* Magna

A. U. 259.

pars plebis urbem relīquit, et in montem trans Aniēnem amnem secessit. Tum patres turbāti Menenium Agrippam misērunt ad plebem, qui eam senatui conciliāret.* Hic iis inter alia fabŭlam narrāvit de ventre et membris humāni corpŏris; quâ popŭlus commōtus est, ut in urbem redīret. Tum primùm tribūni plebis creāti sunt, qui plebem adversùm nobilitātis superbiam defendĕrent.*

28. Octāvo decĭmo anno post exactos reges, Qu. Marcius, Coriolānus* dictus ab urbe Volscōrum Coriŏlis,* quam™ bello cepĕrat, plebi invīsus

A. U. 261.

fiĕri cœpit. Quare urbe* expulsus ad Volscos, acerrĭmos Romanōrum hostes, contendit, et ab iis dux* exercĭtûs factus Romānos sæpe vicit. Jam usque ad quintum milliarium urbis accessĕrat, nec ullis civium suōrum legati-

---

* § 249, II.	ƒ § 162, 7.	* § 274, 1, and 210.
* § 211, R. 4.	* § 274, R. 5.	‡ § 204.
* § 207, R.36,(*a*.)&(*c*.)	* § 221, 1.	™ § 206, (9.)
* § 224.	* § 266, 3.	* § 242.
* § 263, 4.	ʲ § 264. 5.	

onĭbus flecti potĕrat, ut patriæ parcĕret. Deniqᴜe Veturia mater et Volumnia uxor ex urbe ad eum venērunt; qua᷉rum fletu et precĭbus commōtus est, ut exercĭtum remo᷉vēret. Qᴜo facto a Volscis ut prodĭtor[a] occīsus esse dicĭtur.

29. Romāni quum adversùm Veientes bellum gerērent, familia Fabiōrum sola hoc bellum suscēpit. Profecti sunt trecenti sex nobilissĭmi homĭnes, duce[b] Fabio con-
A. U. 274.
sŭle. Quum sæpe hostes vicissent, apud Cremē-ram fluvium castra posuērunt. Ibi Veientes dolo[c] usi eos in insidias pellexērunt. In prœlio ibi exorto[d] omnes periērunt. Unus superfuit ex tantâ familiâ, qui prop-ter ætātem puerīlem duci non potuĕrat ad pugnam. Hic genus propagāvit ad Qu. Fabium Maxĭmum illum,[e] qui Hannibālem prudenti cunctatiōne debilitāvit.

30. Anno trecentesĭmo et altĕro[f] ab urbe con-
A. U. 302.
dītâ decemvīri creāti sunt, qui civitāti leges scri-bērent.[f] Hi primo anno benè egērunt; secundo autem dominatiōnem exercēre cœpērunt. Sed quum unus eōrum Appius Claudius virgĭnem ingenuam, Virginiam, Virginii centuriōnis filiam, corrumpēre vellet, pater eam occidit. Tum ad milites profūgit, eosque ad sediṭiōnem commōvit. Sublāta est decemvīris[h] potestas, ipsique om-nes aut morte aut exilio puniti sunt.

31 In bello contra Veientānos Furius Camillus
A. U. 358.
urbem Falerios obsidēbat. In quâ obsidiōne quum ludi literarii magister princĭpum filios ex urbe in castra hostium duxisset, Camillus hoc donum non accēpit, sed scelestum homĭnem, manĭbus post tergum vinctis,

[a] § 278, R 1.	[d] § 274, 3.	[f] § 264, 5.
[b] § 257, R. 7.	[e] § 207, R. 24.	[h] § 224, R. 2.
[c] § 245.	[f] § 120, 1.	

puĕris Falerios[a] reducendum[b] tradĭdit; virgasque iis dedit, quibus proditōrem in urbem agĕrent.[c]

32. Hac tantâ anĭmi nobilitāte commōti Falisci urbem Romānis tradidĕrunt. Camillo autem apud Romānos crimĭni datum[d] est, quòd albis equis triumphâsset,[e] et præ-dam inĭquè divisisset; damnatusque[f] ob eam cau-sam, et civitāte expulsus est. Paulò pòst Galli Senōnes ad urbem venērunt, Romānos apud flu-men Alliam vicērunt, et urbem etiam occupârunt.[g] Jam nihil præter Capitolium defendi potuit. Et jam præsidi-um fame laborābat, et in eo[h] erant,[i] ut pacem a Gallis auro emĕrent, quum Camillus cum manu milĭtum superveniens hostes magno prœlio superāret.

A. U. 364.

LIBER SECUNDUS.

1. ANNO trecentesĭmo[j] nonagesĭmo quarto post urbem condĭtam Galli itĕrum ad urbem accessĕ-rant, et quarto milliario[k] trans Aniēnem fluvium considĕrant. Contra eos missus est T. Quinctius. Ibi Gallus quidam eximiâ corpŏris magnitudĭne[l] fortissĭmum Romanōrum ad certāmen singulāre provocāvit. T. Man-lius, nobilissĭmus juvĕnis, provocatiōnem accēpit, Gallum occīdit, eumque torque[m] aureo spoliāvit, quo[n] ornātus erat. Hinc et ipse et postĕri ejus Torquāti appellāti sunt. Galli fugam capessivērunt.

A. U 394.

---

[a] § 237.	[f] § 209, R. 4.	[k] § 254, R. 3.
[b] § 274, R. 7.	[g] § 162, 7.	[l] § 211, R. 6.
[c] § 264, 5	[h] § 207, R. 22.	[m] § 251.
[d] § 227.	[i] § 209, R. 11, (1.)	[n] § 249, I.
§ 266, 3	[j] § 120, 2.	

2. Novo bello cum Gallis exorto, anno urbis
quadringentesĭmo sexto, itĕrum Gallus processit
robŏre[a] atque armis insignis, et provocāvit unum ex
Romānis, ut secum armis decernĕret. Tum se M. Valerius, tribūnus milītum, obtŭlit; et, quum processisset armātus, corvus ei[b] supra dextrum brachium sedit. Mox,
commissâ pugnâ, hic corvus alis et unguĭbus Galli ocŭlos
verberāvit. Ita factum est, ut Gallus nullo negotio[c] a Va-
lerio interficerētur,[d] qui hinc Corvīni nomen accēpit.

A. U.
406.

3. Postea Romāni bellum gessērunt cum Sam-
nitĭbus, ad quod[e] L. Papirius Cursor cum honōre
dictatōris profectus est. Qui quum negotii cujusdam causâ Romam ivisset, præcēpit Q. Fabio[f] Rulliāno,
magistro equītum, quem apud exercĭtum relīquit, ne pugnam cum hoste committĕret. Sed ille occasiōnem nactus
felicissĭmè dimicāvit, et Samnītes delēvit. Ob hanc rem a
dictatōre[g] capĭtis[h] damnātus est. At ille in urbem confūgit, et ingenti favōre milītum et popŭli liberātus est; in
Papirium autem tanta exorta est seditio, ut 'pæne ipse
interficerētur.

A. U.
430.

4. Duōbus annis pòst[i] T. Veturius et Spurius Postumius consŭles bellum adversùm Samnītes gerēbant. Hi a
Pontio Thelesīno, duce hostium, in insidias inducti sunt.
Nam ad Furcŭlas Caudīnas Romānos pellexit in
angustias, unde sese expedīre non potĕrant. Ibi
Pontius patrem suum Herennium rogāvit, quid[j] faciendum[k] putāret.[l] Ille respondit, aut omnes occidendos[m]

A. U.
433.

---

[a] § 250.	[f] § 223, R. 2.	[j] § 272.
[b] § 211, R. 5, 1.	[g] § 248, I.	[k] § 270, R. 3.
[c] § 247.	[h] § 217, R. 3.	[l] § 265.
[d] § 262, R. 3.	[i] § 235, R. 10.	[m] § 274, R. 8.
[e] § 225, IV.		

esse, ut Romanōrum vires frangerentur, aut omnes dimittendos, ut beneficio obligarentur. Pontius utrumque consilium improbāvit, omnesque sub jugum misit. Samnites denīque post bellum undequinquaginta annōrum superāti sunt.

5. Devictis Samnitībus, Tarentīnis[a] bellum indictum est, quia legātis Romanōrum injuriam fecissent. Hi Pyrrhum, Epīri regem, contra Romānos auxilium[b] poposcērunt. Is mox in Italiam venit, tumque primùm Romāni cum transmarīno hoste pugnavērunt. Missus est contra eum consul P. Valerius Lævīnus. Hic, quum exploratōres Pyrrhi cepisset, jussit eos per castra duci, tumque dimitti, ut renuntiārent Pyrrho, quæcunque a Romānis agerentur.[c]

A. U
472.

6. Pugnâ commissâ, Pyrrhus auxilio elephantōrum vicit. Nox prœlio finem dedit. Lævīnus tamen per noctem fugit. Pyrrhus Romānos mille[d] octingentos cepit, eosque summo honōre tractāvit. Quum eos, qui in prœlio interfecti fuĕrant, omnes adversis vulnerībus et truci vultu etiam mortuos jacēre vidēret, tulisse ad cœlum manus dicĭtur cum hac voce: *Ego cum talibus viris brevi orbem terrā-rum subigĕrem.*[e]

7. Postea Pyrrhus Romam perrexit; omnia ferro igneque vastāvit; Campaniam depopulātus est, atque ad Prænĕste venit milliario ab urbe octāvo decĭmo. Mox terrōre exercitûs, qui cum consūle sequebātur, in Campaniam se recēpit. Legāti ad Pyrrhum de captivis redimendis[f] missi honorificè ab eo suscepti sunt; captīvos sine pretio reddidit. Unum ex legātis, Fabricium, sic admirātus est,

---

[a] § 224.   [c] § 266, 1.   [e] § 261, 1 and 2, R. 4.
[b] § 231.   [d] § 120, 2.   [f] § 275, III., R. 4.

8

ut ei quartam partem regni sui promittĕret, si ad se transi-
ret;ᵃ sed a Fabricio contemptus est.

8. Quum jam Pyrrhus ingenti Romanōrum admiratiōne
tenerētur, legātum misit Cineam, præstantissĭmum virum,
qui pacem petĕret * eâ conditiōne,ᵇ ut Pyrrhus eam partem
Italiæ, quam armis occupavĕrat, obtinēret. Romāni respondērunt, eumᶜ cum Romānis pacem habēre non posse,
n'si ex Italiâ recessisset. Cineas quum rediisset, Pyrrho
eum interroganti, qualis ipsi Roma visa esset ;* respondit,
se regum patriam vidisse.

9. In altĕroᵈ prœlio cum rege Epīri commisso Pyrrhus
vulnerātus est, elephanti interfecti, viginti millia hostium
cæsa sunt. Pyrrhus Tarentum fugit. Interjecto anno,
Fabricius contra eum missus est. Ad hunc medĭcus
Pyrrhi nocte venit promittens, se Pyrrhum venēno occisū-
rum,ᵉ si munus sibi darētur. Hunc Fabricius vinctum
redūci jussit ad domĭnum. Tunc rex admirātus illum
dixisse fertur ; *Ille † est Fabricius, qui difficiliùs ab honestāte, quàm sol a cursu suo averti potest.* Paulò pòst

A. U.
481.
Pyrrhus tertio etiam prœlio fusus a Tarento reces-
sit, et, quum in Græciam rediisset, apud Argos, Pelo-
ponnēsi urbem, interfectus est.

A. U.
490.
10. Anno quadringentesĭmo nonagesĭmo post
urbem condĭtam Romanōrum exercĭtus primùm in
Siciliamᶠ trajecērunt, regemque Syracusārum Hierōnem, Pœnosque, qui multas civitātes in eâ insūlâ

A. U.
495.
occupavĕrant, superavērunt. Quinto anno hujus
belli, quod contra Pœnos gerebātur, primùm Ro-

---

* Why is this subjunctive used?
† *Ille* is the predicate, "the man," or "one."

ᵃ § 266, 1.   ᶜ § 266, 2.   ᵉ § 270, R. 3.
ᵇ § 249, II.   ᵈ § 120, 1.   ᶠ § 225, IV.

māni, C. Duillio* et Cn. Cornelio Asīńâ consulĭbus, in mari* dimicavērunt. Duillius Carthaginienses vicit, triginta aaves occupāvit, quatuordĕcim mersit, septem millia hostium* cepit, tria millia occidit. Nulla victoria Romāanis gratior fuit. Duillio concessum est, ut, quum a cœnâ redīret, puĕri funalia gestantes et tibĭcen eum comitarentur.

11. Paucis annis interjectis, bellum in Afrĭcam translātum est. Hamilcar, Carthaginiensium dux, pugnâ navālĭ superātur; nam perdĭtis sexaginta A. U. 499 quatuor navĭbus se recēpit; Romāni viginti duas amisērunt. Quum in Afrĭcam venissent, Pœnos in plurĭbus prœliis vicērunt, magnam vim homĭnum cepērunt, septuaginta quatuor civitātes in fidem accepērunt. Tum victi Carthaginienses pacem a Romānis* petiērunt. Quam quum M. Atilius Regŭlus, Romanōrum dux, dare nollet ṇisi durissĭmis conditionĭbus, Carthaginienses auxilium petiērunt a Lacedæmoniis. Hi Xanthippum misēruṇt, qui Romānum exercĭtum magno prœlio vicit. Regŭlus ipse captus et in vincŭla conjectus est.

12. Non tamen ubīque fortūna Carthaginiensĭbus* favit. Quum alĭquot prœliis victi essent, Regŭlum rogavērunt, ut Romam proficiscerētur, et pacem captivorumque permutatiōnem a Romānis obtinēret. Ille quum Romam venisset, inductus in senātum dixit, se desiisse Romānum esse .ex illâ die, quâ* in potestātem Pœnōrum venisset.* Tum Remānis* suasit, ne pacem cum Carthaginiensĭbus facĕrent:* illos* enim tot casĭbus fractos ?pem nullam nisi in pace habēre: tanti* non esse, ut

---

* § 257, R. 7.   * § 223, R. 2.   * § 273, 2.
* § 82, E. 1.   * § 253.   * § 270, R. 2
* § 212.   * § 266, 2.   * § 214.
* § 231, R. 4.

tot millia captivōrum propter se unum et paucos, qui
ex Romānis capti essent, redderentur. Hæc sententia
obtinuit. Regressus igĭtur in Afrĭcam crudelissĭmis suppliciis exstinctus est.

    13. Tandem, C. Lutatio Catŭlo, A. Postumio
A. U.
513. consulĭbus, anno belli Punĭci vicesĭmo tertio magnum prœlium navāle commissum est contra Lily-
bæum, promontorium Siciliæ. In eo prœlio septuaginta tres
Carthaginiensium naves captæ, centum viginti quinque
demersæ, triginta duo millia hostium capta, tredĕcim
millia occīsa sunt. Statim Carthagiuienses pacem petiērunt, eisque pax tribūta est. Captīvi Romanōrum,[a] qui
tenebantur a Carthaginiensĭbus reddĭti sunt. Pœni
Siciliâ,[b] Sardiniâ, et cetĕris insŭlis, quæ inter Italiam
Africamque jacent, decessērunt, omnemque Hispaniam,
quæ citra Ibērum est, Romānis permisērunt.

LIBER TERTIUS.

    1. Anno quingentesĭmo undetricesĭmo ingentes
A. U.
229. Gallōrum copiæ Alpes transiērunt. Sed pro Romānis tota Italia consensit: traditumque est,
octingenta millia homĭnum[a] ad id bellum parāta fuisse.[c]
Res prospĕrè gesta est apud Clusium: quadraginta
millia homĭnum interfecta sunt. Alĭquot annis[d] pòst
pugnātum est[c] contra Gallos in agro Insŭbrum, finitumque
est bellum M. Claudio Marcello, Cn. Cornelio Scipiōne
consulĭbus. Tum Marcellus regem Gallōrum, Viridom-

---

[a] § 212.   [c] § 269.   [e] § 209, R. 3, (2.)
[b] § 242.   [d] § 236.

ārum, manu suâ occīdit, et triumphans spòlia Galli stipīti imposīta humĕris suis vexit.

2. Paulò pòst Punīcum bellum renovātum est per Hannibălem,[a] Carthaginiensium ducem, quem pater Hamilcar novem annos[b] natum aris admovĕrat, ut odium perenne in Romānos jurāret. Hic annum agens vicesĭmum ætātis Saguntum, Hispaniæ civitātem, Romānis amicam, oppugnāre[c] aggressus est. Huic Romāni per legātos denuntiavērunt, ut bello abstinēret.[d] Qui quum legātos admittĕre nollet, Romāni Carthagĭnem misērunt, ut mandarētur Hannibāli,[e] ne bellum contra socios popŭli Romāni gerĕret. Dura responsa a Carthaginiensĭbus reddĭta. Saguntīnis interea fame victis, Romāni Carthaginiensĭbus bellum indixērunt.

A. U. 536.

3. Hannĭbal, fratre Hasdrubăle in Hispaniâ relicto, Pyrenæum[f] et Alpes transiit. Tradĭtur * in Italiam octoginta millia pedĭtum, et viginti millia equĭtum, septem et triginta elephantos abduxisse. Interea multi Ligŭres et Galli Hannibāli[g] se conjunxērunt. Primus ei occurrit P. Cornelius Scipio, qui, prœlio ad Ticīnum commisso, superātus est, et, vulnĕre accepto, in castra rediit. Tum Sempronius Gracchus conflixit ad Trebiam amnem. Is quoque vincĭtur. Multi popŭli se Hannibāli dedidērunt. Inde in Tusciam progressus Flaminium consŭlem ad Trasimēnum lacum supĕrat. Ipse Flaminius interemptus. Romanōrum viginti quinque millia cæsa sunt.

4. Quingentesĭmo et quadragesĭmo anno post urbem condĭtam L. Æmilius Paullus et P. Terentius Varro contra Hannibālem mittuntur. Quamquam

A. U. 540.

---

* Is *tradĭtur* used personally or impersonally ? § 271, R. 2.

[a] § 247, R. 1.   [d] § 273, 2.   [f] § 233, (3.)
[b] § 236.   [e] § 223, R. 2.   [g] § 224.
[c] § 271.

intellectum erat, Hannibălem non alĭter vinci posse[a]
quàm morâ, Varro tamen moræ[b] impatiens apud vicum,
qui Cannæ[c] appellātur, in Apuliâ pugnāvit; ambo consŭles vi͡cti, Paullus interemptus est. In eâ pugnâ consu-
lāres aut prætorii viginti, senatōres triginta capti aut occīsi;
milĭtum quadraginta millia; equĭtum tria millia et quin-
genti̇ periērunt. In his tantis malis nemo tamen pacis
mentiōnem facĕre dignātus est. Servi, quod[d] nunquam
antè factum, manumissi et milītes facti sunt.

5. Post eam pugnam multæ Italiæ civitātes, quæ
Romānis[e] paruĕrant, se ad Hannibălem transtulērunt.
Hannĭbal Romānis obtŭlit,[f] ut captīvos redimĕrent; re-
sponsumque est a senātu, eos cives non esse necessarios,
qui armāti capi potuissent. Hòs omnes ille postea variis
suppliciis interfēcit, et tres modios aureōrum annulōrum ·
Carthagĭnem misit, quos manĭbus[g] equĭtum Romanōrum,
senatōrum, et milĭtum detraxĕrat. Interea in Hispaniâ
frater Hannibălis, Hasdrŭbal, qui ibi remansĕrat cum magno exercĭtu, a duōbus Scipionĭbus vincĭtur, perdĭtque in
pugnâ triginta quinque millia homĭnum.

6. Anno quarto postquàm Hannĭbal in Italiam venĕrat,
M. Claudius Marcellus consul apud Nolam, civitātem Cam-
paniæ, contra Hannibălem benè pugnāvit. Illo tempŏre
Philippus, Demetrii filius, rex Macedoniæ, ad Hannibălem
legātos mittit, eīque auxilia contra Romānos pollicētur.
Qui legāti quum a Romānis capti essent, M. Valerius
Lævīnus cum navĭbus missus est, qui regem impedīret,[h]
quò minùs copias in Italiam trajicĕret.[i] Idem in Macedoniam penĕtrans regem Philippum vicit.

[a] § 272. [d] § 206, (13.) [g] § 224, R. 2.
[b] § 213. [e] § 223, R. 2. [h] § 264, 5.
[c] § 210, R. 2. [f] § 229, R. 5. [i] § 262.

7. In Siciliâ quoque res prospĕrè gesta est. Marcellus magnam hujus insŭlæ[a] partem cepit, quam Pœni occupavĕrant; Syracūsas, nobilissimam urbem, expugnāvit, et ingentem inde prædam Romam misit. Lævinus in Macedoniâ cum Philippo et multis Græciæ popŭlis amicitiam fecit; et in Siciliam profectus Hannōnem, Pœnōrum ducem, apud Agrigentum cepit; quadraginta civitātes in deditiōnem accēpit, viginti sex expugnāvit. Ita omni Siciliâ receptâ, cum ingenti gloriâ Romam regressus est.

8. Interea[b] in Hispaniam,[c] ubi duo Scipiōnes ab Hasdrubăle interfecti erant, missus est P. Cornelius Scipio, vir Romanōrum omnium ferè primus. Hic, puer[d] duodeviginti annōrum, in pugnâ ad Ticīnum, patrem singulāri virtūte[e] servāvit. Deinde post cladem Cannensem[f] multos[g] nobilissimōrum juvĕnum Italiam deserĕre[h] cupientium, auctoritāte suâ ab hoc consilio deterruit. Viginti quatuor annōrum juvĕnis in Hispaniam missus, die, quâ venit, Carthagĭnem Novam cepit, in quâ omne aurum et argentum et belli apparātum Pœni habēbant, nobilissĭmos quoque obsĭdes, quos ab Hispānis accepĕrant. Hos obsĭdes parentĭbus suis[i] reddĭdit. Quare omnes ferè Hispaniæ civitātes ad eum uno anĭmo transiērunt.

9. Ab eo inde tempŏre res Romanōrum in dies lætiōres factæ sunt. Hasdrŭbal a fratre ex[j] Hispaniâ in Italiam evocātus, apud Senam, Picēni civitātem, in insidias incĭdit, et strenuè pugnans occīsus est. Plurĭmæ autem civitātes, quæ in Bruttiis ab Hannibăle tenebantur, Romānis se tradidērunt.

---

[a] § 212.
[b] § 23.
[c] § 20.
[d] § 204.

[e] § 279, 10.
[f] § 128, 6, (a.) & (b.)
[g] § 205, R. 12.

[h] § 271.
[i] § 208, (7.)
[j] § 242, R. 1.

A. U.
550.

10. Anno decīmo quarto postquam in Italiam Hannĭbal venĕrat, Scipio consul creātus, et ın Afrĭcam missus est. Ibi contra Hannōnem, ducem Carthaginiensium, prospĕrè pugnat, totumque ejus exercĭtum delet. Secundo prœlio undēcim millia homĭnum occīdit, et castra cepit cum quatuor millĭbus et quingentis militĭbus. Syphācem, Numidiæ regem, qui se cum Pœnis conjunxĕrat, cepit, eumque cum nobilissĭmis Numīdis et infinītis spoliis Romam misit. Quâ re audītâ, onınis ferè Italia Hannibālem desĕrit. Ipse a Carthaginien-

A. U.
553.

sĭbus in Afrĭcam redīre jubētur. Ita anno decīmo septĭmo Italia ab Hannibāle liberāta est.

11. Post plures pugnas et pacem plùs[a] semel frustrà tentātam, pugna ad Zamam committĭtur, in quâ peritissĭmi duces copias suas ad belium educēbant. Scipio victor recēdit ; Hannĭbal cum paucis equitĭbus evādit. Post hoc prœlium pax cum Carthaginiensĭbus facta est. Scipio, quum Romam rediisset, ingenti gloriâ triumphāvit, atque Africānus appellātus est. Sic finem accēpit secundum Punĭcum bellum pòst[b] annum undevicesĭmum quàm cœpĕrat.

LIBER QUARTUS.

A. U.
556.

1. Finīto Punĭco bello, secūtum est Macedonĭcum[c] contra Philippum regem. Sŭperātus est rex a T. Quinctio Flaminio apud Cynoscephālas, paxque ei data est his legĭbus :[d] *ne Grœciæ civitatĭbus, quas Romāni contra eum defendĕrant, bellum inferret ;*[e]

---

[a] § 256, R. 6.	[c] § 209, R. 2, (1,) (*b*.)	[e] § 262.
[b] § 253, R. 1.	[d] § 249, II.	

*it captivos et transfŭgas reddĕret; quinquag.i.ta svlùm
naves habēret; relīquas Romānis daret; mille talenta
præstāret, et obsĭdem^a daret filium Demetrium.* T
Quinctius etiam Lacedæmoniis intŭlit bellum, et ducem
eōrum Nabīdem[b] vicit.

A. U 563.

2. Finīto bello Macedonico, secūtum est bellum Syriăcum contra Antiŏchum regem, cum quo
Hannĭbal se junxĕrat. Missus est contra eum L. Cornelius Scipio[c] consul, cui frater ejus Scipio Africānus legātus
est addītus. Hannĭbal navāli prœlio victus,[d] Antiŏchus
autem ad Magnesiam, Asiæ civitātem, a Cornelio Scipiōne
consŭle ingenti prœlio fusus est. Tum rex Antiŏchus
pacem petit. Data est ei hâc lege, *ut ex Eurōpá et Asiá
recedĕret, atque intra Taurum se continēret, decem millia
talentōrum et viginti obsĭdes præbēret, Hannibālem, con-
citōrem belli, dedĕret.* Scipio Romam rediit, et ingenti
gloriâ triumphāvit. Nomen et ipse, ad imitatiōnem fratris, Asiatĭci accēpit.

3. Philippo, rege Macedoniæ, mortuo, filius ejus Perseus rebellāvit, ingentĭbus copiis parātis. Dux Romanōrum, P. Licinius consul, contra eum missus, gravi prœlio
a rege victus est. Rex tamen pacem petēbat. Cui
Romāni eam præstāre noluērunt, nisi his conditionĭbus, ut
se et suos Romānis dedĕret. Mox Æmilius Paullus consul
regem ad Pydnam superāvit, et viginti millia pedī-
tum[e] ejus occīdit. Equitātus cum rege fugit.

A. U. 586.

Urbes Macedoniæ omnes, quas rex tenuĕrat, Romānis se dedidērunt. Ipse Perseus ab amīcis desertus in
Paulli potestātem venit. Hic, multis etiam aliis rebus
gestis, cum ingenti pompâ[f] Romam rediit in nave Persei,

---

^a § 230, R. 2.	^c § 279, 9.	^e § 212.
^b § 204.	^d § 209, R. 4.	^f § 247 2.

inusitātæ magnitudĭnis ;" nam sedĕcim remōrum ordĭnes
habuisse dicĭtur. Triumphāvit magnificentissĭmè in curru
aureo, duōbus filiis utrōque latĕre[b] adstantĭbus. Ante
currum inter captīvos duo regis filii et ipse Perseus ducti
sunt.

4. Tertium deinde bellum contra Carthagĭnem
susceptum est sexcentesĭmo et altĕro[c] anno ab
urbe condĭtâ,[d] anno quinquagesĭmo primo postquàm secundum bellum Punĭcum transactum erat. L.
Manlius Censorīnus et M. Manlius consŭles in Afrĭcam
trajecērunt,[e] et oppugnavērunt Carthagĭnem. Multa ibi
præclārè gesta sunt per Scipiōnem, Scipiōnis Afrĭcāni
nepōtem, qui tribūnus in Africâ milītābat. Hujus apud
omnes ingens metus et reverentia erat, neque quidquam
magìs Carthaginiensium duces vitābant, quàm contra eum
prœlium committĕre.

A. U.
602.

5. Quum jam magnum esset Scipiōnis nomen, tertio
anno postquàm Romāni in Afrĭcam trajecĕrant, consul est
creātus, et contra Carthagĭnem missus. Is hanc
urbem a civĭbus acerrimè defensam[f] cepit ac
dĭruit. Ingens ibi præda facta, plurimăque inventa
sunt, quæ multārum civitātum excidiis Carthāgo collegĕ-
rat. Hæc omnia Scipio civitātĭbus Italiæ, Siciliæ, Afrĭcæ
reddĭdit, quæ sua recognoscēbant. Ita Carthāgo septingentesĭmo anno, postquam condĭta erat, delēta est. Scipio
nomen Afrĭcāni juniōris accēpit.

A. U.
608.

6. Intĕrim in Macedoniâ quidam Pseŭdophilippus arma
movit, et P. Juvencium, Romanōrum ducem, ad interneciōnem vicit. Post eum Q. Cæcilius Metellus dux a
Romānis contra Pseudophilippum missus est, et, vigintí

---

[a] § 211, R. 6.   [c] § 120, 1.   [e] § 229, R. 4, 1.
[b] § 254, R. 3.   [d] § 274, R. 5, (a.)   [f] § 274. 3.

quinque millĭbus ex militĭbus ejus occīsis, Macedoı iam recēpit; ipsum etiam Pseudophilippum in potestātem suam redēgit. Corinthiis quoque bellum indictum est, nobilissĭmæ Græciæ civitāti,* propter injuriam Romānis legātis illātam. Hanc Mummius consul cepit ac diruit. Tres igĭtur Romæ simul celeberrĭmi triumphi fuērunt; Scipiōnis* ex Africâ, ante cujus currum ductus est Hasdrŭbal; Metelli* ex Macedoniâ, cujus currum præcessit Andriscus, qui et Pseudophilippus dicĭtur, Mummii* ex Corintho, ante quem signa ænea et pictæ tabŭlæ et alia urbis clarissĭmæ ornamenta prælāta sunt.

A. U. 608.

7. Anno sexcentesĭmo decĭmo post urbem condĭtam Viriāthus in Lusitaniâ bellum contra Romānos excitāvit. Pastor primò fuit, mox latrōnum dux; postrēmò tantos ad bellum popŭlos concitāvit, ut vindex libertātis Hispaniæ existimarētur. Denĭque a suis[b] interfectus est. Quum interfectōres ejus præmium a Cæpiōne consŭle petĕrent, responsum est, nunquam Romānis placuisse,† imperatōrem a militĭbus suis interfĭci.

A. U. 610.

8. Deinde bellum exortum est cum Numantīnis, civitāte Hispaniæ. Victus ab his Qu. Pompēius, et post eum C. Hostilius Mancīnus consul, qui pacem cum iis fecit infāmem, quam popŭlus et senātus jussit infringi, atque ipsum Mancīnum hostĭbus tradi. Tum P. Scipio Africānus in Hispaniam missus est. Is primùm milĭtem ignāvum et corruptum correxit; tum multas Hispaniæ civitātes partim bello cepit, partim in deditiōnem accēpit. Postrēmò ipsam Numantiam fame ad deditiōnem coēgit, urbemque evertit; relīquam provinciam in fidem accēpit.

A. U 621.

---

* What is understood?
† What is the subject of *placuisse?* § 269.

[a] § 204, R. 3.   [b] § 205, R. 7, (1.) N. 1.

9. P. Scipiōne Nasīcâ et L. Calpurnio Bestiâ con
sulĭbus, Jugurthæ, Numidārum regi, bellum illātum est, quòd
Adherbālem et Hiempsălem, Micipsæ filios, patruēles suos,
interemisset.* Missus adversùs eum consul Calpurnius
Bestia corruptus regis pecuniâ pacem cum eo flagitiosis-
sĭmam fecit, quæ a senātu improbāta est. Denĭque Qu.
Cæcilius Metellus consul Jugurtham variis prœliis vicit,
elephantos ejus occĭdit vel cepit, multas civitātes ipsĭus in
deditiōnem accēpit. Ei successit C. Marius, qui bello
⸳erminum posuit, ipsumque Jugurtham cepit. Ante

A. U.
648.

currum triumphantis Marii Jugurtha cum duōbus
filiis ductus est vinctus, et mox jussu consŭlis in
carcĕre strangulātus.

LIBER QUINTUS.

1. Dum bellum in Numidiâ contra Jugurtham geritur,
Cimbri et Teutŏnes aliæque Germanōrum et Gallōrum
gentes Italiæ* minabantur, aliæque Romanōrum exercĭtus
fudērunt. Ingens fuit Romæ* timor, ne* itĕrum Galli
urbem occupārent. Ergo Marius consul* creātus, eīque
bellum contra Cimbros et Teutŏnes decrētum est; bellō-
que protracto, tertius ei et quartus consulātus delātus est.
In duōbus prœliis cum Cimbris ducenta millia hostium
cecĭdit, octoginta millia cepit, eorumque regem Theutobŏ-
chum; propter quod merĭtum absens quintò Consul creā-

A. U.
653.

tus est. Interea Cimbri et Teutŏnes, quorum
copia adhuc infinīta erat, in Italiam transiērunt.
Itĕrum a C. Mario et Qu. Catŭlo contra eos

---

a § 266, 3.   *c* § 221, I.   *e* § 210.

b § 223, R. 2.   *d* § 262, R. 7.

dimicātum est* ad Verōnam. Centum et quadraginta millia aut in pugnâ aut in fugâ cæsa sunt; sexaginta millia capta. Tria et triginta Cimbris᭢ signa sublāta sunt.

2. Sexcentesimo quinquagesimo nono anno ab urbe condītâ in Italiâ gravissimum bellum exarsit. A. U. 659. Nam Picentes, Marsi, Pelignique, qui multos annos populo Romāno obediērant, æqua cum illis jura sibi dari postulābant. Perniciōsum admŏdum hoc bellum fuit. P. Rutilius consul in eo occīsus est; plures exercītus fusi fugatīque. Tandem L. Cornelius Sulla cùm᭣ alia egregiè gessit, tum Cluentium, hostium ducem, cum magnis copiis,᭤ fudit. Per quadriennium cum gravi utriusque partis calamitāte hoc bellum tractum est. Quinto demum anno L. Cornelius Sulla ei imposuit finem. Romāni tamen, id᭣ quod priùs negavērant, jus civitātis, bello finīto, sociis tribuērupt.

3. Anno urbis condītæ sexcentesimo sexagesimo sexto primum Romæ bellum civīle exortum A. U. 666. est; eōdem anno etiam Mithridatīcum. Causam bello civīli C. Marius dedit. Nam quum Sullæ bellum adversùs Mithridātem regem Ponti decrētum esset, Marius ei᭢ hunc honōrem eripēre conātus est. Sed Sulla, qui adhuc cum legionībus suis in Italiâ morabātur, cum exercītu Romam venit, et adversarios cùm interfēcit, tum fugāvit. Tum rebus Romæ utcunque compositis, in Asiam profectus est, pluribusque prœliis Mithridātem cœgit, ut pacem a Romānis petēret,᭦ et Asiâ, quam invasěrat, relictâ, regni sui finībus contentus esset.

4. Sed dum Sulla in Græciâ et Asiâ Mithridātem vincit, Marius, qui fugātus fuěrat, et Cornelius Cinna, unus

---

ex consulĭbus, bellum in Italiâ reparârunt, et ingressi Ro
mam nobilissimos ex senatu* et consulăres viros interfecĕ-
runt; multos proscripsērunt; ipsius Sullæ domo eversâ,
filios et. uxōrem ad fugam compulērunt. Universus relĭquus senātus ex urbe fugiens ad Sullam in Græciam
venit, orans ut patriæ subvenīret. Sulla in Italiam trajēcit, hostium exercĭtus vicit, mox etiam urbem ingressus
est, quam cæde* et sanguĭne civium replēvit. Quatuor
millia inermium, qui se dedidĕrant, interfĭci jussit; duo millia equĭtum et senatōrum proscripsit. Tum de Mithridāte
triumphāvit. Duo hæc bella funestissĭma, Italĭcum, quod
et sociāle dictum est, et civīle, consumpsērunt ultra centum
et quinquagĭnta millia homĭnum, viros consulăres vigĭnti
quatuor, prætorios septem, ædilĭtios sexaginta, senatōres
ferè ducentos.

LIBER SEXTUS.

A. U.
676.
1. ANNO urbis condītæ* sexcentesĭmo* septua
gesĭmo sexto, L. Licinio Lucullo* et M. Aurelio
Cottâ consulĭbus, mortuus est Nicomēdes, rex Bi-
thyniæ, et testamento popŭlum Romānum fecit herēdem.′
Mithridātes, pace ruptâ,* Asiam. rursus voluit invadĕre.
Adversùs eum ambo consŭles missi variam habuêre fortūnam. Cotta apud Chalcedŏnem victus prœlio, a rege
etiam intra oppidum obsessus est. Sed quum se inde
Mithridātes Cyzīcum* transtulisset, ut, hac urbe captâ,

---

* § 212, R. 2, N. 4.   d § 120, 2.   * § 257, R. 5.
b § 249, I.   * § 279, 9.   ʌ § 237.
o § 274, R. 5, (a.)   ſ § 230.

totam Asiam invadĕret, Lucullus ei,[a] alter consul, occurrit, ac dum Mithridātes in obsidiōne Cyzĭci commorātur, ipse eum a tergo obsēdit, famēque consumptum multis prœliis vicit. Postrēmò Byzantium[b] fugāvit ; navāli quoque prœlio ejus duces oppressit. Ita unâ hiĕme[c] et æstāte a Lucullo centum ferè millia milītum regis exstincta sunt.

2. Anno urbis sexcentesĭmo septuagesĭmo octāvo novum in Italiâ bellum commōtum est. Septuaginta enim quatuor gladiatōres, ducĭbus[d] Spartāco, Crixo, et Œnomao, e ludo gladiatorio, qui Capuæ[e] erat, effugērunt, et per Italiam vagantes pæne non levius bellum, quàm Hannĭbal,[f] movērunt. Nam contraxērunt exercĭtum ferè sexaginta millium armatōrum, multosque duces et duos Romānos consūles vicērunt. Ipsi victi sunt in Apuliâ a M. Licinio Crasso proconsūle, et, post multas calamitātes Italiæ,[*] tertio anno huic bello finis est impositus.   •

A. U. 678.

3. Intĕrim L. Lucullus bellum Mithridatĭcum persecūtus regnum Mithridātis invāsit, ipsumque regem apud Cabīra civitātem, quò ingentes copias ex omni regno adduxĕrat Mithridātes, ingenti prœlio superātum fugāvit, et castra ejus diripuit. Armenia quoque Minor, quam tenēbat, eīdem† erepta est. Susceptus est Mithridātes a Tigrāne, Armeniæ rege, qui tum ingenti gloriâ imperābat ; sed hujus quoque regnum Lucullus est ingressus. Tigranocerta, nobilissĭmam Armeniæ civitātem, cepit ; ipsum regem, cum magno exercĭtu venientem, ita vicit, ut rcbur

---

[*] Is this genitive *subjective* or *objective?* § 211, R. 2.
† i. e. *Mithridāti.*

[a] § 224.	[c] § 253.	[e] § 221, l.
[b] § 237.	[d] § 257, R. 7.	[f] § 278.

militum Armeniōrum delēret. Sed quum Lucullus finem
bello impōnēre parāret, successor ei* missus est.

4. Per illa tempŏra pirātæ omnia maria infestābant ita,
ut[b] Romānis, toto orbe[c] terrārum victorībus, sola navigatio
tuta non esset. Quare id bellum Cn. Pompēio decrētum
est, quod intra paucos menses incredibĭli felicitāte
et celeritāte confēcit. Mox ei delātum bellum
contra regem Mithridātem et Tigrānem. Quo sus-
cepto, Mithridātem in Armeniâ Minōre nocturno prœlio
vicit, castra diripuit, et quadraginta millĭbus ejus occīsis,
viginti tantùm de exercĭtu suo perdĭdit et duos centuriōnes.
Mithridātes fugit cum uxōre et duōbus comitĭbus, neque
multò pòst, Pharnācis filii sui seditiōne coactus, venēnum
hausit. Hunc vitæ finem habuit Mīthridātes, vir ingentis
industriæ[d] atque consilii. Regnāvit annis[e] sexaginta, vixit
septuaginta duōbus: contra Romānos bellum habuit annis
quadraginta.

A. U
687.

5. Tigrāni deinde Pompēius bellum intŭlit. Ille[f] se[g]
ei[h] dedĭdit, et in castra Pompēii venit, ac diadēma suum[g]
in ejus[h] manĭbus collocāvit, quod ei Pompēius[i] reposuit.
Parte[j] regni eum multāvit et grandi pecuniâ. Tum alios
etiam reges et popŭlos superāvit. Armeniam Minōrem
Deiotăro, Galatiæ regi, donāvit, quia auxilium contra
Mithridātem tulěrat. Seleuciam, vicīnam Antiochīæ civitātem, libertāte[k] donāvit, quòd regem Tigrānem non recepisset.[l] Inde in Judæam transgressus, Hierosolўmam,
caput gentis, tertio mense cepit, duodĕcim millĭbus Judæōrum occīsis, cetěris in fidem receptis. His gestis finem

---

[a] § 211, R. 5.	[e] § 236.	[i] § 9, 1.
[b] § 262, R. 1.	[f] § 207, R. 23.	[j] § 251.
[c] § 254, R. 3.	[g] § 208.	[k] § 249, 1.
[d] § 211, R. 6.	[h] § 208, (6.)	[l] § 266, 3.

antiquissĭmo bello imposuit. Ante triumphantis* currum ducti sunt filii Mithridātis, filius Tigrānis, et Aristobūlus, rex Judæōrum. Prælāta ingens pecunia, auri atque argenti infinītum.† Hoc tempŏre nullum per orbem terrārum grave bellum erat.

6. M. Tullio Cicerōne oratōre et C. Antonio consulĭbus, anno ab urbe condĭtâ sexcentesĭmo undenonagesĭmo L. Sergius Catilīna, nobilissĭmi genĕris vir, sed ingenii pravissĭmi, ad delendam patriam conjurāvit cum quibusdam claris quidem⁴ sed audacĭbus viris. A Cicerōne urbe⁵ expulsus est, socii ejus deprehensi et in carcĕre strangulāti sunt. Ab Antonio, altĕro consŭle, Catilīna ipse prœlio victus est et interfectus.

A U. 689.

7. Anno urbis condĭtæ sexcentesimo nonagesĭmo tertio C. Julius Cæsar cum L. Bibŭlo consul est factus. Quum ei Gallia decrēta esset, semper vincendo⁶ usque ad Oceănum Britannĭcum processit. Domuit autem annis⁴ novem ferè omnem Galliam, quæ inter Alpes, flumen Rhodănum, Rhenum et Oceănum est. Britannis mox bellum intŭlit, quibus ante eum ne nomen quidem Romanōrum cognĭtum erat; Germānos quoque trans Rhenum aggressus, ingentĭbus prœliis vicit.

A. U. 693.

8. Circa eădem tempŏra M. Licinius Crassus contra Parthos missus est. Et quum circa Carras contra omina et auspicia prœlium commisisset, a Surēnâ, Orōdis regis duce, victus et interfectus est cum filio, clarissĭmo et præstantissĭmo juvĕne. Reliquiæ exercĭtûs per C. Cassium quæstōrem servātæ sunt.

A. U. 700.

---

* Supply *Pompĕii*.   † Supply *pondus*.

⁴ § 279, 3, (*a.*) & (*d.*)   ⁵ § 242.   ⁶ § 275, R. 4.   ⁴ § 253.

9*

9. Hinc jam bellum civīle success.t, quo Ro-
A. U.
705.
māni nomĭnis fortūna mutāta est. Cæsar enim
victor e Galliâ rediens, absens cœpit poscēre altē-
rum consulātum ; quem quum aliqui sine dubitatiōne de-
ferrent,[a] contradictum est[b] a Pompēio et aliis, jussusque est,
dimissis exercitĭbus, in urbem redīre. Propter hanc injuriam ab Arimĭno, ubi milĭtes congregātos habēbat, infesto
exercĭtu Romam contendit. Consŭles cum Pompēio,
senatusque omnis atque universa nobilĭtas ex urbe fugit, et
in Græciam transiit ; et, dum senātus bellum contra Cæ-
sărem parābat, hic vacuam urbem ingressus dictatōrem
se fecit.

10. Inde Hispanias petit, ibĭque Pompēii legiōnes superāvit ; tum in Græciâ adversùm Pompēium ipsum dimicāvit. Primo prœlio victus est et fugātus ; evāsit tamen,
quia nocte interveniente Pompēius sequi noluit ; dixitque
Cæsar, nec[c] Pompēium scire vincĕre, et illo tantùm die se
potuisse superāri. Deinde in Thessaliâ apud Pharsālum
ingentĭbus utrinque copiis commissis dimicavērunt. Nunquam adhuc Romānæ copiæ majōres neque meliorĭbus
ducĭbus[d] convenĕrant. Pugnātum est[e] ingenti contentiōne, victusque ad postrēmum Pompēius, et castra ejus di-
repta sunt. Ipse fugātus Alexandrĭam petiit, ut a rege
Ægypti, cui tutor a senātu datus fuĕrat, accipĕret auxilia.
At hic fortūnam magìs quàm amicitiam secūtus, occĭdit
Pompēium, caput ejus et annŭlum Cæsāri misit. Quo
conspecto, Cæsar lacrўmas fudisse dicĭtur, tanti viri intuens caput, et genĕri * quondam sui.

---

* Pompey married Julia, the daughter of Cæsar ; but she was now
dead.

a § 145, II 4.   c § 278, R. 7.   e § 209, R. 3, (2.)
b § 184, 2.   d § 249, III., & R.

11. Quum ad Alexandriam venisset Cæsar, Ptolemæus ei insidias parāre voluit, quâ de causâ regi bellum illātum est. Rex victus in Nilo periit, inventumque est corpus ejus cum loricâ aureâ. Cæsar, Alexandriâ potītus,
regnum Cleopătræ dedit. Tum inde profectus Pompeia-
nārum partium reliquias est persecūtus, bellisque civilī-
bus toto terrārum orbe compositis, Romam rediit. Ubi
quum insolentiùs agĕre cœpisset, conjurātum* est in eum
a sexaginta vel ampliùs senatorĭbus, equitibusque Romānis. Præcipui fuērunt inter conjurātos Bruti duo ex
genĕre illīus Bruti, qui, regĭbus expulsis, primus Romæ
consul fuĕrat, C. Cassius et Servilius Casca. Ergo Cæsar, quum in curiam venisset, viginti tribus A. U.
709.
vulnerĭbus confossus est.

12. Interfecto Cæsăre, anno urbis septingentesĭmo nono bella civilia reparāta sunt. Senātus favēbat Cæsăris
percussorĭbus,ᵇ Antonius consul a Cæsăris partĭbus stabat.
Ergo turbātâ republĭcâ, Antonius, multis scelerĭbus commissis, a senātu hostis judicātus est. Fusus fugatusque Antonius, amisso exercĭtu, confūgit ad Lepĭdum, qui Cæsări ᶜ
magister equĭtum fuĕrat, et tum grandes copias milĭtum habēbat; a quo susceptus est. Mox Octaviānus cum Antonio pacem fecit, et quasi vindicatūrusᵈ patris * sui mortem, a quo per testamentum fuĕrat adoptātus, Romam
cum exercĭtu profectus extorsit, ut sibi juvĕni viginti an-
nōrumᵉ consulātus darētur. Tum junctus cum Antonio
et Lepĭdo rempublīcam armis tenēre cœpit, senatumque
proscripsit. Per hos etiam Cicĕro orator occisus est, mul-
tīque alii nobĭles.

---

* i. e. *Julii Cæsăris.*

ª § 184, 2. ᶜ § 211, R. 5, (1.) ᵉ § 211, R. 6.
ᵇ § 223 R. 2. ᵈ § 274, R. 6.

13. Interea Brutus et Cassius, interfectōres Cæsaris
ingens bellum movērunt. Profecti contra eos Cæsar Octaviānus, qui postea Augustus est appellātus, et M. Antonius,

A. U. 712.

apud Philippos, Macedoniæ urbem, contra eos pugnavērunt. Primo prœlio victi sunt Antonius et
Cæsar; periit tamen dux nobilitātis Cassius; secundo Brutum et infinītam nobilitātem, quæ cum illis bellum suscepĕrat, victam* interfecērunt. Tum victōres
rempublīcam ita inter se divisērunt, ut Octaviānus Cæsar
Hispanias, Gallias, Italiam tenēret; Antonius Orientem,
Lepīdus Afrīcam accipĕret.

14. Paulò pòst Antonius, repudiātâ sorōre Cæsāris
Octaviāni, Cleopātram, regīnam Ægypti, uxōrem duxit.
Ab hâc incitātus ingens bellum commōvit, dum Cleopātra
cupiditāte muliĕbri optat Romæ regnāre. Victus est ab

A. U. 723.

Augusto navāli pugnâ clarâ et illustri apud Actium,
qui locus in Epīro est. Hinc fugit in Ægyptum,
et, desperātis rebus, quum omnes ad Augustum
transīrent, se ipse[b] interēmit. Cleopātra quoque aspīdem
sibi admīsit, et venēno ejus exstincta est. Ita bellis toto
orbe confectis, Octaviānus Augustus Romam rediit anno
duodecīmo* quàm consul fuĕrat. Ex eo inde tempōre
rempublīcam per quadraginta et quatuor annos solus obtinuit. Antè enim duodĕcim annis cum Antonio et Lepīdo
tenuĕrat.† Ita ab initio principātûs ejus usque ad finem
quinquaginta sex anni fuēre.

---

* Supply *post*. § 253, R. 1.   † What is understood?

   [a] § 205, R. 2, E.   [b] § 207, R. 28.

OF THE GEOGRAPHY AND THE NATIONS OF ANTIQUITY. ·

1. UNIVERSUS terrārum orbis in tres partes dividītur, Eurōpam,[a] Asiam, Āfrīcam. Eurōpa ab Afrĭcâ sejungĭtur freto Gaditāno, in cujus utrâque parte montes sunt altissĭmi, Abÿla in Afrĭcâ, in Eurōpâ Calpe, qui montes Hercŭlis columnæ appellantur. Per idem fretum mare internum, quod littorĭbus Eurōpæ, Asiæ, et Afrĭcæ includĭtur, jungĭtur cum Oceāno.

2. Eurōpa termĭnos[b] habet ab oriente Tanaim fluvium, pontum Euxīnum, et palūdem Mæotĭda;[c] a meridie, mare internum; ab occidente, mare Atlantĭcum sive Oceănum; a septentriōne, mare Britannĭcum Mare internum tres maxĭmos sinus habet. Quorum is, qui Asiam a Græciâ sejungit, Ægæum mare vocâtur; secundus, qui est inter Græciam et Italiam, Ionium; tertius denīque, qui occidentāles Italiæ oras alluit, a Romānis Tuscum, a Græcis Tyrrhēnum mare appellātur.

3. In eâ Eurōpæ parte, quæ ad occāsum vergit, prima terrārum est Hispania, quæ a tribus laterĭbus mari circumdāta per Pyrenæos montes cum Galliâ cohæret. Quum

---

[a] § 204, R. 10.　　　[b] § 230, R. 2.　　　[c] § 80, I.

universa Hispania dives sit[a] et fœcunda, ea tamen regio, quæ a flumine Bæti[b] Bætica vocătur, cetĕras fertilitāte[c] antecellit. Ibi Gades sitæ, insŭla cum urbe a Tyriis condĭtâ, quæ freto Gaditāno nomen dedit. Tota illa regic viris,[d] equis, ferro, plumbo, ære, argento, aurōque abundat, et ubi penuriâ aquārum minùs est fertĭlis, linum tamen aut spartum alit. Marmŏris quoque lapicidīnas habet. In Bæticâ minium reperĭtur.

4. Gallia posĭta est inter Pyrenæos montes et Rhenum; orientālem oram Tuscum mare alluit, occidentālem Oceănus. Ejus pars illa, quæ Italiæ[e] est opposĭta, et Narbonensis vocātur, omnium * est lætissĭma. In eâ orâ sita est Massilia, urbs a Phocæis condĭta, qui, patriâ a Persis devictâ, quum servitūtem ferre non possent, Asiâ relictâ, novas in Eurōpâ sedes quæsivĕrant. Ibĭdem est campus lapideus, ubi Hercŭles dicĭtur contra Neptūni libĕros dimicâsse. Quum tela defecissent, Jupĭter filium imbre lapĭdum adjūvit. Credas[f] pluisse; † adeò multi passim jacent.

5. Rhodănus fluvius, haud longè a Rheni fontĭbus ortus, lacu Lemāno excipĭtur, servatque impĕtum, ita ut per medium lacum intĕger fluat, tantusque, quantus venit, egrediātur. Inde ad occāsum versus, Gallias aliquandiu dirĭmit; donec, cursu in meridiem flexo, aliōrum amnium accessu auctus in mare effundĭtur.

6. Ea pars Galliæ, quæ ad Rhenum porrigĭtur, frumenti[g] pabulīque feracissĭma est, cœlum salūbre; noxia animalium genĕra pauca alit. Incŏlæ superbi et superstitiōsi, ita ut deos humānis victĭmis[h] gaudēre existĭment.

---

* Supply *partium*.   † Supply *illos*, i. e. *lapĭdes*.

[a] § 263, 5, R. 1.   [d] § 250, 2, (2.)   [g] § 213.
[b] § 82, E. 2, (b.)   [e] § 224.   [h] § 247, 1, (2.)
[c] § 250.   [f] § 261, R. 4.

Magistri religiōnum et sapientiæ sunt Druīdæ, qui, quæ* se scire profitentur, in antris abditisque silvis docent. Anīmas æternas esse credunt, vitamque altĕram post mortem incipĕre. Hanc ob causam cum defunctis arma cremant aut defodiunt, eamque doctrīnam homines ad bellum* alacriōres facĕre existĭmant.

7. Universa Gallia divīsa est inter tres magnos popŭlos, qui fluviis terminantur. A Pyrenæo monte usque ad Garumnam Aquitāni habĭtant; inde ad Sequănam Celtæ; Belgæ denĭque usque ad Rhenum pertĭnent.

8. Garumna amnis, ex Pyrenæo monte delapsus, diu vadōsus est et vix navigabĭlis. Quanto* magis procēdit, tanto fit latior; ad postrēmum magni freti* simīlis, non solùm majōra navigia tolĕrat, verùm etiam more maris exsurgit, navigantesque* atrocīter jactat.

9. Sequăna ex Alpĭbus ortus in septentriōnem pergit. Postquàm se haud procul Lutetiâ* cum Matrŏnâ conjunxit, Oceāno* infundĭtur. Hæc flumĭna opportunissima sunt mercĭbus* permutandis et ex mari* interno in Oceănum transvehendis.

10. Rhenus itĭdem ex Alpĭbus ortus haud procul ab origĭne lacum effĭcit Venĕtum, qui etiam Brigantīnus appellātur. Deinde longo spatio* per fines Helvetiōrum, Mēdiomatricōrum, et Trevirōrum continuo alveo fertur, aut modĭcas insŭlas* circumfluens; in agro Batăvo autem, ubi Oceăno appropinquāvit, in plures amnes divĭditur; nec jam amnis, sed ripis longè recedentĭbus, ingens lacus,

---

* § 206, (4.)   ᵉ § 205, R. 7, (1,) N.·1.   ⁱ § 82, E. 1.
ᵇ § 213, R. 4, (2.)   ᶠ § 241, R. 2.   ʲ § 236.
ᶜ § 256, R. 16, & (2.)   ᵍ § 224.   ᵏ § 233.
ᵈ § 222, R 2.   ʰ § 275, R. 2.

Flevo appellātur, ejusdemque nomĭnis insŭlam amp exus. fit itĕrum arctior et fluvius itĕrum in mare emittĭtur.

11. Trans Rhenum Germāni habĭtant usque ad·Vistŭ lam, quæ finis est Germaniæ ad orientem. Ad meridiein termĭnātur Alpĭbus, ad septentriōnem mari Britannĭco et Baltico. Incŏlæ corpŏrum proceritāte excellunt. Anĭmos bellando* corpŏra laborĭbus exercent. Hanc ob causam crebrò bella gerunt cum finitĭmis, non tam finium prolatan- dōrum* causâ, aut imperii cupiditāte, sed ob belli amōrem. Mites tamen sunt erga supplĭces* et boni hospitĭbus. Urbes mœnĭbus cinctas aut fossis aggeribusque munitas non habent. Ipsas domos ad breve tempus struunt non lapidĭbus aut laterĭbus coctis sed lignis, quæ frondĭbus tegunt. Nam diu eōdem in loco morāri* periculōsum arbitrantur libertāti.

12. Agricultūræ* Germāni non admŏdùm student, nec quisquam agri modum cerſum aut fines proprios habet. Lacte vescuntur et caseo et carne. Ubi fons, campus, ne- musve iis placuērit,* ibi domos figunt, mox aliò transitūri cum conjugĭbus et libĕris. Interdum etiam hiĕmein in subterraneis specŭbus dicuntur transigĕre.

13. Germania altis montĭbus, silvis, paludibusquė invia reddĭtur. Inter silvas* maxĭma est Hercynia, cujus latitui dĭnem Cæsar novem diērum iter* patēre narrat. Inse- quenti tempŏre magna pars ejus excĭsa est. Flumĭna sunt in Germaniâ multa et magna. Inter hæc clarissĭmum nomen Rheni, de quo supra dix̄mu̇s, et Danubii. Clar- quoque amnes, Mœnus, Visurgis, Alh· Danubius om-

----

* § 275, III., R. 4. * § 269, R. 1.
* § 275, III., R. 1. * § 223.
* § 222, R. 4, (3.) * § 223, R. 2.

nium Europæ fluminum maximus, apud Rhætos oritur, .
flexōque ad ortum solis cursu, receptisque sexaginta amni-
bus, in. Pontum Euxinum sex vastis ostiis effunditur.

14. Britanniam insulam Phœnicibus innotuisse, eosque
stannum inde et plumbum pellesque petivisse, probabile
est. Romānis eam Julius Cæsar primus aperuit; neque
tamen priùs cognita esse cœpit quàm Claudio[a] imperante.
Hadriānus eam, muro ab oceăno Germanīco ad Hibernī-
cum mare ducto, in duas partes divīsit, ut inferiōrem insūlæ partem, quæ Romānis parēbat, a barbarōrum populōrum, qui in Scotiâ habităbant, incursionĭbus tuerētur.

15. Maxĭma insūlæ pars campestris, collĭbus passim
silvisque distincta. Incŏlæ Gallos proceritāte[b] corpŏrum
vincunt, ceterùm ingenio[b] Gallis simīles, simpliciōres tamen
illis[c] magisque barbāri. Nemŏra habĭtant pro urbĭbus.
Ibi tuguria exstruunt et stabŭla pecŏri, sed plerùmque ad
breve tempus. Humanitāte cetĕris præstant ii, qui Can
tium incŏlunt. Tota hæc regio est maritīma. Qui in
teriōrem insūlæ partem habĭtant, frumenta non serunt; lacte[d] et carne vi/unt. Pro vestĭbus indūti sunt pellĭbus.[e]

16. Italia ab Alpĭbus usque ad fretum Sicŭlum porrigitur inter mare Tuscum et Adriatĭcum. Multo[f] longior
est quàm latior.[g] In medio se attollit Apennīnus mons,
qui, postquàm continenti jugo progressus est usque ad
Apuliam, in duos quasi ramos dividĭtur. Nobilissĭma regio
ob fertilitātem soli cœlīque salubritātem. Quum longè
in mare procurrat, plurĭmos habet portus populōrum inter
se[h] patentes commercio.[i] Neque ulla facīlè[j] est regio.

---

[a] § 257. [e] § 249. [h] § 208, (5.)
[b] § 259. [f] § 256, R. 16, & (2.) [i] § 223.
[c] § 256, 2. [g] § 256, R. 12. [j] § 277, R. 7.
[d] § 245, 1. 4.

quæ tot tamque pulchras urbes habeat,[a] inter quas Roma et magnitudine et nominis famâ eminet.

17. Hæc urbs, orbis terrārum caput, septem montes complectĭtur.   Initio quatuor portas habēbat; Augusti ævo triginta septem.   Urbis magnificentiam augēbant fora, templa, portĭcus, aquæductus, theātra, arcus triumphāles, horti denĭque, et id genus[b] alia, ad quæ vel lecta animus stupet.   Quare rectè de eâ prædicāre videntur, qui nullĭus urbis in toto orbe terrārum magnificentiam ei[c] comparāri posse dixērunt.

18. Felicissĭma in Italiâ regio est Campania.   Multi ibi vitifēri colles, ubi nobilissĭma vina gignuntur, Setīnum, Cæcŭbum, Falernum, Massĭcum.   Calĭdi ibīdem fontes[d] saluberrĭmi.   Nusquam generosior olea.   Conchylio[c] quoque et pisce nobīli maria vicīna scatent.

19. Clarissĭmi amnes Italiæ sunt Padus et Tibĕris. Et Padus quidem in superiōre parte, quæ Gallia Cisalpīna vocātur, ab imis radicībus Vesŭli montis exorĭtur; primùm exīlis, deinde aliis amnĭbus ita alĭtur, ut se per septem ostia in mare effundat.   Tibĕris, qui antiquissĭmis temporĭbus Albŭlæ nomen habēbat, ex Apennīno orĭtur; deinde duōbus et quadraginta fluminĭbus auctus fit navigabĭlis.   Plurīmas in utrâque ripâ villas adspĭcit, præcipuè autem urbis Romānæ magnificentiam.   Placidissĭmus amnium rarò ripas egredĭtur.

20. In inferiōre parte Italiæ clara quondam urbs Tarentum, quæ maris sinui, cui adjăcet, nomen dedit.   Soli fertilītas cœlique jucunda temperies in causâ fuisse vidētur, ut incōlæ luxuriâ et deliciis enervarentur.   Quumque[f]

---

[a] § 264, 7.   [c] § 224.   [e] § 250, 2, (2.)
[b] § 231, R. 5, & 6.   [d] § 209, R. 4.   [f] § 263, 5, R. 1.

aliquandıu potentiâ* florērent, copiasque haud contemnen-
das alērent, peregrīnis tamen plerùmque ducītus in bellis
utebantur, ut Pyrrho, rege Epīri, quo superāto, urbs in
Romanōrum potestātem venit.

21. Proxĭma Italiæ est Sicilia, insŭla omnium* maris
interni maxĭma. Antiquissĭmis temporĭbus eam cum Italiâ
cohæsisse, marisque impĕtu, aut terræ motu inde divulsam
esse, verisimĭle est. Forma triangulāris, ita ut littĕræ,
quam Græci Delta vocant, imagĭnem refĕrat. A tribus
promontoriis vocātur Trinacria. Nobilissĭmus ibi mons
Ætnæ, qui urbi Catănæ immĭnet, tum ob altitudĭnem,
tum etiam ob ignes, quos effundit; quare Cyclōpum in illo
monte officīnam esse poëtæ dicunt. Cinēres e craterĭbus
egesti agrum circumjacentem fœcundum et ferācem red-
·dĕre existimantur. Sunt ibi Piōrum campi, qui nomen
habent a duōbus juvenĭbus Catanensĭbus, qui, flammis
quondam repentè ingruentĭbus, parentes senectūte confec-
tos, humĕris sublātos, flammæ* eripuisse feruntur. Nomĭna
fratrum Amphinōmus et Anāpus fuērunt.

22. Inter urbes Siciliæ nulla est illustrior Syracūsis,
Corinthiōrum coloniâ, ex quinque urbĭbus conflātâ. Ab
Atheniensĭbus bello petīta, maxĭmas hostium copias delēvit:
Carthaginienses etiam magnis interdum cladĭbus affēcit.
Secundo bello Punĭco per triennium oppugnāta, Archĭmē-
dis potissĭmùm ingenio et arte defensa, a M. Marcello
capta est. Vicīnus huic urbi fons Arethūsæ Nymphæ[c]
sacer, ad quam Alphēus[d] amnis ex Peloponnēso per mare
Ionium lapsus† comissāri‡ dicĭtur. Nam si quid ad
Olympiam in illum amnem jactum fuĕrit, id in Arethūsæ

---

* Supply *insulārum*.   † Supply *esse*.
‡ Infinitive denoting a purpose after *lapsus esse*. § 271, N. 3.
[a] § 250   [b] § 224, R. 2.   [c] § 222, 3.   [d] § 293. N.

fonte reddi.* De illâ fabŭlâ quid statuendum sit,* sponte appāret.

23. In mari Ligustĭco insŭla est Corsĭca, quam Græci Cyrnum vocant. Terra aspēra multisque locis[b] invia, cœlum grave, mare circà[c] importūnum. Incŏlæ latrociniis dediti feri sunt et horrĭdi. Mella quoque illīus insŭlæ amāra esse dicuntur corporibusque[d] nocēre. Proxĭma ei est Sardinia, quæ a Græcis mercatorĭbus Ichnūsa vocātur, quia formam humāni vestigii habet. Solum[e] quàm cœlum melius. Illud fertĭle, hoc grave ac noxium. Noxia quoque animalia herbasque venenātas gignit. Multum inde frumenti[f] Romam mittĭtur; unde hæc insŭla et Sicilia nutrices urbis vocantur.

24. Græcia nomĭnis celebritāte[g] omnes ferè alias orbis terrārum regiōnes superāvit. Nulla enim magnōrum ingeniōrum[h] fuit feracior; neque ulla belli pacisque artes majōre studio excoluit. Plurĭmas eădem colonias in omnes terræ partes deduxit. Multùm ităque terrâ marīque valuit, et gravissĭma bella magnâ cum gloriâ gessit.

25. Græcia inter Ionium et Ægæum mare porrigĭtur. In plurĭmas regiōnes divīsa est, quarum amplissĭmæ sunt Macedonia et Epīrus — quamquam hæ a nonnullis a Græciâ sejunguntur — tum Thessalia. Macedoniam Philippi et Alexandri regnum illustrāvit; quorum ille[i] Græciam subēgit, hic[i] Asiam latissĭmè domuit, ereptumque Persis[j] imperium in Macedōnes transtŭlit. Centum ejus regiōnis et quinquaginta urbes numerantur; quarum septuaginta

---

* Supply *dicĭtur*.

[a] § 265.	[e] § 209, R. 4.	[h] § 213.
[b] § 254, R. 3.	[f] § 212, R. 3.	[i] § 207, R. 23.
[c] § 235, R. 10.	[g] § 250.	[j] § 224, R. 2.
[d] § 223 R. 2.		

 quas, Perseo, ultimo Macedoniæ rege, superāto, Paullus
Æmilius diripuit.

26. Epīrus, quæ ab Acrocerauniis incīpit montĭbus,
desīnit in Achelŏo flumĭne. Plures eam popūli incŏlunt.
Illustris ibi Dodōna in Molossōrum finĭbus, vetustissĭmo
Jovis oracŭlo inclÿta. Columbæ ibi ex arborĭbus oracŭla
dedisse narrantur; quercusque ipsas et lebētes æneos
inde suspensos deōrum voluntātem tinnĭtu significâsse[a]
fama est.

27. Achelōi fluvii ostiis insŭlæ alĭquot objăcent, quarum maxĭma est Cephallenia. Multæ præterea insŭlæ
littŏri Epīri adjăcent, interque eas Corcÿra, quam Homērus Scheriam appellâsse existimātur. In hâc Phæācas
posuit ille et hortos Alcinoi. Coloniam huc deduxērunt
Corinthii, quo[b] tempŏre Numa Pompilius Romæ[c] regnāvit. Vicīna ei Ithăca, Ulyssis patria, aspĕra montĭbus,
sed Homēri carminĭbus adeò nobilitāta, ut[d] ne fertilissĭmis
quidem regionĭbus cedat.

28. Thessalia latè patet inter Macedoniam et Epīrum,
fœcunda regio, generōsis præcipuè equis[e] excellens, unde
Thessalōrum equitātus celebērrĭmus. Montes ibi memo-
rabĭles Olympus, in quo deōrum sedes esse existimātur,
Pelion et Ossa, per quos[f] gigantes cœlum petivisse dicuntur; Œta denĭque, in cujus vertĭce Hercŭles, rogo con-
scenso, se ipsum[g] cremāvit. Inter Ossam[h] et Olympum
Penēus, limpidissĭmus amnis, delabĭtur, vallem amœnissĭ-
mam, Tempe vocātam, irrĭgans.

29. Inter relĭquas Græciæ regiōnes nomĭnis claritāte
emĭnet Attĭca, quæ etiam Atthis vocātur. Ibi Athēnæ,

---

[a] § 272.   [d] § 262, R. 1.   [g] § 207, R. 28.
[b] § 206, (3.)   [e] § 250.   [h] § 235, R. 2.
[c] § 221, 1   [f] § 247, R. 4.

de quâ urbe deos inter se certâsse fama est. Certius est,[a] nullam unquam urbem tot poëtas tulisse, tot oratōres, tot philosŏphos, totque in omni virtūtis genēre claros viros. Res autem bello eas gessit, ut huic soli[b] gloriæ[c] studēre viderētur; pacisque artes ita excoluit, ut hac laude magis etiam quàm belli gloriâ splendēret. Arx ibi sive Acropŏlis[d] urbi imminens, unde latus in mare prospectus patet. Per propylæa ad eam adscendĭtur,[e] splendĭdum Periclis opus. Cum ipsâ urbe per longos muros conjunctus est portus Piræeus, post bellum Persĭcum secundum a The mistŏcle munītus. Tutissĭma ibi statio navium.

30. Attĭcam attingit Bœotia, fertilissĭma regio. Incŏlæ magis corporĭbus[f] valent quàm ingeniis. Urbs celeberrĭma Thebæ,[g] quas Amphĭon musĭces ope mœnĭbus cinxisse dicĭtur. Illustrāvit eam Pindāri poëtæ ingenium, Epaminondæ virtus. Mons[d] ibi Helĭcon,[*] Musārum sedes, et Cithæron plurĭmis poëtārum fabŭlis celebrātus.

31. Bœotiæ[*] Phocis finitĭma, ubi Delphi urbs clarissĭma. In quâ urbe oracŭlum Apollĭnis quantam apud omnes gentes auctoritātem habuĕrit,[f] quot quàmque præclāra munĕra ex omni ferè terrārum orbe Delphos[h] missa fuĕrint, nemo ignōrat. Immĭnet urbi Parnassus mons, in cujus verticĭbus Musæ habitāre dicuntur, unde aqua fontis Castalii poëtārum ingenia inflammāre existimātur.

32. Cum eâ parte Græciæ, quam hactĕnus descripsĭmus, cohæret ingens peninsŭla, quæ Peloponnēsus vocātur, platăni folio simillĭma. Angustus ille trames intet

---

* What is the predicate of this proposition?

[a] § 260.	[d] § 209, R. 4.	[g] § 265.
[b] § 107.	[e] § 209, R. 3, (2.)	[h] § 237.
[c] § 223	[f] § 250.	

Ægæum mare et Ionium, per quem cum Megar de rohæ-
ret, Isthmus appellātur. In eo templum Neptūni est, ad
quod ludi celebrantur Isthmīci. Ibidem in ipso Peloponn-
nēsi adītu, Corinthus sita est, urbs antiquissīma, ex cujus
summā" arce, (Acrocorinthon* appellant,*) utrumque mare
conspicītur. Quum opību̇s florēret, maritimisque valēret
copiis, gravia bella gessit. In bello Achaïco, quod Romāni cum Græcis gessērunt, pulcherrīma urbs, quam Cicēro
Græciæ lumen appellat, a L. Mummio expugnāta fundītus-
que delēta est. Restituit eam Julius Cæsar, colonosque'
eò milītes veterānos misit.

33. Nobīlis est in Peloponnēso urbs Olympīa, templo
Jovis Olympii ac statuâ illustris. Statua ex ebōre facta,
Phidiæ summi artifīcis opus præstantissīmum. Prope
illud templum ad Alphēi flumīnis ripas ludi celebrantur
Olympīci, ad quos videndos* ex totâ Græciâ concurrītur.*
Ab his ludis Græca gens res gestas suas numērat.

34. Nec Sparta prætereunda est, urbs nobilissīma,
quam Lycurgi leges, civiumque virtus et patientia illustrāvit.' Nulla ferè gens bellīcâ laude* magis floruit, pluresque viros fortes constantesque genuit. Urbi immīnet
mons Taÿgĕtus, qui usque ad Arcadiam procurrit. Proxī-
mè urbem* Eurōtas fluvius delabītur, ad cujus ripas Spar-
tāni se exercēre solēbant. In Sinum Laconīcum effundītur. Haud procul inde abest promontorium Tænārum,
ubi altissīmi specus, per quos Orpheum ad infēros de-
scendîsse narrant.'

35. Mare Ægæum, inter Græciam Asiamque patens,

---

* Supply *quam*. § 230.

a § 205, R. 17.	*d* § 275, III., R. 3.	*g* § 250.
b § 54.	*e* § 184, 2.	*h* § 235, (5,) R. 11.
c § 230. R. 2.	*f* § 209, R. 12, (3.)	*i* § 209, R. 2, (2.)

plurīmis insŭlis distinguĭtur. Illustres inter eas sunt Cȳclă des, sic appellātæ, quia in orbem jacent. Media eārum[a] est Delus, quæ repentè e mari enāta esse dicĭtur. In eâ insŭlâ Latōna Apollĭnem et Diānam pepĕrit, quæ numĭna ibi unà cum matre summâ religiōne coluntur. Urbi immĭnet Cynthus, mons excelsus et arduus. Inŏpus amnis parĭter cum Nilo decrescĕre et augēri dicĭtur. Mercātus in Delo celeberrĭmus, quòd ob portûs commoditātem templíque religiōnem mercatōres ex toto orbe terrārum eò confluēbant. Eandem ob causam civitātes Græciæ, post secundum Persĭcum bellum, tribūta ad belli usum in eam insŭlam, tanquam in commūne totíus Græciæ ærarium, conferēbant; quam pecuniam insequenti tempŏre Athenienses in suam urbem transtulērunt.

36. Eubœa insŭla littŏri[b] Bœotiæ et Attĭcæ prætendītur, angusto freto a continenti distans. Terræ motu a Bœotiâ avulsa esse credĭtur; sæpiùs eam concussam esse[c] constat. Fretum, quo a Græciâ sejungĭtur, vocātur Euripus, sævum et æstuōsum mare, quod continuo motu agitātur. Nonnulli dicunt septies quovis die statis tempŏrĭbus fluctus alterno motu agitāri; alii hoc negant, dicentes, mare temērè in venti modum huc illuc movēri. Sunt, qui narrent,[d] Aristotĕlem philosŏphum, quia hujus miracŭli causas investigāre non posset,[e] ægritudĭne confec tum esse.

37. Jam ad Boreāles regiōnes pergāmus.[f] Supra Ma cedoniam Thracia porrigĭtur a Ponto Euxīno usque ad Illyriam. Regio frigĭda et in iis tantùm partĭbus fœcundior, quæ propiōres sunt mari. Pomĭfēræ arbōres raræ; frequentiōres vites; sed uvæ non maturescunt, nisi frigus

---

studiŏsè arcĕtur. Sola Thasus, insŭla littŏri Thᵊaciæ ad-
jăcens, vino excellit. Amnes sunt celeberrimi˙ Hebrus, ad
quem Orpheus a Mænadĭbus discerptus esse dicĭtur ; Nestus
et Strymon. Montes altissĭmi, Hæmŭs, ex cujus vertĭce
Pontus et Adria conspicĭtur ; Rhodŏpe et Orbēlus.

38. Plures Thraciam gentes incŏlunt nominĭbus diveɪ-
sæ et morĭbus. Inter has Getæ omnium sunt ferocissĭmi
et ad mortem paratissĭmi.ᵃ Anĭmas enim post mortem
reditūras existĭmant. Recens nati apud eos deflentur ;
funĕra autem cantu lusūque celebrantur. Plures singŭli
uxōɪes habent. Hæ omnes, viro defuncto, mactāri simulque cum eo sepelīri cupiunt, magnōque id certamĭne a
judicĭbusᵇ contendunt. Virgĭnes non a parentĭbus traduntur viris, sed aut publĭcè ducendæ locantur, aut vene-
unt. Formōsæ in pretio sunt ; cetĕræ maritos mercēde
datâ inveniunt.

39. Inter urbes Thraciæ memorabĭle est Byzantĭum,
ad Bospŏrum Thracium, urbs natūrâ munīta et arte, quæ
cùmᶜ ob soli fertilitātem, tum ob vicinitātem maris omnium
rerum, quas vita requīrit, copiâᵈ abundat. Nec Sestos
prætereunda est silentio, urbs ad Hellespontum posita, quam
amor Herûs et Leandri memorabĭlem reddīdit ; nec Cynossēma, tumŭlus Hecŭbæ, ubi illa, post Trojam dirŭtam, in
canem mutāta et sepulta esse dicĭtur. Nomen etiam habet
in iisdem regionĭbus urbs Ænos, ab Æneâ e patriâ pro-
fŭgo condīta ; Zone, ubi nemŏra Orpheum canentem
secūta esse narrantur ; Abdēra denĭque, ubi Diomēdes rex
advĕnas equis suis devorandos objiciēbat, donec ipse ab
Hercŭle iisdem objectus est. Quæ urbs quum ranārum
muriumque multitudĭne ĭnfestarētur, incŏlæ, relicto patriæ

ᵃ § 222, R. 4.   ᵇ § 231, R. 2.   ᶜ § 278, R. 7.   ᵈ § 250, (2.)

solo, novas sedes quæsivērunt.   Hos Cassander, rex Macedoniæ, in˙ societātem accepisse, agrosque in extrēmā˙
Macedoniâ assignâsse dicītur.

40. Jam de Scythis pauca dicenda sunt.   Terminātur
Scythia ab uno latēre Ponto Euxīno, ab altēro montĭbus
Rhipæis, a tergo Asiâ et Phasĭde flumĭne.   Vasta regĭœ
nullis ferè. intus finĭbus dividĭtur.   Scythæ enim nec
agrum exercent, nec certas sedes habent, sed armenta et
pecŏra pascentes per incultas solitudĭnes errāre solent.
Uxōres liberosque secum in plaustris vehunt.   Lacte et
melle vescuntur; aurum et argentum, cujus nullus apud
eos usus est, aspernantur.   Corpŏra pellĭbus[b] vestiunt.

41. Diversæ sunt Scythārum gentes, diversique mores.
Sunt, qui funĕra parentum festis sacrificiis celĕbrent,[c]
eorumque capitĭbus affābrè expolītis aurōque vinctis pro
pocŭlis utantur.   Agathyrsi ora et corpŏra pingunt, idque[*]
tanto[d] magis, quanto quis[e] illustriorĭbus gaudet majorĭbus.[f]
Ii, qui Tauricam Chersonēsum incŏlunt, antiquissĭmis
'emporĭbus advēnas Diānæ mactābant.   Interiùs habitantes cetēris[g] rudiōres sunt.   Bella amant, et quò quis[e] plures hostes interemĕrit, eò[d] majōre existimatiōne apud suos[h]
babētur.   Ne fœdĕra quidem incruenta sunt.   Sauciant
se qui paciscuntur, sanguinemque permistum degustant.
Id fidei pignus certissĭmum esse putant.

42. Maxĭma flumĭnum Scythicōrum sunt Ister, qui et
Danubius vocātur, et Borysthēnes.   De Istro suprà dictum
est.[i]   Borysthēnes, ex ignōtis fontĭbus ortus, liquidissĭmas

---

* Supply *faciunt.*

[a] § 205, R, 17.	[d] § 256, R. 16.	[f] § 256, 2.
[b] § 249, I.	[e] § 137, 1, R. (3.)	[h] § 205, R. 7, (1,) N. 1.
[c] § 264, 6.	[f] § 247, 1, (2.)	§ 225, III., R. 1.

aquas trahit et potātu°˙ jucundas. Placĭdus idem latissĭma pabŭla alit. Magno spatio navigabĭlis juxta urbem Borysthenida˙ in Pontum effundĭtur.

43. Ultra Rhipæos montes et Aquilōnem gens habitāre existimātur felicissĭma, Hyperborēos * appellant. Regio aprĭca, felix cœli temperies omnīque afflātu' noxio carens. Semel in anno sol iis orĭtur solstitio,ᵈ brumâ semel occĭdit. Incŏlæ in nemorĭbus et lucis habĭtant; sine omni discordiâ et ægritudĭne vivunt. Quum vitæ' eos˙ tædet, epŭlis sumptis ex rupe se in mare præcipĭtant. Hoc enim sepultūræ genus beatissĭmum esse existĭmant.

44. Asia˙ cetēris terræ partĭbus est amplior. Oceănus eam alluit, ut locis ita nominĭbus diffērens; Eōus ab oriente, a meridie Indĭcus, a septentriōne Scythĭcus. Asiæ nomĭne appellātur etiam peninsŭla, quæ a mari Ægæo usque ad Armeniam ˛patet. In hac parte est Bithynia ad Propontĭdem sita, ubi Granĭcus in mare effundĭtur, ad quem amnem Alexander, rex Macedoniæ, primam victoriam de Persis reportāvit. Trans illum amnem sita est Cyzĭcus in cervĭce peninsŭlæ, urbs nobilissĭma, a Cyzĭco appellāta, qui in illis regionĭbus ab Argonautis pugnâ occīsus est. Haud procul ab illâ urbe Rhyndācus in mare effundĭtur, circa quem angues nascuntur, non solùm ob magnitudĭnem mirabĭles, sed etiam ob id, quòd, quum ex aquâ emergunt et hiant, supervolantes aves absorbent.

45. Propontis cum Ponto jungĭtur per Bospŏrum,' quod fretum quinque stadia latum Eurōpam ab Asiâ sepărat. Ipsis in faucĭbus Bospŏri oppĭdum est Chalcēdon,† ab

---

* Supply *quam*. ˙   † Supply *condĭta*.

ᵃ § 276, III.   ᵈ § 253.   ᶠ § 229, R. 6.
ᵇ § 80, I.   ᵉ § 215, (1.)   ᵍ § 247, R. 4.
ᶜ § 250, (2.)

Argiâ, Megarensium princĭpe, et templum Jovis, ab Jasŏne condĭtum. Pontus ipse ingens est maris sinus, non molli neque arenōso circumdătus littŏre, tempestatĭbus* obnoxi\
us, raris stationĭbus.ᵇ Olim ob sævitātem populōrum, qui circà habĭtant, Axēnus appellātus fuisse dicĭtur; postea, mollĭtis illōrum morĭbus, dictus est Euxīnus.

46. In littŏre Ponti, in Mariandynōrum agro, urbs est Heraclēa, ab Hercūle, ut fertur, condĭta. Juxta eam spe\
lunca est Acherusia, quam ad Manes perviam esse existi\
mant.ᶜ Hinc Cerbĕrus ab Hercūle extractus fuisse dicĭtur. Ultra fluvium Thermodonta Mossȳni habĭtant. Hi totum corpus distinguunt notis. Reges suffragio elīgunt; eosdem in turre ligneâ inclūsos arctissĭmè custodiunt, et, si quid perpĕram imperitavĕrint,ᵈ inediâ totĭus diēi afficiunt. Ex\
trēmum Ponti angūlum Colchi tenent ad Phasīdem; quæ loca fabūla de vellēre aureo et Argonautārum expeditio illustrāvit.

47. Inter provincias Asiæ propriè dictæ illustris est Ionia, in duodĕcim civitātes divīsa. Inter eas est Milētus, belli pacisque artĭbus inclȳta; eíque vicīnum Panionium, sacra regio, quò omnes Iōnum civitātes statis temporĭbus legātos solēbant mittĕre. Nulla facĭlèᵉ urbs plures colo\
nias misit, quàm Milētus. Ephĕsi, quamᶠ urbem Amaz\
ōnes condidisse traduntur, templum est Diānæ, quod sep\
tem mundi miracūlisᵍ annumerāri solet. Totīus templi longitūdo est quadringentōrum viginti quinque pedum,ʰ latitūdo ducentōrum viginti; columnæ centum viginti sep\
tem numĕro, sexaginta pedum altitudīne; ex iis triginta sex cælātæ. Opĕri præfuit Chersĭphron architectus.

ᵃ § 222, 3. ᵈ § 209, R. 2, (1,) (b.) ᵍ § 224.

ᵇ § 211, R. 6. ᵉ § 277, R. 7. ʰ § 211, R. 6.

ᶜ § 219, R. 2, (2.) ᶠ § 206, (3.)

48. Æŏlis olim Mysia appellāta,[*] et, ubi Hellespontum attingit. Troas. Ibi Ilium fuit situm ad radīces montis Idæ, urbs bello, quod per decem annos cum universâ Græciâ gessit, clarissïma. Ab Idæo monte Scamander defluit et Simŏis, amnes famâ quàm natūrâ majōres. Ipsum montem certāmen[*] deārum Paridisque judicium illustrem reddidit. In littŏre claræ sunt urbes Rhœtēum et Dardania; sed sepulcrum Ajācis, qui ibi post certāmen cum Ulysse gladio incubuit, utrâque[†] clarius.

49. Ionībus[b] Cares sunt finitïmi, popūlus armōrum[c] oellïque adeò amans, ut aliēna etiam bella mercēde acceptâ gerēret. Princeps Cariæ urbs Halicarnassus, Argivōrum colonia, regum sedes olim. Unus eōrum Mausōlus fuit. Qui quum vitâ[d] defunctus esset, Artemisia conjux desiderio marīti flagrans, ossa ejus cineresque contūsa cum aquâ miscuit ebibitque, splendidumque præterea sepulcrum exstruxit, quod inter septem orbis terrārum miracŭla censētur.

50. Cilicia sita est in intïmo recessu maris, ubi Asia propriè sic dicta cum Syriê conjungïtur. Sinus ille ab urbe Isso Issīci nomen habet. Fluvius ibi Cydnus aquâ[e] limpidissïmâ et frigidissïmâ, in quo Alexander Macēdo quum lavāret,[f] parum abfuit, quin frigōre enecarētur.[g] Antrum Corycium in iisdem regionïbus ob singulārem natūram memorabīle est. Ingenti illud hiātu patet in monte arduo, altēque demissum undïque viret lucis pendentïbus. Ubi ad ima perventum est,[h] rursus aliud antrum apeiitur. Ibi sonïtus cymbalōrum ingredientes[i] terrēre

---

[*] See "MYTHOLOGY," section 11.   [†] Supply *urbe.*

[a] § 209, R. 4.   [d] § 245, 1.   [g] § 262.
[b] § 222, 3.   [e] § 211, R. 6.   [h] § 184, 2.
[c] § 213.   [f] § 229, R. 4, 1.   [i] § 205, R. 7, (1,) N. 1.

dicitur. Totus hic specus augustus est et verè sacer, et a diis habitāri existimātur.

51. E Ciliciâ egressos[a] Syria excīpit, cujus pars est Phœnīce in littŏre maris interni posīta. Hanc regiōnem sollers hominum genus colit. Phœnīces enim litterārum fonnas a se inventas aliis popūlis tradidērunt; alias eliam artes, quæ ad navigatiōnem et mercatūram spectant, studiōsè coluērunt. Cetĕrùm fertīlis regio,[b] crebrisque fluminibus rigāta, quorum ope terræ marisque opes facīli negotio inter se[c] permutantur. Nobilissīmæ Phœnīces urbes Sidon, antĕquam a Persis caperētur, maritimārum urbium maxīma, et Tyrus, aggĕre cum terrâ conjuncta. Purpŭra hujus urbis omnium pretiosissīma. Conficitur ille color ex succo in conchis, quæ etiam purpŭræ vocantur, latente.

52. Ex Syriâ descendĭtur[d] in Arabiam, peninsŭlam inter duo maria, Rubrum et Persĭcum, porrectam. Hujus ea pars, quæ ab urbe Petrâ Petrææ nomen accēpit, planè est sterīlis; hanc excĭpit ea, quæ ob vastas solitudīnes Deserta vocātur. His partībus adhæret Arabia Felix, regio angusta, sed cinnămi, thuris aliorumque odōrum, feracissīma. Multæ ibi gentes sunt, quæ fixas sedes non habeant,[e] Nomădes a Græcis appellātæ. Lacte et carne ferinâ vescuntur. Multi etiam Arābum popūli latrociniis[f] vivunt. Primus e Romānis Ælius Gallus in hanc terram cum exercītu penetrāvit.

53. Camēlos inter armenta pascit Oriens. Duo harum sunt genĕra, Bactriānæ et Arabiæ. Illæ bina habent in dorso tubĕra, hæ singŭla; unum autem sub pectŏre, cui incumbant. Dentium ordĭne[g] superiōre carent. Sitim[h]

---

[a] § 205, R. 7, (1,) N. 1.	[d] § 184, 2.	[g] § 250, (2.)
[b] § 209, R. 4.	[e] § 264, 1, (a.)	[h] § 79, 2.
[c] § 208, (5.)	[f] § 245, II. 4.	

quatriduo tolĕrant; aquam, antĕquam bibant, pedĭbus turbant. Vivunt quinquagēnis annis;[a] quaedam etiam centēnis.[b]

54. Ex Arabiâ pervenītur in Babyloniam, cui Babўlon nomen dedit, Chaldaicārum gentium caput, urbs et magni tudῐne et divitiis clara. Semirāmis eam condidĕrat, vel, ut multi credidĕrunt, Belus, cujus regia ostendĭtur. Murus exstructus latercŭlo[c] coctῑli, triginta et duos pedes[a] est latus, ita ut quadrigæ inter se occurrentes sine pericŭlo commeāre dicantur; altitūdo ducentōrum pedum; turres autem denis[b] pedῑbus[d] quàm murus altiōres sunt. Totius opĕris ambῑtus sexaginta millia passuum complectῐtur. Mediam urbem[e] permeat Euphrātes. Arcem habet viginti stadiōrum[f] ambῑtu;[g] super ea pensῑles horti conspiciun·tur, tantæque sunt moles tamque firmæ, ut onĕra nemŏrum sine detrimento ferant.

55. Amplissima Asiæ regio[h] India primùm patefacta est armis Alexandri Magni, regis Macedoniæ, cujus exemplum successōres secūti in interiōra[i] Indiæ penetravĕrunt. In eo tractu, quem Alexander subēgit, quinque millia[j] oppidŭ-rum fuisse, gentesque novem, Indiamque tertiam partem esse terrārum omnium, ejus comῑtes scripsĕrunt. Ingentes ibi sunt amnes, Indus et Indo[k] major Ganges. Indus in Paropamiso ortus undeviginti amnes recῑpit, totῐdem Ganges interque eos plures navigabῑles.

56. Maxῑma in Indiâ gignuntur animalia. Canes ibi grandiōres cetĕris. Arbōres tantæ proceritātis esse tra·duntur, ut sagittis superjăci nequeant. Hoc[l] efficit uber-

---

[a] § 236.	[e] § 233.	[i] § 212, R. 3, N. 4.
[b] § 119, 111.	[f] § 211, R. 6.	[j] § 272.
[c] § 249. 1.	[g] § 250.	[k] § 256, 2.
[d] § 256, R. 16.	[h] § 204.	[l] § 206, (13.)

tas soli, temperies cœli, aquārum abundantia. Immānes quoque serpentes alit, qui elephantos morsu et ambītu corpōris conficiunt. Solum tam pingue et ferax, ut mella frondibus* defluant, sylvæ lanas ferant, arundīnum internodia fissa cymbārum usum præbeant, binosque, quædam etiam ternos homines, vehant.

57. Incolārum habĭtus moresque diversi. Lino[b] alii vestiuntur et lanis arbŏrum, alii ferārum aviumque pellĭbus, pars nudi[c] incēdunt.[d] Quidam animalia occidĕre eorumque carnĭbus vesci nefas putant;* alii piscĭbus tantùm aluntur. Quidam parentes et propinquos, priùs quàm annis et macie conficiantur, velut hostias cædunt eorumque viscerĭbus[e] epulantur; ubi senectus eos morbusve invādit, mortem in solitudine æquo animo exspectant. Ii, qui sapientiam profitentur, ab ortu solis ad occāsum stare solent, solem immobilĭbus ocŭlis intuentes; ferventĭbus arēnis toto die alternis pedĭbus insistunt. Mortem non exspectant, sed sponte arcessunt in rogos incensos se præcipitantes.

58. Maxĭmos India elephantos gignit, adeōque ferōces, ut Afri elephanti illos paveant, nec contuēri audeant. Hoc animal cetĕra omnia docilitāte supĕrat. Discunt arma jacĕre, gladiatōrum more congrĕdi, saltāre et per funes incedĕre. Plinius narrat, Romæ unum segniōris ingenii sæpius castigātum esse verberĭbus, quia tardiùs[f] accipiēbat, quæ tradebantur; eundem repertum esse noctu eādem meditantem. Elephanti gregātim semper ingrediuntur. Ducit agmen maxĭmus natu,[f] cogit is, qui ætāte ei est

---

* What are the accusatives after *putant* ? § 230.

[a] § 242.	[d] § 209, R. 11.	[g] § 250.
[b] § 249.	[e] § 245, II. 4.	
[c] § 205, R. 3.	[f] § 256, R. 9, & (a.)	

proxĭmus. Amnem transitūri minĭmos præιnittun:. Capiuntur foveis. In has ubi elĕphas decidérit, cetĕri ramos
congĕrunt, aggĕres construunt, omnique vi conantur extra-
hĕre. Domantur fame et verberĭbus. Domĭti militant et
turres armatōrum in hostes ferunt, magnâque ex parte
Orientis bella conficiunt. Totas acies prosternunt, armātos
protĕrunt. Ingens dentĭbus pretium. In Græciâ ebur ad
deōrum simulācra tanquam pretiosissĭma materia adhibĕ-
tur; in extrēmis[b] Afrīcæ postium vicem in domiciliis præ-
bet, sepesque in pecōrum stabŭlis elephantōrum dentĭbus
fiunt. Inter omnia animalia[a] maxĭmè odĕrunt[c] murem.
Infestus elephanto etiam rhinocĕros, qui nomen habet a
cornu, quod in naso gerit. In pugnâ maxĭmè adversarii.
alvum petit, quam scit esse molliōrem. Longitudĭne
elephantum ferè exæquat; crura multo breviōra; color
buxeus.

59. Etiam Psittăcos India mittit. Hæc avis humānas
voces optĭmè reddit. Quum loqui discit, ferreo radio ver-
berātur, aliter enim non sentit ictus. Capīti[d] ejus eādem
est duritia, quæ rostro. Quum devōlat, rostro se excīpit,
eīque innitĭtur.

60. Testudĭnes tantæ magnitudĭnis Indĭcum mare emit-
tit, ut singulārum testis casas intĕgant.[e] Insŭlas[f] rubri
præcipuè maris his navĭgant cymbis. Capiuntur obdor-
miscentes in summâ aquâ, id[g] quod prodĭtur stertentium
sonĭtu. Tum terni adnātant, a duōbus in dorsum vertĭtur,
a tertio laqueus injicĭtur, atque ita a plurĭbus in littōre
stàntĭbus trahĭtur. In mari testudĭnes conchyliis vivunt;
tanta enim oris est duritia, ut lapĭdes comminuant; in

---

[a] § 212, R. 2, N. 4.   [d] § 226.   [f] § 237, R. 5.
[b] § 212, R. 3, N. 4.   [e] § 209, R. 2, (2.)   [g] § 206, (13.)
[c] § 183, 3 N.

11*

terram egressæ, herbis.* Pariunt ova ovis avium similia, ad centēna numēro; eāque extra aquam defossâ terrâ cooperiunt.

61. Margarītæ Indici oceăni omnium maxĭmè laudan tur. Inveniuntur in conchis scopŭlis adhærentĭbus. Maxĭma laus est in candōre, magnitudĭne, lævōre, pondĕre. Rarò duæ inveniuntur, quæ sibi ex omni parte sint simĭles. Has aurĭbus[a] suspendĕre,[b] feminārum est gloria. Duos maxĭmos uniōnes Cleopătra, Ægypti regīna, habuisse dicĭtur. Horum unum, ut Antonium magnificentiâ superāret, in cœnâ acēto solvit, solūtum hausit.

62. Ægyptus, inter Catabathmum et Arăbas posĭta, a plurĭmis ad Asiam refertur; alii Asiam Arabĭco sinu termināri existĭmant. Hæc regio, quanquam expers[c] est imbrium,[d] mirè tamen est fertĭlis. Hoc[e] Nilus effĭcit, omnium fluviōrum, qui in mare internum effunduntur, maxĭmus. Hic in desertis Afrĭcæ orĭtur, tum ex Æthiopiâ descendit in Ægyptum, ubi de altis rupĭbus præcipitātus usque ad Elephantĭdem urbem fervens adhuc decurrit. Tum demum fit placidior. Juxta Cercasōrum oppĭdum in plures amnes dividĭtur, et tandem per septem ora effundītur in mare.

63. Nilus, nivĭbus in Æthiopiæ montĭbus solūtis, crescĕre incĭpit Lunâ novâ post solstitium per quinquaginta ferè dies; totĭdem diēbus minuĭtur. Justum incrementum est cuhitōrum sedĕcim. Si minōres sunt aquæ, non omnia rigant. Maxĭmum incrementum fuit cubitōrum duodeviginti; minĭmum quinque. Quum stetēre aquæ, aggĕres aperiuntur, et arte aqua in agros immittĭtur. Quum omnis recessĕrit, agri irrigāti et limo obducti seruntur.

---

* Supply *vivunt*.

[a] § 224.   [c] § 213.   [e] § 206, (13.)
[b] § 269.   [d] §§ 82, E. 5, and 83. II. 1.

64. Nilus crocodīlum alit, belluam quadrupĕdem, in terrâ non minùs quàm in flumīne hominībus infestam. Unum hoc anīmal terrestre linguæ usu caret; dentium plures habet ordīnes; maxilla inferior est immobĭlis. Magnitudĭne excĕdit plerùmque duodeviginti cubĭta. Parit ova anserinis* non majōra. Unguĭbus etiam armātus est, et cute contra omnes ictus invictâ. Dies in terrâ agit, noctes in aquâ. Quum satur est, et in littŏre somnum capit ore hiante, trochĭlus, parva avis, dentes ei faucesque purgat. Sed hiantem conspicātus ichneumon, per easdem fauces ut telum alĭquod immissus, erōdit alvum. Hebĕtes ocŭlos dicĭtur habēre in aquâ, extra aquam acerrīmos. Tentyrītæ in insŭlâ Nili habitantes, diræ huic belluæᵃ obviàm ire audent, eamque incredibĭli audaciâ expugnant.

65. Aliam etiam belluam Nilus alit, hippopotămum; ungŭlisᵇ binis, dorsoᶜ equi et jubâ et hinnītu; rostro resimo, caudâ et dentĭbus aprōrum. Cutis ĭmpenetrabĭlis, præterquam si humōre madeat. Primus hippopotămum et quinque crocodĭlos M. Scaurus ædilitātis suæ ludisᵈ Romæ ostendit.

66. Multa in Ægypto mira sunt et artis et natūræ opĕra. Inter ea, quæ manĭbus hominum facta sunt, emĭnent pyramīdes, quarum maxĭmæ sunt et celeberrĭmæ in monte sterĭli inter Memphin oppĭdum et eam partem Ægypti, quæ Delta vocātur. Amplissĭmam eārum trecenta sexaginta sexᵉ hominum millia annis viginti exstruxisse traduntur. Hæc octo jugĕra soli occŭpat; unumquodque latus octingentos octoginta tres pedes longum est; altitūdo a

* Supply ovis.

ᵃ § 228. ᶜ § 211, R. 6, (1.) ᵉ § 279, 7.
ᵇ § 211, R. 6. ᵈ § 253

cacumĭnæ pedum quindĕcim millium. Intus in eâ est puteus octoginta sex cubitōrum. Ante has pyramĭdes Sphinx 'est posĭta miræ magnitudĭnis. Capĭtis ambĭtus centum[a] duos pedes habet; longitūdo est pedum centum quadra ginta trium; altitūdo a ventre usque ad summum capĭtis apĭcem sexaginta duōrum.

67. Inter miracŭla Ægypti commemorātur etiam Mœris lacus, quingenta millia passuum in circuĭtu patens; Labyrinthus ter mille domos et regias duodēcim uno parĭĕte amplexus, totus marmŏre[b] exstructus tectusque; turris denĭque in insŭlâ Pharo, a Ptolemæo, Lagi filio, condīta. Usus[c] ejus navĭbus noctu ignes ostendēre ad prænuntianda[d] vada portûsque introĭtum.

68. In palustrĭbus Ægypti regionĭbus papȳrum nascĭtur. Radicĭbus incŏlæ pro ligno utuntur; ex ipso autem papȳro navigia texunt, e libro vela, tegĕtes, vestem ac funes. Succi causâ etiam mandunt modò crudum, modò decoctum. Præparantur ex eo[e] etiam chartæ. Chartæ ex papȳro usus post Alexandri demum victorias repertus est. Primò enim scriptum[*] in palmārum foliis, deinde in libris quarundam arbŏrum; postea publĭca monimenta plumbeis tabŭlis confĭci, aut marmorĭbus mandāri cœpta sunt. Tandem æmulatio regum Ptolemæi et Eumĕnis in bibliothēcis condendis occasiōnem dedit membrānas[c] Pergāmi inveniendi. Ab eo inde tempŏre libri modò in chartâ ex papȳro factâ, modò in membrānis scripti sunt.

69. Mores incolārum Ægypti ab aliōrum populōrum moribus vehementer discrĕpant. Mortuos nec cremant, nec sepeliunt; verùm arte medicātos intra penetralia collŏ-

---

* Supply *est ab hominĭbus.* § 141, R. 2.

[a] § 120, 2.   [c] § 209, R. 4.   [e] § 275, 1.
[b] § 249.   [d] § 275. R. 3.

cant. Negotia extra domos feminæ, viri domos et res domesticas curant; onĕra illæ humĕris, hi capitĭbus gerunt. Colunt effigies multōrum animalium et ipsa animalia. Hæc interfecisse[a] capitāle est; morbo exstincta lugent et sepeliunt.

70. Apis omnium Ægypti populōrum numen est; bos niger cum candĭdâ in dextro latĕre maculâ; nodus sub linguâ, quem canthārum appellant. Non fas est eum certos vitæ annos excedĕre. Ad hunc vitæ termĭnum quum pervenĕrit, mersum in fonte enĕcant. Necātum lugent, aliumque quærunt, quem ei substituant; nec tamen unquam diu quærĭtur. Delūbra ei sunt gemĭna, quæ thalāmos vocant, ubi popŭlus auguria captat. Altĕrum * intrâsse lætum est; in altĕro dira portendit. Pro bono etiam habētur signo, si e manĭbus consulentium cibum capit. In publĭcum procedentem grex puerōrum comitātur, carmenque in ejus honōrem canunt,[b] idque vidētur intelligĕre.

71. Ultra Ægyptum Æthiŏpes habĭtant. Horum popŭli quidam Macrobii vocantur, quia paulò quàm nos diutiùs vivunt. Plus auri[c] apud eos reperītur, quàm æris; hanc ob causam æs illis vidētur pretiosius. Ære se exornant, vincŭla auro[d] fabrĭcant. Lacus est apud eos, cujus aqua tam est liquĭda atque levis, ut nihil eōrum, quæ immittuncur, sustinēre queat; quare arbŏrum quoque folia non in nātant aquæ, sed pessum aguntur.

72. Africa ab oriente terminātur Nilo; a cetĕris partĭbus mari. Regiōnes ad mare posītæ eximiè sunt fertĭles; interiōres incultæ et arēnis sterilĭbus tectæ, et ob nimium

---

* Supply thus: [Apim] altĕrum [thalămum] intrĂsse lætum est.

[a] § 269   [c] § 212, R. 3.   [d] § 249, 1.
[b] § 209 R. 11, (2.)

calōrem desertæ. Prima pars ab occidente est Maɟrita
nia. Ibi mons præaltus Abўla, Calpæ monti in Hispaniâ
oppositus. Hi montes columnæ Herculis appellantur.
Fama est, ante Herculem mare internum terris inclūsum
fuisse, nec exitum habuisse in Oceănum ; Herculem autem
junctos montes diremisse et mare junxisse cum Oceăno.
Ceterùm regio illa est ignobilis et parvis tantùm oppidis
habitātur. Solum melius quàm incōlæ.

73. Numidia magis culta et opulentior. Ibi satìs longo
a littŏre intervallo saxa cernuntur attrīta fluctĭbus, spinæ
piscium, ostreorumque fragmenta, ancŏræ etiam cautĭbus
infixæ, et alia ejusmödi signa maris olim usque ad ea loca
effūsi. Finitīma regio, a promontorio Metagonio ad aras
Philænōrum, propriè vocātur Africa. Urbes in eâ celeber-
rīmæ Utica et Carthāgo, ambæ a Phœnicĭbus condītæ.
Carthaginem divitiæ, mercatūrâ imprimis comparātæ, tum
bella cum Romānis gesta, excidium denique illustrāvit.[a]

74. De aris Philænōrum hæc narrantur. Pertinacis-
sĭma fuĕrat contentio inter Carthaginem et Cyrēnas de
finĭbus. Tandem placuit,[b] utrinque eōdem tempōre juvĕnes mitti, et locum, quò convenissent, pro finĭbus habēri.
Carthaginiensium legāti, Philæni fratres, paulò ante tempus constitūtum egressi esse dicuntur. Quod quum Cyre-
nensium legāti intellexissent, magnāque exorta esset contentio, tandem Cyrenenses dixērunt, se tum demum hunc
locum pro finĭbus habitūros esse, si Philæni se ibi vivos
obrui passi essent.[c] Illi conditiōnem accepērunt. Carthaginienses autem animōsis juvenĭbus in illis ipsis locis,
ubi vivi sepulti sunt, aras consecravērunt, eorumque virtūtem æternis honorĭbus prosecūti sunt.   •

---

[a] § 209. R. 12, (3.)   [b] § 269.   [c] § 266, R. 4.

75. Inde ad Catabathmum Cyrenaïca porrigitur, ubi Ammōnis oracŭlum et fons quidam, quem Solis esse * dicunt. Hic fons mediâ nocte fervet,ᵃ tum paulātim tepescit; sole oriente fit frigĭdus; per meridiem maxĭmè riget. Catabathmus vallis est devexa versùs Ægyptum. Ibi finītur Afrĭca. Proximi his popŭli urbes non habent, sed in tuguriis vivunt. quæ mapalia vocantur. Vulgus pecŭdum vestĭtur pellĭbus. Potus est lac succusque baccārum; cibus caro. Interiōres etiam incultiùs vivunt. Sequuntur greges suos, utque hi pabŭlo ducuntur, ita illi tuguria sua promŏvent. Leges nullas habent, nec in commūne consultant. Inter hos Troglodȳtæ in specŭbus habĭtant, serpentibusque aluntur.

76. Ferārum Afrĭca feracissĭma. Pardos, panthēras, leōnes gignit, quod belluārum genus Eurōpa ignōrat. Leōni ᵇ præcipua generositas. Prostrātis parcĕre dicĭtur; in infantes nonnisi summâ fame sævit. Anĭmi † ejus index cauda, quam, dum placĭdus est, immōtam servat; dum irascĭtur, terram et se ipsumᶜ eâ flagellat. Vis summa in pectōre. Si fugĕre cogĭtur, contemptim cedit, quàm diu spectāri potest; in silvis acerrĭmo cursu fertur. Vulnerātus percussōrem novit,ᵈ et in quantâlībet multitudīne appĕtit. Hoc tam sævum anĭmal gallinacei cantus terret. Domātur etiam ab homĭnĭbus. Hanno Pœnus primus leōnem mansuefactum ostendisse dicĭtur. Marcus autem Antonius triumvir primus, post pugnam in campis Philippĭcis, Romæ leōnes ad currum junxit.

77. Struthiocamēli Afrĭci altitudĭnem equĭtis equoᵉ insidentis exæquant, celeritātem vincunt. Pennæ ad hoc demum videntur datæ, ut currentes adjŭvent; nam a terrâ

---

* Supply *fontem*. † What is the predicate of this clause?

ᵃ § 145, .1. ᶜ § 207, R. 28. ᵉ § 224.

ᵇ § 226. ᵈ § 183, 3, N.

tolli non possunt. Ungŭlæ cervĭnis sunt simĭles. His in
fugâ comprehendunt lapĭdes, eosque contra sequentes jacu
lantur. Omnia concŏquunt. Cetĕrùm magna iis stolidi
tas, ita ut, quum caput et collum frutĭce occultavĕrint, se
latĕre existĭment. Pennæ eōrum quæruntur ad ornātum.

78. Afrĭca serpentes genĕrat vicēnûm[a] cubitōrum;
nec minōres India. Certè Megasthĕnes scribit, serpentes
ibi in tantam magnitudĭnem adolescĕre, ut solĭdos hauriant
cervos taurosque. In primo Punĭco bello ad flumen Ba-
grādam serpens centum viginti pedum a Regŭlo, impera-
tōre Romāno, ballistis et tormentis expugnāta esse fertur.
Pellis ejus et maxillæ diu Romæ in templo quodam asser-
vātæ sunt. In Indiâ serpentes perpetuum bellum cum
elephantis gerunt. Ex arborĭbus se in prætereuntes *
præcipĭtant gressusque ligant nodis. Hos nodos elephanti
manu resolvunt. At dracōnes in ipsas elephantōrum nares
caput condunt spiritumque præclūdunt plerùmque in illâ
dimicatiōne utrique commoriuntur, dum victus elĕphas corruens serpentem pondĕre suo elĭdit.

---

[a] § 119, III.   * Supply *illos.*

DICTIONARY.

EXPLANATION OF ABBREVIATIONS.

a. . . . . . . active.	*f.* . . . . . . feminine.	*num.* . . . numeral.
adj. . . . . . adjective.	*freq.* . . . . frequentative.	*part.* . . participle.
adv. . . . . . adverb.	*imp.* . . . . impersonal.	*pass.* . . . passive.
c. . . . . . . common gender.	*inc.* . . . . inceptive.	*pl.* . . . . . plural.
comp. . . . comparative.	*ind.* . . . . indeclinable.	*prep.* . . . preposition.
conj. . . . conjunction.	*int.* . . . . interjection.	*pret.* . . . . preteritive.
d. . . . . . doubtful gender.	*irr.* . . . . irregular.	*pro.* . . . . pronoun.
def. . . . . . defective.	*m.* . . . . . . masculine.	*rel.* . . . . . relative.
dep. . . . . deponent.	*n.* . . . . . . neuter.	*subs.* . . . . substantive.
dim. . . . . diminutive.	*neut. pass.* neuter passive.	*sup.* . . . . . superlative.

§ This character refers to the sections of Andrews and Stoddard's Latin Grammar.

A., *an abbreviation of* Aulus. § 328.

A, ab, abs, prep. *from :* ab oriente, *on the east :* a meridie, *on the south.* Before the agent of a passive verb, *by.* § 195, R. 2.

Abdēra, æ, f. *a maritime town of Thrace.*

Abdītus, a, um, part. & adj. *hidden ; concealed ; removed ; secret ;* from

Abdo, abdēre, abdĭdi, abdĭtum, a. (ab & do, § 172,) *to remove from view ; to hide ; to conceal.*

Abdūco, abducēre, abduxi, ab-ductum, a. (ab & duco,) *to lead away.*

Abductus, a, um, part. (abdūco.)

Abeo, abīre, abii, abītum, irr. n. (ab & eo,) *to go away ; to depart.*

Aberro, āre, āvi, ātum, n. (ab & erro,) *to stray ; to wander, to lose the way.*

Abjectus, a, um, part. from

Abjicio, abjicēre, abjēci, abjec-tum, a. (ab & jacio, § 172,) *to cast, to cast away ; to throw aside.*

Abluo, ēre, i, tum, a. (ab & luo,) *to wash away ; to purify.*

12

Abrumpo, abrumpĕre, abrŭpi, abruptum, a. *to break.*

Abscindo, abscindĕre, abscĭdi, abscissum, a. (ab & scindo,) *to cut off.*

Absens, tis, part. (absum, § 154,) *absent.*

Absolvo, absolvĕre, absolvi, absolŭtum, a. (ab & solvo,) *to loose; to release.*

Absorbeo, absorbĕre, absorbui & absorpsi, a. (ab & sorbeo, § 168,) *to suck in; to swallow.*

Absterreo, ĕre, ui, ĭtum, a. (abs & terreo,) *to frighten away; to deter.*

Abstinentia, æ, f. *abstinence; disinterestedness; freedom from avarice;* from

Abstineo, abstinĕre, abstinui, a. (abs & teneo, § 168,) *to keep from; to abstain.*

Absum, abesse, abfui, irr. n. (ab & sum,) *to be absent* or *distant; to be gone:* parum abesse, *to want but little; to be near.*

Absŭmo, absumĕre, absumpsi, absumptum, a. (ab & sumo,) *to consume; to destroy; to waste.*

Absumptus, a, um, part.(absŭmo.)

Absurdus, a, um, adj. (ab & surdus, deaf; senseless,) *senseless; absurd.*

Abundantia, æ, f. *plenty; abundance;* from

Abundo, āre, āvi, ātum, n. (ab & undo, to boil,) *to overflow; to abound.*

Abȳla, æ, f. *Abyla; a mountain in Africa, at the entrance of the Mediterranean sea, opposite to mount Calpe in Spain. These mountains were anciently called the Pillars of Hercules.*

Ac, atque, conj. *and; as; than.* § 198, R. 1.

Acca, æ, f. *Acca Laurentia, the wife of Faustulus, and nurse of Romulus and Remus.*

Accĕdo, accedĕre, accessi, accessum, n. (ad & cedo, § 196 I. 2,) *to draw near; to approach; to advance; to engage in; to undertake.*

Accendo, accendĕre, accendi, accensum, a. (ad & candeo, §§ 172 and 189, 1,) *to set on fire.*

Accensus, a, um, part. (accendo,) *set on fire; kindled; lighted, inflamed; burning.*

Acceptus, a, um, part. (accipio.)

Accessus, ūs, m. (accĕdo,) *approach; access; accession.*

Accĭdo, ĕre, i, n. (ad & cado, § 172,) *to fall down at* or *before:* accĭdit, imp. *it happens,* or *it happened.*

Accipio, accipĕre, accēpi, acceptum, a. (ad & capio, § 189, 5.) *to take* or *receive; to learn; to hear; to understand; to accept:* accipĕre finem, *to come to an end; to terminate.*

Accipĭter, tris, § 71, m. *a hawk.*

Accumbc, accunıbĕre, accubui, n. (ad & cubo, § 165,) *to sit* or *recline at table.*

Accurātĕ, adv. (ad & cura,) *accurately; carefully.*

Accurro, accurrĕre, accurri *or* accucurri, n. (ad & curro,) *to run to.*

Accūso, āre, āvi, ātum, a. (ad & causor, *to allege,*) *to accuse;* *to blame; to find fault with.*

Acer, acris, acre, § 108; comp. acrior; sup. acerrĭmus, § 125, 1; adj. *sharp; sour; eager; vehement; rapid; courageous; fierce; violent; acute; keen; piercing.*

Acerbus, a, um, adj. *sour; unripe; vexatious; harsh; morose; disagreeable.*

Acerrĭmĕ, adv. sup. *See* Acrĭter.

Acervus, i, m. *a heap.*

Acétum, i, n. *vinegar.*

Achaïcus, a, um, adj. *Achæan, Grecian.*

Achelōus, i, m. *a river of Epirus.*

Acherusia, æ, f. *a lake in Campania;* also, *a cave in Bithynia.*

Achilles, is & eos, m. *the son of Peleus and Thetis, and the bravest of the Grecian chiefs at the siege of Troy.*

Acĭdus, a, um, adj. *sour; sharp; acid.*

Acies, ēi, f. *an edge; a line of* soldiers; *an army in battle array; a squadron; a rank, an army; a battle.*

Acĭnus, i, m. *a berry; a grapestone.*

Acrĭter, acriùs, acerrĭmĕ, adv *sharply; ardently; fiercely; courageously.*

Acroceraunia, ōrum, n. pl. § 96; *lofty mountains between Albania and Epirus.*

Acrocorinthos, i, f. *the citadel of Corinth.*

Acropŏlis, ıs, f. *the citadel of Athens.*

Actio, ōnis, f. (ago,) *an action; operation; a process.*

Actium, i, n. *a promontory of Epirus, famous for a naval victory of Augustus over Antony and Cleopatra.*

Actus, a, um, part. (ago,) *driven; led.*

Aculeus, i, m. *a sting; a thorn; a prickle; a porcupine's quill.*

Acūmen, ĭnis, n. (acuo,) *acuteness; perspicacity.*

Acus, ûs, f. *a needle.*

Ad, prep. *to; near; at; towards;* with a numeral, *about.*

Adămas, antis, m. *adamant; a diamond.*

Addĭtus, a, um, part. from

Addo, addĕre, addĭdi, addĭtum, a. (ad & do,) *to add; to annex; to appoint; to give.*

Addūco, adducĕre, adduxi, adductum, a. (ad & duco,) *to*

lead; *to bring*: in dubitatiōnem, *to bring into question.*

Ademptus, a, um, part. (adīmo.)

Adeò, adv. *so*; *therefore*; *so
much*; *to such a degree*; *so
very.*

Adeo, adire, adii, adītum, irr. n.
(ad & eo,) *to go to.* § 182, 3.

Adhærens, tis, part. from

Adhæreo, adhærére, adhæsi, n.
(ad & hæreo,) *to stick to*; *to
adhere*; *to adjoin*; *to lie contiguous.*

Adherbal, ălis, m. *a king of Numidia, put to death by his
cousin Jugurtha.*

Adhibeo, adhibére, adhibui, ad-
hibītum, a. (ad & habeo, § 189,
4,) *to admit*; *to apply*; *to use*;
to employ.

Adhuc, adv. *hitherto*; *yet*; *as
yet*; *still.*

Adīmo, adimére, adèmi, ademp-
tum, a. (ad & emo,) *to take
away.*

Adītus, ûs, m. (adeo,) *a going
to*; *entrance*; *access*; *approach.*

Adjaceo, ére, ui, ītum, n. (ad &
jaceo,) *to adjoin*; *to lie near*;
to border upon.

Adjungo, adjungère, adjunxi, ad-
junctum, a. (ad & jungo,) *to
join*; *to unite with.*

Adjūtus, a, um, part. from

Adjuvo, adjuvàre, adjūvi, adjū-
tum, a. ad & juvo,) *to assist*;
to help to aid.

Admětus, i, m. *a king of Thessaly.*

Administer, tri, m. *a servant
an assistant.*

Administro, àre, àvi, àtum, a.
(ad & ministro,) *to administer*; *to manage.*

Admiratio, ōnis, f. (admiror,) *ad-
miration.*

Admiràtus, a, um, part. from

Admiror, àri, àtus sum, dep. *to
admire.*

Admissus, a, um, part. from

Admitto, admittěre, admisi, ad-
missum, a. (ad & mitto,) *to
admit*; *to allow*; *to receive.*

Admŏdum, adv. (ad & modus,)
very; *much*; *greatly.*

Admoneo, ére, ui, ītum, a. (ad &
moneo,) *to admonish*; *to
warn*; *to put in mind.*

Admonĭtus, a, um, part. (admoneo.)

Admoveo, admovére, admōvi, ad-
mōtum, a. (ad & moveo,) *to
bring to*; *to move to.*

Adnăto, àre, àvi, àtum, freq. (ad
& nato,) *to swim to.*

Adolescens, tis, adj. (adolesco,)
(comp. ior, § 126, 4,) *young*:
subs. *a young man or woman*;
a youth.

Adolescentia, æ, f. *youth,* from

Adolesco, adolescère, adolévi,
adultum, inc. *to grow*; *to increase*; *to grow up.*

Adopto, àre, àvi, àtum, a. (ad &
opto,) *to adopt*; *to take for a
son*; *to assume.*

Adorior, oriri, ortus sum, dep. § 177, (ad & orior,) *to attack; to accost; to address; to undertake.*

Adria, æ, m. *the Adriatic sea.*

Adriatĭcus, a, um, adj. *Adriatic:* mare Adriaticum, *the Adriatic sea or gulf;* now, *the gulf of Venice.*

Adscendo, *or* ascendo, adscendĕre, adscendi, adscensum, a. (ad & scando,) *to ascend; to rise:* adscenditur, *the ascent is,* or *they ascend.*

Ad- *or* as- sisto, sistĕre, stĭti, n. (ad & sisto,) *to stand by; to assist; to help.*

Adspectūrus, a, um, part. (aspicio.)

Ad- *or* as- spergo, gĕre, si, sum, a. (ad & spargo,) *to sprinkle.*

Ad- *or* as- spicio, spicĕre, spexi, spectum, a. (ad & specio,) *to look at; see; regard; behold.*

Ad- *or* as- stans, tis, part. from

Ad- *or* as- sto, stăre, stĭti, n. (ad & sto,) *to stand by; to be near.*

Adsum, adesse, adfui, adfutūrus, irr. n. (ad & sum,) *to be present; to aid; to assist.*

Adulātor, ōris, m. (adŭlor,) *a flatterer.*

Aduncus, a, um, adj. *bent; crooked.*

Advectus, a, um, part. from

Advĕho, advehĕre, advexi, advectum, a. (ad & veho,) *to carry; to convey.*

12 *

Advĕna, æ, c. § 31, (advenio,) *a stranger.*

Adveniens, tis, part. from

Advenio, advenire, advĕni, adventum, n. (ad & venio,) *to arrive; to come.*

Adventus, ùs, m. *an arrival; a coming.*

Adversarius, i, m. (adversor,) *an adversary; an enemy.*

Adversùs & adversùm, prep. *against; towards.*　　　•

Adversus, a, um, adj. (adverto) *adverse; opposite; unfavorable; bad; fronting:* adversa cicătrix, *a scar in front* adverso corpŏre, *on the breast.*

Advŏco, āre, āvi, ātum, a. (ad & voco,) *to call for* or *to; to call; to summon.*

Advŏlo, āre, āvi, ātum, n. (ad & volo,) *to fly to.*

Ædifĭco, āre, āvi, ātum, a. (ædes & facio,) *to build.*

Ædilĭtas, ātis, f. *the office of an edile; edileship.*

Ædilĭtius, (vir,) i, m. *one who has been an edile.*

Ægæus, a, um, adj. *Ægæan:* Ægæum mare, *the Ægæan sea, lying between Greece and Asia Minor. It is now called the Archipelăgo.*

Æger, ra, rum, adj. *sick; weak; infirm; diseased.*

Ægrè, adv. *grievously; with difficulty.*

Ægritúdo, ĭnis, f. *sorrow; grief.*

Ægyptus, i, f. § 29, 2 ; *Ægypt.*

Ælius, i, m. *the name of a Ro-man family.*

Æmilius, i, m. *the name of several noble Romans of the* gens Æmilia, *or Æmilian tribe.*

Æmulatio, ōnis, f. (æmŭlor,) *emulation ; rivalry ; competition.*

Æmŭlus, a, um, adj. *emulous.*

Æmŭlus, i, m. *a rival ; a com-petitor.*

Ænēas, æ, m. *a Trojan prince, the son of Venus and An-chises.*

Æneus, a, um, adj. *brazen.*

Ænos, i, f. § 29, 2; *a town in Thrace, at the mouth of the Hebrus, named after its foun-der, Æneas.*

Æŏlis, ĭdis, f. *a country on the western coast of Asia Minor, between Troas and Ionia.*

Æquālis, e, adj. *equal.*

Æqualĭter, adv. *equally.*

Æquĭtas, ātis, f. *equity ; justice ; moderation.*

Æquus, a, um, adj. *equal :* æquus anĭmus, *or* æqua mens, *equa-nimity.*

Aër, is, m. *the air ; the atmos-phere.*

Ærarium, i, n. *the treasury ;* from

Æs, æris, n. *brass ; money.*

Æschўlus. i, m. *a celebrated Greek tragic poet.*

Æsculap·is, i, m. *the son of Apo'lo, and god of medicine.*

Æs·as, ātis, f. *summer.*

Æstimandus, a, um, part. *to be esteemed, prized, or regarded ;* from

Æstīmo, āre, āvi, ātum, a. *to esteem ; to value ; to regard ; to judge of ; to estimate.*

Æstuo, āre, āvi, ātum, n. *to be very hot.*

Æstuōsus, a, um, adj. *stormy ; boiling ; surging ; turbulent.*

Æstus, ûs, m. *heat.*

Ætas, ātis, f. *age.*

Æternus, a, um, adj. *eternal ; immortal.*

Æthiopia, æ, f. *Ethiopia, a coun-try in Africa, lying on both sides of the equator.*

Æthiops, ŏpis, m. *an Ethiopian.*

Ætna, æ, f. *a volcanic mountain in Sicily.*

Ævum, i, n, *time ; an age.*

Afer, ra, rum, adj. § 106, *of Africa.*

Affăbrè, adv. *artfully ; ingeni-ously ; curiously ; in a work-manlike manner.*

Affectus, a, um, part. *affected : afflicted.*

Affĕro, afferre, attŭli, allātum, irr. a. (ad & fero,) *to bring ; to carry.*

Afficio, icĕre, ēci, ectum, a. (ad & facio,) *to affect :* inediā, *to deprive of food :* cladĭbus, *to overthrow.*

Afficior, ĭci, ectus sum, pass. *to be affected :* gaudio, *to be af-fected with joy ; to rejoice :* fe-bri, *to be attacked with a fever.*

Affĭgo, affigĕre, affixi, affixum, a. (ad & figo,) *to fasten; to affix:* cruci, *to crucify.*

Affĭnis, e, adj. *neighboring; contiguous.*

Affĭnis, is, c. *a relation.*

Affirmo, ăre, āvi, ātum, a. (ad & firmo,) *to affirm; to confirm.*

Affixus, a, um, part. (affīgo.)

Afflātus, ūs, m. *a blast; a breeze; a gale; inspiration.*

Afrĭca, æ, f. *Africa; also a part of the African continent, lying east of Numidia, and west of Cyrene.*

Africānus, i, m. *the cognomen or surname of two of the Scipios, derived from their conquest of Africa.*

Afrĭcus, a, um, adj. *belonging to Africa; African..*

Agamemnon, ŏnis, m. *a king of Mycenæ, and the commander-in-chief of the Grecian forces at the siege of Troy.*

Agathyrsi, ōrum, m. pl. *a barbarous tribe living near the* palus Mæōtis.

Agellus, i, m. dim. (ager,) *a small farm.*

Agēnor, ŏris, m. *a king of Phœnicia.*

Agens, tis, part. (ago.)

Ager, ri, m. *a field; land; a farm; an estate; ground; a territory; the country.*

Agger, ĕris, m. *a heap; a pile;* *a mound; a bulwark; a bank; a rampart; a dam; a mole.*

Aggredior, ĕdi, essus sum, dep. (ad & gradior, § 189, 1,) *to go to; to attack.*

Aggressus, a, um, part. *having attacked.*

Agitātor, ōris, m. *a driver;* from

Agĭto, ăre, āvi, ātum, freq. (ago,) *to drive; to agitate; to revolve.*

Aglāus, i, m. *a very poor Arcadian.*

Agmen, ĭnis, n. (ago,) *a train; a troop upon the march; a band; an army.*

Agnĭtus, a, um, part. from

Agnosco, agnoscĕre, agnōvi, agnĭtum, a. (ad & nosco,) *to recognize; to know.*

Agnus, i, m. *a lamb.*

Ago, agĕre, ēgi, actum, a. *to conduct; to drive; to lead; to act; to do; to reside; to live:* funus, *to perform funeral rites:* annum centesĭmum, *to be spending,* or *to be in his one hundredth year:* bene, *to behave well:* ago gratias, *to thank.*

Agor, agi, actus sum, pass. *to be led:* agĭtur, *it is debated:* res de quâ agĭtur, *the point i t debate:* pessum agi, *to sink.*

Agricŏla, æ, m. (ager & colo) *a husbandman; a farmer.*

Agricultūra, æ, f. *agriculture.*

Agrigentum, ı, n. *a town upon*

the southern coast of Sicily, now *Girgenti.*

Agrippa, æ, m. *the name of several distinguished Romans.*

Ahēnum, i, n. *a kettle; a caldron; a brazen vessel.*

Aio, ais, ait, def. verb, (§ 183, 4,) *I say.*

Ajax, ácis, m. *the name of two distinguished Grecian warriors at the siege of Troy.*

Ala, æ, f. *a wing; an arm-pit; an arm.*

Alācer, ácris, ácre, adj. *lively; courageous; ready; fierce; spirited.*

Alba, æ, f. Alba Longa; *a city of Latium, built by Ascanius.*

Albánus, i, m. *an inhabitant of Alba.*

Albánus, a, um, adj. *Alban:* mons Albánus, *mount Albanus, at the foot of which Alba Longa was built, 16 miles from Rome.*

Albis, is, m. *a large river of Germany,* now *the Elbe.*

Albŭla, æ, m. *an ancient name of the Tiber.*

Albus, a, um, adj. *white.*

Alcestis, ĭdis, f. *the daughter of Pelias, and wife of Admētus.*

Alcibiădes, is, m. *an eminent Athenian, the pupil of Socrates.*

Alcinoüs, i, m. *a king of Phœacia* or *Corcyra, whose gardens were very celebrated.*

Alcyōne, es, f. *the daughter of* Æōlus, *and wife of Ceyx: she and her husband were changed into sea birds, called* Alcyōnes.

Alcyon, is, m. *kingfisher.*

Alcyonēus, a, um, adj. *halcyon.*

Alexander, dri, m. *surnamed the Great, was the son of Philip king of Macedon.*

Alexandrīa, æ, f. *the capital of Egypt; founded by Alexander the Great.*

Algeo, algēre, alsi, n. *to be cold.*

Alicunde, adv. (alĭquis & unde,) *from some place.*

Alienátus, a, um, part. *alienated; estranged.*

Aliëno, āre, āvi, ātum, a. *to alienate; to estrange.*

Aliēnŭs, a, um, adj. *foreign; of or belonging to another; another man's; another's.*

Aliò, adv. *to another place; elsewhere.*

Aliquandiu, adv. (aliquis & diu,) *for some time.*

Aliquando, adv. *once; formerly; at some time; at length: sometimes.*

Aliquantum, n. adj. *something; somewhat; a little.*

Alĭquis, alĭqua, alĭquod & alĭquid, pro. (§ 138,) *some; some one; a certain one.*

Alĭquot, ind. adj. *some.*

Alīter, adv. *otherwise.*

Alīter — alīter, *in one way — in another.*

Alius, a, ud, adj. § 107, R. 1; *another; other:* alii — alii, *some — others.*

Allätus, a, um, part. (affěro,) *brought.*

Allectus, a, um, part. (allicio.)

Allěvo, āre, āvi, ātum, a. (ad & levo,) *to raise up; to allevi-ate; to lighten.*

Allia, æ, f. *a small river of Italy, flowing into the Tiber.*

Allicio, -licěre, -lexi, -lectum, (ad & lacio,) a. *to allure; to entice.*

Alligātus, a, um, part. *bound; confined;* from

Allīgo, āre, āvi, ātum, a. (ad & ligo,) *to bind to; to fasten; to bind or tie.*

Allocūtus, a, um, part. *speaking,* or *having spoken to;* from

Allŏquor, -lŏqui, -locūtus sum, dep. (ad & loquor,) *to speak to; to address; to accost.*

Alluo, -luěre, -lui, a. (ad & luo,) *to flow near; to wash; to lave.*

Alo, a:ěre, alui, alĭtum or altum, a. *to nourish; to feed; to sup-port; to increase; to main-tain; to strengthen.*

Alŏeus, i, m. *a giant, son of Ti-tan and Terra.*

Alpes, ium, f. pl. *the Alps.*

Alpheus, i, m. *a river of Pelo-ponnesus.*

Alpīnus, a, um, adj. *of or be-longing to the Alps; Alpine:* Alpini inures, *marmots.*

Altè, iis, issĭmè, adv. *o.t high, highly; deeply; low; loudly.*

Alter, ěra, ěrum, adj. § 107; *the one (of two); the other; the second.* § 120, 1.

Alternus, a, um, adj. *alternate; by turns.*

Althæa, æ, f. *the wife of Œneus, and mother of Meleager.*

Altitūdo, ĭnis, f. *height;* from

Altus, a, um, adj. (ior, issĭmus,) *high; lofty; deep; loud.*

Alumnus, i, m. *a pupil; a foster-son; a fosterling.*

Alveus, i, m. *a channel.*

Alvus, i, f. *the belly.*

Amans, tis, part. and adj. (ior, issĭmus,) *loving; fond of.*

Amārus, a, um, adj. *bitter.*

Amātus, a, um, part. (amo.)

Amâzon, ŏnis; pl. Amazŏnes, um, f. *Amazons, a nation of female warriors, who original-ly inhabited a part of Sarma-tia, near the river Don, ana afterwards passed over into Asia Minor.*

Ambitio, ŏnis, f. (ambio,) *ambition.*

Ambītus, ûs, m. *compass; ex-tent; circuit; circumference; an encompassing; an encir-cling; a coiling around.*

Ambo, æ, o, adj. pl. § 118, 1; *both; each.*

Ambŭlo, āre, āvi, ātum, n. *to walk.*

Amicitia, æ, f. *friendship;* from

Amicus, a, um, adj. *friendly.*

Amicus, i, m. (amo,) *a friend.*

Amissus, a, um, part. from

Amitto, amittĕre, amisi, amissum, a. (a & mitto,) *to lose; to relinquish.*

Ammon, ŏnis, m. *a surname of Jupiter, to whom, under this name, a temple was erected in the Lybian desert.*

Amnis, is, d. § 63, 1 ; *a river.*

Amo, ăre, ăvi, ătum, a. *to love.* § 155.

Amœnus, a, um, adj. (ior, issĭmus,) *pleasant; agreeable; delightful.*

Amor, ŏris, m. (amo,) *love.*

Amphinómus, i, m. *a Catanean, distinguished for his filial affection.*

Amphion, ŏnis, m. *a son of Jupiter and Antiope, and the husband of Niobe. He is fabled to have built Thebes by the sound of his lyre.*

Ample, adv. (ius, issĭmè,) *amply;* (amplus.)

Amplector, ecti, exus sum, dep. (amb & plector, § 196, (b.) *to embrace.*

Amplexus, a, um, part. *having embraced; embracing.*

Amplio, ăre, ăvi, ătum, a. *to enlarge.*

Amplius, adv. (amplè,) *more.*

Amplus, a, um, adj. (ior, issĭmus,) *great; abundant; large; spacious.*

Amulius, i, m. *the son of Silvius*

Procas, and brother of Numitor.

Amyclæ, ărum, f. pl. *a town upon the western coast of Italy, near Fundi.*

Amȳcus, i, m. *a son of Neptune, and king of Bebrycia.*

An, conj. *whether; or.*

Anacreon, tis, m. *a celebrated lyric poet of Teos in Ionia.*

Anápus, i, m. *a Catanean, the brother of Amphinomus.*

Anaxagŏras, æ, m. *a philosopher of Clazomene, a city of Ionia.*

Anceps, cipĭtis, adj. *uncertain; doubtful.*

Anchises, æ, m. *a Trojan, the father of Æneas.*

Anchŏra, or Ancŏra, æ, f. *an anchor.*

Ancilla, æ, f. *a female servant; a maid.*

Ancus, i, m. (Martius,) *the fourth king of Rome.*

Andriscus, i, m. *a person of mean birth, called also Pseudophilippus, on account of his pretending to be Philip, the son of Persis, king of Macedon.*

Andromĕda, æ, f. *the daughter of Cepheus and Cassiope, and wife of Perseus.*

Ango, angĕre, anxi, a. *to trouble, to disquiet; to torment; to vex.*

Anguis, is, c. *a snake; a serpent.*

Angŭlus, i, m. *a corner.*

Angustiæ, ārum, f. pl. *narrowness ; a narrow pass ; a defile.*

Angustus, a, um, adj. *narrow ; limited ; straitened ; pinching.*

Anĭma, æ, f. *breath ; life ; the soul.*

Animadverto, -vertĕre, -verti, -versum, a. (anĭmus, ad, & verto,) *to attend ; to observe ; to notice.*

Anĭmal, ālis, n. (anĭma,) *an animal.*

Anĭmōsus, a, um, adj. *courageous ; bold ; undaunted ;* from

Anĭmus, i, m. *the mind ; disposition ; spirit ; courage ; a design :* uno anĭmo, *unanimously :* mihi est anĭmus, *I have a mind*

Anio, ēnis, m. *a branch of the Tiber, which enters it three miles above Rome.* It is now called *the Teverone.*

Annecto, -nectĕre, -nexui, -nexum, a. (ad & necto,) *to annex ; to tie or fasten to.*

Annŭlus, i, m. *a ring.*

Annumĕro, āre, āvi, ātum, a. (ad & numĕro,) *to number ; to reckon ; to reckon among.*

Annuo, -nuĕre, -nui, n. (ad & nuo, to nod,) *to assent ; to agree.*

Annus, i, m. *a year.*

Annuus, a, um, adj. *annual ; yearly ; lasting a year.*

Anser, ĕris, m. *a goose.*

Anserinus, a, um, adj. *of or belonging to a goose :* ova. *goose-eggs.*   •

Antè, adv. *before ; sooner.*

Ante, prep. *before.*

Antea, adv. (ante & is,) *before ; heretofore.*

Antecello, -cellĕre, a. (ante & cello,) *to excel ; to surpass ; to exceed ; to be superior to.*

Antepōno, -ponĕre, -posui, -posĭtum, a. (ante & pono,) *to prefer ; to set before.*

Anteposĭtus, a, um, part. (antepōno.)

Antĕquam, adv. *before ; before that.*

Antigōnus, i, m. *a king of Macedonia.*

Antiochia, æ, f. *the capital of Syria.*

Antiŏchus, i, m. *a king of Syria.*

Antiŏpe, es, f. *the wife of Lycus, king of Thebes, and the mother of Amphion.*

Antiquus, a, um, adj. (ior, issĭmus,) *ancient ; old ; of long continuance.*

Antipăter, tris, m. *a Sidonian poet.*

Antium, i, n. *a maritime town of Italy.*

Antonius, i, m. *Antony, the name of a Roman family.*

Antrum, i, n. *a cave.*

Apelles, is, m. *a celebrated painter of the island of Cos.*

Apenninus, i, m. *the Apennines.*

Aper, ri, m. § 48; *a boar; a wild boar.*

Aperio, -perire, -perui, -pertum, a. (ad & pario,) *to open; to discover; to disclose; to make known.*

Apertus, a, um, part. (aperio.)

Apex, ĭcis, m. *a point; the top; the summit.*

Apis, is, f. *a bee.*

Apis, is, m. *an ox worshipped as a deity among the Egyptians.*

Apollo, ĭnis, m. *the son of Jupiter and Latona, and the god of music and poetry.*

Apparātus, ûs, m. *a preparation; apparatus; equipment; habiliment.*

Appareo, ĕre, ui, n. (ad & pareo,) *to appear; .to be manifest or clear.*

Appellandus, a, um, part. from

Appello, āre, āvi, ātum, a. (ad & pello,) *to name* or *call; to address; to call upon.*

Appendo, -pendĕre, -pendi, -pensum, a. (ad & pendo,) *to hang upon* or *to; to weigh out; to pay.*

Appĕtens, tis, part. *seeking after;* from

Appĕto, -petĕre, -petīvi, -petītum, a. (ad & peto,) *to desire; to strive for; to aim at; to attack.*

Appius, i, m. *a Roman prænōmen belonging to the Claudian gens or tribe.*

Appōno, -ponĕre, -posui, -posĭtum, a. (ad & pono,) *to set* or *place before; to put to; to join.*

Apposĭtus, a, um, part. (appōno.)

Apprópinquo, āre, āvi, ātum, n. (ad & propinquo,) *to approach; to draw near.*

Aprĭcus, a, um, adj. *sunny; serene; warm.*

Apto, āre, āvi, ātum, a. *to fit; to adjust.*

Apud, prep. *at; in; among; before; to:* with the name of a person, it signifies *in his house;* with that of an author, it signifies *in his writings.*

Apulia, æ, f. *a country in the eastern part of Italy, near the Adriatic.*

Aqua, æ, f. *water.*

Aquæductus, ûs, m. (aqua & duco,) *an aqueduct; a conduit.*

Aquĭla, æ, f. *an eagle.*

Aquĭlo, ōnis, m. *the north wind.*

Aquitania, æ, f. *a country of Gaul.*

Aquitāni, ōrum, m. pl. *the inhabitants of Aquitania.*

Ara, æ, f. *an altar.*

Arabia, æ, f. *Arabia.*

Arabĭcus, a, um, adj. *Arabian; of* or *belonging to Arabia;* Arabĭcus sinus, *the Red sea.*

Arabius, a, um, adj. *Arabian.*

Arabs, ăbis, m. *an Arabian*

Arbitrātus, a, um, part. *having thought;* from

Arbĭtror, āri, ātus sum, dep. *to believe; to think.*

Arbor, & Arbos, ŏris, f. *a tree.*

Arca, æ, f. *a chest.*

Arcadia, æ, f. *Arcadia, a country in the interior of the Peloponnesus.*

Arcas, ădis, m. *a son of Jupiter and Calisto; also, an Arcadian.*

Arceo, ēre, ui, a. *to drive away; to ward off; to keep from; to restrain.*

Arcessitus, a, um, part. from

Arcesso, ēre, ivi, ĭtum, a. *to send for; to invite; to summon; to call.*

Archimēdes, is, m. *a famous mathematician and mechanician of Syracuse.*

Architectus, i, m. *an architect; a builder.*

Archȳtas, æ, m. *a Pythagorean philosopher of Tarentum.*

Arctè, adv. (iùs, issĭmè,) *straitly; closely; strictly;* from

Arctus, a, um, adj. (ior, issĭmus,) *narrow; close.*

Arcus, ùs, m. *a bow; an arch.*

Ardea, æ, f. *a city of Latium, the capital of the Rutuli.*

Ardens, tis, part. & adj. *burning; hot;* from

Ardeo, ardère, arsi, arsum, n. *to burn; to sparkle; to be consumed by fire.*

Arduus, a, um, adj. *high; lofty; steep; arduous; difficult.*

Arēna, æ, f. *sand.*

Arenōsus, a, um, adj. *sandy.*

Arethūsa, æ, f. *the name of a nymph of Elis, who was changed into a fountain in Sicily.*

Argentum, i, n. *silver.*

Argias, æ, m. *a chief of the Megarensians.*

Argīvus, a, um, adj. *of Argos; Argive.*

Argīvi, ōrum, m. pl. *Argives; inhabitants of Argos.*

Argonautæ, ārum, m. pl. *the Argonauts; the crew of the ship Argo, who sailed with Jason to Colchis.*

Argos, i, n. sing., & Argi, ōrum, m. pl. *a city in Greece, the capital of Argolis.*

Arguo, uēre, ui, ūtum, a. *to show, to prove; to convict.*

Arimĭnum, i, n. *a city of Italy, on the coast of the Adriatic.*

Aristobūlus, i, m. *a name of several of the high priests and kings of Judæa.*

Aristotēles, is, m. *Aristotle, a Greek philosopher, born at Stagira, a city of Macedonia.*

Arma, ōrum, n. pl. § 96; *arms.*

Armātus, a, um, part. *armed:* pl. armāti, ōrum, *armed men; soldiers.*

Armenia, æ, f. (Major,) *a country of Asia, lying between the*

13

Taurus and the Caucasus. Armenia (Minor,) *a small country, lying between Cappadocia and the Euphrates.*

Armenius, a, um, adj. *Armenian.*

Armentum, i, n. *a herd.*

Armilla, æ, f. *a bracelet* or *ring worn on the left arm by soldiers who had been distinguished in battle.*

Armo, āre, āvi, ātum, a. *to arm.*

Aro, āre, āvi, ātum, a. *to plough; to cover with the plough.*

Arreptus, a, um, part. from

Arripio, -ripĕre, -ripui, -reptum, a. (ad & rapio, § 189, 5.) *to seize upon.*

Arrŏgo, āre, āvi, ātum, a. (ad & rogo,) *to arrogate; to claim.*

Ars, tis, f. *art; contrivance; skill; employment; occupation; pursuit.*

Arsi. *See* Ardeo.

Artemisia, æ, f. *the wife of Mausōlus, king of Caria.*

Artĭfex, ĭcis, c. (ars & facio,) *an artist.*

Arundo, ĭnis, f. *a reed; a cane.*

Aruns, tis, m. *the eldest son of Tarquin the Proud.*

Arx, cis, f. *a citadel; a fortress.*

Ascanius, i, m. *the son of Æneas and Creüsa.*

Ascendo. *See* Adscendo.

Asia, æ, f. *Asia; Asia Minor;* also, *proconsular Asia,* or *the Roman province.*

Asiatĭcus, i m. *an agnōmen or*

surname of L. Cornelius Scipio, on account of his victories in Asia.

Asīna, æ, m. *a cognōmen or surname of a part of the Cornelian family.*

Asinus, i, m. *an ass.*

Aspectūrus, a, um, part. (aspicio.

Asper, ĕra, ĕrum, adj. *rough, rugged.*

Aspergo. *See* Adspergo.

As- or ad- spernor, āri, ātus sum, dep. *to spurn; to despise; to reject.*

Aspicio. *See* Adspicio.

Aspis, ĭdis, f. *an asp.*

Assecūtus, a, um, part. from

As- or ad- sĕquor, -sequi, -secūtus sum, dep. (ad & sequor,) *t obtain; to overtake.*

As- or ad- servo, āre, āvi, ātum, a. (ad & servo,) *to preserve; to keep.*

As- or ad- signo, āre, āvi, ātum, a. (ad & signo,) *to assign; to appoint; to allot; to distribute.*

Assisto. *See* Adsisto.

Assuesco,-suescĕre, -suēvi, -suētum, inc. *to be accustomed; to be wont.*

Assurgo, -surgĕre, -surrexi, -surrectum, n. (ad & surgo,) *to rise; to arise.*

Astronomia, æ, f. *astronomy.*

Astūtus, a, um, adj. (ior, :ssĭmus,) *cunning; crafty.*

Asȳlum, i, n. *an asylum.*

At, conj. § 198, II. 9; *but.*

Atalanta, æ, f. *the daughter of Schœneus, king of Arcadia.*

Athênæ, ārum, f. pl. *Athens, the capital of Attica.*

Atheniensis, is, m. *an Athenian; an inhabitant of Athens.*

Atilius, i, m. *a Roman proper name.*

Atlantĭcus, a, um, adj. *Atlantic; relating to Atlas:* mare Atlantĭcum, *the Atlantic ocean.*

Atque, conj. *and.*

Atrocĭter, adv. (iùs, issĭmè,) (atrox,) *fiercely; violently; severely.*

Attălus, i, m. *a king of Pergāmus.*

Attĕro, -terĕre, -trivi, -tritum, a. (ad & tero,) *to rub off; to wear.*

Atthis, ĭdis, f. *the same as Attĭca.*

Attĭca, æ, f. *Attica, a country in the southern part of Greece proper.*

Attingo, -tingĕre, -tĭgi, -tactum, a. (ad & tango,) *to touch; to border upon; to attain; to reach.*

Attollo, ĕre, a. (ad & tollo,) *to raise up.*

Attritus, a, um, part. (attĕro,) *rubbed away; worn off.*

Auctor, ōris, c. (augeo,) *an author.*

Auctorĭtas, ātis, f. *authority; influence; reputation.*

Auctus, a, um, part. (augeo,) *increased enlarged; augmented.*

Audacia, æ, f. *audacity; boldness;* from

Audax, ācis, adj. *bold; daring; audacious; desperate.*

Audeo, audēre, ausus sum, neut. pass. *to dare.* § 142, 2.

Audio, ire, ivi, itum, a. *to hear.*

Audītus, a, um, part.

Audītus, ûs, m. *the hearing.*

Aufĕro, auferre, abstŭli, ablātum, irr. a. (ab & fero,) *to take away; to remove.*

Aufugio, -fugĕre, -fūgi, -fugĭtum, n. (ab & fugio, § 196, 1,) *to fly away; to run off; to escape; to flee.*

Augendus, a, um, part. from

Augeo, augēre, auxi, auctum, a. *to increase; to augment; to enlarge; to rise.*

Augurium, i, n. *augury; divination.*

Augustè, adv. *nobly;* from

Augustus, a, um, adj. *august; grand; venerable.*

Augustus, i, m. *an honorary appellation bestowed by the senate upon Cæsar Octavianus; and succeeding emperors took the same name.*

Aulis, ĭdis, f. *a seaport town in Bœotia.*

Aulus, i, m. *a common prænōmen among the Romans.*

Aurelius, i, m. *the name of several Romans.*

Aureus, a, um, adj. (aurum,) *golden.*

Auriga, æ, m. *a charioteer.*

Auris, is, f. *the ear.*

Aurum, i, n. *gold.*

Auspicium, i, n. *an auspice; a species of divination, from the flight, &c. of birds.*

Ausus, a, um, part. (audeo,) *daring ; having dared.*

Aut, conj. § 198, 2; *or ; aut—aut, either—or.*

Autem, conj. § 198, 9; *but ; yet.*

Autumnus, i, m. *autumn.*

Auxi. See Augeo.

Auxilium, i, n. *help ; aid ; assistance.*

Avaritia, æ, f. *avarice ;* from

Avārus, a, um, adj. *avaricious ; covetous.*

Avĕho, -vehĕre, -vexi, -vectum, a. (a & veho,) *to carry off or away.*

Avello, -vellĕre, -velli *or* -vulsi, -vulsum, a. (a & vello,) *to carry away ; to pull away.*

Aventinus, i, m. *mount Aventine, one of the seven hills on which Rome was built.*

Aversus, a, um, part. *turned away :* cicătrix aversa, *a scar in the back :* from

Averto, -vertĕre, -verti, -versum, a. (a & verto,) *to avert ; to turn ; to turn away.*

Avicŭla, æ, f. dim. (avis,) *a small bird.*

Avĭdus, a, um, adj. (ior, issĭmus,) *ravenous ; greedy ; eager.*

Avis, is, f. *a bird.*

Avŏco, âre, âvi, âtum, a. (a &

voco,) *to call away, to divert to withdraw.*

Avolatūrus, a, um, part. from

Avŏlo; âre, âvi, âtum, n. (a & volo,) *to fly away or off.*

Avulsus, part. (avello.)

Avuncŭlus, i, m. *an uncle.*

Avus, i, m. *a grandfather.*

Axĕnus, i, m. (from the Greek "Αξενος, inhospitable ;) *the Euxine sea ; anciently so called, on account of the cruelty of the neighboring tribes.*

B.

Babўlon, ōnis, f. *the metropolis of Chaldea, lying upon the Euphrates.*

Babylonia, æ, f. *the country about Babylon.*

Bacca, æ, f. *a berry.*

Bacchus, i, m. *the son of Jupiter and Semĕle, and the god of wine.*

Bactra, ōrum, n. *the capital of Bactriāna, situated upon the sources of the Oxus.*

Bactriáni, ōrum, m. pl. *the inhabitants of Bactriāna.*

Bactriānus, a, um, adj. *Bactrian, pertaining to Bactra or Bactriāna.*

Bacŭlum, i, n. *a staff.*

Bætĭca, æ, f. *a country in the southern part of Spain, watered by the river Bætis.*

Bætis, is, m. *a river in the south-*

ern part of Spain, now *the Guadalquivir.*

Bagrāda, æ, m. *a river of Africa, between Utica and Carthage.*

Ballista, æ, f. *an engine for throwing stones.*

Baltĭcus, a, um, adj. *Baltic :* mare Baltĭcum, *the Baltic sea.*

Barbărus, a, um, adj. *barbarous ; rude ; uncivilized ; savage :* subs. barbări, *barbarians.*

Batăvus, a, um, adj. *Batavian ; belonging to Batavia,* now *Holland.*

Beatitūdo, ĭnis, f. *blessedness ; happiness ;* from

Beātus, a, um, adj. (ior issĭmus,) *happy ; blessed.*

Bebrycia, æ, f. *a country of Asia.*

Belgæ, árum, m. pl. *the inhabitants of the north-east part of Gaul ; the Belgians.*

Belgĭcus, a, um, adj. *of or pertaining to the Belgæ.*

Bellérophon, tis, m. *the son of Glaucus, king of Ephȳra.*

Bellicōsus, a, um, adj. (ior, issĭmus, bellum, § 128, 4,) *warlike.*

Bellĭcus, a, um, adj. (bellum, § 128, 2,) *warlike.*

Belligĕro, āre, āvi, ātum, n. (bellum & gero,) *to wage war ; to carry on war.*

Bello, āre, āvi, ātum, n. *to war ; to wag war ; to contend ; to fight.*

Bellua, æ, f. *a beast ; a brute.*

Bellum, i. n. *war*

Belus, i, m. *the founder of the Babylonish empire.*

Benè, adv. (comp. meliùs, sup. optĭmè,) *well ; finely ; very :* benè pugnāre, *to fight successfully.*

Beneficium, i, n. (benè & facio,) *a benefit ; a kindness.*

Benevolentia, æ, f. (benè & volo,) *benevolence ; good will.*

Benignè, adv. *kindly ;* from

Benignus, a, um, adj. *kind ; benign.*

Bestia, æ, f. *a beast.*

Bestia, æ, m. *the surname of a Roman consul.*

Bias, antis, m. *a philosopher born at Priéne, and one of the seven wise men of Greece.*

Bibliothēca, æ, f. *a library.*

Bibo, bibēre, bibi, bibĭtum, a. *to drink ; to imbibe.*

Bibŭlus, i, m. *a colleague of Julius Cæsar in the consulship.*

Bini, æ, a, num. adj. § 119, III ; *two by two ; two.*

Bipes, ĕdis, adj. (bis & pes,) *two-footed.*

Bis, num. adv. *twice.*

Bithynia, æ, f. *a country of Asia Minor, east of the Propontis.*

Blanditia, æ, f. *a compliment :* blanditiæ, pl. *blandishments ; caresses ; flattery :* from

Blandus, a, um, adj (ior, issĭmus,)

flattering ; enticing ; inviting ; tempting.

Bœotia, æ, f. *a country of Greece, north of Attica.*

Bonĭtas, ātis, f. *goodness ; excellence ;* from

Bonus, a, um, adj. (melior, optĭmus,) *good ; happy ; kind.*

Bonum, i, n. *a good thing ; an endowment ; an advantage ; profit :* bona, n. pl. *an estate ; goods.*

Boreālis, e, adj. *northern ;* from

Boreas, æ, m. *the north wind.*

Borysthĕnes, æ, m. *a large river of Scythia, flowing into the Euxine ; it is now called the Dneiper.*

Borysthĕnis, ĭdis, f. *the name of a town at the mouth of the Borysthenes.*

Bos, bovis, c. *an ox ; a cow.* §§ 83, R. 1, & 84, E. 1.

Bosphŏrus, *or* Bospŏrus, i, m. *the name of two straits between Europe and Asia ; one, the* Bosphŏrus Thracius, *Thracian Bosphorus,* now the *straits of Constantinople ;* the other, the Bosphŏrus Cimmĕrius, *the Cimmerian Bosphorus,* now *the straits of Caffa.*

Brachium, i, n. *the arm.*

Brevi, adv. *shortly ; briefly ; in a short time ;* from

Brevis, e, adj. (ior, issĭmus,) *short; brief.*

Brevĭtas, ātis, f. *shortness ; brevity.*

Brigantinus, a, um, adj. *belonging to Brigantium, a town of the Vindelici :* Brigantĭnus lacus, *the lake of Constance.*

Britannia, æ, f. *Great Britain.*

Britannĭcus, a, um, adj. *belonging to Britain ; British :* oceānus Britannĭcus, *and* mare Britannĭcum, *the North sea, including a part of the Baltic.*

Britannus, a, um, adj. *British :* Britanni, *the Britons.*

Bruma, æ, f. *the winter solstice ; the shortest day.*

Bruttium, i, n. *a promontory of Italy.*

Bruttii, ōrum, m. pl. *a people in the southern part of Italy.*

Brutus, i, m. *the name of an illustrious Roman family.*

Bucephălus, i, m. *the name of Alexander's war-horse.*

Bucephălos, i, f. *a city of India near the Hydaspes, built by Alexander, in memory of his horse.*

Buxeus, a, um, adj. *of box ; of a pale yellow color, like boxwood.*

Byzantium, i, n. *now Constantinople, a city of Thrace, situated upon the Bosphŏrus.*

C.

C., *an abbreviation of Caius.*

Cabira, ind. *a town of Pontus.*

Cacūmen, ĭnis, n. *the top; the peak; the summit.*

Cadens, tis, part. (cado.)

Cadmus, i, m. *a son of Agēnor, king of Phœnicia.*

Cado, cadĕre, cecĭdi, casum, n. *to fall.*

Cæcilius, i, m. *the name of several Romans.*

Cæcŭbum, i, n. *a town of Campania, famous for its wine.*

Cæcŭbus, a, um, adj. *Cæcuban; of Cæcubum.*

Cædes, is, f. *slaughter; carnage; homicide; murder;* from

Cædo, cædĕre, cecīdi, cæsum, a. *to cut; to kill; to slay; to beat.*

Cælātus, a, um, part. from

Cælo, are, āvi, ātum, a. *to carve; to engrave; to sculpture; to emboss.*

Cæpe, *or* Cepe, n. indec. *an onion.*

Cæpio, ōnis, m. *a Roman consul who commanded in Spain.*

Cæsar, ăris, m. *a* cognómen *or surname given to the Julian family.*

Cæstus, ùs, m. *a gauntlet; a boxing glove.*

Cæsus, a, um, part. (cædo,) *cut; slain; beaten.*

Caius, i, m. *a Roman* prænôr en

Calais, is, m. *a son of Boreas.*

Calamĭtas, ātis, f. *a calamity; a misfortune;* from

Calāmus, i, m. *a reed.*

Calathiscus, i, m. *a small basket.*

Calefacio, calefacĕre, calefēci, calefactum, a. (caleo & facio,) *to warm.*

Calefio, fiĕri, făctus sum, irr. § 180, N.; *to be warmed.*

Calefactus, a, um, part. (calefio,) *warmed.*

Calĭdus, a, um, adj. *warm.*

Callĭdus, a, um, adj. *cunning; shrewd.*

Calor, ōris, m. *warmth; heat.*

Calpe, es, f. *a hill* or *mountain in Spain, opposite to Abȳla in Africa.*

Calpurnius, i, m. *the name of a Roman family.*

Calydonius, a, um, adj. *of or belonging to Calydon, a city of Ætolia; Calydonian.*

Camēlus, i, c. *a camel.*

Camillus, i, m. (M. Furius,) *a Roman general.*

Campania, æ, f. *a pleasant country of Italy, between Latium and Lucania.*

Campester, tris, tre, adj. *even; plain; level; champaign; flat.*

Campus, i, m. *a plain; a field, the Campus Martius.*

Cancer, cri, m. *a crab.*

Candĭdus, a, um, adj. *white.*

Candor, ŏris, m. *brightness;
whiteness; clearness.*

Canens, tis, part. *singing.*

Canis, is, c. *a dog.*

Cannæ, ārum, f. pl. *a village in
Apulia, famous for the defeat
of the Romans by Hannibal.*

Cannensis, e, adj. *belonging to
Cannæ.*

Cano, canĕre, cecĭni, cantum, a.
*to sing; to sound or play upon
an instrument.*

Cantans, tis, part. (canto.)

Canthărus, i, m. *a beetle; a knot
under the tongue of the god
Apis.*

Cantium, i, n. *now the county of
Kent, on the eastern coast of
England.*

Canto, āre, āvi, ātum, freq.
(cano,) *to sing; to repeat
often.*

Cantus, ûs, m. *singing; a song:*
cantus galli, *the crowing of
the cock.*

Capesso, ĕre, īvi, ītum, a. (capio,)
§ 187, II. 5; *to take; to take
the management of:* fugam
capessĕre, *to flee.*

Capiendus, a, um, part. (capio.)

Capiens, tis, part. from

Capio, capĕre, cepi, captum, a.
*to take; to capture; to take
captive; to enjoy; to derive.*

Capitālis, e, adj. (caput,) *capital;
mortal; deadly; pernicious:*
capitāle, ('sc. crimen,) *a capital crime.*

Capitolium, i, n. *the capitol; th
Roman citadel on the Capito
line hill.*

Capra, æ, f. *a she-goat.*

Captivus, a, um, adj. *captive.*

Capto, āre, āvi, ātum, freq. § 187,
II. 1, (capio,) *to catch at; to
seek for; to hunt for.*

Captus, a, um, part. (capio,)
taken; taken captive.

Capua, æ, f. *the principal city of
Campania.*

Caput, ĭtis, n. *a head; life; the
skull; a capital city:* capĭtis
damnāre, *to condemn to death.*

Carbonarius, i, m. (carbo, *a coal;*)
*a collier; a maker of char-
coal.*

Carcer, ĕris, m. *a prison.*

Careo, ēre, ui, ĭtum, n. *to be
without; to be free from; to
be destitute; not to have; to
want.*

Cares, ium, m. pl. *Carians; the
inhabitants of Caria.*

Caria, æ, f. *a country in the southeastern part of Asia Minor.*

Carĭca, æ, f. *a fig.*

Carmen, ĭnis, n. *a song; a poem.*

Carneădes, is, m. *a philosopher
of Cyrēne, distinguished for
his acuteness.*

Caro, carnis, f. *flesh.*

Carpentum, i, n. *a chariot; a
wagon.*

Carpetāni, ōrum, m. pl. *a people
of Spain, on the borders of the
Tagus.*

Carpo, carpĕre, carpsi, carptum, a. *to pluck; to tear.*

Carræ, ārum, f. pl. *a city of Mesopotamia, near the Euphrates.*

Carthaginiensis, e, adj. *of or belonging to Carthage; Carthaginian:* subs. *a Carthaginian.*

Carthago, ĭnis, f. *Carthage, a maritime city in Africa:* Carthago Nova, *Carthagena, a town of Spain.*

Carus, a, um, adj. (ior, issĭmus,) *dear.*

Casa, æ, f. *a cottage; a hut.*

Casca, æ, m. *the* cognōmen *or surname of P. Servilius, one of the conspirators against Cæsar.*

Caseus, i, m. *cheese.*

Cassander, dri, m. *the name of a Macedonian.*

Cassiŏpe, es, f. *the wife of Cepheus, king of Ethiopia, and mother of Andromeda.*

Cassius, i, m. *the name of several Romans.*

Castalius, a, um, adj. *Castalian; of Castalia, a fountain of Phocis, at the foot of mount Parnassus.*

Castigātus, a, um, part. from

Castigo, āre, āvi, ātum, a. *to chastise; to punish.*

Castrum, i, n. *a castle:* castra, ōrum, pl. *a camp:* castra ponĕre, *to pitch a camp; to encamp.*

Casus, ûs, m. *accident; chance; an event; a misfortune; a disaster; a calamity.*

Catabathmus, i, m. *a declivity; a gradual descent; a valley between Egypt and Africa proper.*

Catăna, æ, f. *now Catania, a city of Sicily, near to mount Etna.*

Catanensis, e, adj. *belonging to Catana; Catanean.*

Catiēnus, i, m. Catiēnus Plotinus, *a Roman who was greatly distinguished for his attachment to his patron.*

Catilina, æ, m. *a conspirator against the Roman government, whose plot was detected and defeated by Cicero.*

Cato, ōnis, m. *the name of a Roman family.*

Catūlus, i, m. *the name of a Roman family of the Lutatian tribe.*

Catŭlus, i, m. *the young of beasts; a whelp.*

Caucăsus, i, m. *a mountain of Asia, between the Black and Caspian seas.*

Cauda, æ, f. *a tail.*

Caudinus, a, um, adj. *Caudine; of or belonging to Caudium, a town of Italy.*

Caula, æ, f. *a fold.*

Causa, æ, f. *a cause; a reason; a lawsuit:* in causâ est, *or* causa est, *is the reason:* ali

cūjus rei causâ, *for the pur-*
pose, or *for the sake of a*
thing.

Cautes, is, f. *a rock ; a crag ; a*
cliff.

Caveo, cavēre, cavi, cautum, n.
& a. *to beware ; to avoid ; to*
shun : cavēre sibi ab aliquo,
to secure themselves ; to guard
against.

Caverna, æ, f. *a cave ; a cavern.*

Cavus, a, um, adj. *hollow*

Cecidi. *See* Cædo.

Cecidi. *See* Cado.

Cecini. *See* Cano.

Cecropia, æ, f. *an ancient name*
of Athens ; from

Cecrops, ōpis, m. *the first king*
of Athens.

Cedo, cedēre, cessi, cessum, n.
to yield ; to give place ; to
retire ; to retreat ; to submit.

Celĕber, bris, brc, adj. (rior, errĭmus,) *crowded ; much visited;*
renowned ; famous ; distin-
guished.

Celebratus, a, um, part. (celébro.)

Celebrĭtas, ātis, f. (celĕber,)
fame ; glory ; celebrity ; re-
nown.

Celĕbro, āre, āvi, ātum, a. *to*
visit ; to celebrate ; to make
famous ; to perform.

Celerĭtas, ātis, f. (celer, swift,)
speed ; swiftness ; quickness.

Celerĭter, adv. (ius, rīme,) *swift-*
ly.

Celeus, i m. *a king of Eleusis.*

Celo, āre, āvi, ātum, a *to hide ;*
to conceal.

Celtæ, ārum, m. pl. *the Celts, a*
people of Gaul.

Censco, ēre, ui, um, a. *to judge ;*
to believe ; to count ; to reckon.

Censor, is, m. *a censor ; a cen-*
surer ; a fault-finder ; a critic.

Censorinus, i, m. (L. Manlius,)
a Roman consul in the third
Punic war.

Censorius, i, m. *one who has been*
a censor ; a surname of Cato
the elder.

Census, ûs, m. *a census ; an*
enumeration of the people ; a
registering of the people, their
ages, &c.

Centēni, æ, a, num. adj. pl. *every*
hundred ; a hundred.

Centesĭmus, æ, um, num. adj. *the*
hundredth.

Centies, num. adv. *a hundred*
times.

Centum, num. adj. pl. ind. *a hun-*
dred.

Centurio, ōnis, m. *a centurion ·*
a captain of a hundred men.

Cephallenia, æ, f. *an island in*
the Ionian sea, now Cefalo-
Cepe, see Cæpe.   [nia.

Cepi. See Capio.

Cera, æ, f. *wax.*

Cerbĕrus, i, m. *the name of the*
three-headed dog which guard-
ed the entrance of the infernal
regions.

Cercasōrum, i, n. *a town of Egypt.*

Ceres, ĕris, f. *Ceres, the goddess of corn.*

Cerno, cernĕre, a. § 172; *to see; to perceive.*

Certāmen, īnis, n. (certo,) *a contest; a battle; zeal; eagerness; strife; contention; debate; a game or exercise:* Olympĭcum certāmen, *the Olympic games.*

Certè, adv. (iùs, issĭmè,) (certus,) *certainly.*

Certo, āre, āvi, ātum, a. & n. *to contend; to strive; to fight.*

Certus, a, um, adj. (ior, issĭmus,) *certain; fixed.*

Cerva, æ, f. *a female deer; a hind.*

Cervinus, a, um, adj. *belonging to a stag or deer.*

Cervix, īcis, f. *the neck; an isthmus.*

Cervus, i, m. *a male deer; a stag.*

Cessātor, is, m. *a loiterer; a lingerer; an idler.*

Cesso, āre, āvi, ātum, n. *to cease; to loiter.*

Cetĕrus, cetĕra, cetĕrum, adj. (§ 105,) *other; the other; the rest.*

Cetĕrùm, adv. *but; however; as for the rest.*

Cetus, i, m. *a whale.*

Ceÿx, ÿcis, m. *the son of Hesperus, and husband of Alcyŏne.*

Chalcédon, ŏnis, t. *a city of Bithynia opposite to Byzantium.*

Chaldaĭcus, a, um, adj *(Chaldæa,) Chaldean.*

Charta, æ, f. *paper.*

Chersĭphron, ŏnis, m. *a distinguished architect, under whose direction the temple at Ephesus was built.*

Chersonēsus, i, f. *a peninsula.*

Chilo, ŏnis, m. *a Lacedæmonian philosopher, and one of the seven wise men of Greece.*

Christus, i, m. *Christ.*

Cibus, i, m. *food; nourishment.*

Cicātrix, īcis, f. *a wound; a scar; a cicatrice.*

Cicĕro, ŏnis, m. *a celebrated Roman orator.*

Ciconia, æ, f. *a stork.*

Cilicia, æ, f. *a country in the southeastern part of Asia Minor.*

Cimbri, ōrum, m. pl. *a nation formerly inhabiting the northern part of Germany.*

Cinctus, a, um, part. (cingo.)

Cineas, æ, m. *a Thessalian, the favorite minister of Pyrrhus.*

Cingo, cingĕre, cinxi, cinctum, a. *to surround; to encompass; to encircle; to gird.*

Cinis, ĕris, d. *ashes; cinders.*

Cinna, æ, m. (L. Cornelius,) *a consul at Rome, in the time of the civil war.*

Cinnāmum, i, n. *cinnamon.*

Circa, & Circum, pr. & adv *about; around; in the neighborhood of.*

Circuĭtus, ûs, m. *a circuit; a circumference.*

Circumdătus, a, um, part. from

Circumdo, dăre, dĕdi, dătum, a. (circum & do,) *to surround; to put around; to environ; to invest.*

Circumeo, īre, ii, ītum, irr. n. (circum & eo, § 182, 3,) *to go round; to visit.*

Circumfluo, -fluĕre, -fluxi, -fluxum, n. (circum, & fluo,) *to flow round.*

Circumiens, euntis, part. (circumeo.)

Circumjaceo, ēre, ui, n. (circum & jacĕo,) *to lie around; to border upon.*

Circumsto, stăre, stĕti, n. (circum & sto,) *to stand round.*

Circumvenio, -venīre, -vēni, -ventum, a. (circum & venio,) *to surround; to circumvent.*

Circumventus, a, um, part.

Ciris, is, f. *the name of the fish into which Scylla was changed.*

Cisalpinus, a, um, adj. (cis & Alpes,) *Cisalpine; on this side of the Alps; that is, on the side nearest to Rome.*

Cithæron, ŏnis, m. *a mountain of Bœotia, near Thebes, sacred to Bacchus.*

Citò, adv. (iùs, issīmè,) *quickly;* from

Citus, a, um, adj. (ior, issīmus,) *quick.*

Citra, pr. & adv. *on this side.*

Civĭcus, a, um, adj. (civis,) *civic* corŏna civĭca, *a civic crown, given to him who had saved the life of a citizen by killing an enemy.*

Civilis, e, adj. *of or belonging to a citizen; civil.*

Civis, is, c. *a citizen.*

Civĭtas, ātis, f. *a city; a state; the inhabitants of a city; the body of citizens; a constitution; citizenship; freedom of the city.*

Clades, is, f. *an overthrow; discomfiture; defeat; disaster; slaughter.*

Clam, pr. *without the knowledge of:*—adv. *privately; secretly.*

Clamo, āre, āvi, ātum, a. *to cry out; to call on.*

Clamor, ōris, m. *a clamor; a cry.*

Clandestīnus, a, um, adj. (clam,) *secret; clandestine.*

Claritas, ātis, f. *celebrity; fame;* from

Clarus, a, um, adj. (ior issīmus,) *clear; famous; renowned; celebrated; loud.*

Classis, is, f. *a fleet.*

Claudius, i, m. *the name of several Romans, belonging to the tribe hence called Claudian.*

Claudo, claudĕre, clausi, clausum, a. *to close; to shut.*

Claudus, a, um, adj. *lame.*

Clausus, a, um, part. (claudo,) *shut up.*

Clavus, i, m. *a nail; a spike.*

Clemens, tis, adj. *merciful.*

Clementia, æ, f. *clemency; mildness.*

Cleopătra, æ, f. *an Egyptian queen, celebrated for her beauty.*

Cloăca, æ, f. *a drain; a common sewer.*

Cluentius, i, m. *the name of several Romans.*

Clusium, i, n. *a city of Etruria.*

Clypeus, i, m. *a shield; a buckler.*

Cn., *an abbreviation of*

Cneius, i, m. *a Roman prænomen.*

Coactus, a, um, part. (cogo,) *collected; assembled; compelled.*

Coccyx, ȳgis, m. *a cuckoo.*

Cocles, ītis, m. *a Roman, distinguished for his bravery.*

Coctĭlis, e, adj. (coquo, § 129, 4,) *dried; burnt; baked.* .

Coctus, a, um, part. (coquo,) *baked; burnt; boiled.*

Cœlum, i, n. sing. m. pl. § 92, 4; *heaven; the climate; the sky; the air; the atmosphere.*

Cœna, æ, f. *a supper.*

Cœpi, isse, def. § 183, 1; *I begin, or I began.*

Cœptus, a, um, part. *begun.*

Coërceo, ēre, ui, ĭtum, a. (con & arceo,) *to check; to restrain; to control.*

Cogĭtatio, ŏnis, f. (cogĭto,) · a *thought; a reflection.*

Cogitātum, i, n. *a thought.*

Cogĭto, āre, āvi, ātum, a. *to think; to consider; to meditate.*

Cognĭtus, a, um, part. (cognosco.)

Cognōmen, ĭnis, n. *a surname* from

Cognosco, •noscĕre, -nōvi, -nī tum, a. (con & nosco,) *to know; to learn:* de causā, *to try or decide a suit at law.*

Cogo, cogĕre, coēgi, coactum, a. (con & ago,) *to drive; to compel; to force; to urge; to collect:* agmen, *to bring up the rear; to march in the rear.*

Cohæreo, -hærēre, -hæsi, -hæsum, n. (con & hæreo,) *to adhere; to be united; to be joined to.*

Cohibeo, -hibēre, -hibui, -hibĭtum, a.(con & habeo, § 189, 4,) *to hold back; to restrain.*

Cohors, tis, f. *a cohort; the tenth part of a legion.*

Colchi, ōrum, m. *the people of Colchis.*

Colchis, ĭdis, f. *a country of Asia, east of the Euxine.*

Collābor, -lābi, -lapsus sum, dep. (con & labor,) *to fall.*

Collāre, is, n. (collum,) *a collar; a necklace.*

Collatīnus, i, m. *a surname of Tarquinius, the husband of Lucretia.*

Collectus, a, um, part. (collĭgo.)

Collēga, æ, m. *a colleague.*

Collegium, i, n. *a college; a company.*

Colligo, -ligĕre, -lēgi, -lectum, a. (con & lego,) *to collect.*

Collis, is, m. *a hill.*

Collocâtus, a, um, part. from

Collŏco, âre, âvi, âtum, a. (con & loco,) *to place:* statuam, *to erect; to set up.*

Colloquium, i, n. *conversation; an interview;* from

Collŏquor, -lōqui, -locûtus sum, dep. (con & loquor,) *to speak together; to converse.*

Collum, i, n. *the neck.*

Colo, colĕre, colui, cultum, a. *to cultivate; to exercise; to pursue; to practise; to respect; to regard; to venerate; to worship; to inhabit.*

Colonia, æ, f. *a colony.*

Colônus, i, m. *a colonist.*

Color, & Colos, ōris, m. *a color.*

Columba, æ, f. *a dove; a pigeon.*

Columbâre, is, n. *a dovecote.*

Columna, æ, f. *a pillar; a column.*

Combûro, -urĕre, -ussi, -ustum, a. (con & uro, § 196, 5,) *to burn; to consume.*

Comedendus, a, um, part. from

Comĕdo, edĕre, ĕdi, ĕsum & estum, a. (con & edo,) *to eat up; to devour.*

Comes, ĭtis, c. *a companion.*

Comêtes, æ, m. *a comet,* § 45.

Comissor, âri, âtus sum, dep. *to revel; to riot; to banque ; to carouse.*

Comĭtans, tis, part. (comĭtor)

Comĭtâtus, a, um, part. from

Comĭtor, âri, âtus sum, dep. (comes,) *to accompany; to attend; to follow.*

Commĕmŏro, âre, âvi, âtum, a. (con & memŏro,) *to commemorate; to mention.*

Commendo, âre, âvi, âtum, a. (con & mando,) *to commend; to recommend; to commit to one's care.*

Commeo, âre, âvi, âtum, n. (con & meo,) *to go to and fro; to go and come; to pass.*

Commercium, i, n. (con & merx,) *commerce; traffic; intercourse.*

Commĭgro, âre, âvi, âtum, n. (con & migro,) *to emigrate; to remove.*

Commĭnuo, -minuĕre, -minui, -minûtum, a. (con & minuo,) *to dash or break in pieces; to crush.*

Commĭnûtus, a, um, part. *diminished; broken in pieces.*

Committo, -mittĕre, -misi, -missum, a. (con & mitto,) *to commit; to intrust:* pugnam, *to join battle; to commence or fight a battle.*

Commissus, a, um, part. *intrusted; perpetrated; committed commenced:* prœlium commissum, *a battle begun or fought :* copiis commissis, *forces being engaged.*

Commodĭtas, ătis, f. (commŏdus,) *a convenience ; commodious-ness.*

Commŏdum, i, n. *an advantage ; gain.*

Commorior, -mŏri &. -morĭri, -mortuus sum, dep. (con & morior,) *to die together.*

Commŏror, ări, ătus sum, dep. (con & moror,) *to reside ; to stay at ; to remain ; to continue.*

Commŏtus, a, um, part. from

Commoveo, -mŏvēre, -mŏvi, -mŏtum, a. (con & moveo,) *to move ; to excite ; to stir up ; to influence ; to induce.*

Communĭco, āre, āvi, ātum, a. *to communicate ; to impart ; to tell ;* from

Commūnis, e, adj. *common :* in commūne consulĕre, *to consult for the common good.*

Comœdia, æ, f. *a comedy.*

Compăro, āre, āvi, ātum, a. (con & paro,) *to gain ; to procure ; to get ; to compare.*

Compello, -pellĕre, -pŭli, -pulsum, a. (con & pello,) *to drive ; to compel ; to force :* in fugam, *to put to flight.*

Compenso, āre, āvi, ātum, a. (con & penso,) *to compensate ; to make amends for.*

Comperio, -perire, -pĕri, -pertum, a. (con & pario, § 189, 1,) *to learn ; to discover.*

Complector, -plecti, -plexus sum. dep. (con & plector,) *to embrace ; to comprise ; to comprehend ; to reach ; to extend :* complecti amŏre, *to love.*

Compŏno, -ponēre, -posui, -posĭtum, a. (con & pono,) *to compose ; to put together ; to arrange ; to construct ; to finish ; to compare.*

Composĭtus, a, um, part. *finished ; composed ; quieted.*

Comprehendendus, a, um, part. from

Comprehendo, -prehendĕre, -prehensi, -prehensum, a. (con & prehendo,) *to comprehend ; to seize ; to apprehend.*

Comprehensus, a, um, part.

Compulsus, a, um, part. (compello.)

Conātus, a, um, part. (conor,) *having endeavored.*

Concēdo, -cedĕre, -cessi, -cessum, a. (con & cedo,) *to yield ; to permit ; to grant.*

Conceptus, a, um, part. (concipio,) *conceived ; couched ; expressed.*

Concessus, a, um, part. (concēdo.)

Concha, æ, f. *a shell-fish.*

Conchylium, i, n. *a shell-fish.*

Concilio, āre, āvi, ātum, a. *to conciliate ; to unite ; to reconcile ; to acquire for one's self ; to gain ; to obtain ;* from

Concilium, i, n. *a council.*

Concio, ōnis, f. (concieo,) *an*

assembly; an assembly of the people.

Concipio, -cipĕre, -cépi, -ceptum, a. (con & capio, § 189, 5,) to conceive; to imagine; to form; to draw up; to comprehend.

Concito, āre, āvi, ātum, freq. (con & cito,) to excite; to raise.

Concitor, ōris, m. one who excites; an exciter; a mover; a disturber.

Concŏquo, -coquĕre, -coxi, -coctum, a. (con & coquo,) to boil; to digest.

Concordia, æ, f. (concors,) concord; agreement; harmony.

Concrēdo, -credĕre, -credīdi, -credītum, a. (con & credo,) to trust; to intrust.

Concrēmo, āre, āvi, ātum, a. (con & cremo,) to burn with; to burn; to consume.

Concurro, -currĕre, -curri, -cursum, n. (con & curro,) to run together: concurrĭtur, pass. imp. a crowd assemble; there is an assemblage.

Concussus, a, um, part. shaken; moved; from

Concutio, -cutĕre, -cussi, -cussum, a. (con & quatio,) to shake; to agitate; to tremble.

Conditio, ōnis, f. (condo,) condition; situation; a proposal; terms.

Conditus, a, um, part. from

Condo, -dĕre, -dīdi, -dĭtum, a. (con & do,) to found; to build; to make; to form; to hide; to bury; to conceal.

Conduco, -ducĕre, -duxi, -ductum, a. (con & duco,) to hire.

Confectus, a, um, part. (conficio.)

Confĕro, conferre, contŭli, collātum, irr. a. (con & fero,) to bring together; to heap up; to bestow; to give: se conferre, to betake one's self; to go.

Conficio, -ficĕre, -fēci, -fectum, a. (con & facio,) to make; to finish; to waste; to wear out; to terminate; to consume; to ruin; to destroy; to kill.

Confligo, -fligĕre, -flixi, -flictum, a. (con & fligo,) to contend, to engage; to fight.

Conflo, āre, āvi, ātum, a. (con & flo,) to blow together; to melt, to unite; to compose.

Confluo, -fluĕre, -fluxi, -fluxum, n. (con & fluo,) to flow together; to flock; to assemble.

Confodio, -fodĕre, -fōdi, -fossum, a. (con & fodio,) to dig; to pierce; to stab.

Confossus, a, um, part. (confodio.)

Confugio, -fugĕre, -fūgi, -fugītum, n. (con & fugio,) to fly to; to fly for refuge; to flee.

Congĕro, -gerĕre, -gessi, -gestum, a. (con & gero,) to bring together; to collect; to heap up.

Congredior, -grĕdi, -gressus sum, dep. (con & gradior, § 189, 1,) *to encounter; to engage; to fight.*

Congrĕgo, āre, āvi, ātum, a. (con & grex,) *to assemble in flocks; to assemble.*

Conjectus, a, um, part. from

Conjicio, -jicĕre, -jēci, -jectum, a. (con & jacio,) *to cast; to throw; to conjecture.*

Conjugium, i, n. (con & jugo,) *marriage.*

Conjungo, -jungĕre, -junxi, -junctum, a. (con & jungo,) *to unite; to bind; to join.*

Conjurātus, a, um, part. *conspired:* conjurāti, subs. *conspirators:* from

Conjūro, āre, āvi, ātum, a. (con & juro,) *to swear together; to combine; to conspire:* conjurātum est, *a conspiracy was formed.*

Conjux, ŭgis, c. (con & jugo,) *a spouse; a husband or wife.*

Conor, āri, ātus sum, dep. *to attempt; to venture; to endeavor; to strive.*

Conquĕror, -quĕri, -questus sum, dep. (con & queror,) *to complain; to lament.*

Conscendo, -scendĕre, -scendi, -scensum, a. (con & scando,) *to climb; to ascend.*

Conscensus, a, um, part. (conscendo.)

Conscisco, -sciscĕre, -scivi, scitum, a. (con & scisco,) *to decree; to execute:* sibi mortem consciscĕre, *to lay violent hands on one's self; to commit suicide.*

Consĕcro, āre, āvi, ātum, a. (con & sacro,) *to consecrate; to dedicate; to devote.*

Consēdi. *See* Consido.

Consenesco, -senescĕre, -senui, inc. (con & senesco,) *to grow old.*

Consentio, -sentire, -sensi, -sensum, n. (con & sentio,) *to consent; to agree; to unite.*

Consēquor, -sĕqui, -secūtus sum, dep. (con & sequor,) *to gain; to obtain.*

Consecūtus, a, um, part. *having obtained.*

Consĕro, -serĕre, -serui, -sertum, a. (con & sero,) *to join; to put together:* pugnam, *to join battle; to fight.*

Conservandus, a, um, part. from

Conservo, āre, āvi, ātum, a. (con & servo,) *to preserve; to maintain; to perpetuate.*

Consīdens, tis, part. from

Consido, -sidĕre, -sēdi, -sessum, n. (con & sido,) *to sit down; to encamp; to take one's seat; to perch; to light.*

Consilium, i, n. (consŭlo,) *counsel; design; intention; a council; deliberation; advice, a plan; judgment; discretion; prudence; wisdom.*

Consisto, -sistĕre, -stĭti, n. (con & sisto,) *to stand; to consist.*

Consŏlor, āri, ātus sum, dep. (con & solor,) *to comfort; to console.*

Conspectus, a, um, part. (conspicio.)

Conspectus, ûs, m. *a sight; a view.*

Conspicātus, a, um, part. (conspĭcor.)

Conspicio, -spicĕre, -spexi, -spectum, a. (con & specio, § 189, 2,) *to behold; to see.*

Conspĭcor, āri, ātus sum, dep. *to behold; to see.*

Conspicuus, a, um, adj. *conspicuous; distinguished.*

Constans, tis, part. & adj. *firm; determined; constant; steady.*

Constituo, -stituĕre, -stitui, -stitūtum, a. (con & statuo,) *to appoint; to establish.*

Consto, -stāre, -stĭti, n. (con & sto,) *to consist of:* constat, imp. *it is certain, manifest, clear, evident, known.*

Construo, -struĕre, -struxi, -structum, a. (con & struo,) *to construct; to build; to compose; to form; to heap up.*

Consuesco, -suescĕre, -suēvi, -suētum, n. (con & suesco,) *to be accustomed.*

Consue'ūdo, ĭnis, f. *habit; custom.*

Consul, ŭlis, m. *a consul.*

Consulāris, e, adj. *of or pertain ing to the consul; consular.* vir consulāris, *one who has been a consul; a man of consular dignity.*

Consulātus, ûs, m. *the consulship.*

Consŭlo, -sulĕre, -sului, -sultum, a. *to advise; to consult.*

Consulto, āre, āvi, ātum, freq. (consŭlo,) *to advise together; to consult.*

Consūmo, -sumĕre, -sumpsi, -sumptum, a. (con & sumo,) *to consume; to wear out; to exhaust; to waste; to destroy.*

Consumptus, a, um, part.

Contagiōsus, a, um, adj. (contingo,) *contagious.*

Contemnendus, a, um, part. from

Contemno, -temnĕre, -tempsi, -temptum, a. (con & temno,) *to despise; to reject with scorn.*

Contemplātus, a, um, part. *observing; regarding; considering;* from

Contemplor, āri, ātus sum, dep. *to contemplate; to regard; to consider; to look at; to gaze upon.*

Contemptim, adv. *with contempt; contemptuously; scornfully;* from

Contemptus, a, um, part. contemno.)

Contemptus, ûs, m. *contempt.*

Contendo, dĕre, di, tum, a. & n.

(con & tendo,) *to dispute ; to fight ; to contend ; to go to ; to direct one's course :* aliquid ab aliquo, *to request ; to solicit ; to beg something of some one.*

Contentio, ōnis, f. *contention ; a debate ; a controversy ; exertion ; an effort ; a strife.*

Contentus, a, um, adj. *content ; satisfied.*

Contĕro, -terĕre, -trĭvi, -tritum, a. (con & tĕro,) *to break ; to pound ; to waste.*

Contĭnens, tis, part. & adj. *joining ; continued ; uninterrupted ; temperate :* subs. f. *the continent,* or *main land :* from

Contineo, -tinēre, -tinui, -tentum, a. (con & teneo,) *to hold in ; to contain.*

Contingo, -tingĕre, -tĭgi, -tactum, a. (con & tango,) *to touch :* contingit, imp. *it happens :* mihi, *it happens to me ; I have the fortune.*

Continuus, a, um, adj. *continued ; adjoining ; incessant ; uninterrupted ; continual ; without intermission ; in close succession :* continuo alveo, *in one entire* or *undivided channel.*

Contra, prep. *against ; opposite to :* adv. *on the other hand.*

Contractus, a, um, part. (contrăho.)

Contradico, -dicĕre, -dixi, -dictum. a. (contra & dico,) *to speak against ; to contradict ; to oppose.*

Contradictus, a, um, part. *contradicted ; opposed.*

Contrăho, -trahĕre, -traxi, -tractum, a. (con & traho,) *to contract ; to draw together ; to assemble ; to collect.*

Contrarius, a, um, adj. *contrary : opposite.*

Contueor, -tuēri, -tuĭtus sum, dep. (con & tueor,) *to regard, to behold ; to view ; to look steadfastly at ; to gaze upon ; to survey.*

Contundo,-tundĕre,-tŭdi,-tūsum, a (con & tundo,) *to beat ; to bruise ; to crush ; to pulverize.*

Contūsus, a, um, part.

Convalesco, -valescĕre, -valui, inc. (con & valesco,) *to grow well ; to recover.*

Convenio, -venire, -vēni, -ventum, n. (con & venio,) *to meet ; to assemble ; to come together.*

Converto, -vertĕre, -verti, -versum, a. (con & verto,) *to turn ; to resort to ; to appropriate ; to convert into ; to change :* se in preces, *to turn to entreating.*

Conversus, a, um, part.

Convicium, i, n. *loud noise. scolding ; reproach ; abuse.*

Convivium, i, n. (con & vivo,) *a feast ; a banquet ; an entertainment.*

Convŏco, âre, âvi, âtum, a. (con & voco,) *to call together; to assemble.*

Convolvo, -volvĕre, -volvi, -volû-tum, a. (con & volvo,) *to roll together :* pass. *to be rolled to-gether :* se, *to roll one's self up.*

Cŏöperio, -perire, -perui, -per-tum, a. (con & operio,) *to cover.*

Copia, æ, f. *an abundance; a multitude; a swarm :* copiæ, pl. *forces; troops.*

Copiŏsè, adv. (iùs, issĭmè,) *co-piously; abundantly.*

Coquo, coquĕre, coxi, coctum, a. *to bake; to boil; to roast; to cook.*

Coquus, i, m. *a cook.*

Cor, cordis, n. *the heart.*

Coram, prep. *in the presence of; before :* adv. *openly.*

Corcȳra, æ, f. *an island on the coast of Epirus,* now *Corfu.*

Corinthus, i, f. *Corinth, a city of Achaia, in Greece.*

Corinthius, a, um, adj. *Corinth-ian, belonging to Corinth :* Corinthii, subs. *the Corinthi-ans.*

Coriŏli, ŏrum, m. pl. *a town of Latium.*

Coriolânus, i, m. *a distinguished Roman general.*

Corium, ı, n. *the skin; the skin or hide of a beast.*

Cornelĭa, æ, f. *a noble Roman lady.*

Cornelĭus, i, m. *the name of an illustrious tribe,* or *clan, at Rome, containing many fam-ilies.*

Cornix, ĭcis, f. *a crow.*

Cornu, u, n. § 87 ; *a horn.*

Corŏna, æ, f. *a crown.*

Corpus, ŏris, n. *a body; a corpse*

Correptus, a, um, part. (corripio.)

Corrĭgo, -rigĕre, -rexi, -rectum, a. (con & rego,) *to straight-en; to make better; to cor-rect.*

Corripio, -ripĕre, -ripui, -reptum, a. (con & rapio,) *to seize.*

Corrŏdo, -rodĕre, -rôsi, -rôsum, a. (con & rodo,) *to gnaw; to corrode.*

Corrôsus, a, um, part.

Corruens, tis, part. (corruo.)

Corrumpo, -rumpĕre, -rûpi, -rup-tum, a. (con & rumpo,) *to corrupt; to bribe; to hurt; to violate; to seduce; to im-pair; to destroy.*

Corruo, -ruĕre, -rui, n. (con & ruo,) *to fall; to decay.*

Corruptus, a, um, part. & adj. (corrumpo,) *bribed; vitiated; foul; corrupt.*

Corsĭca, æ, f. *an island in the Mediterranean sea, north of Sardinia.*

Corvĭnus, i, m. *a surname given to M. Valerius.*

Corvus, i, m. *a raven.*

Corycius, a, um, adj. *Corycian, of Corycus.*

Corȳcus, i, m. *the name of a city and mountain of Cilicia.*

Cos., *an abbreviation of* consul; Coss., *of* consules ; § 328.

Cotta, æ, m. *a Roman* cognōmen, *belonging to the Aurelian tribe.*

Crater, ĕris, m. *a goblet; a crater; the mouth of a volcano.*

Crates, ētis, m. *a Theban philosopher.*

Crassus, i, m. *the name of a Roman family of the Lucinian tribe.*

Creātus, a, um, part. (creo.)

Creber, crebra, crebrum, adj. *frequent.*

Crĕbrò, adv. (creber,) *frequently.*

Credo, -dĕre, -dīdi, -dĭtum, a. *to believe ; to trust.*

Cremĕra, æ, f. *a river of Etruria, near which the Fabian family were defeated and destroyed.*

Cremo, āre, āvi, ātum, a. *to burn ; to consume.*

Creo, āre, āvi, ātum, a. *to choose ; to create ; to elect.*

Cresco, crescĕre, crevi, cretum, n. *to increase ; to grow.*

Creta, æ, f. *Crete,* now *Candia, an island in the Mediterranean sea, south of the Cyclădes.*

Cretensis, e, adj. *belonging to Crete, Cretan.*

Crevi. *See* Cresco.

Crimen, nĭs, n. *a crime ; a fault ;* an accusation : alĭcui crimĭni dare, *to charge as a crime against one.*

Crinis, is, m. *the hair.*

Crixus, i, m. *the name of a celebrated gladiator.*

Crocodilus, i, m. *a crocodile.*

Cruciātus, a, um, part. (crucio.)

Cruciātus, ūs, m. *torture ; torment ; distress ; trouble ; affliction.*

Crucio, āre, āvi, ātum, a. (crux,) *to torment ; to torture.*

Crudēlis, e, adj. (ior, issĭmus,) *cruel.*

Crudelĭter, adv. *cruelly.*

Crudus, a, um, adj. *crude ; raw.*

Cruor, ōris, m. *blood ; gore.*

Crus, uris, n. *the leg.*

Crux, crucis, f. *a cross.*

Cubītus, ı, m., & Cubĭtum, i, n. *a cubit.*

Cucurri. *See* Curro.

Cui, & Cujus. *See* Qui, & Quis

Culex, ĭcis, m. *a gnat.*

Culpa, æ, f. *a fault ; guilt, blame.*

Culpo, āre, āvi, ātum, a. *to blame.*

Cultellus, i, m. (dim. from culter,) *a little knife ; a knife.*

Cultus, a, um, part. (colo,) *cultivated ; improved ; dressed.*

Cum, pr. *with :* adv. the same as quum, *when :* cùm — tum, *not only — but also ; as well — as also.*

Cunctatio, ōnis, f. (cunctor,) *delay ; a delaying ; hesitation.*

Cunicŭlus, i, m. *a rabbit; a cony.*

Cupidĭtas, ātis, f. (cupio,) *desire; cupidity.*

Cupīdo, ĭnis, f. *desire.*

Cupīdus, a, um, adj. *desirous.*

Cupiens, tis, part. from

Cupio, ĕre, ivi, itum, a. *to desire; to wish; to long for.*

Cur, adv. *why; wherefore.*

Cura, æ, f. *care; anxiety.*

Cures, ium, f. pl. *a city of the Sabines.*

Curia, æ, f. *a curia or ward; one of thirty parts into which the Roman people were divided; the senate-house.*

Curiatii, ōrum, m. pl. *the name of an Alban tribe. Three brothers belonging to this tribe fought with the Horatii.*

Curo, āre, āvi, ātum, a. (cura,) *to take care of; to care; to be concerned; to cure or heal.*

Curro, currĕre, cucurri, cursum, n. *to run.*

Currus, ûs, m. *a chariot.*

Cursor, ōris, m. *a runner; also, a surname given to L. Papirius.*

Cursus, ûs, m. *a course; a running.*

Curvus, a; um, adj. *crooked.*

Custodia, æ, f. (custos,) *a prison; a guard.*

Custodio, ire, ivi, itum, a. *to preserve; to keep safely; to guard; to watch;* from

Custos, ōdis, c. *a guard; a keeper.*

Cutis, is, f. *the skin.*

Cyaneus, a, um, adj. *dark blue.*

Cyclădes, um, f. pl. *a cluster of islands in the Archipelago, which derive their name from the Greek* κύκλος, *a circle.*

Cyclōpes, um, m. pl. *the Cyclops, giants of Sicily, living near Ætna.*

Cydnus, i, m. *a river of Cilicia.*

Cyllēne, es, f. *a mountain in Arcadia.*

Cymba, æ, f. *a boat; a skiff; a canoe.*

Cymbălum, i, n. *a cymbal.*

Cynicus, i, m. *a Cynic. The Cynics were a sect of philosophers founded by Antisthĕnes.*

Cynocephălæ, ārum, f. pl. *small hills near Scotussa, in Thessaly.*

Cynocephăli, ōrum, m. pl. *a people of India with heads like dogs.*

Cynocephălus, i, m. *an Egyptian deity.*

Cynossēma, ātis, n. *a promontory of Thrace, near Sestos, where queen Hecŭba was buried.*

Cynthus, i, m. *a hill near the town of Delos.*

Cyrēnæ, ārum, f. pl. *Cyrene, a city of Africa, the capital of Cyrenaica.*

Cyrenaica, æ, f. *a country in the*

northern part of Africa, so called from its capital, Cyrēnæ.

Cyrenæus, a, um, adj. *Cyrenean; belonging to Cyrēnæ.*

Cyrenensis, e, adj. *Cyrenean; of Cyrēnæ.*

Cyrnus, i, f. *a Greek name of the island of Corsica.*

Cyrus, i, m. *Cyrus, the name of a Persian king.*

Cyzicus, i, f. *the name of an island, near Mysia, containing a town of the same name.*

D.

Dædālus, i, m. *an ingenious Athenian artist, the son of Euphēmus.*

Damno, āre, āvi, ātum, a. *to condemn.*

Damnōsus, a, um, adj. *injurious; hurtful.*

Danäus, i, m. *an ancient king of Argos, and brother of Ægyptus.*

Dandus, a, um, part. (do.)

Dans, tis, part. (do.)

Danubius, i, m. *the Danube, a river of Germany, called also, after its entrance into Illyricum, the Ister; the largest river in Europe.*

Daps, dapis, f. § 94; *a feast; a meal.*

Daidania, æ, f. *a country and*

city of Asia Minor, near the Hellespont.

Datūrus, a, um, part. (do.)

Datus, a, um, part. (do.)

De, prep. *from; of; concerning; on account of.*

Dea, æ, f. § 43, 2; *a goddess.*

Debello, āre, āvi, ātum, a. (de & bello,) *to conquer; to subdue.*

Debeo, ēre, ui, ītum, a. (de & habeo,) *to owe; to be obliged;* with an infinitive, *ought* or *should.*

Debeor, ēri, ītus sum, pass. *to be due.*

Debilīto, āre, āvi, ātum, a. (debilis,) *to weaken; to enfeeble.*

Debītus, a, um, part. (debeo,) *due; deserved; owing.*

Decēdo, -cedēre, -cessi, -cessum, n. (de & cedo,) *to depart; to retire; to withdraw; to yield; to die.*

Decerno, -cernēre, -crēvi, -crētum, a. (de & cerno,) *to judge; to decide; to fight; to contend; to discern; to decree:* bellum decrētum est, *the management of the war was de-*

Decem, num. adj. *ten.* [creed.

Decemvĭri, ōrum, m. pl. *decemvirs, ten men appointed to prepare a code of laws for the Romans, and by whom the laws of the twelve tables were formed.*

Decerpo, -cerpēre, -cerpsi, -cerptum, a. (de & carpo,) *to pluck off; to pick; to gather.*

Decĭdo, -cidĕre, -cĭdi, n. (de & cado,) *to fall:* dentes decĭdunt, *the teeth fail,* or *come out.*

Decĭmus, a, um, num. adj. (decem,) *the tenth.*

Decius, i, m. *the name of several Romans, three of whom were distinguished for their patriotism.*

Declăro, āre, āvi, ātum, a. (de & claro,) *to declare; to show.*

Decoctus, a, um, part. from

Decŏquo, -coquĕre, -coxi, -coctum, a. (de & coquo,) *to boil.*

Decŏrus, a, um, adj. *handsome; adorned; decorous; beautiful.*

Decrĕtus, a, um, part. (decerno.)

Decresco, -crescĕre, -crēvi, n. (de & cresco,) *to decrease; to diminish; to subside; to fall; to decay.*

Decumbo, -cumbĕre, -cubui, n. (de & cubo,) *to lie down.*

Decurro, -currĕre, -curri, -cursum, n. (de & curro,) *to flow down; to run.*

Dedi. *See* Do.

Dedĭdi. *See* Dedo.

Deditio, ōnis, f. (dedo,) *a surrender.*

Dedĭtus, a, um, part. (dedo.)

Dedo, dedĕre, dedĭdi, dedĭtum, a. *to surrender; to deliver up; to give up; to addict* or *devote one's self.*

Dedūcĕ, -ducĕre, -duxi, -ductum, a. (de & duco,) *to lead forth; to bring; to lead.*

Defatĭgo, āre, āvi, ātum, a. (de & fatigo,) *to weary; to fatigue.*

Defendo, -fendĕre, -fendi, -fensum, a. (de & fendo, § 172,) *to defend; to protect.*

Defensus, a, um, part. (defendo.)

Defĕro, -ferre, -tŭli, -lātum, irr. a. (de & fero,) *to bring; to convey; to proffer; to confer; to give; to bestow.*

Deficiens, tis, part. from

Deficio, -ficĕre, -fēci, -fectum, a. & n. (de & facio,) *to fail; to be wanting; to decrease; to be eclipsed.*

Defleo, ēre, ēvi, ētum, a. (de & fleo,) *to deplore; to bewail; to lament; to weep for.*

Defluo, -fluĕre, -fluxi, -fluxum, n. (de & fluo,) *to flow down.*

Defodio, -fodĕre, -fōdi, -fossum, a. (de & fodio,) *to bury; to inter.*

Deformĭtas, ātis, f. (deformis,) *deformity; ugliness.*

Defossus, a, um, part. (defodio.)

Defunctus, a, um, part. *finished:* defunctus *or* defunctus vitâ, *dead:* from

Defungor, -fungi, -functus sum, dep. (de & fungor,) *to execute; to perform; to be free from; to finish.*

Degens, tis, part. from

Dego, degĕre, degi, a. & n

(de & ago,) *to lead ; to live ; to dwell.*

Degusto, åre, åvi, åtum, a. (de & gusto,) *to taste.*

Deinde, adv. (de & inde,) *then ; further ; after that ; next.*

Deiotărus, i, m. *a man who was made king of Galatia, by the Roman senate, through the favor of Pompey.*

Dejectus, a, um, part. from

Dejicio, -jicĕre, -jēci, -jectum, a. (de & jacio,) *to throw* or *cast down.*

Delābor, -lābi, -lapsus sum, dep. (de & labor,) *to fall ; to glide down ; to flow.*

Delapsus, a, um, part. *descending ; having fallen.*

Delātus, a, um, part. (defĕro,) *conferred.*

Delecto, åre, åvi, åtum, a. (de & lacto, § 189, 1,) *to delight ; to please.*

Delectus, a, um, part. (delīgo.)

Delendus, a, um, part. *to be destroyed ;* from

Deleo, ēre, ēvi, ētum, a. *to extinguish ; to destroy ; to ruin.*

Deliciæ, årum, f. pl. *pastimes ; diversions ; pleasures ; delights.*

Delictum, i, n. (delinquo,) *a crime; a fault.*

Delīgo, -ligĕre, -lēgi, -lectum, a. (de & lego,) *to select; to choose.*

Delinquo, -linquĕre, -liqui, -lictum, a. (de & linquo.) *to offend to do wrong.*

Delphĭcus, a, um, adj. *Delphic, belonging to Delphi.*

Delphi, ōrum, m. pl. *a town of Phocis, where were a famous temple and oracle of Apollo.*

Delphĭnus, i, m. *a dolphin.*

Delta, æ, f. *a part of Egypt, so called from its resemblance to the Greek letter delta, Δ.*

Delūbrum, i, n. *a temple ; a shrine.*

Delus or -os, i, f. *an island, containing a city of the same name, situated in the Ægean sea ; the birthplace of Apollo and Diana.*

Demarātus, i, m. *a Corinthian, the father of the elder Tarquin.*

Demergo, -mergĕre, -mersi, -mersum, a. (de & mergo,) *to plunge ; to sink.*

Demersus, a, um, part.

Demetrius, i, m. *a Greek proper name.*

Demissus, a, um, part. *cast down ; descending ;* from

Demitto, -mittĕre, -mīsi, -missum, a. (de & mitto,) *to send down ; to let down ; to drop.*

Democrĭtus, i, m. *a Grecian philosopher, who was born at Abdēra.*

Demonstro, åre, åvi, åtum, a. (de & monstro,) *to demonstrate ; to show ; to prove.*

Demosthĕnes, is, m. *the most celebrated of the Athenian orators.*

15

Demum, adv. *at length ; not till ; at last ; only.*

Deni, æ, a, num. adj. pl. § 119, III. *every ten ; ten.*

Denïque, adv. *finally ; at last.*

Dens, tis, m. *a tooth.*

Densus, a, um, adj. *thick.*

Dentâtus, i, m. (Siccius,) *the* cognòmen, *or surname, of a brave Roman soldier.*

Denuntio *or* -cio, âre, âvi, âtum, a. (de & nuntio,) *to denounce ; to foreshow ; to proclaim ; to declare.*

Depascor, -pasci, -pastus sum, dep. (de & pascor,) *to feed ; to eat up ; to feed upon.*

Depingo, -pingĕre, -pinxi, -pic- tum, a. (de & pingo,) *to paint ; to depict ; to describe ; to ex- hibit.*

Deplóro, âre, âvi, âtum, a. (de & ploro,) *to weep for ; to deplore ; to mourn.*

Depóno, -ponĕre, -posui, -posĭ- tum, a. (de & pono,) *to lay down* or *aside.*

Depopulâtus, a, um, part. from

Depopŭlor, âri, âtus sum, dep. (de & popŭlus,) *to lay waste.*

Deprehendo, -prehendĕre, -pre- hensi, -prehensum, a. (de & prehendo,) *to seize ; to catch ; to detect.*

Deprehensus, a, um, part.

Depulso, âre, âvi, âtum, freq. (de & pulso,) *to push away ; to keep off   to repel.*

Descendo, -scendĕre, -scenɪli, -scensum, n. (de & scando, § 189, 1,) *to descend :* in cer- tâmen descendĕre, *to engage in a contest :* descendĭtur, imp. *one descends ; we de- scend.*

Describo, -scribĕre, -scripsi, -scriptum, a. (de & scribo,) *to describe ; to divide ; to or- der.*

Desĕro, -serĕre, -serui, -sertum, a. (de & sero,) *to desert ; to forsake ; to abandon.*

Desertum, i, n. *a desert.*

Desertus, a, um, part. & adj. *deserted ; waste ; desolate ; desert.*

Desiderium, i, n. *a longing for ; a desire ; love ; affection ; re- gret ; grief.*

Desĭno, -sinĕre, -sīvi, -sĭtum, n. (de & sino,) *to leave off ; to terminate ; to cease ; to end ; to renounce.*

Desperâtus, a, um, part. & aoj. *despaired of ; past hope ; des- perate ; hopeless.*

Despéro, âre, âvi, âtum, a. (de & spero,) *to despair.*

Desponsâtus, a, um, part. from

Desponso, âre, âvi, âtum, a. *to promise in marriage ; to be- troth ; to affiance.*

Destĭno, âre, âvi, âtum, a. *to de- sign ; to appoint ; to deter- mine ; to aim at.*

Desum, -esse, -fui, -futûrus, irr.

n. (de & sum,) *to be want-ing.*

Deterior, adj. comp. (sup. deter-rimus, § 126, 1,) *worse.*

Deterreo, ēre, ui, ītum, a. (de & terreo,) *to deter ; to frighten.*

Detestor, āri, ātus sum, dep. (de & testor,) *to detest.*

Detractus, a, um, part. from

Detrăho, -trahĕre, -traxi, -trac-tum, a. (de & traho,) *to take down* or *away; to draw off; to take from.*

Detrimentum, i, n. (detĕro,) *det-riment ; damage ; harm ; loss ; injury.*

Deus, i, m. § 52 ; *God ; a god.*

Devĕho, -vehĕre, -vexi, -vectum, a. (de & veho,) *to carry away.*

Devexus, a, um, adj. *sloping ; inclining.*

Devictus, a, um, part. from

Devinco, -vincĕre, -vici, -vic-tum, a. (de & vinco,) *to con-quer ; to subdue ; to overcome.*

Devŏlo, āre, āvi, ātum, n. (de & volo,) *to fly down ; to fly away.*

Devŏro, āre, āvi, ātum, a. (de & voro,) *to devour ; to eat up.*

Devŏtus, a, um, part. from

Devovĕo, -vovēre, -vōvi, -vōtum, a. (de & voveo,) *to vow ; to devote ; to consecrate.*

Dexter, ĕra, ĕrum, or ra, rum, § 106, adj. *right ; on the right hand.*

Dextra, æ, f. *the right hand.*

Diadēma, ătis, n. *a diadem ; a white fillet worn upon the heads of kings.*

Diagŏras, æ, m. *a Rhodian who died from excessive joy, be-cause his three sons were vic-torious at the Olympic games.*

Diāna, æ, f. *the daughter of Ju-piter and Latŏna, and sister of Apollo*

Dĭco, āre, āvi, ātum, a. *to conse-crate ; to dedicate.*

Dico, dicĕre, dixi, dictum, a. *to say ; to name ; to call.*

Dictātor, ōris, m. *a dictator ; a chief magistrate, elected on special occasions, and vested with absolute authority ;* from

Dicto, āre, āvi, ātum, freq. *to dic-tate ; to say often.*

Dictum, i, n. *a word ; an ex-pression.*

Dictus, a, um, part. (dico.)

Dies, ēi, m. or f. in sing., m. in pl., § 90 ; *a day :* in dies, *dai-ly ; every day.*

Diffĕrens, tis, adj. *different ; dif-fering ;* from

Diffĕro, differre, distŭli, dilā-tum, irr. a. & n. (dis & fero,) *to carry up and down ; to scatter ; to disperse ; to spread abroad ; to publish ; to defer ; to be different.*

Difficĭlè, adv. (iùs, lĭmè,) *diffi-cultly ; with difficulty ;* from

Difficĭlis, e, adj. (dis & facĭlis, *difficult.*

Difficultas, ātis, f. § 101, 1,&(2.) *difficulty; trouble; embarrassment; poverty.*

Digitus, i, m. *a finger; a finger's breadth.*

Dignātus, a, um, part. (dignor,) *vouchsafing; thought worthy.*

Dignĭtas, ātis, f. (dignus,) *dignity; honor; office.*

Dignor, āri, ātus sum, dep. *to think worthy; to vouchsafe; to deign;* from

Dignus, a, um, adj. (ior, issimus,) *worthy.*

Dilanio, āre, āvi, ātum, a. (dis & lanio,) *to tear* or *rend in pieces.*

Diligenter, adv. (iùs, issĭmè,) *diligently; carefully.*

Diligo, -ligĕre, -lexi, -lectum, a. (dis & lego,) *to love.*

Dimĭcatio, ōnis, f. *a fight; a contest; a battle;* from

Dimīco, āre, āvi, (or ui,) ātum, a. (dis & mico,) *to fight:* dimicatum est, *a battle was fought.*

Dimissus, a, um, part. from

Dimitto, -mittĕre, -misi, -missum, a. (dis & mitto,) *to dismiss; to let go.*

Diogénes, is, m. *an eminent Cynic philosopher, born at Sinŏpe, a city of Asia Minor.*

Diomēdes, is, m. *a Grecian warrior;* also, *a cruel king of Thrace.*

Dionysius, i, m. *the name of two tyran's of Syracī se.*

Diremptūrus, a, um, part. (dirĭmo,) *about to decide.*

Direptus, a, um, part. (diripio.)

Dirĭmo, -imĕre, -ēmi, -emptum, a. (dis & emo, § 196, 13,) *to divide; to part; to separate; to decide.*

Diripio, -ripĕre, -ripui, -reptum, a. (dis & rapio,) *to rob; to plunder; to pillage; to sack; to destroy.*

Diruo, -ruĕre, -rui, -rūtum, a. (dis & ruo,) *to destroy; to overthrow; to raze.*

Dirus, a, um, adj. *frightful; terrible; direful; ominous.*

Dirūtus, a, um, part. (diruo.)

Discēdo, -cedĕre, -cessi, -cessum, n. (dis & cedo,) *to depart; to go away.*

Discerpo, -cerpĕre, -cerpsi, -cerptum, a. (dis & carpo,) *to tear in pieces.*

Discerptus, a, um, part. (discerpo.)

Discipŭlus, i, m. (disco,) *a pupil; a scholar.*

Disco, discĕre, didĭci, a. *to learn.*

Discordia, æ, f. (discors,) *dissension; disagreement; discord.*

Discordo, āre, āvi, ātum, n. *to be at variance; to differ.*

Discrĕpo, āre, āvi or ui, ĭtum, n. (dis & crepo,) *to differ; to disagree.*

Disertè, adv. (iùs, issĭmè,) *clearly; eloquently.*

Disputatio, ŏnis, f. *a dispute; a discourse; a discussion;* from

Dispŭto, āre, āvi, ātum, a. (dis & puto,) *to discourse; to dispute; to discuss.*

Dissemĭno, āre, āvi, ātum, a. (dis & semĭno,) *to spread abroad; to scatter; to promulgate.*

Dissĕro, -serĕre, -serui, -sertum, a. (dis & sero,) *to discourse; to reason; to debate; to say.*

Dissidium, i, n. *a disagreement; a dissension.*

Dissimĭlis, e, adj. *unlike; dissimilar.*

Distans, tis, part. (disto,) *differing; distant; being divided, or separated.*

Distinguo, -stinguĕre, -stinxi, -stinctum, a. (di & stinguo,) *to distinguish; to mark; to adorn; to variegate; to spot; to sprinkle.*

Disto, stāre, n. (di & sto,) *to be distant or apart; to be divided; to differ.*

Distribuo, -tribuĕre, -tribui, -tribūtum, a. (dis & tribuo,) *to distribute; to divide.*

Ditis, e, adj. (ior, issĭmus,) *rich.*

Diu, adv. (utiùs, utissĭmè, § 194,) *long; for a long time:* tam diu — quàm diu, *so long — as.*

Diurnus, a, um, adj. *daily.*

Diutĭnus, a, um, adj. *lasting; long.*

Diuturnĭtas, ātis, f. *long continuance; duration.*

Diuturnus, a, um, adj. *long; lasting.*

Divello, -vellĕre, -velli or -vulsi, -vulsum, a. (di & vello,) *to separate; to disjoin; to tear off.*

Diversus, a, um, adj. *different.*

Dives, ĭtis, adj. *rich; wealthy; fertile; fruitful.*

Divĭdo, dividĕre, divisi, divisum, a. *to divide; to distribute; to separate.*

Divinus, a, um, adj. *divine; heavenly.*

Divisus, a, um, part. (divĭdo.)

Divitiæ, ārum, f. pl. *riches; wealth.*

Divulsus, a, um, part. (divello.)

Do, dare, dedi, datum, a. *to give; to grant; to surrender:* pœnas, *to suffer punishment:* crimĭni, *to impute as a crime; to accuse:* finem, *to termĭnate:* causam, *to occasion:* nomen, *to give name.*

Doceo, ĕre, ui, tum, a. *to teach.*

Docilĭtas, ātis, f. *docility; teachableness.*

Doctrĭna, æ, f. *instruction; education; doctrine.*

Doctus, a, um, part. & adj. (doceo,) *taught; learned.*

Dodōna, æ, f. *a town and forest of Epirus, where were a temple and oracle of Jupiter.*

Doleo, ēre, ui, n. *to grieve; to sorrow; to be in pain.*

Dolor, ōris, m. *pain; sorrow; grief.*

Dolus, i, m. *a device; a trick; a stratagem; guile; artifice.*

Domestĭcus, a, um, adj. (domus,) *domestic.*

Domicilium, i, n. *a habitation; a house; an abode.*

Domĭna, æ, f. (domĭnus,) *a mistress.*

Dominatio, ōnis, f. *government; power; dominion; usurpation; domination; despotism.*

Domĭnus, i, m. *master; owner; lord.*

Domĭtus, a, um, part. from

Domo, āre, ui, ĭtum, a. *to subdue; to tame; to overpower; to conquer; to vanquish.*

Domus, ûs & i, f. § 89, & (a.) *a house:* domi, *at home:* domo, *from home:* domum, *home.*

Donec, adv. *until; as long as.*

Dono, āre, āvi, ātum, a. (donum,) *to give; to present.*

Donum, i, n. *a gift; an offering; a present.*

Dormio, ire, īvi, ītum, n. *to sleep.*

Dorsum, i, n. *the back.*

Dos, dotis, f. *a portion; a dowry.*

Draco, ōnis, m. *a dragon; a species of serpent.*

Druĭdæ, ārum, m. pl. *Druids,* *priests of the ancient Britons and Gauls.*

Dubitatio, ōnis, f. *a doubt; hesitation; question;* from

Dubĭto, āre, āvi, ātum, n. *to hesitate; to doubt.*

Ducenti, æ, a, num. adj. pl. *two hundred.*

Duco, cĕre, xi, ctum, a. *to lead; to conduct:* uxōrem, *to take a wife; to marry:* exequias, *to perform funeral rites;* murum, *to build a wall.*

Ductus, a, um, part. *led.*

Duillius, i, m (Caius,) *a Roman commander, who first conquered the Carthaginians in a naval engagement.*

Dulcis, e, adj. (ior, issĭmus,) *sweet; pleasant.*

Dum, adv. & conj. *while; whilst; as long as; until.*

Duo, æ, o, num. adj. pl. § 118. *two.*

Duodĕcim, num. adj. ind. pl. *twelve.*

Duodecĭmus, a, um, num. adj. *the twelfth.*

Duodeviginti, num. adj. ind. pl. § 118, 4; *eighteen.*

Duritia, æ, & Durĭties, ēi, f. § 101, 1; *hardness;* from

Durus, a, um, adj. (ior, issĭmus,) *hard; severe; harsh; unfavorable.*

Dux, cis, c. *a leader; a guide; a commander.*

E.

E, ex, prep. *out of; from; of; among.*

Ea. *See* Is.

Ebĭbo, -bibĕre, -bībi, -bibĭtum, a. (e & bibo,) *to drink up.*

Ebriĕtas, ātis, f. (ebrius,) *drunkenness.*

Ebur, ŏris, n. *ivory.*

Edīco, -dicĕre, -dixi, -dictum, a. (e & dico,) *to proclaim; to announce; to publish; to order.*

Edīdi. *See* Edo.

Edītus, a, um, part. *published; uttered; produced;* from

Edo, -dĕre, -dīdi, -dītum, a. *to publish; to cause; to occasion; to produce; to make:* spectacŭlum edĕre, *to give an exhibition.*

Edo, edĕre *or* esse, edi, esum, irr. a. § 181; *to eat; to consume.*

Educātus, a, um, part. from

Edūco, āre, āvi, ātum, a. *to educate; to instruct.*

Edūco, -ducĕre, -duxi, -ductum, a. (e & duco,) *to lead forth; to bring forth; to produce; to draw out.*

Efficio, -ficĕre, -fēci, -fectum, a. (e & facio,) *to effect; to make; to form; to cause; to accomplish.*

Effigies, iēi, f. *an image; an effigy.*

Efflo, āre, āvi, ātum, a. (e & flo,) *to breathe out:* anĭmam, *to die; to expire.*

Effugio, -fugĕre, -fūgi, -fugĭtum, a. & n. (e & fugio,) *to escape; to fly from; to flee.*

Effundo, -fundĕre, -fūdi, -fūsum, a. (e & fundo,) *to pour out; to spill; to discharge; to waste; to overflow; to extend or spread.*

Effūsus, a, um, part. *poured out; wasted.*

Egeria, æ, f. *a nymph of the Aricinian grove, from whom Numa professed to receive instructions respecting religious rites.*

Egĕro, -gerĕre, -gessi, -gestum, a. (e & gero,) *to carry out; to cast forth; to throw out.*

Egestus, a, um, part.

Egi. *See* Ago.

Ego, mei, subs. pro. *I;* § 133.

Egredior, -grĕdi, -gressus sum, dep. (e & gradior,) *to go out; to overflow; to go beyond.*

Egregiè, adv. *in a distinguished manner; excellently; famously;* from

Egregĭus, a, um, adj. (e & grex,) *distinguished; eminent; choice.*

Egressus, a, um, part. (egredior.)

Ejusmŏdi, pro. (genitive of is & modus, § 134, 5,) *such; such like; of the same sort.*

Elābor, -lābi, -lapsus sum, dep.

(e & labor,) *to glide away; to escape.*

Elapsus, a, um, part. *having passed.*

Elephantis, ĭdis, f. *an island and city in the southern part of Egypt.*

Elephantus, i, & Elĕphas, antis, m. *an elephant.*

Eleusinii, ōrum, m. pl. *the Eleusinians ; the inhabitants of Eleusis.*

Eleusis & -in, inis, f. *a town of Attica, sacred to Ceres*

Elĭdo, -lidĕre, -lisi, -lisum, a. (e & lædo,) *to crush.*

Elĭgo, -ligĕre, -lēgi, -lectum, a. (e & lego,) *to choose; to select.*

Elŏquens, tis, adj. (ior, issĭmus,) (elŏquor,) *eloquent.*

Eloquentia, æ, f. *eloquence.*

Elŏquor, -lŏqui, -locūtus sum, dep. (e & loquor,) *to say ; to declare ; to tell.*

Eluceo, -lucĕre, -luxi, n. (e & luceo,) *to shine forth.*

Emergo, -mergĕre, -mersi, -mersum, n. (e & mergo,) *to emerge; to come out ; to rise up.*

Emineo, ĕre, ui, n. *to be eminent ; to rise above; to be conspicuous ; to be distinguished ; to appear.*

Emitto, -mittĕre, -misi, -missum, a. (e & mitto,) *to send forth ; to discharge.*

Emo, emĕre, emi, emptum, a. o *buy; to purchase.*

Emorior, -mŏri or -moriri, -mortuus sum, dep. *to die.*

Emptus, a, um, part. (emo.)

Enascor, -nasci, -nātus sum, dep. *to arise; to be born ; to spring from.*

Enātus, a, um, part. *born of.*

Enĕco, -necāre, -necāvi or -necui, -necātum or -nectum, a. (e & neco,) *to kill.*

Enervo, āre, āvi, ātum, a. *to enervate ; to enfeeble ; to weaken.*

Enim, conj. § 279, 3 ; *for ; but ; truly ; indeed.*

Enna, æ, f. *a town of Sicily.*

Ennius, i, m. *a very ancient Roman poet.*

Enuntio, āre, āvi, ātum, a. *to proclaim ; to disclose ; to divulge.*

Eo, ire, ivi, itum, irr. n. § 182 ; *to go.*

Eŏ, adv. *thither ; to that degree ; to that pitch ; to that degree of eminence.*

Eŏus, i, m. *the morning star.*

Eŏus, a, um, adj. *eastern; the eastern.*

Epaminondas, æ, m. *a distinguished Theban general.*

Ephĕsus, i, m. *a city on the western coast of Ionia, rear the river Caÿster.*

Ephialtes, is, m. *a giant, the son of Neptune or of Alöeus, ana brother of Otos.*

Epimenĭdes, is, m. *a poet of Gnossus, in Crete.*

Epīrus, i, f. *a country in the western part of Greece.*

Epistŏla, æ, f. *an epistle; a letter.*

Epŭlor, āri, ātus sum, dep. *to feast; to feast upon; to eat; from*

Epŭlum, i, n. sing., & Epŭlæ, ārum, f. pl. *a banquet; a feast.*

Eques, ĭtis, m. (equus,) *a knight; a horseman:* equĭtes, pl. *knights; horsemen; cavalry.*

Equĭdem, conj. (ego & quidem,) *indeed; I for my part.*

Equĭtātus, ūs, m. *cavalry.*

Equus, i, m. *a horse.*

Eram, Ero, &c. *See* § 153.

Ereptus, a, um, part. (erĭpio.)

Erga, prep. *towards.*

Ergo, conj. § 198, 6; *therefore.*

Erinaceus, i, m. *a hedgehog.*

Erĭpio, -rĭpĕre, -rĭpui, -reptum, a. (e & rapio,) *to tear from; to take from; to rescue; to take away; to deliver.*

Erro, āre, āvi, ātum, n. *to wander; to err; to stray; to roam.*

Erŏdo, -rodĕre, -rōsi, -rōsum, a. (e & rodo,) *to gnaw away; to consume; to eat into.*

Erudio, ire, ivi, itum, a. (e & rudis,) *to instruct; to form.*

Erudĭtio, ōnis, f. *instruction; learning.*

Erudĭtus, a um, part. (erudio.)

Esse, Essem, &c. *See* Sum.

Esuriens, tis, par *hungry; being hungry.*

Esurio, ire, ivi, ĭtum, n. *to be hungry.*

Et, conj. § 198, 1; *and; also; even :* et — et, *both — and.*

Etiam, conj. (et & jam,) *also; especially;* with an adjective or adverb in the comparative degree, *even.*

Etruria, æ, f. *a country of Italy north and west of the Tiber, Tuscany.*

Etrusci, ōrum, m. pl. *the people of Etruria; the Tuscans or Etrurians.*

Etruscus, a, um, adj. *belonging to Etruria; Tuscan or Etrurian.*

Eubœa, æ, f. *a large island in the Ægean sea, near Bœotia.*

Eumĕnes, is, m. *a general in Alexander's army;* also, *the name of several kings of Pergamus.*

Euphēmus, i, m. *the father of Dædălus.*

Euphrātes, is, m. *a large river which forms the western boundary of Mesopotamia.*

Euripĭdes, is, m. *a celebratea Athenian tragic poet.*

Euripus, i, m. *a narrow strait between Bœotia and Eubœa.*

Europa, æ, f. *the daughter of Agenor, king of Phœnicia.*

From her, Europe, one of the quarters of the earth, is supposed to have been named.

Eurôtas, æ, m. *a river of Laconia, near Sparta.*

Euxinus, i, m. (from Εὔξεινος, hospitable,) (pontus,) *the Euxine, now the Black sea.*

Evado. -vadĕre. -vāsi. -vasum. a. & n. (e & vado,) *to go out; to escape; to become.*

Everto, -vertĕre, -verti, -versum, a. (e & vertu,) *to overturn; to destroy.*

Eversus, a, um, part. *overturned; destroyed.*

Evôco, āre, āvi, ātum, a. (e & voco,) *to call out; to summon; to impure.*

Evôlo, āre, āvi, ātum, n. (e & volo,) *to fly out or away.*

Evŏmo, -vomĕre, -vomui, -vomĭtum, a. (e & vomo,) *to vomit forth; to eructate; to discharge.*

Ex, prep. *See E.*

Exactus, a, um, part. (exĭgo,) *banished; driven away.*

Exæquo, āre, āvi, ātum, a. (ex & æquo,) *to equal.*

Exanĭmo, āre, āvi, ātum, a. (ex & anima,) *to kill; to deprive of life; to render lifeless.*

Exardesco, -ardescĕre, -arsi, inc. *to burn; to become inflamed; to kindle; to become excited; to be enraged:* bellum exarsit, *a war broke out.*

Exaspĕro, āre, ā⸱i, ātum, a. *to exasperate; to incense.*

Excæco, āre, āvi, ātum, a. (ex & cæcus,) *to blind; to make blind.*

Excēdo, -cedĕre, -cessi, -cessum, n. (ex & cedo,) *to depart; to exceed; to surpass; to go beyond.*

Excello. -celĕre, -celui. -celsum, n. (ex & cello,) *to be high; to excel; to be eminent.*

Excelsus, a, um, adj. *high; lofty.*

Excidium, i, n. (ex & cædo,) *a destruction; ruin.*

Excĭdo, -cidĕre, cĭdi, n. (ex & cado,) *to fall; to fall out or from; to drop.*

Excido, -cidĕre, -cĭdi, -cisum, a. (ex & cædo,) *to cut out; to cut down; to hew out.*

Excisus, a, um, part.

Excipio, -cipĕre, -cēpi, -ceptum, a. (ex & capio,) *to sustain; to receive; to support; to follow; to succeed.*

Excitandus, a, um, part. from

Excĭto, āre, āvi, ātum, a. freq. (excieo,) *to excite; to awaken. to arouse; to stir up.*

Exclāmo, āre, āvi, ātum, a. (ex & clamo,) *to cry out; to exclaim.*

Exclŭdo, -cludĕre, -clŭsi, -clŭsum, a. (ex & claudo,) *to exclude; to hatch.*

Excŏlo, -colĕre, -colui, -cultum, a. (ex & colo,) *to cultivate, to exercise.*

Excrucio, áre, ávi, átum, a. (ex & crucio,) *to torment; to trouble.*

Excubiæ, árum, f. pl. (excúbo,) *a guard; a watch; a sentinel.*

Excusatio, ónis, f. (excúso,) *an excusing; an excuse; an apology.*

Exédo, -edĕre & -esse, -édi, -ésum, irr. a. (ex & ĕdo, § 181,) *to eat; to eat up; to devour.*

Exemplum, i, n. *an example; an instance.*

Exequiæ. *See* Exsequiæ.

Exerceo, ére, ui, ítum, a. (ex & arceo,) *to exercise; to train; to discipline; to practise:* agrum, *to cultivate the earth:* dominationem, *to be tyrannical.*

Exercĭtus, ús, m. *an army.*

Exhaurio, -haurire, -hausi, -haustum, a. (ex & haurio,) *to exhaust; to drain; to wear out; to impoverish.*

Exĭgo, -igĕre, -égi, -actum, a. (ex & ago,) *to drive away; to banish.*

Exiguus,a,um, adj. *small; scanty.*

Exĭlis, e, adj. *slender; small; thin.*

Exilium, i, n. (ex & solum,) *exile; banishment.*

Eximiè, adv. *remarkably; very;* from

Eximius, a, um, adj. (exĭmo,) *extraordinary; remarkable.*

Existĭmatio, ónis, f. *opinion; reputation; respect;* from

Existĭmo, áre, ávi, átum, a. (ex & æstĭmo,) *to believe; to think; to imagine; to suppose.*

Exitium, i, n. (exeo,) *destruction · ruin.*

Exĭtus, ús, m. *an exit; the event; the issue; an outlet.*

Exorátus, a, um, part. (exóro,) *entreated; influenced; induced.*

Exorior, -oriri, -ortus sum, dep. § 177, (ex & orior,) *to rise; to arise; to appear.*

Exorno, áre, ávi, átum, a. (ex & orno,) *to adorn; to deck.*

Exóro, áre, ávi, átum, a. (ex & oro,) *to entreat or beseech earnestly.* § 197, 9.

Exortus, a, um, part. (exorior,) *risen; having arisen.*

Expecto or -specto, áre, ávi, átum, a. (ex & specto,) *to look for; to wait for.*

Expedio, íre, ívi, ítum, a. (ex & pes,) *to free; to extricate:* expĕdit, imp. *it is fit; it is expedient.*

Expeditio, ónis, f. *an expedition.*

Expello, -pellĕre, -pŭli, -pulsum, a. (ex & pello,) *to expel; to banish.*

Expers, tis, adj. (ex & pars,) *without; devoid; void of; destitute of.*

Expĕto, ĕre, ívi, ítum, a. (ex & peto,) *to ask; to demand; to strive after; to seek earnestly.*

Expio, āre, āvi, ātum, a. (ex & pio,) *to expiate ; to appease.*

Expleo, ēre, ēvi, ētum, a. (ex & pleo,) *to fill.*

Explico, āre, āvi & ui, ātum & ītum, a. (ex & plico,) *to unfold ; to spread ; to explain.*

Explorător, ōris, m. (exploro,) *a spy ; a scout.*

Expolio, ire, īvi, ītum, a. (ex & polio,) *to polish ; to adorn ; to improve ; to finish.*

Expōno, -ponĕre, -posui, -posītum, a. *to explain ; to set forth ; to expose.*

Exprŏbro, āre, āvi, ātum, a. (ex & probrum,) *to upbraid ; to blame ; to reproach ; to cast in one's teeth.*

Expugno, āre, āvi, ātum, a. (ex & pugno,) *to take by assault ; to conquer ; to vanquish ; to subdue ; to take by storm.*

Expulsus, a, um, part. (expello.)

Exsequiæ, ārum, f. pl. (exsĕquor,) *funeral rites.*

Exsilio, *or* Exilio, īre, ii & ui, n. (ex & salio,) *to spring up* or *out ; to leap forth.*

Exspiro *or* -piro, āre, āvi, atum, a. (ex & spiro,) *to breathe forth ; to expire ; to die.*

Exstinctus, *or* Extinctus, a, um, part. *dead ;* from

Exstinguo, -stinguĕre, -stinxi, -stinctum, a. (ex & stinguo,) *to extinguish ; to kill ; to put to death ; to destroy*

Exstructus, *or* Extructus, a, um, part. from

Exstruo, *or* Extruo, -struĕre, -struxi, -structum, a. (ex & struo,) *to build ; to pile up ; to construct.*

Exsurgo, -surgĕre, -surrexi, -sur rectum, n. (ex & surgo,) *to rise up ; to arise ; to swell ; to surge.*

Exter, *or* Extĕrus, a, um, adj. § 125, 4, (exterior, extĭmus *or* extrēmus,) *foreign ; strange ; outward.*

Exto, extāre, extĭti, n. (ex & sto,) *to be ; to remain ; to be extant.*

Extorqueo, -torquēre, -torsi, -tortum, a. (ex & torqueo,) *to extort ; to wrest from , to obtain by force.*

Extra, prep. *beyond ; without ; except.*

Extractus a, um, part. from

Extrăho, -trahĕre, -traxi, -tractum, a. (ex & traho,) *to draw out ; to extract ; to extricate ; to free ; to rescue ; to liberate.*

Extrēmus, a, um, adj. (sup. of extĕrus,) *extreme ; the last ; the farthest.*

F.

Faba, æ, f. *a bean.*

Fabius, i, m. *the name of an illustrious Roman family.*

Fabricius, i, m. *a Roman, distinguished for his integrity.*

Fabrĭco, āre, āvi, ātum, a. (faber,) to make; to forge; to manufacture.

Fabŭla, æ, f. (fari,) a story; a fable; a tradition; a play.

Fabŭlōsus, a, um, adj. fabulous.

Faciendus, a, um, part. (facio.)

Faciens, tis, part. (facio.)

Facies, iēi, f. a face; appearance.

Facĭlĕ, adv. (iùs, lĭmè,) easily; willingly; clearly; undoubtedly; from

Facĭlis, e, adj. (facio,) easy.

Facĭnus, ŏris, n. a deed; a crime; an exploit; from

Fac.o, facĕre, feci, factum, a. to do; to make; to value: facĕre iter, to perform a journey; to travel: malè facĕre, to injure; to hurt: sacra facĕre, to offer sacrifice: facĕre pluris, to value higher: fac, take care; cause.

Factum, i, n. an action; a deed.

Factūrus, a, um, part. (facio.)

Factus, a, um, part. made; done: facta obviàm, meeting: prædà factâ, having been taken.

Facundus, a, um, adj. eloquent.

Falerii, ōrum, m. pl. a town of Etruria.

Falernus, i, m. a mountain of Campania, famous for its wine.

Falernus, a, um, adj. belonging to Falernus; Falernian.

Falisci, ōrum, m. p. the inhabitants of Falerii.

Fama, æ, f. fame; reputation; report.

Famelĭcus, a, um, adj. hungry; from

Fames, is, f. hunger; famine.

Familia, æ, f. a family; servants.

Familiāris, e, adj. of the same family; familiar.

Familiarĭtas, ātis, f. friendship; intimacy; confidence.

Familiarĭter, adv. familiarly; on terms of intimacy.

Famŭla, æ, f. a maid; a female servant or slave.

Fas, n. ind. right; a lawful thing.

Fascis, is, m. a bundle; a fagot: fasces, pl. bundles of birchen rods, carried before the Roman magistrates, with an axe bound up in the middle of them.

Fatālis, e, adj. fatal; ordained by fate.

Fateor, fatēri, fassus sum, dep. to confess.

Fatidĭcus, a, um, adj. (fatum & dico,) prophetic.

Fatigātus, a, um, part. from

Fatĭgo, āre, āvi, ātum, a. to weary.

Fatum, i, n. fate; destiny: fata, pl. the fates.

Fauce, abl. f. the throat: pl. fauces, the throat; the jaws; the straits. (§ 94.)

Faustŭlus, i, m. the shepherd by

16

whom Romŭlus and Remus were brought up.

Faveo, favére, favi, fautum, n. *to favor.* .

Favor, óris, m. *favor; good will; partiality; applause.*

Febris, is, f. *a fever.*

Feci.   *See* Facio.

Felicĭtas, átis, f. (felix, § 101, 2,) *felicity; good fortune; happiness.*

Felicĭter, adv. (ius, issĭmè,) *fortunately; happily; successfully.*

Felis, is, f. *a cat.*

Felix, icis, adj. (ior, issĭmus,) *happy; fortunate; fruitful; fertile; opulent; auspicious; favorable.*

Femĭna, æ, f. *a female; a woman.*

Femineus, a, um, adj. *female; feminine; pertaining to females.*

Fera, æ, f. *a wild beast.*

Ferax, ácis, adj. (ior, issĭmus,) (fero,) *fruitful; productive; fertile; abounding in.*

Ferè, adv. *almost; nearly; about:* ferè nullus, *scarcely any one.*

Ferens, tis, part. (fero.)

Ferĭnus, a, um, adj. (fera,) *of wild beasts.*

Fero, ferre, tuli, latum, irr. a. *to bear; to carry; to relate; to bring; to produce :* ferre manum, *to stretch forth; to extend :* ferunt, *they say.*

Feror, ferri, latus sum, pass. *to be carried; to flow; to mov rapidly; to fly :* fertur, imp. *it is said.*

Ferox, ócis, adj. (ior, issĭmus,) *wild; fierce; savage; ferocious.*

Ferreus, a, um, adj. *iron; obdurate :* from

Ferrum, ı, n. *iron; a sword; a knife.*

Fertĭlis, e, adj. (ior, issĭmus,) (fero,) *fertile; fruitful.*

Fertilĭtas, átis. f. *fertility; richness; fruitfulness.*

Ferŭla, æ, f. *a staff; a reed.*

Ferus, a, um, adj. *wild; rude; uncultivated; uncivilized; savage.*

Ferveo, fervére, ferbui, n. *to boil; to seethe; to foam; to be hot; to glow.*

Fessus, a, um, adj. *weary; tired; fatigued.*

Festum, i, n. *a feast;* from

Festus, a, um, adj. *festive; joyful; merry.*

Ficus, i & ûs, f. *a fig-tree; a fig.*

Fidélis, e, adj. *faithful;* from

Fides, ĕi, f. *fidelity; faith :* in fidem, *in confirmation :* in fidem accipĕre, *to receive under one's protection.*

Figo, figĕre, fixi, fixum, a. *to fix; to fasten.*

Filia, æ, f. § 43, 2 ; *a daughter.*

Filius, i, m. § 52 ; *a son.*

Findo, findĕre, fidi, fissum, a. *to split; to cleave.*

Fingens, tis, part. *feigning; pretending;* from

Fingo, fingĕre, finxi, fictum, a. *to pretend; to devise; to feign; to form; to make.*

Finio, ire, ivi, itum, a. *to end; to finish; to terminate;* from

Finis, is. d. *the end; a boundary; a limit:* fines, m. pl. § 63, 1; *the limits of a country. &c.*

Finitus, a, um, part. (finio.)

Finitimus, a, um, adj (finis,) *neighboring.*

Fio, fiĕri, factus sum, irr. pass. § 180, (facio,) *to be made; to become; to happen:* fit, *it happens:* factum est, *it happened; it came to pass.*

Firmàtus, a, um, part. (firmo.)

Firmiter, adv. (iùs, issĭmè,) (firmus,) *firmly; securely.*

Firmo, àre, àvi, àtum, a. *to confirm; to establish;* from

Firmus, a, um, adj. *firm; strong; secure.*

Fissus, a, um, part. (findo.)

Fixus, a, um, part. (figo,) *fixed; permanent.*

Flagello, àre, àvi, àtum, a. *to whip; to scourge; to lash.*

Flagitiòsus, a, um, adj. (ior, issĭmus,) *shameful; infamous; outrageous;* from

Flagitium, i, n. *a shameful action; an outrage; a crime; a dishonor; villany.*

Flagro, àre, àvi, àtum, n. *to burn; to be on fire; to suffer · to be oppressed; to be violent.*

Flaminius, i, m. *a Roman.*

Flavus, a, um, adj. *yellow.*

Flamma, æ, f. *a flame.*

Flecto, flectĕre, flexi, flexum, a. *to bend; to bow; to turn; to move; to prevail upon.*

Fleo, ĕre, ĕvi, ĕtum, a. *to weep; to lament.*

Fletus, ùs, m. *weeping; tears.*

Flevo, onis, m. *a lake near the mouth of the Rhine, now the Zuyder-zee.*

Flexus, a, um, part. (flecto,) *bent; changed; turned.*

Floreo, ĕre, ui, n. (flos, § 187, I. 1,) *to bloom; to blossom; to flourish; to be distinguished.*

Flos, flòris, m. *a flower; a blossom.*

Fluctus, ùs, m. (fluo,) *a wave.*

Fluo, fluĕre, fluxi, fluxum, n. *to flow.*

Fluvius, i, m. *a river.*

Flumen, ĭnis, n. (fluo,) *a river.*

Fodio, fodĕre, fodi, fossum, a. *to dig; to pierce; to bore.*

Fœcundĭtas, àtis, f. *fruitfulness;* from

Fœcundus, a, um, adj. (ior, issĭmus,) *fruitful; fertile.*

Fœdus, ĕris, n. *a league; a treaty.*

Folium, i, n. *a leaf.*

Fons, tis, m. *a fountain; a source; a spring.*

Forem, def. verb, § 154, 3; *I would* or *should be:* fore, *to*

be about to be; it would or
will come to pass.

Foris, adv. *abroad.*

Forma, æ, f. *a form; shape;
figure; beauty.*

Formica, æ, f. *an ant.*

Formido, ĭnis, f. *fear; dread;
terror.*

Formidolósus, a, um, adj. *fear-
ful; timorous.*

Formositas, ātis, f. *beauty; ele-
gance;* from

Formósus, a, um, adj. (ior, issĭmus,)(forma,)*beautiful; handsome.*

Fortasse, adv. (fors,) *perhaps.*

Forté, adv. (fors,) *accidentally;
by chance.*

Fortis, e, adj. (ior, issĭmus,)
bold; brave; courageous.

Fortiter, adv. (iùs, ıssīmè,) (fortis,) *bravely.*

Fortitudo, ĭnis, f. (fortis,) *boldness; bravery.*

Fortuna, æ, f. (fors,) *fortune;
chance.*

Forum, i, n. *the market-place; the
forum; the court of justice.*

Fossa, æ, f. (fodio,) *a ditch; a
trench; a moat.*

Fovea, æ, f. *a pit.*

Foveo, fovēre, fovi, fotum, a. *to
keep warm; to cherish.*

Fractus, a, um, part. (frango.)

Fragĭlis, e, adj. (frango,) *frail;
perishable.*

Fragilitas, ātis, f. (fragĭlis,) *frail-
ty; weakness.*

Fragmentum, i, n. (frango *a
fragment; a piece.*

Frango, frangĕre, fregi, frac-
tum, a. *to break; to break in
pieces; to weaken; to de-
stroy.*

Frater, tris, m. *a brother.*

Fraudulentus, a, um, adj. (fraus,
§ 128, 4,) *fraudulent; deceit-
ful; treacherous.*

Frequens, tis, adj. (ior, issĭmus,)
frequent; numerous.

Fretum, i, n. *a strait; a sea.*

Frico, fricāre, fricui, frictum &
fricātum, a. *to rub.*

Frigĭdus, a, um, adj. (ior, issĭmus,) *cold;* from

Frigus, ŏris, n. *cold.*

Frons, frondis, f. *a leaf of a tree;
a branch with leaves.*

Fructus, ùs, m. (fruor,) *fruit;
produce.*

Frugis, gen. f. (frux, nom. scarcely used, § 94,) *corn:* frŭges,
um, pl. *fruits; the various
kinds of corn.*

Frumentum, i, n. (fruor,) *corn;
wheat.*

Fruor, frui, fruĭtus & fructus, dep.
to enjoy.

Frustrà, adv. *in vain; to no purpose.*

Frustrātus, a, um, part. from

Frustror, āri, ātus sum, dep.
(frustrà,) *to frustrate; to deceive.*

Frutex, ĭcis, m. *a shrub; a bush.*

Fuga, æ, f. *a flight.*

Fugax, ācis, adj. *swift; fleeting.*

Fugiens, tis, part. from

Fugio, fugĕre, fugi, fugītum, n. & a. *to fly; to escape; to avoid; to flee; to flee from.*

Fugo, āre, āvi, ātum, a. *to put to flight; to drive off; to chase.*

Fui, Fuĕram, &c. *See* Sum.

Fulgeo, fulgĕre, fulsi, n. *to shine.*

Fuligo, ĭnis, f. *soot.*

Fullo, ōnis, m. *a fuller.*

Fulmen, ĭnis, n. (fulgeo,) *thunder; a thunderbolt; lightning.*

Funāle, is, n. (funis,) *a torch.*

Fundĭtus, adv. (fundus,) *from the foundation; utterly.*

Fundo, fundĕre, fudi, fusum, a. *to pour out:* lacrȳmas, *to shed tears:* hostes, *to scatter; to rout; to discomfit.*

Fundus, i, m. *the bottom of any thing;* also, *a farm; a field.*

Funestus, a, um, adj. (ior, issĭmus,) (funus,) *fatal; destructive.*

Fungor, fungi, functus sum, dep. *to perform* or *discharge an office; to do; to execute:* fato, *to die.*

Funis, is d. *a rope; a cable.*

Funus, ĕris, n. *a funeral; funeral obsequies.*

Fur, furis, c. *a thief.*

Furcŭla, æ, f. dim. (furca,) *a little fork:* Furcŭlæ Caudinæ, *the Caudine Forks, a narrow defile in the country*

of the Hirpini, in Italy, where the Romans were defeated by the Samnites.

Furiōsus, a, um, adj. (furo,) *furious; mad.*

Furius, i, m. *the name of several Romans, as of M. Furius Camillus, a distinguished general.*

Fusus, a, um, part. (fundo.)

Futūrus, a, um, part. (sum,) *about to be; future.*

G.

Gades, ium, f. pl. *the name of an island and town in Spain, near the straits of Gibraltar,* now *Cadiz.*

Gaditānus, a, um, adj. *of Gades* or *Cadiz:* fretum Gaditānum, *the straits of Gibraltar.*

Galatia, æ, f. *a country in the interior of Asia Minor.*

Gallia, æ, f. *Gaul, a country formerly extending from the Pyrenees to the Rhine, and along the northern part of Italy to the Adriatic.*

Galliæ, pl. *the divisions of Gaul.*

Gallĭcus, a, um, adj. *belonging to Gaul; Gallic.*

Gallina, æ, f. *a hen.*

Gallinaceus, i, m. *a cock.*

Gallus, i, m. *a cock.*

Gallus, i, m. *an inhabitant of Gallia · a Gaul;* also, *a cognomen of several Romans.*

Ganges, is, m. *the name of a large river in India.*

Garumna, æ, f. *the Garonne, a river of Aquitania.*

Gaudeo, gaudēre, gavisus sum, n. pass. § 142, 2; *to rejoice; to delight; to be pleased with.*

Gaudium, i, n. *joy; gladness.*

Gavisus, a, um, part. (gaudeo,) *rejoicing; having rejoiced.*

Gemĭnus, a, um, adj. *double:* gemĭni filii, *twin sons.*

Gemmātus, a, um, part. *adorned with gems; gemmed; glittering.*

Gemmo, āre, āvi, ātum, a. (gemma,) *to adorn with gems.*

Gener, eri, m. § 46; *a son-in-law.*

Genĕro, āre, āvi, ātum, a. (genus,) *to beget; to produce.*

Generosĭtas, ātis, f. *nobleness of mind; magnanimity;* from

Generōsus, a, um, adj. (ior, issĭmus,) *noble; spirited; brave; generous; fruitful; fertile.*

Genĭtus, a, um, part. (gigno,) *born; produced.*

Gens, tis, f. *a nation; a tribe; a family; a clan.*

Genui. *See* Gigno.

Genus, ĕris, n. *a race; a family; a sort* or *kind.*

Geometria, æ, f. *geometry.*

Gerens, tis, part. (gero,) *bearing; conducting.*

Germānus, i, m. *a German; an inhabitant of Germany.*

Germania, æ, f. *Germany.*

Germanĭcus, a, um, adj. *German; of Germany.*

Gero, gerĕre, gessi, gestum, a. *to bear; to carry; to do:* res eas gessit, *performed such exploits:* odium, *to hate:* onus, *to bear a burden:* bellum, *to wage* or *carry on war:* res prospĕrè gesta est, *affairs were managed successfully,* or *a successful battle was fought.*

Gerўon, m. *a giant who was slain by Hercules, and whose oxen were driven into Greece.*

Gestans, tis, part. from

Gesto, āre, āvi, ātum, freq. (gero,) *to bear; to carry about.*

Gestus, a, um, part. *borne; performed:* res gestæ, *see* Res.

Getæ, ārum, m. pl. *a savage people of Dacia, north of the Danube.*

Gigas, antis, m. *a giant.*

Gigno, gignĕre, genui, genĭtum, a. *to bring forth; to bear; to beget; to produce.*

Glaber, bra, brum, adj. *bald; bare; smooth.*

Glacialis, e, adj. *icy; freezing.*

Glacies, ēi, f. *ice.*

Gladiātor, ōris, m. (gladius,) *a gladiator.*

Gladiatorius, a, um, adj. *belonging to a gladiator; gladiatorial;* from

Gladius, i, m. *a sword.*

Glans, dis, f. *mast ; an acorn.*

Glisco, ĕre, n. *to increase.*

Gloria, æ, f. *glory ; fame.*

Glorior, āri, ātus sum, dep. *to boast.*

Gorgias, æ, m. *a celebrated soph- ist and orator. He was born at Leontini, in Sicily, and was hence surnamed Leontinus.*

Gracĭlis, e, adj. (ior, līmus, § 125, 2,) *slender ; lean ; delicate.*

Gracchus, i, m. *the name of an illustrious Roman family.*

Gradior, gradi, gressus sum, dep. *to go ; to walk.*

Gradus, ûs, m. *a step ; a stair.*

Græcia, æ, f. *Greece.*

Græcus, a, um, adj. *Grecian ; Greek :*—subs. *a Greek.*

Grandis, e, adj. (ior, issĭmus,) *large ; great.*

Granicus, i, m. *a river of Mysia, emptying into the Propontis.*

Grassor, āri, ātus sum, dep. freq. (gradior,) *to advance ; to march ; to proceed ; to make an attack.*

Grates, f. pl. (gratus,) § 94 ; *thanks :* agĕre grates, *to thank.*

Gratia, æ, f. (gratus,) *grace ; favor ; thanks ; return ; re- quital ; gratitude :* habēre, *to feel indebted* or *obliged ; to be grateful :* in gratiam, *in fa- vor of :* gratiâ, *for the sake.*

Gratulatus, a, um, part. *having congratulated ;* from

Gratŭlor, āri, ātus sum, dep. *to congratulate ; from*

Gratus, a, um, adj. (ior, issĭmus,) *acceptable ; pleasing ; grate- ful.*

Gravis, e, adj. (ior, issĭmus,) *heavy ; severe ; great ; grave ; important ; violent ; unwhole- some ; noxious :* gravis som- nus, *sound sleep.*

Gravĭtas, ātis, f. *heaviness ; grav- ity ; weight.*

Gravĭter, adv. (iùs, issĭmè,) *hard- ly ; heavily ; grievously ; se- verely.*

Gravo, āre, āvi, ātum, a. *to load ; to oppress ; to burden.*

Gregātim, adv. (grex,) *in herds.*

Gressus, ûs, m. (gradior,) *a step ; a pace ; a gait.*

Grex, gis, c. *a flock ; a herd ; a company.*

Grus, gruis, c. *a crane.*

Gubernātor, ōris, m. (guberno,) *a pilot ; a ruler.*

Gyărus, i, f. *one of the Cyclă- des.*

Gyges, is, m. *a rich king of Lydia.*

Gymnosophistæ, ārum, m. *Gym- nosophists ; a sect of Indian philosophers.*

H.

Habens, tis, part. from

Habeo, ĕre, ui, ĭtum, a. *to have ; to possess ; to hold ; to esteem, to suppose; to take :* habére consilium, *to deliberate.*

Habíto, áre, ávi, átum, freq. (habeo,) *to dwell; to inhabit.*

Habitúrus, a, um, part. (habeo.)

Habítus, a, um, part. (habeo.)

Habítus, ûs, m. *habit; form; dress; attire; manner.*

Hactěnus, adv. (hic & tenus,) *hitherto; thus far.*

Hadriánus, i, m. *Adrian, the fifteenth emperor of Rome.*

Hæmus, i, m. *a mountain of Thrace, from whose top, both the Euxine and Adriatic seas can be seen.*

Halcyon, or Alcyon, ŏnis, f. *the halcyon or kingfisher.* — See Alcyŏne.

Halicarnassus, i, f. *a maritime city of Caria, the birthplace of Herodŏtus.*

Hamilcar, áris, m. *a Carthaginian general.*

Hannïbal, ălis, m. *a brave Carthaginian general, the son of Hamilcar.*

Hanno, ŏnis, m. *a Carthaginian general.*

Harmonia, æ, f. *the wife of Cadmus, and daughter of Mars and Venus.*

Harpyiæ, árum, f. pl. *the Harpies; winged monsters, having the faces of women and the bodies of vultures.*

Haruspex, ïcis, m. *a soothsayer; a diviner; one who pretended* to a knowledge of future events from inspecting the entrails of victims.

Hasdrúbal, ălis, m. *a Carthaginian general, the brother of Hannibal.*

Hasta, æ, f. *a spear; a lance.*

Haud, adv. *not.*

Haurio, haurìre, hausi, haustum, a. *to draw out; to drink, to swallow.*

Haustus, a, um, part. *swallowed.*

Haustus, ûs, m. *a draught.*

Hebes, ětis, adj. *dull; obtuse; dim.*

Hebesco, ěre, inc. (hebes,) *to become dull; to grow dim.*

Hebrus, i, m. *a large river of Thrace.*

Hecŭba, æ, f. *the wife of Priam, king of Troy.*

Heděra, æ, f. *ivy.*

Hegesias, æ, m. *an eloquent philosopher of Cyrêne.*

Helěna, æ, f. *Helen, the daughter of Jupiter and Leda, and wife of Menelàus.*

Helĭcon, ŏnis, m. *a mountain of Bœotia, near to Parnassus, and sacred to Apollo and the Muses.*

Helvetia, æ, f. *a country in the eastern part of Gaul, now Switzerland.*

Helvetii, ŏrum, m. pl. *Helvetians; the inhabitants of Helvetia.*

Hellebŏrum, i, n. or Hellebŏrus, i, m. *the herb hellebore.*

Hellespontus, i, m. *a strait be-*

tween Thrace and Asia Minor, now called *the Dardanelles.*

Heraclĕa, æ, f. *the name of several cities in Magna Græcia, in Pontus, in Syria,* &c.

Herba, æ, f. *an herb; grass.*

Herbĭdus, a, um, adj. *grassy; full of herbs* or *grass.*

Hercŭles, is, m. *a celebrated hero, the son of Jupiter and Alcmēna.*

Hercynius, a, um, adj. *Hercynian:* Hercynia silva, *a large forest in Germany,* now the *Black Forest.*

Heres, *or* Hæres, ēdis, c. *an heir.*

Herennius, i, m. *a general of the Samnites, and the father of Pontius Thelesinus.*

Hero, ûs, (§ 69, E. 4,) f. *a priestess of Venus, who resided at Sestos, and who was beloved by Leander, a youth of Abȳdos.*

Hespĕrus, i, m. *a son of Iapĕtus, who settled in Italy, and from whom that country was called Hesperia;* also *the evening star.*

Heu! int. *alas! ah!*

Hians, tis, part. (hio.)

Hiātus, ûs, m. *an opening; a chasm; an aperture.*

Hibernĭcus, a, um, adj. *Irish:* mare Hibernĭcum, *the Irish sea.*

Hibernus, a, um, adj. *of winter; wintry.*

Hic, adv. *here; in this place.*

Hic, Hæc, Hoc, pro. § 134; *this; he; she,* &c.

Hiempsal, ălis, m. *a king of Numidia.*

Hiems, ēmis, f. *winter.*

Hiĕro, ōnis, m. *a tyrant of Syracuse.*

Hierosolȳma, æ, f. & Hierosolȳma, ōrum, n. pl. *Jerusalem, the capital of Judea.*

Hinc, adv. *hence; from hence; from this; from this time:* hinc — hinc, *on this side, and on that.*

Hinnio, īre, īvi, ītum, n. *to neigh.*

Hinnītus, ûs, m. *a neighing.*

Hinnuleus, i, m. *a fawn.*

Hio, āre, āvi, ātum, n. *to gape; to yawn; to open the mouth.*

Hipparchus, i, m. *the son of Pisistrătus, tyrant of Athens.*

Hippolȳtus, i, m. *the son of Theseus.*

Hippomĕnes, is, m. *the son of Megareus, and husband of Atalanta.*

Hippopotămus, i, m. *the hippopotamus* or *river-horse.*

Hispania, æ, f. *Spain.*

Hispănus, a, um, adj. *Spanish:* subs. m. *a Spaniard.*

Hodie, adv. (hic & dies,) *to-day; at this time; now-a-days.*

Hodiĕque, *to this day; to this time.*

Hœdus, i, m. *a kid; a young goat.*

Homērus, i, m. *Homer, the most*

ancient and illustrious of the Greek poets.

Homo, ĭnis, c. *a man; a person; one.*

Honestas, ātis, f. *virtue; dignity; honor;* from

Honestus, a, um, adj. *honorable; noble;* from

Honor & -os, ŏris. m. *honor; respect; an honor; a dignity; an office.*

Honorifĭcè, adv. (honorificus, § 125, 3,) *honorably:* parum honorifice, *slightingly; with little respect.*

Hora, æ, f. *an hour.*

Horatius, ı, m. *Horace; the name of several Romans:* Horatii, pl. *three Roman brothers, who fought with the three Curiatii.*

Hortensius, i, m. *the name of several Romans.*

Horrĭdus, a, um, adj. *rough; rugged; rude; unpolished; barbarous.*

Hortātus, ùs, m. *an exhortation; instigation; advice;* from

Hortor, ári, átus sum, dep. *to exhort.*

Hortus, i, m. *a garden.*

Hospes, ĭtis, c. *a stranger; a guest.*

Hospĭtium, i, n. *hospitality:* hospitio accipĕre, *to entertain.*

Hostia, æ, f. *a victim.*

Hostilius, i, m. (Tullus,) *the third king of Rome: a* cognŏmen *among the Romans.*

Hostis, is, c. *an enemy.*

Huc, adv. *hither:* huc --- illuc, *hither — thither; now here --- now there.*

Hujusmŏdi, adj. ind. (hic & modus, § 134, 5, *of this sort or kind.*

Humanĭtas, ātis, f. *humanity; kindness; gentleness;* from

Humānus, a, um, adj. (homo,) *human.*

Humérus, i, m. *the shoulder.*

Humĭlis, e, adj. (ior, lĭmus, § 125, 2,) *humble:* humĭli loco natum esse, *to be born in a humble station or of obscure parents.*

Humor, ŏris, m. *moisture;* pl *liquids; humors.*

Humus, i, f. *the ground:* humi, *on the ground.* § 221, 1., R. 3.

Hyæna, æ, f. *the hyena.*

Hydrus, i, m. *a water-snake.*

Hymnus, i, m. *a hymn; a song of praise.*

Hyperboreus, a, um, adj. (ὑπὲρ βορέας,) properly, *living beyond the source of the north wind; northern:* Hyperborei, ŏrum, m. pl. *people inhabiting the northern regions; beyond Scythia.*

Hystrix, ĭcis, f. *a porcupine.*

I.

Iapĕtus, *the son of Cælus and Terra.*

Ibérus, ı, m. *a river of Spain, now the Ebro.*

Ibi, adv. *there ; here ; then.*

Ibidem, adv. *in the same place.*

Ibis, ĭdis, f. *the ibis, the Egyptian stork.*

Icărus, i, m. *the son of Dædălus.*

Icarius, a, um, adj. *of Icărus ; Icarian.*

Ichneumon, ŏnis, m. *the ichneumon* or *Egyptian rat.*

Ichnūsa, æ, f. *an ancient Greek name of Sardinia, derived from the Greek ἴχνος, a footstep ; a track.*

Ico, icĕre, ici, ictum, a. *to strike :* fœdus, *to make, ratify,* or *conclude a league* or *treaty.*

Ictus, a, um, part.

Ictus, ūs, m. *a blow ; a stroke.*

Ida, æ, f. *a mountain of Troas, near Troy.*

Idæus, a, um, adj. *belonging to Ida :* mons Idæus, *mount Ida.*

Idem, eădem, idem, pro. § 134, 6 ; *the same.*

Idoneus, a, um, adj. *fit ; suitable.*

Igĭtur, conj. *therefore.*

Ignărus, a, um, adj. (in & gnarus,) *ignorant.*

Ignāvus, a, um, adj. (in & gnavus,) *idle ; inactive ; cowardly.*

Ignis, is, m. *fire ; flame.*

Ignobĭlis, e, adj. (in & nobĭlis,) *ignoble ; mean ; unknown.*

Ignŏro, āre, āvi, ātum, a. (ignōtus,) *to be ignorant ; not to know.*

Ignŏtus, a, um, part. & adj. (in & notus,) *unknown.*

Ilium, i, n. *Ilium* or *T. oy, the principal city of Troas.*

Illātus, a, um, part. (from infĕro,) *brought in ; inflected upon ; inferred.*

Ille, a, ud, pro. § 134 ; *that ; he she ; it ; the former :* pl. *they those.*

Illecĕbra, æ, f. *an allurement an enticement.*

Illĭco, adv. (in & loco,) *in that place ; immediately ; instantly.*

Illuc, adv. *thither :* huc — illuc, *now here — now there.*

Illustris, e, adj. (ior, issĭmus,) *illustrious ; famous ; celebrated.*

Illustro, āre, āvi, ātum, a. (in & lustro,) *to enlighten ; to illustrate ; to render famous ; to celebrate ; to make renowned.*

Illyria, æ, f. *a country opposite to Italy, and bordering on the Adriatic.*

Imāgo, ĭnis, f. *an image ; a picture ; a figure ; a resemblance.*

Imbecillis, e, adj. (ior, lĭmus, § 125, 2,) *weak ; feeble.*

Imber, bris, m. *a shower ; a rain.*

Imitatio, ōnis, f. *imitation :* ad imitatiónem, *in imitation :* from

Imĭtor, āri, ātus sum, dep. *to imitate ; to copy.*

Immānis, e, adj. *monstrous ; cruel ; huge · enormous ; dreadful.*

Immensus, a, um, adj. (in & mensus,) *immeasurable; boundless; immoderate.*

mmeritus, a, um, part. (in & meritus,) *not deserving; undeserved.*

Imminens, tis, part. *hanging over; threatening;* from

immineo, ēre, ui, n. *to hang over; to impend; to threaten; to be near.*

mmissus, a, um, part. *admitted; sent in; darted in;* from

Immitto, -mittĕre, -misi, -missum, a. (in & mitto,) *to let in; to send to, into, against, or upon; to throw at.*

Immobilis, e, adj. (in & mobilis,) *immovable; steadfast.*

Immŏlo, āre, āvi, ātum, a. (in & mola,) *to sacrifice; to immolate.*

Immortālis, e, adj. (in & mortālis,) *immortal.*

Immŏtus, a, um, part. (in & motus,) *unmoved; still; motionless.*

Immutātus, a, um, part. *altered; changed;* from

Immūto, āre, āvi, ātum, a. (in & muto,) *to change.*

Impatiens, tis, adj. (in & patiens,) *impatient; not able to endure.*

Impedītus, a, um, part. *impeded; hindered; encumbered; entangled;* from

Impedio, īre, ivi, ītum, a. (in & pes,) *to impede; to disturb to obstruct; to check; to delay; to prevent.*

Impendeo, -pendēre, -pendi -pensum, n. (in & pendeo, *to hang over; to impend; to threaten.*

Impenetrabĭlis, e, adj. (in & penetrabĭlis,) *impenetrable.*

Impensè, adv. *exceedingly; greatly.*

Imperātor, ōris, m. (impĕro,) *a commander; a general.*

Imperīto, āre, āvi, ātum, freq (impĕro,) *to command; to rule; to govern.*

Imperitus, a, um, adj. (ior, issĭmus,) (in & peritus,) *inexperienced; unacquainted with.*

Imperium, i, n. *a command government; reign; authority; power;* from

Impĕro, are, āvi, ātum, a. *to command; to order; to direct; to govern; to rule over.*

Impertiens, tis, part. from

Impertio, īre, ivi, ītum, a. (in & partio,) *to impart; to share, to give.*

Impĕtro, āre, āvi, ātum, a. (in & patro,) *to obtain; to finish.*

Impĕtus, ûs, m. (in & peto *force; violence; impetuosity, an attack.*

Impius, a, um, adj. (in & pius,) *impious; undutiful.*

Impleo, ēre, ēvi, ētum, a. *to fill; to accomplish; to perform.*

Implicĭtus, a, um, part. *entangled; attacked.*

Implico, āre, āvi *or* ui, ātum *or* ītum, a. (in & plico,) *to entangle; to implicate.*

Implĭcor, āri, ātus *or* ītus sum, pass. *to be entangled :* morbo, *to be attacked with; to be sick.*

Implŏro, āre, āvi, ātum, a. (in & ploro,) *to implore; to beseech; to beg.*

Impŏno, -ponĕre, -posui, -posĭtum, a. (in & pono,) *to lay* or *place upon; to impose; to put.*

Importūnus, a, um, adj. *dangerous; perilous; troublesome; cruel : outrageous; craving; ungovernable.*

Imposĭtus, a, um, part. (impŏno.)

Improbātus, a, um, part. *disallowed; disapproved; rejected.*

Imprŏbo, āre, āvi, ātum, a. (in & probo,) *to disapprove; to reject.*

Imprŏbus, a, um, adj. *wicked; bad.*

Imprūdens, tis, adj. (in & prudens,) *imprudent; inconsiderate.*

Impugnatūrus, a, um, part. from

Impugno, āre, āvi, ātum, a. *to attack.*

Impūnè, adv. (in & pœna,) *with impunity; without hurt; without punishment.*

Imus, a, um, adj. (sup. of infĕrus, § 125, 4,) *the lowest; the deepest.*

In, prep. with the accusative, signifies *into; towards; upon; until; for; against :* with the ablative, *in; upon; among; at;* § 235, (2 :) in dies, *from day to day :* in eo esse, *to be on the point of :* in sublime, *aloft.*

Inānis, e, adj. *vain; empty; ineffectual; foolish.*

Inaresco, -arescĕre, -arŭi, inc. § 173; *to grow dry.*

Incĕdo, -cedĕre, -cessi, -cessum, n. (in & cedo,) *to go; to walk; to come.*

Incendo, dĕre, di, sum, a. (in & candeo,) *to light; to kindle, to set fire to; to inflame.*

Incensus, a, um, part. *lighted; kindled; burning; inflamed.*

Incertus, a, um, adj. (ior, issĭmus,) (in & certus,) *uncertain.*

Inchoo, āre, āvi, ātum, a. *to begin.*

Incĭdens, tis, part. from

Incĭdo, -cidĕre, -cĭdi, n. (in & cado,) *to fall into* or *upon; to chance to meet with.*

Incipio, -cipĕre, -cĕpi, -ceptum, a. (in & capio,) *to commence; to begin.*

Incĭto, āre, āvi, ātum, a. (in & cito,) *to instigate; to encourage; to animate.*

Inclūdo, dĕre, si, sum, a. (in & claudo,) *to shut in; to include; to inclose; to encircle; to encompass.*

17

Ínclûsus, a, um, part. (ĭnclŭdo.)

Inclytus, a, um, adj. (comp. not used; sup. issĭmus,) *famous; celebrated; renowned.*

Incŏla, æ, c. *an inhabitant.*

Incŏlo, colĕre, colui, cultum, a. (in & colo,) *to inhabit; to dwell.*

Incŏlūmis, e, adj. *unhurt; unpunished; safe.*

Incompertus, a, um, adj. *unknown; uncertain.*

Inconsiderātē, adv. *inconsiderately; rashly.*

Incredibĭlis, e, adj. (in & credibĭlis,) *incredible; wonderful.*

Incredibilĭter, adv. *incredibly.*

Incrementum, i, n. (incresco,) *an increase.*

Increpo, āre, ui, ĭtum, a. (in & crepo,) *to reprove; to chide; to blame.*

Incruentus, a, um, adj. (in & cruor,) *bloodless.*

Incultē, adv. (iùs, issĭmè,) *rudely; plainly;* from

Incultus, a, um, part. & adj. (in & colo,) *uncultivated; uninhabited; desert.*

Incumbo, -cumbĕre, -cubui, -cubĭtum, n. (in & cubo,) *to lean; to lie; to rest or recline upon; to apply to:* gladio, *to fall upon one's sword; to slay one's self with a sword.*

Incursio, ŏnis, f. (incurro,) *an attack; an incursion; an inroad.*

Inde, adv. *thence; from thence.*

Index, ĭcis, d. (indĭco,) *an index; a mark; a sign.*

India, æ, f. *a country of Asia, deriving its name from the river Indus.*

Indico, cĕre, xi, ctum, a. (in & dico,) *to indicate; to announce; to declare; to proclaim.*

Indictus, a, um, part.

Indĭcus, a, um, adj. *of India; Indian.*

Indigĕna, æ, c. (in & geno,) *a native.*

Indōles, is, f. (in & oleo, to grow,) *the disposition; nature; inherent quality.*

Indūco, cĕre, xi, ctum, a. (in & duco,) *to lead in; to induce; to persuade.*

Inductus, a, um, part.

Induo, -duĕre, -dui, -dūtum, a. *to put on; to dress; to clothe.*

Indus, i, m. *a large river in the western part of India.*

Industria, æ, f. *industry; diligence.*

Indūtus, a, um, part. (induo.)

Inedia, æ, f. (in & edo,) *want of food; fasting; hunger.*

Ineo, ire, ii, ĭtum, irr. n. & a. (in & eo,) *to go or enter into; to enter upon; to make; to form.*

Inermis, e, adj. (in & arma,) *defenceless; unarmed.*

Inertia, æ, f. (iners,) *laziness, sloth; idleness.*

Infămis, e, adj. (in & fama,) *infamous ; disgraceful.*

Infans, tis, c. *an infant ; a child.*

Infĕri, ōrum, m. pl. (inferus,) *the infernal regions ; Hades ; Orcus ; the infernal gods ; the shades.*

Inferior, us, adj. comp. *See* Infĕrus.

.nfĕro, inferre, intŭli, illātum, irr. a. (in & fero,) *to bring in or against ; to bring upon ; to inflict upon :* bellum, *to make war upon.*

Infĕrus, a, um, adj. (inferior, infĭmus *or* imus, § 125, 4,) *low ; humble.*

Infesto, āre, āvi, ātum, a. *to infest ; to disturb ; to molest ; to vex ; to plague ; to trouble ; to annoy ; from*

Infestus, a, um, adj. *hostile : inimical.*

Infigo, gĕre, xi, xum, a. (in & figo,) *to fix ; to fasten ; to drive in.*

Infinitus, a, um, adj. (in & finio,) *infinite ; unbounded ; vast ; immense :* infinitum argenti, *an immense quantity of silver :* infinita nobilitas, *a vast number.*

Infirmus, a, um, adj. *weak ; infirm.*

Infixus, part. (infigo.)

Inflammo, āre, āvi, ātum, a. *to inflame ; to excite ; to stimulate ; to animate.*

Inflatus, a, um, part. *blown upon ; puffed up.*

Infligo, gĕre, xi, ctum, a. (in & fligo,) *to inflict.*

Inflo, āre, āvi, ātum, a. (in & flo,) *to blow upon.*

Infrendens, tis, part. from

Infrendeo, ēre, ui, n. (in & frendeo,) *to gnash with the teeth.*

Infringo, -fringĕre, -frēgi, -fractum, a. (in & frango,) *to break or rend in pieces ; to disannul ; to make void.*

Infundo, -fundĕre, -fūdi, -fūsum, a. (in & fundo,) *to pour in :* infunditur, *it empties.*

Ingenium, i, n. *the disposition ; genius ; talents ; character.*

Ingens, tis, adj. *great ; very great.*

Ingenuus, a, um, adj. *free-born ; free ; noble ; ingenuous.*

Ingredior, -grĕdi, -gressus sum, dep. (in & gradior,) *to go in ; to enter ; to come in ; to walk ; to walk upon ; to go.*

Ingressus, a, um, part.

Ingruo, -gruĕre, -grui, n. *to invade ; to assail ; to pour down ; to fall upon suddenly.*

Inhæreo, -hærēre, -hæsi, -hæsum, n. (in & hæreo,) *to cleave or stick to or in :* cogitationĭbus, *to be fixed or lost in thought.*

Inhio, āre, āvi, ātum, a. & n. (in & hio,) *to gape for ; to desire.*

Inimicus, a, um, adj. (in & amicus,) *inimical ; hostile.*

Inimicus, i, m. *an enemy.*

Iniquè, adv. (iniquus,) *unjustly; unequally.*

Initium, i, n. (ineo,) *a commencement; a beginning.*

Initūrus, a, um, part. (ineo,) *about to enter upon or begin.*

Injicio, -jicĕre, -jēci, -jectum, a. (in & jacio,) *to throw in or upon.*

Injuria, æ, f. (injurius,) *an injury; an insult.*

Innăto, āre, āvi, ātum, n. (in & nato,) *to swim or float upon.*

Innitor, -nitī, -nīsus *or* -nixus sum, dep. (in & nitor,) *to lean or depend upon; to rest upon.*

Innocentia, æ, f. (in & nocens,) *innocence.*

Innotesco, -notescĕre, -notui, inc. (in & notesco,) *to be known; to become known.*

Innoxius, a, um, adj. (in & noxius,) *harmless.*

Innumerabĭlis, e, adj. (in & numerabilis,) *innumerable.*

Innumĕrus, a, um, adj. (in & numĕrus,) *innumerable.*

Inopia, æ, f. (inops,) *want.*

Inōpus, i, m. *a fountain or river of Delos, near which Apollo and Diana were said to have been born.*

In- *or* im- primis, adv. (in & primus,) *chiefly; especially.*

Inquam, *or* Inquio, def. *I say;* § 183, 5.

nquīno, āre, āvi, ātum, a. *to pollute; to stain; to soil.*

Inquiro, -quirĕre, -quisī , -quisi tum, a. (in & quæro,) *to inquire; to investigate.*

Insania, æ, f. (insānus,) *madness.*

Insanio, īre, ivi, ītum, n. *to be mad.*

Inscribo, -scribĕre, -scripsi, -scriptum, a. (in & scribo,) *to inscribe; to write upon.*

Inscriptus, a, um, part.

Insectum, i, n. (insēco,) *an insect.*

Insēquens, tis, part. *succeeding; subsequent; following;* from

Insĕquor, -sĕqui, -secūtus sum, dep. (in & sequor,) *to follow.*

Insīdens, tis, part. from

Insideo, -sidēre, -sēdi, -sessum, n. (in & sedeo,) *to sit upon.*

Insidiæ, ārum, f. pl. *an ambush; ambuscade; treachery; deceit:* per insidias, *treacherously.*

Insidians, tis, part. from

Insidior, āri, ātus sum, dep. *to lie in wait; to lie in ambush; to deceive.*

Insigne, is, n. *a mark; a token; an ensign;* from

Insignis, e, adj. (in & signum,) *distinguished; eminent.*

Insisto, -sistĕre, -stiti, -stĭtum, n. (in & sisto,) *to stand upon, to insist.*

Insolabilĭter, adv. *inconsolably.*

Insŏlens, tis, adj. (ior, issĭmus,) *insolent; haughty.*

Insolenter, adv. (iùs, issĭmè,) *haughtily, insolently.*

Inspectans, tis, part. from

Inspecto, āre, ávi, átnin, freq. *to inspect; to look upon.*

Instatūrus, a, um, part. (insto.)

Instituo, -stituĕre, -stitui, -stitū-tum, a. (in & statuo,) *to appoint; to institute; to make; to order.*

Institūtum, i, n. *an institution; a doctrine;* from

Institūtus, a, um, part. (instituo.)

Insto, -stāre, -stĭti, n. (in & sto,) *to be near to; to urge; to persist; to harass; to pursue closely; to beg earnestly.*

Instrumentum, i, n. *an instrument; utensil; implement;* from

nstruo, -struĕre, -struxi, -struc-tum, a. (in & struo,) *to prepare; to teach; to supply with; to furnish.*

Insùbres, um, m. pl. *a people living north of the Po, in Cisalpine Gaul.*

Insuesco, -suescĕre, -suèvi, -suè-tum, inc. (in & suesco,) *to grow accustomed.*

Insūla, æ, f. *an island.*

Insŭper, adv. (in & super,) *moreover.*

Intĕger, gra, grum, adj. (rior, errĭmus,, *whole; entire; unhurt; just.*

Intĕgo, -tegĕre, -tɛxi, -tectum, a. (in & tego,) *to cover.*

Integrĭtas, ātis, f. (intĕger,) *integrity; probity; honesty.*

Intellectus, a, um, part. from

Intelligo, -ligĕre, -lexi, -lec-tum, a. (inter & lego,) *to understand; to perceive; to discern; to know; to learn.*

Inter, prep. *between; among :* inter se, *mutually :* occurrentes inter se, *meeting each other.*

Intercipio, -cipĕre, -cēpi, -cep-tum, a. (inter & capio,) *to intercept; to usurp; to take away fraudulently.*

Interdico, -dicĕre, -dixi, -dictum a. (inter & dico,) *to forbid; to prohibit.*

Interdictus, a, um, part.

Interdiu, adv. *by day; in the day-time.*

Interdum, adv. *sometimes.*

Interea, adv. (inter & is,) *in the mean time.*

Interemptus, a, um, part. (inter-imo.)

Intereo, íre, ii, ĭtum, irr. n. (inter & eo, § 182,) *to perish.*

Intĕrest, imp. (intersum,) *it concerns :* mea, *it concerns me.*

Interfector, ōris, m. *a murderer; a slayer; a destroyer.*

Interfectus, a, um, part. *killed.*

Interficio, -ficĕre, -fēci, -fectum, a. (inter & facio,) *to kill; to slay.*

Intĕrim, adv. *in the mean time.*

Interīmo, -imĕre, -ēmi, -emptum, a. (inter & emo,) *to kill; to put to death; to slay.*

Interior, us, adj. (sup. intŭmus, § 126, 1,) *inner; the interior.*

Interiùs, adv. *farther in the interior.*

nterjectus, a, um, part. *cast between:* anno interjecto, *a year having intervened; a year after.*

Interjicio, -jicĕre, -jēci, -jectum, a. (inter & jacio,) *to throw between.*

Internecio, ōnis, f. (internĕco,) *ruin; destruction:* ad interneciōnem, *with a general massacre.*

Internodium, i, n. (inter & nodus,) *the space between two knots; a joint.*

Internus, a, um, adj. *internal:* mare internum, *the Mediterranean sea.*

Interpres, ĕtis, c. *an interpreter.*

Interregnum, i, n. (inter & regnum,) *an interregnum; a vacancy of the throne.*

Interrŏgo, āre, āvi, ātum, a. (inter & rogo,) *to ask.*

Intersum, esse, fui, irr. n. (inter & sum,) *to be present at.*

Intervallum, i, n. (inter & vallum,) *an interval; a space; a distance.*

Interveniens, tis, part. from

Intervenio, venire, vēni, ventum,

n. (inter & venio,) *to come between; to intervene.*

Intexo, ĕre, ui, tum, a. (in & texo,) *to interweave.*

Intŭmus, a, um, adj. sup. (comp. interior, § 126, 1,) *innermost; inmost; intimate; familiar; much beloved.*

Intra, prep. *within:*—adv. *inward.*

Intrepĭdus, a, um, adj. (in & trepĭdus,) *fearless; intrepid.*

Intro, āre, āvi, ātum, a. *to enter.*

Introdŭco, -ducĕre, -duxi, -ductum, a. (intro & duco,) *to lead in; to introduce.*

Introïtus, ûs, m. (introeo,) *an entrance.*

Intuens, tis, part. from

Intueor, ēri, ītus sum, dep. (in & tueor,) *to look upon; to consider; to behold; to gaze at.*

Intus, adv. *within.*

Inusitātus, a, um, adj. *unaccustomed; unusual; extraordinary.*

Inutĭlis, e, adj. *useless.*

Invādo, -vadĕre, -vāsi, -vāsum, a. (in & vado,) *to invade; to attack; to assail; to fall upon.*

Invenio, -venire, -vēni, -ventum, a. (in & venio,) *to find; to get; to procure; to obtain, to invent; to discover.*

Inventus, a, um, part.

Investigo, āre, āvi, ātum, a. (in & vestigo,) *to investigate; to trace* or *find out; to discover.*

Invĭcem, adv. (in & vicis,) *mutually*; *in turn*: se invĭcem occidērunt, *slew one another.*

Invictus, a, um, part. (in & vietus,) *unconquered*; *impenetrable*; *invulnerable.*

Invidia, æ, f. (invĭdus,) *envy*; *hatred.*

Invisus, a, um, adj. (in & visus,) *hated*; *hateful*; *obnoxious* : plebi, *unpopular.*

Invitātus, a, um, part. *invited*; *entertained* :—subs. *a guest.*

Invito, āre, āvi, ātum, a. *to invite.*

Invius, a, um, adj. (in & via,) *inaccessible*; *impassable*; *impenetrable.*

Invŏco, āre, āvi, ātum, a. (in & voco,) *to call upon*; *to invoke.*

Iōnes, um, m. pl. *Ionians*; *the inhabitants of Ionia.*

Ionia, æ, f. *Ionia*; *a country on the western coast of Asia Minor.*

Ionius, a, um, adj. *of Ionia*; *Ionian*: mare, *that part of the Mediterranean which lies between Greece and the south of Italy.*

Iphicrătes, is, m. *an Athenian general.*

Iphigenia, æ, f. *the daughter of Agamemnon and Clytemnestra, and priestess of Diana.*

Ipse, a, um, pro. § 135; *he himself*; *she herself*; *itself*; or simply *he*; *she*; *it*: et ipse, *he also*; before a verb of the first or second person, *I*; *thou* : ego ipse, *I myself*; tu ipse, *thou thyself*, &c.

Ira, æ, f. *anger*; *rage.*

Irascor, irasci, dep. § 174; *to be angry.*

Irātus, a, um, adj. *angry.*

Ire. *See* Eo.

Irreparabĭlis, e, adj. *irreparable*; *irrecoverable.*

Irretio, ire, īvi, ītum, a. (in & rete,) *to entangle*; *to insnare.*

Irretitus, part. *entangled*; *caught.*

Irridens, tis, part. from

Irrideo, dēre, si, sum, a. (in & rideo,) *to deride*; *to laugh at.*

Irrĭgo, āre, āvi, ātum, a. (in & rigo,) *to water*; *to bedew*; *to moisten.*

Irrīto, āre, āvi, ātum, a. *to irritate*; *to provoke*; *to incite.*

Irruens, tis, part. from

Irruo, uĕre, ui, n. (in & ruo,) *to rush*; *to rush in*, *into*, or *upon*; *to attack.*

Is, ea, id, pro. § 134; *this*; *he*; *she*; *it* : in eo esse, i. e. in eo statu, *to be in that state*; *to be upon the point.*

Issus, i, f. *a maritime city of Cilicia.*

Issĭcus, a, um, adj. *of or belonging to Issus.*

Isocrătes, is, m. *a celebrated Athenian orator.*

Iste, a, ud, pro. § 134; *that*; *that*

person or *thing*; *he*; *she*; *it.*
§ 207, R. 25.

Ister, tri, m. *the name of the Danube after it enters Illyricum.*

Isthmĭcus, a, um, adj. *Isthmian; belonging to the Isthmus of Corinth*: ludi, *games celebrated at that place.*

Isthmus, i, m. *an isthmus; a neck of land separating two seas.*

Ita, adv. *so; in such a manner; even so; thus.*

Italia, æ, f. *Italy.*

Itălus, a, um, adj. *Italian.*

Ităli, subs. *the Italians.*

Italĭcus, a, um, adj. *belonging to Italy; Italian.*

Ităque, adv. *and so; therefore.*

Iter, itinĕris, n. *a journey; a road; a march.*

Itĕrum, adv. *again; once more; a second time.*

Ithăca, æ, f. *a rocky island in the Ionian sea, with a city of the same name.*

Itŭdem, adv. *in like manner; likewise; also.*

Itûrus, a, um, part. (eo.)

Ivi. *See* Eo.

J.

ɹacens, tis, part. from

Iacĕo, ĕre, ui, n. *to lie; to be situated.*

Jacio, jacĕre, jēci, jactum, a. *to throw; to cast; to fling; to hurl.*

Jacto, āre, āvi, ātum, freq. (jacio, *to throw about; to toss; to agitate.*

Jactus, a, um, part. (jacio,) *cast; thrown.*

Jacŭlor, āri, ātus sum, dep. *to hurl; to dart; to shoot.*

Jam, adv. *now; already; presently; even.*

Jamdûdum, adv. *long ago.*

Janicŭlum, i, n. *one of the seven hills of Rome.*

Jason, ŏnis, m. *the son of Æson, king of Thessaly, and leader of the Argonauts*; also, *an inhabitant of Lycia.*

Jejûnus, a, um, adj. *fasting; hungry.*

Jovis. *See* Jupĭter.

Juba, æ, f. *the mane.*

Jubeo, jubēre, jussi, jussum, a. *to command; to bid; to order; to direct.*

Jucundus, a, um, adj. (jocus,) *sweet; agreeable; delightful; pleasant.*

Judæa, æ, f. *Judēa.*

Judæus, a, um, adj. *belonging to Judēa*:—subs. *a Jew.*

Judex, ĭcis, c. *a judge.*

Judicium, i, n. *a judgment; decision.*

Judĭco, āre, āvi, ātum, a. *to judge; to deem; to determine; to decide.*

Jugĕrum, i, n. § 93, 1; *an acre of land.*

Jugum. i, n. *a yoke; a ridge* or

chain of mountains; in war, an instrument consisting of two spears placed erect, and a third laid transversely upon them.

Jugurtha, æ, m. a king of Numidia.

Julius, i, m. a name of Cæsar, who belonged to the gens Julia.

Junctus, a, um, part. (jungo.)

Junior, adj. (comp. from juvĕnis,) younger.

Junius, i, m. the name of a Roman tribe which included the family of Brutus.

Jungo, jungĕre, junxi, junctum, a. to unite; to connect; to join: currui, to put in; to harness to.

Juno, ŏnis, f. the daughter of Saturn and wife of Jupiter.

Jupĭter, Jovis, m. § 85; the son of Saturn, and king of the gods.

Jurgiŏsus, a, um, adj. (jurgium,) quarrelsome; scolding; brawling.

Juro, ăre, ăvi, ătum, a. to swear.

Jus, juris, n. right; justice: jus civitātis, the freedom of the city; citizenship: jure, with reason; rightly; deservedly.

Jussi. See Jubeo.

Jussus, a, um, part. (jubeo.)

Jussu, abl. m. § 94; a command.

Justitia, æ, f. justice; from

Justus, a, um, adj. just; right; full; regular; ordinary; exact.

Juvenca, æ, f. a cow; a heifer.

Juvencius, i, m. a Roman general, conquered by Andriscus.

Juvĕnis, e, adj. (comp. junior, § 126, 4,) young; youthful.

Juvĕnis, is, c. a young man or woman; a youth.

Juventus, ūtis, f. youth.

Juvo, juvāre, juvi, jutum, a. to help; to assist.

Juxta, prep. near; hard by:— adv. alike; even; equally.

L.

L., an abbreviation of Lucius. § 328.

Labor, & Labos, ŏris, m. labor; toil.

Labor, labi, lapsus sum, dep. to fall; to glide; to glide away; to flow on.

Laboriŏsus, a, um, adj. (labor,) laborious.

Labŏro, ăre, ăvi, ătum, n. to work or labor; to suffer with, to be distressed.

Labyrinthus, i, m. a labyrinth.

Lac, lactis, n. milk.

Lacedæmonius, a, um, adj. belonging to Lacedæmon; Lacedæmonian; Spartan.

Lacedæmon, ŏnis, f. Lacedæmon, or Sparta, the capital of Laconia.

Lacerātus, a, um, part. from

Lacĕro, āre, āvi, ātum, a. *to tear in pieces.*

Lacessitus, a, um, part. from

Lacesso, ĕre, īvi, ītum, a. *to disturb ; to trouble ; to provoke ; to stir up.*

Lacrȳma, æ, f. *a tear.*

Lacus, ûs, m. *a lake.*

Laconĭcus, a, um, adj. *Laconic ; Spartan ; Lacedæmonian.*

Lædo, lædĕre, læsi, læsum, a. *to injure ; to hurt.*

Lætātus, a, um, part. (lœtor.)

Lætitia, æ, f. (lætus,) *joy.*

Lætor, āri, ātus sum, dep. *to rejoice ; to be glad ; to be delighted with.*

Lætus, a, um, adj. (ior, issĭmus,) *glad ; joyful ; full of joy ; fortunate ; prosperous ; fruitful ; abundant.*

Lævinus, ı, m. *the name of a Roman family ; (P. Valerıus,) a Roman consul.*

Lævor, ōrıs, ın. *smoothness.*

Lagus, ı. m. *a Macedonian, who adopted as his son that Ptolemy who afterwards became king of Egypt.*

Lana, æ, f. *wool.*

Lanātus, a, um, adj. *bearing wool ; woolly.*

Laniātus, a, um, part. from

Lanio, āre, āvi, ātum, a. *to tear in pieces.*

Lapicidina, æ, f. (lapis & cædo,) *a quarry.*

Lapideus, a, um, adj. *stony ;* from

Lapis, ĭdis, m. *a stone.*

Lapsus, a, um, part. (labor.)

Laqueus, i, m. *a noose ; a snare.*

Largitio, ōnis, f. *a present.*

Latè, adv. (iùs, issĭmè,) *widely, extensively.*

Latĕbra, æ, f. *a lurking-place ; a hiding-place ; a retreat.*

Latens, tis, part. from

Lateo, ēre, ui, n. *to be hidden ; to be concealed ; to be unknown.*

Later, ĕris, m. *a brick.*

Latercŭlus, i, m. dim. (later,) *a little brick ; a brick.*

Latinus, i, m. *an ancient king of the Laurentes, a people of Italy.*

Latinus, a, um, adj. *Latin ; of Latium :* Latini, subs. *the Latins.*

Latitūdo, ĭnis, f. (latus,) *breadth.*

Latium, i, n. *Latium.*

Latmus, i, m. *a mountain in Caria, near the borders of Ionia.*

Latòna, æ, f. *the daughter of the giant Cœus, and mother of Apollo and Diana.*

Latro, āre, āvi, ātum, n. & a. *to bark ; to bark at.*

Latro, ōnis, m. *a robber.*

Latrocinium, i, n. *robbery ; piracy.*

Latūrus, a, um, part. (fero.)

Latus, a, um, adj. (ior, issĭmus,) *broad ; wide.*

Latus, ĕris, n. *a side.*

Laudātus, a, um, part. from

Laudo, āre, āvi, ātum, a. *to praise; to extol; to commend.*

Laurentia, æ, f. *See* Acca.

Laus, dis, f. *praise; glory; honor; fame; repute; estimation; value.*

Lautè, adv. *sumptuously; magnificently.*

Lavinia, æ, f. *the daughter of Latinus, and the second wife of Æneas.*

Lavinīum, i, n. *a city in Italy, built by Æneas.*

Lavo, lavāre & lavēre, lavi, lotum, lautum, & lavātum, a. § 165; *to wash; to bathe.*

Leæna, æ, f. *a lioness.*

Leander, & Leandrus, dri, m. *a youth of Abȳdos, distinguished for his attachment to Hero.*

Lebes, ētis, m. *a kettle; a caldron.*

Lectus, a, um, part. (lego,) *read; chosen.*

Leda, æ, f. *the wife of Tyndarus, king of Sparta, and the mother of Helēna.*

Legatio, ōnis, f. (lego, āre,) *an embassy.*

Legātus,i,m.(lego, āre,) *a deputy; a lieutenant; an ambassador*

Legio, ōnis, f. (lego, ēre,) *a legion; ten cohorts of soldiers.*

Legislātor, ōris, m. (lex & fero,) *a legislator; a lawgiver.*

Lego, legēre, legi, lectum, a. *to read; to choose; to collect.*

Lemān is, i, m. *the name of a lake in Gaul, bordering upon the country of the Helvetii, now the lake of Geneva.*

Leo, ōnis, m. *a lion.*

Leonīdas, æ, m. *a brave king of Sparta, who fell in the battle of Thermopylæ.*

Leontīnus, a, um, adj. *belonging to Leontini, a city and a people of the same name, on the eastern coast of Sicily.*

Lepīdus, i, m. *the name of an illustrious family, of the Æmilian clan:* M. Lepidus, *one of the triumvirs with Augustus and Antony.*

Lepus, ōris, m. *a hare.*

Letālis, e, adj. *fatal; deadly;* from

Letum, i, n. *death.*

Levis, e, adj. (ior, issīmus,) *light; trivial; inconsiderable; smooth.*

Levītas, ātis, f. *lightness.*

Levo, āre, āvi, ātum, a. *to ease; to relieve; to lighten; to alleviate.*

Lex, gis, f. *a law; a condition.*

Libens, tis, part. (libet,) *willing.*

Libenter, adv. *willingly.*

Libet, *or* Lubet, libuit, imp. *it pleases.*

Libenter, adv. (libens,) *freely; willingly.*

Liber, libēra, libērum, adj. *free.*

Liber, libri, m. *the inner bark of a tree; a book.*

Liberalīter, adv. (liberālis,) *liberally; kindly.*

Liberātus, a, um, part. (libĕro,) *liberated; set at liberty.*

Libĕrè, adv. *freely; without restraint.*

Libĕri, ōrum, m. pl. § 96; *children.*

Libĕro, āre, āvi, ātum, a. *to free; to liberate; to deliver.*

Libertas, ātis, f. *liberty.*

Libya, æ, f. properly *Libya, a kingdom of Africa, lying west of Egypt; sometimes it comprehends the whole of Africa.*

Licinius, i, m. *a name common among the Romans.*

Licet, uit, ĭtum est, imp. § 169; *it is lawful; it is permitted; you may; one may.*

Licèt, conj. *although.*

Lienōsus, a, um, adj. *splenetic.*

Ligneus, a, um, adj. *wooden;* from

Lignum, i, n. *wood; a log of wood; timber.*

Ligo, āre, āvi, ātum, a. *to bind.*

Liguria, æ, f. *Liguria, a country in the west of Italy.*

Ligus, ŭris, m. *a Ligurian.*

Ligustĭcus, a, um, adj. *Ligurian:* mare, *the gulf of Genöa.*

Lilybæum, i, n. *a promontory on the western coast of Sicily.*

Limpĭdus, a, um, adj. (ior, issĭmus,) *transparent; limpid; clear.*

Limus, i, m. *mud; clay.*

Lingua, æ, f. *the tongue; a language.*

Linum, i, n. *flax; linen.*

Liquĭdus, a, um, adj. (ior, issĭmus,) *liquid; clear; pure; limpid.*

Lis, litis, f. *a strife; a contention; a controversy.*

Littĕra, or Litĕra, æ, f. *a letter of the alphabet:* (pl.) *letters; literature; learning; a letter; an epistle.*

Litterarius, a, um, adj. *belonging to letters; literary.*

Littus, or Litus, ōris, n. *the shore.*

Loco, āre, āvi, ātum, a. *to place, set, dispose, or arrange; to give* or *dispose of in marriage;* from

Locus, i, m. in sing.; m. & n. in pl. § 92, 2 ; *a place.*

Locusta, æ, f. *a locust.*

Longè, adv. (iùs, issĭmè,) (longus,) *far; far off.*

Longinquus, a, um, adj. (comp. ior,) *far; distant; long; foreign.*

Longitūdo, ĭnis, f. *length;* from

Longus, a, um, adj. (ior, issĭmus,) *long,* applied both to time and space; *lasting.*

Locūtus, a, um, part. (loquor,) *having spoken.*

Locutūrus, a, um, part. *about to speak;* from

Loquor, loqui, locūtus sum, dep. *to speak.*

Lorica, æ, f. *a coat of mail; corselet; breast-plate; cuirass.*

Lorum, i, n. *a thong.*

Lubens, tis, part. (lubet.)

Lubenter, adv. (ius, issïmè.) *See* Libenter.

Lubet. *See* Libet.

Lubido, *or* Libido, ïnis, f. *lust; desire.*

Lubricus, a, um, adj. *slippery.*

Luceo, lucëre, luxi, n. *to shine.*

Lucius, i, m. *a Roman* prænömen.

Lucretia, æ, f. *a Roman matron, the wife of Collatinus.*

Lucretius, i, m. *the father of Lucretia.*

Luctus, ùs, m. (lugeo,) *mourning; sorrow.*

Lucullus, i, m. *a Roman celebrated for his luxury, his patronage of learned men, and his military talents.*

Lucus, i, m. *a grove.*

Ludo, ludëre, lusi, lusum, a. *to play; to be in sport; to deceive.*

Ludus, i, m. *a game; a play; a place of exercise; a school:* gladiatorïus, *a school for gladiators.*

Lugeo, lugëre, luxi, n. *to mourn; to lament.*

Lumen, ïnis, n. (luceo,) *light; an eye.*

Luna, æ, f. *the moon.*

Lupa, æ, f. *a she-wolf.*

Lupus, i, m. *a wolf.*

Luscinia, æ, f. *a nightingale.*

Lusitania, æ, f. *a part of* Hispania, now *Portugal.*

Lustro, are, ävi, ätum, a. *to puri-fy; to appease; to expiate:* exercïtum, *to review; to muster*

Lustrum, i, n. *the lair of wild beasts; a den.*

Lusus, ùs, m. *a game; a play.* per lusum, *in sport; sportively.*

Lutatius, i, m. *the name of a Roman tribe:* C. Lutatius Catülus, *a Roman consul in the first Punic war.*

Lutetia, æ, f. *a city of Gaul,* now *Paris.*

Lutum, i, n. *clay.*

Lux, lucis, f. *light.*

Luxuria, æ, f. *luxury; excess; voluptuousness.*

Lycius, a, um, adj. *Lycian; of Lycia, a country of Asia Minor.*

Lycomëdes, is, m. *a king of Scyros.*

Lycurgus, i, m. *the Spartan lawgiver.*

Lydia, æ, f. *a country of Asia Minor.*

Lysander, dri, m. *a celebrated Lacedæmonian general.*

Lysimächus, i, m. *one of Alexander's generals, who was afterwards king of a part of Thrace.*

M.

M., *an abbreviation of* Marcus. § 328.

Macëdo, önis, m. *a Macedonian*

Macedonia, æ, f. *a country of Europe, lying west of Thrace, and north of Thessaly and Epirus.*

Macedonĭcus, a, um, adj. *of Macedonia ; Macedonian ;* also, *an agnōmen or surname of Q. Metellus.*

Macies, ĕi, f. *leanness ; decay.*

Macrobii, ōrum, m. pl. *a Greek word signifying* long-lived ; *this name was given to certain tribes of Ethiopians, who were distinguished for the simplicity and purity of their manners, and for their longevity.*

Mactātus, a, um, part. from

Macto, āre, āvi, ātum, a. *to sacrifice ; to slay.*

Macŭla, æ, f. *a spot ; a stain.*

Madeo, ēre, ui, n. *to be moist ; to be wet.*

Mænādes, um, f. pl. *priestesses of Bacchus ; bacchants ; bacchanals.*

Mæōtis, ĭdis, adj. *Mæotian :* palus Mæōtis, *a lake* or *gulf, lying north of the Euxine,* now called *the sea of Azoph.*

Magis, adv. (sup. maxĭmè, § 194,) *more ; rather ; better.*

Magister, tri, m. *a teacher ; a master :* magister equĭtum, *the commander of the cavalry, and the dictator's lieutenant.*

Magistrātus, ùs, m. *a magistracy ; a civil office ; a magistrate.*

Magnesia, æ, f. *a town of Ionia.*

Magnifĭcè, adv. (entiùs, entissĭmè,) (magnifĭcus,) *magnificently ; splendidly.*

Magnificentia, æ, f. *magnificence, splendor ; grandeur ;* from

Magnifĭcus, a, um, adj. (entior, entissĭmus,) (magnus & facio,) *magnificent ; splendid.*

Magnitūdo, ĭnis, f. (magnus,) *greatness ; magnitude ; size.*

Magnopēre, adv. (magnus & opus,) *greatly ; very ; earnestly.*

Magnus, a, um, adj. (comp. major, sup. maxĭmus,) *great ; large.*

Major, comp. (magnus,) *greater ; the elder.*

Majōres, um, m. pl. *forefathers ; ancestors.*

Male, adv. (pejùs, pessĭmè,) (malus,) *badly ; ill ; hurtfully.*

Maledĭco, -dicĕre, -dixi, -dictum, a. (malè & dico,) *to revile ; to rail at ; to abuse ; to reproach.*

Maledĭcus, a, um, adj. (entior, entissĭmus,) *reviling ; railing ; scurrilous ; abusive.*

Malefĭcus, a, um, adj. (entior, entissĭmus,) (malè & facio,) *wicked ; hurtful ; mischievous ; injurious :*—subs. *an evil-doer.*

Malo, malle, malui, irr. § 178, 3; *to prefer ; to be more willing, to wish rather.*

Malum, i, n. *an apple.*

Malum, i, n. (malus,) *evil ; misfortune ; calamity ; sufferings ; evil deeds.*

Malus, a, um, adj. (pejor, pessĭmus, § 125, 5,) *bad ; wicked :* mali, *bad men.*

Mancinus, i, m. *a Roman consul who made a disgraceful peace with the Numantians.*

Mando, mandĕre, mandi, mansum, a. *to chew ; to eat.*

Mando, āre, āvi, ātum, a. *to command ; to intrust ; to commit ; to bid ; to enjoin :* mandāre marmorĭbus, *to engrave upon marble.*

Mane, ind. n. *the morning,* § 94:— adv. *early in the morning.*

Maneo, ēre, si, sum, n. *to remain ; to continue.*

Manes, ium, m. pl. *the dead ; the manes ; ghosts or shades of the dead.*

Manlius, i, m. *a Roman proper name.*

Mano, āre, āvi, ātum, n. *to flow.*

Mansuefacio, -facĕre, -fēci, -factum, a. (mansues & facio,) *to tame ; to make tame.*

Mansuefio, -fĭĕri, -factus sum, irr. § 180, N., *to be made tame.*

Mansuefactus, a, um, part.

Mantinèa, æ, f. *a city of Arcadia.*

Manubiæ, ārum, f. pl. *booty ; spoils ; plunder.*

Manumissus, a, um, part. from

Manumitto, -mittĕre, -misi, -missum, a. (manus & mitto,) *to set free, at liberty ; to free ; to manumit.*

Manus, ūs, f. *a hand ; the trunk of an elephant ; a band or body of soldiers.*

Mapāle, is, n. *a hut or cottage of the Numidians.*

Marcellus, i, m. *the name of a Roman family which produced many illustrious men.*

Marcius, i, m. *a Roman name and* cognōmen *or surname.*

Marcus, i, m. *a Roman* prænōmen.

Mare, is, n. *the sea.*

Margarita, æ, f. *a pearl.*

Mariandȳni, ōrum, m. pl. *a people of Bithynia.*

Marinus, a, um, adj. (mare,) *marine ; pertaining to the sea ;* aqua marina, *sea-water.*

Maritĭmus, a, um, adj. *maritime ; on the sea-coast :* copiæ, *naval forces.*

Maritus, i, m. *a husband.*

Marius, i, m. (C.) *a distinguished Roman general, who was seven times elected consul.*

Marmor, ōris, n. *marble.*

Mars, tis, m. *the son of Jupiter and Juno, and god of war.*

Marsi, ōrum, m. pl. *a people of Latium, upon the borders of lake Ticinus.*

Marsȳas, æ, m. *a celebrated Phrygian musician ; also, a brother of Antigŏnus, the king of Macedonia.*

Massa, æ, f. *a mass; a lump.*

Massīcus, a, um, adj. *Massic, of Massicus, a mountain in Campania, famous for its wine:* vinum, *Massic wine.*

Massilia, æ, f. *a maritime town of* Gallia Narbonensis, now *Marseilles.*

Mater, tris, f. *a mother; a matron.*

Materia, æ, f. *a material; matter; stuff; timber.*

Matrimonium, i, n. *matrimony; marriage.*

Matrŏna, æ, f. *a matron; a married woman.*

Matrŏna, æ, f. *a river of Gaul,* now *the Marne.*

Maturesco, maturescĕre, maturui, inc. *to ripen; to grow ripe;* from

Matūrus, a, um, adj. (ior, rĭmus or issĭmus,) *ripe; mature; perfect.*

Maurıtania, æ, f. *a country in the western part of Africa, extending from Numidia to the Atlantic ocean.*

Mausŏlus, i, m. *a king of Caria.*

Maxil.a, æ, f. *a jaw; a jawbone.*

Maxĭmè, adv. (sup. of magĭs,) *most of all; especially; greatly.*

Maxĭmus, i, m. *a Roman surname:* Qu. Fabius Maxĭmus, *a distinguished Roman general.*

Maxĭmus, a, um, adj. (sup. of magnus,) *greatest   eldest:* maxĭmus natu. *See* Natu.

Mecum, (me & cum, § 133, 4,) *with me.*

Medeor, ēri, dep. § 170; *to cure; to heal.*

Medicina, æ, f. *medicine.*

Medīco, āre, āvi, ātum, a. *to heal; to administer medicine; to medicate; to prepare medically; to embalm.*

Medīcus, i, m. *a physician.*

Meditātus, a, um, part. *designed; practised;* from

Medĭtor, āri, ātus sum, dep. *to meditate; to reflect; to practise.*

Medius, a, um, adj. *middle; the midst, § 205, R. 17:* medium, *the middle.*

Mediomatrĭci, ōrum, m. pl. *a people of Belgic Gaul.*

Medūsa, æ, f. *one of the three Gorgons.*

Megăra, æ, f. *the capital of Megaris.*

Megarenses, ium, m. pl. *Megarensians; the inhabitants of Megăra.*

Megăris, ĭdis, f. *a small country of Greece.*

Megasthĕnes, is, m. *a Greek historian, whose works have been lost.*

Mehe-cŭlè, adv. *by Hercules; truly; certainly.*

Mel, lis, n. *honey.*

Meleăgrus & -ăger, gri, m. *a king of Calydonia.*

Melior, us, adj. (comp. of bonus, § 125, 5,) *better.*

Meliùs, adv. (comp. of benè,) *better.*

Membrāna, æ, f. *a thin skin; a membrane; parchment.*

Membrum, i, n. *a limb; a member.*

Memĭni, def. pret. § 183; *I remember; I relate.*

Memor, ŏris, adj. *mindful.*

Memorabĭlis, e, adj. *memorable; remarkable; worthy of being mentioned.*

Memoria, æ, f. *memory.*

Memŏro, āre, āvi, ātum, a. *to remember; to say; to mention.*

Memphis, is, f. *a large city of Egypt.*

Mendacium, i, n. *a falsehood;* from

Mendax, ăcis, adj. *false; lying.*

Menelăus, i, m. *a king of Sparta, the son of Atreus, and husband of Helen.*

Menenius, i, m. (Agrippa,) *a Roman, distinguished for his success in reconciling the plebeians to the patricians.*

Mens, tis, f. *the mind; the will; the understanding.*

Mensis, is, m. *a month.*

Mentio, ŏnis, f. (memĭni,) *mention* or *a speaking of.*

Mentt or iri, itus sum, dep. *to lie;*

to assert falsely; to feign; to deceive.

Mercător, ŏris, m. (mercor,) *a merchant; a trader.*

Mercatūra, æ, f. § 102, R. 2; *merchandise; trade.*

Mercátus, ûs, m. *a market; a mart; a fair; an emporium; a sale.*

Merces, ēdis, f. (mereo,) *wages; a reward; a price.*

Mercurius, i, m. *Mercury, the son of Jupiter and Maia. He was the messenger of the gods.*

Mereo, ēre, ui, ĭtum, n. *to deserve; to gain; to acquire.*

Mercor, ēri, ĭtus sum, dep. *to deserve; to earn.*

Mergo, mergĕre, mersi, mersum, a. *to sink; to dip under.*

Meridiānus, a, um, adj. *southern; south; at noon-day;* from

Meridies, iēi, m. (medius & dies,) *noon; mid-day; south.*

Merĭtò, adv. *with reason; with good reason; deservedly.*

Merĭtum, i, n. (mereo,) *merit; desert.*

Mersi. *See* Mergo.

Mersus, a, um, part. (mergo.)

Merŭla, æ, f. *a blackbird.*

Merx, cis, f. *merchandise.*

Messis, is, f. (meto,) *the harvest.*

Meta, æ, f. *a goal; a limit.*

Metagonium, i, n. *a promontory in the northern part of Africa.*

Metallum, i, n. *metal; a mine.*

18 *

Metanira, æ, f. *the wife of Celeus, king of Eleusis.*

Metellus, i, m. *the name of an illustrious family at Rome.*

Metior, metiri, mensus sum, dep. *to measure.*

Metius, i, m. (Suffetius,) *an Alban general, put to death by Tullus Hostilius.*

Meto, metĕre, messui, messum, a. *to reap; to mow.*

Metuo, metuĕre, metui, a. *to fear;* from

Metus, ûs, m. *fear.*

Meus, a, um, pro. § 139; (ego,) *my; mine.*

Micipsa, æ, m. *a king of Numidia.*

Mico, âre, ui, n. *to shine.*

Midas, æ, m. *a king of Phrygia, distinguished for his wealth.*

Migro, âre, âvi, âtum, n. *to remove; to migrate; to wander.*

Mihi. *See Ego.*

Miles, ĭtis, c. *a soldier; the soldiery.*

Milêtus, i, f. *the capital of Ionia, near the borders of Caria.*

Militia, æ, f. (miles,) *war; military service.*

Milĭto, âre, âvi, âtum, n. *to serve in war.*

Mille, n. ind. (in sing.) *a thousand:* millia, um, pl. mille, adj. ind. § 118, 6.

Milliarium, i, n. *a milestone; a mile* or 5000 *Roman feet:*

ad quintum millia iⅬⅰⅠ urbis, *within five miles of the city.*

Miltiădes, is, m. *a celebrated Athenian general, who conquered the Persians.*

Milvius, i, m. *a kite.*

Minæ, ârum, f. pl. § 96; *threats.*

Minâtus, a, um, part. (minor.)

Minerva, æ, f. *the daughter of Jupiter, and goddess of war and wisdom.*

Minĭmè, adv. (sup. of parum,) *least; at least; not at all.*

Minĭmus, a, um, adj. (sup. of parvus,) *the least; the smallest.*

Ministerium, i, n. (minister,) *service; labor.*

Minium, i, n. *red lead; vermilion.*

Minor, âri, âtus sum, dep. *to threaten; to menace.*

Minor, ôris, adj. (comp. of parvus,) *less; smaller; weaker.*

Minos, ôis, m. *a son of Europa, and king of Crete.*

Minuo, minuĕre, minui, minûtum, a. *to diminish.*

Minùs, adv. (minor,) (comp. of parum,) *less:* quò minùs *or* quomĭnus, *that—not.*

Miracŭlum, i, n. (miror,) *a miracle; a wonder.*

Mirabĭlis, e, adj. *wonderful; astonishing.*

Mirâtus, a, um, part. (miror,) *wondering at.*

Mirè, adv. (mirus,) *wonderfully*; *remarkably*.

Miror, âri, âtus sum, dep. *to wonder at; to admire;* from

Mirus, a, um, adj. *wonderful; surprising*.

Misceo, miscêre, miscui, mistum or mixtum, a. *to mingle; to mix*.

Miser, êra, êrum, adj. *miserable; unhappy; wretched; sad*.

Miserâtus, a, um, part. (misêror.)

Misereor, miserêri, miserîtus *or* misertus sum, dep. *to have compassion; to pity*.

Misêret, miseruit, miserîtum est, imp. *it pitieth:* me misêret, *I pity*.

Misericordia, æ, f. (misericors,) *pity; compassion*.

Misêror, âri, âtus sum, dep. *to pity*.

Misi. *See* Mitto.

Mistus, & Mixtus, a, um, part. (misceo.)

Mithridâtes, is, m. *a celebrated king of Pontus*.

Mithridatïcus, a, um, adj. *belonging to Mithridates; Mithridatic*.

Mitis, e, adj. (ior, issïmus,) *mild; meek; kind; humane*.

Mitto, mittêre, misi, missum, a. *to send; to throw; to bring forth; to produce; to afford:* mittêre se in aquam, *to plunge into the water*.

Mixtus. *See* Mistus.

Modïcus, a, um, adj. *moderate; of moderate size; small*.

Modius, i, m. *a measure; a half-bushel*.

Modò, adv. *now; only; but:* modò — modò, *sometimes — sometimes:*—conj. (*for* si modò or dumïnôdo,) *provided that; if only*.

Modus, i, m. *a measure; a manner; a way; degree; limit; moderation*.

Mœnia, ųm, n. pl. *the walls of a city*.

Mœnus, i, m. *the Maine, a river of Germany, and a branch of the Rhine*.

Mœrens, tis, part. from

Mœreo, mœrêre, neut. pass. *to be sad; to mourn*.

Mœris, is, m. *a lake in Egypt*.

Moles, is, f. *a mass; a bulk; a burden; a weight; a pile*.

Molestus, a, um, adj. (ior, issï-mus,) *irksome; severe; troublesome; oppressive; unwelcome*.

Mollio, îre, îvi, îtum, a. *to soften, to moderate;* from

Mollis, e, adj. (ior, issïmus,) *soft; tender*.

Molossi, ôrum, m. pl. *the Molossians, a people of Epirus*.

Momordi. *See* Mordeo.

Monens, tis, part. from

Moneo, êre, ui, îtum, a. *to advise; to remind; to warn; to admonish*.

Monimentum *or* -umentum, i, n. § 102, 4; *a monument; a memorial; a record.*

Mons, tis, m. *a mountain; a mount.*

Monstro, äre, ävi, ätum, a. *to show; to point out.*

Mora, æ, f. *delay.*

Morbus, i, m. *a disease.*

Mordax, ācis, adj. *biting; sharp; snappish;* from

Mordeo, mordēre, momordi, morsum, a. *to bite.*

Mores. *See Mos.*

Moriens, tis, part. from

Morior, mori & moriri, mortuus sum, dep. § 174; *to die.*

Moror, äri, ätus sum, dep. *to delay; to tarry; to stay; to remain:* nihil moror, *I care not for; I value not.*

Morösus, a, um, adj. *morose; peevish; fretful; cross.*

Mors, tis, f. *death.*

Morsus, ûs, m. *a bite; biting.*

Mortälis, e, adj. *mortal.*

Mortuus, a, um, part. (morior,) *dead.*

Mos, moris, m. *a custom:* more, *after the manner of; like:* mores, *conduct; deportment; manners; customs.*

Mossȳni, örum, m. pl. *a people of Asia Minor, near the Euxine.*

Motus, ûs, m. *motion:* terræ motus, *an earthquake.*

Motus, a, um, part. from

Moveo, movēre, movi motum, a *to move; to stir; to excite.*

Mox, adv. *soon; soon after; by and by.*

Mucius, i, m. (Scævöla,) *a Roman, celebrated for his fortitude.*

Muliěbris, e, adj *womanly; female;* from

Mulier, ēris, f. *a woman.*

Multitūdo, īnis, f. (multus,) *a multitude.*

Multo *or* -cto, äre, ävi, ätum, a. *to punish; to fine; to impose a fine; to sentence to pay a fine.*

Multò, & Multùm, adv. *much; by far.*

Multus, a, um, adj. *much; many.*

Mummius, i, m. *a Roman general.*

Mundus, i, m. *the world; the universe.*

Muniendus, a, um, part. from

Munio, ire, īvi, ītum, a. *to fortify:* viam, *to open or prepare a road.*

Munus, ěris, n. *an office; a gift; a present; a favor; a reward.*

Murälis, e, adj. *pertaining to a wall:* corōna, *the mural crown, given to him who first mounted the wall of a besieged town;* from

Murus, i, m. *a wall; a wall of a town.*

Mus, muris, m. *a mouse.*

Musa, æ, f. *a muse; a song.*

Musca, æ, f. *a fly.*

Muscŭlus, i, m. dim. (mus, § 100, 3,) *a little mouse.*

Musĭce, es, & Musĭca, æ, f. (musa,) *music; the art of music.*

Musĭcus, a, um, adj. *musical.*

Muto, âre, âvi, âtum, a. *to change; to transform.*

Mygdonia, æ, f. *a small country of Phrygia.*

Myrmecĭdes, is, m. *an ingenious artist of Milêtus.*

Myndius, i, m. *a Myndian; an inhabitant of Myndus.*

Myndus, i, f. *a city in Caria, near Halicarnassus.*

Mysia, æ, f. *a country of Asia Minor, having the Propontis on the north, and the Ægean sea on the west.*

N.

Nabis, ĭdis, m. *a tyrant of Lacedæmon.*

Næ, adv. *verily; truly.*

Nactus, a, um, part. (nanciscor,) *having found.*

Nam, conj. § 198, 7; *for; but.*

Nanciscor, nancisci, nactus sum, dep. *to get; to find; to meet with.*

Narbonensis, e, adj. Narbonensis Gallia, *one of the four divisions of Gaul, in the southeastern part, deriving its name* *from the city of Narbo, now Narbonne.*

Naris, is, f. *the nostril.*

Narro, âre, âvi, âtum, a. *to relate; to tell; to say.*

Nascor, nasci, natus sum, dep. *to be born; to grow; to be produced.*

Nasica, æ, m. *a surname of Publius Cornelius Scipio.*

Nasus, i, m. *a nose.*

Natâlis, e, adj. *natal:* dies natâlis, *a birth-day.*

Natans, tis, part. from

Nato, âre, âvi, âtum, freq. (no,) *to swim; to float.*

Natu, abl. sing. m. *by birth:* natu minor, *the younger:* minĭmus, *the youngest:* major, *the elder:* maxĭmus, *the oldest.* § 126, 4, R. 1.

Natûra, æ, f. (nascor,) *nature; creation; power.*

Naturâlis, e, adj. *natural.*

Natus, a, um, part. (nascor,) *born:* octoginta annos natus *eighty years old.*

Natus, i, m. *a son.*

Naufragium, i, n. *a shipwreck.*

Nauta, æ, m. *a sailor.*

Navâlis, e, adj. (navis,) *naval; belonging to ships.*

Navigabĭlis, e, adj. *navigable.*

Navigatio, ônis, f. (navigo,) *navigation.*

Navigium, i, n. *a ship; a vessel.*

Navigo, âre, âvi, âtum, a. (navis & ago,) *to navigate; to sail:*

navigātur, imp. *navigation is carried on ; they sail.*

Navis, is, f. *a ship.*

Ne, conj. *not — lest ; lest that ; that — not :* ne quidem, *not even.* § 279, 3.

Ne, conj. enclitic : in *direct* questions, it is often omitted in the translation ; in *indirect* questions, *whether :* in a second question, or. § 265, R. 2.

Nec, conj. (ne & que,) *and not ; but not ; neither ; nor.*

Necessarius,a,um, adj.(necesse,) *necessary :*—subs. *a friend.*

Necessitas, ātis, f. *necessity ; duty.*

Neco, āre, āvi *or* ūi, ātum, a. *to kill ; to destroy ; to slay.*

Nefas, n. ind. (ne & fas,) *impiety ; wrong.*

Neglectus, a, um, part. from

Negligo, -ligĕre, -lexi, -lectum, a. (nec & lego,) *to neglect ; not to care for ; to disregard.*

Nego, āre, āvi, ātum, a. *to deny ; to refuse ; to declare that not.*

Negotium, i, n. (ne & otium,) *business ; labor ; pains ; difficulty :* facīli *or* nullo negotio, *easily.*

Nemo, ĭnis, c. (ne & homo,) *no one ; no man.*

Nemus, ōris, n. *a forest ; a grove.*

Nepos, ōtis, m. *a grandson.*

Neptūnus, i, m. *Neptune, a son of Saturn and Ops, and the god of the sea.*

Nequāquam, adv. *by no means.*

Neque, conj. (ne & que,) *neither ; nor ; and — not.*

Nequeo, ire, ivi, itum, irr. n. (ne & queo, § 182, 3,) *I cannot ; I am not able.*

Nequis, -qua, -quod *or* -quid, pro. § 138 ; *lest any one ; that no one* or *no thing.*

Nereis, ĭdis, f. *a Nereid ; a sea-nymph. The Nereids were the daughters of Nereus and Doris.*

Nescio, ire, ivi, itum, n. (ne & scio,) *to be ignorant of ; not to know ; can not.*

Nestus, i, m. *a river in the western part of Thrace.*

Neuter, tra, trum, adj. (ne & uter, § 107,) *neither of the two ; neither.*

Nicomēdes, is, m. *a king of Bithynia.*

Nidifīco, āre, āvi, ātum, a. (nidus & facio,) *to build a nest.*

Nidus, i, m. *a nest.*

Niger, gra, grum, adj. *black.*

Nihil, n. ind., *or* Nihĭlum, i, n. (ne & hilum,) *nothing :* nihil habeo quod, *I have no reason why.*

Nihilomĭnŭs, adv. *nevertheless.*

Nilus, i, m. *the Nile ; the largest river of Africa.*

Nimius, a, um, adj. *too great ; excessive ; immoderate.*

Nimiŭm, & Nimiŏ, adv. *too much.*

Ninus, i, m. *a king of Assyria.*

Niŏbe, es, f. *the wife of Amphion, king of Thebes.*

Nisi, adv. (ne & si,) *unless; except; if not.*

Nisus, i, m. *a king of Megāris, and the father of Sylla.*

Nitĭdus, a, um, adj. (niteo,) *shining; bright; clear.*

Nitor, ōris, m..(niteo,) *splendor; gloss; brilliancy.*

Nitor, niti, nisus & nixus sum, dep. *to strive.*

Nix, nivis, f. *snow.*

No, nare, navi, natum, n. *to swim.*

Nobĭlis, e, adj. (ior, issĭmus,) *noble; celebrated; famous; of high rank.*

Nobilĭtas, ātis, f. *nobility; the nobility; the nobles; a noble spirit; nobleness.*

Nobilĭto, āre, āvi, ātum, a. *to ennoble; to make famous.*

Noceo, ēre, ui, ĭtum, a. *to hurt; to injure; to harm.*

Noctu, abl. sing. *by night; in the night time.* § 94.

Nocturnus, a, um, adj. *nightly; nocturnal.*

Nodus, i, m. *a knot; a tumor.*

Nola, æ, f. *a city of Campania.*

Nolo, nolle, nolui, irr. n. (non & volo, § 178, 2,) *to be unwilling:* the imperative of nolo, with an infinitive, is translated by *not,* and the infinitive, by an imperative; as, esse noli, *be not.*

Nomădes, um, m. pl. *a name given to those tribes who wander from place to place, with their flocks and herds, having no fixed residence.*

Nomen, ĭnis, n. *a name.*

Non, adv. *not.*

Nonagesĭmus, a, um, num. adj. *the ninetieth.*

Nonne, adv. (instead of num non,) *not?* (in a question.)

Nonnĭhil, n. ind. *something.*

Nonnĭsi, adv. *only; not; except.*

Nonnullus, a, um, adj. *some.*

Nonus, a, um, num. adj. *the ninth.*

Nos. See Ego.

Nosco, noscĕre, novi, notum, a. § 183, 3, N.; *to know; to understand; to learn.*

Noster, tra, trum, pro. *our.* § 139.

Nota, æ, f. *a mark.*

Notans, tis, part. from

Noto, āre, āvi, ātum, a. *to mark; to observe; to stigmatize.*

Notus, a, um, part. (from nosco,) *known.*

Novem, ind. num. adj. pl. *nine.*

Novus, a, um, adj. (comp. not used; sup. issĭmus,) *new; recent; fresh.*

Nox, noctis, f. *night:* de nocte, *by night.*

Noxius, a, um, adj. *hurtful; injurious.*

Nubes, is, f. *a cloud.*

Nubo, nubĕre, nupsi & nupta

sum, nuptum, n. *to cover;
to veil; to marry; to be married;* (used only of the wife.)

Nudátus, a, um, part. *laid open;
stripped; deprived;* from

Nudo, áre, ávi, átum, a. *to make
naked; to lay open;* from

Nudus, a, um, adj. *naked; bare.*

Nullus, a, um, gen. ĭus, § 107,
adj. (non ullus,) *no; no one.*

Num, adv.: in translating *direct*
questions, it is commonly
omitted; in *indirect* questions,
it signifies *whether.*

Numa, æ, m. (Pompilius,) *the
second king of Rome, and the
successor of Romulus.*

Numantia, æ, f. *a city of Spain,
which was besieged by the Romans for twenty years.*

Numantini, ōrum, m. pl. *Nu-
mantines; the people of Numantia.*

Numen, ĭnis, n. (nuo,) *a deity; a
god.*

Numĕro, áre, ávi, átum, a. *to
count; to number; to reckon;*
from

Numĕrus, i, m. *a number.*

Numĭdæ, árum, m. pl. *the Numidians.*

Numidia, æ, f. *a country of Africa.*

Numītor, ōris, m. *the father of
Rhea Silvia, and grandfather
of Romulus and Remus.*

Nummus, i, m. *money.*

Nunc, adv. *now:* nunc etiam,
even now; still.

Nuncŭpo, áre, ávi, átum, a. *to
name.*

Nunquam, (ne & unquam,) adv.
never.

Nuntiátus, a, um, part. from

Nuntio *or* -cio, áre, ávi, átum, a.
(nuntius,) *to announce; to tell.*

Nuptiæ, árum, f. pl. *nuptials;
marriage; a wedding.*

Nusquam, adv. (ne & usquam,)
nowhere; in no place.

Nutriendus, a, um, part. *to b
nourished.*

Nutrio, íre, ívi, ítum, a. *to nour
ish.*

Nutrītus, a, um, part.

Nutrix, ícis, f. *a nurse.*

Nympha, æ, f. *a nymph; a god
dess presiding over fountains
groves,* or *rivers,* &c

O.

O! int. *O! ah!*

Ob, prep. *for; on account of;
before.*

Obdormisco, -dormiscĕre, -dor-
mivi, inc. (ob & dormisco,) *to
fall asleep; to sleep.*

Obdūco, -ducĕre, -duxi, -duc-
tum, a. (ob & duco,) *to draw
over; to cover over.*

Obductus, a, um, part. *spread
over; covered over.*

Obedio, íre, ívi, ítum, n. (ob &
audio,) *to obey; to comply
with; to be subject to.*

Obeo, íre, ívi & ii, ítum, irr. n.

& a. (ob & eo,) *to go to; to discharge; to execute; to die.*

Overro, āre, āvi, ātum, n. (ob & erro,) *to wander; to wander about.*

Obītus, ūs, m. (obeo,) *death.*

Objaceo, ére, ui, ītum, n. (ob & jaceo,) *to lie against or before; to be opposite.*

Objectus, a, um, part. *thrown to,* or *in the way; exposed.*

Objicio, -jicĕre, -jĕci, -jectum, a. (ob & jacio,) *to throw before; to throw to; to give; to object; to expose.*

Oblīgo, āre, āvi, ātum, a. (ob & ligo,) *to bind; to oblige; to obligate.*

Obliquè, adv. *indirectly; obliquely;* from

Obliquus, a, um, adj. *oblique; indirect; sidewise.*

Oblitus, a, um, part. *forgetting; having forgotten.*

Obliviscor, oblivisci, oblītus sum, dep. *to forget.*

Obnoxius, a, um, adj. *obnoxious; subject; exposed to; liable.*

Obruo, -ruĕre, -rui, -rūtum, a. (ob & ruo,) *to overwhelm; to cover; to bury.*

Obrūtus, a, um, part. *buried; covered; overwhelmed.*

Obscūro, āre, āvi, ātum, a. (obscūrus,) *to obscure; to darken.*

Obsĕcro, āre, āvi, ātum, a. (ob & sacro,) *to beseech; to conjure.*

19

Obsĕquor, -sĕqui, -secūtus sum, dep. (ob & sequor,) *to follow; to serve.*

Observo, āre, āvi, ātum, a. (ob & servo,) *to observe; to watch.*

Obses, ĭdis, c. (obsideo,) *a hostage.*

Obsessus, a, um, part. *besieged;* from

Obsideo, -sidēre, -sēdi, -sessum, a. (ob & sedeo,) *to besiege; to invest; to blockade.*

Obsidio, ōnis, f. *a siege.*

Obsidionâlis, e, adj. *belonging to a siege; obsidional:* corōna, *a crown given to him who had raised a siege.*

Obstĕtrix, īcis, f. *a midwife.*

Obtestâtus, a, um, part. from

Obtestor, āri, ātus sum, dep. (ob & testor,) *to conjure; to beseech; to entreat.*

Obtineo, -tinēre, -tinui, -tentum, a. (ob & teneo,) *to hold; to retain; to obtain:* obtīnet sententia, *the opinion prevails.*

Obtūlit. *See* Offĕro.

Obviàm, adv. *in the way; meeting; to meet:* fio or eo obviàm, *I meet; I go to meet.*

Occasio, ōnis, f. *an occasion; a good opportunity.*

Occāsus, ūs, m. *the setting of the heavenly bodies; the descent; evening; the west.*

Occīdens, tis, m. *the west; the setting sun; evening.*

Occidentàlis, e, adj. *western ; occidental.*

Occido, occidĕre, occīdi, occisum, a. (ob & cædo,) *to kill ; to slay ; to put to death.*

Occĭdo, occidĕre, occĭdi, occâsum, n. (ob & cado,) *to fall ; to fall down ; to set.*

Occisûrus, a, um, part. (occido.)

Occisus, a, um, part. (occido.)

Occœcâtus, a, um. part. from

Occœco, âre, âvi, âtum, a. *to blind ; to dazzle.*

Occulto, âre, âvi, âtum, freq. (occŭlo,) *to conceal ; to hide.*

Occultor, âri, âtus sum, pass. *to be concealed ; to hide one's self.*

Occŭpo, âre, âvi, âtum a. *to occupy ; to seize upon ; to take possession of.*

Occurro, -currĕre, -curri & -cucurri, -cursum, n. (ob & curro,) *to meet ; to go to meet ; to encounter.*

Oceänus, i, m. *the ocean ; the sea.*

Octaviânus, i, m. (Cæsar,) *the nephew and adopted son of Julius Cæsar, called, after the battle at Actium, Augustus.*

Octâvus, a, um, num. adj. (octo,) *eighth.*

Octingenti, æ, a, num. adj. pl. *eight hundred.*

Octo, ind. num. adj. pl. *eight.*

Octoginta, ind. num. adj. pl. *eighty.*

Ocŭlus, i, m. *an eye.*

Odi, odisse, def. pret. § 183, 1 *to hate ; to detest.*

Odium, i, n. *hatred.*

Odor, ôris, m. *a smell :* pl. odôres, *odors ; perfumes.*

Odôror, âri, âtus sum, dep. *to smell.*

Œneus, ei & eos, m. *a king of Calÿdon, and father of Meleâger and Dejanira.*

Œnomâus, i, m. § 9; *the name of a celebrated gladiator.*

Œta, æ, m. *a mountain in Thessaly, on the borders of Doris.*

Offĕro, offerre, obtûli, oblâtum, irr. a. (ob & fero, § 196, 9,) *to offer ; to present.*

Officina, æ, f. *a work-shop ; an office.*

Officio, -ficĕre, -fēci, -fectum, a. (ob & facio,) *to stand in the way of ; to injure ; to hurt.*

Officium, i, n. *duty ; a kindness ; an obligation ; politeness ; civility ; attention.*

Olea, æ, f. *an olive-tree.*

Oleum, i, n. *oil.*

Olim, adv. *formerly ; sometime.*

Olor, ôris, m. *a swan.*

Olus, ĕris, n. *herbs ; potherbs.*

Olympia, æ, f. *a town and district of the Peloponnêsus, upon the Alpheus.*

Olympĭcus, a, um, adj. *Olympic; pertaining to Olympia.*

Olympius, a, um, adj. *Olympian;*

pertaining to Olympus *or to* Olympia.

Olympus, i, m. *a high mountain between Thessaly and Macedon.*

Omen, inis, n. *an omen; a sign.*

Omnis, e. adj. *all; every; every one:* omnes, *all:* omnia, *all things:* with sine, it may signify *any;* as, sine omni discordiâ, *without any discord.*

Onus, ĕris, n. *a burden; a load.*

Onustus, a, um, adj. *laden; full of.*

Opĕra, æ, f. *labor; pains:* dare opĕram alicui, *to attend to a thing; to devote one's self to it.*

Opĕror, āri, ātus sum, dep. *to labor; to work.*

Opīmus, a, um, adj. (comp. ior,) *rich; fruitful; fat; dainty.*

Oportet, ēre, uit, imp. *it behoves; it is meet, fit, or proper; it is a duty; we ought.*

Oppĭdum, i, n. *a walled town; a town.*

Oppōno, -ponĕre, -posui, -posĭtum, a. (ob & pono,) *to oppose; to set against.*

Opportūnus, a, um, adj. (ior, issĭmus,) *seasonable; commodious; convenient; favorable.*

Opposĭtus, a, um, part. *opposed; opposite.*

Opprĭmo, -primĕre, pressi, -pressum, a. (ob & premo,) *to op-*

press; to overpowe; to subdue.

Oppugnātus, a, um, part. from

Oppugno, āre, āvi, ātum, a. (ob & pugno,) *to assault; to besiege; to attempt to take by force; to storm.*

(Ops, nom., not in use, § 94,) opis, gen. f. *aid; help; means; assistance:* opes, pl. *wealth; riches; resources; power.*

Optĭmè, adv. (sup. of benè,) *very well; excellently; best.*

Optĭmus, a, um, adj. (sup. of bonus,) *best; most worthy.*

Optio, ōnis, f. *a choice; an option;* from

Opto, āre, āvi, ātum, a. *to desire.*

Opŭlens, & Opŭlentus, a, um, adj. (ior, issīmus,) *rich; opulent; wealthy.*

Opus, ĕris, n. *a work; a labor; a task.*

Ora, æ, f. *a coast; a shore.*

Ora, pl. *See* Os.

Oracŭlum, i, n. (oro,) *an oracle; a response.*

Orans, tis, part. (oro.)

Oratio, ōnis, f. (oro,) *a discourse; an oration.*

Orātor, ōris, m. (oro,) *an orator; an ambassador.*

Orbātus, a, um, part. (orbo,) *bereaved or deprived of.*

Orbēlus, i, m. *a mountain of Thrace or Macedonia.*

Orbis, is, m. *an orb; a circle:* in

orbem jacĕre, *to lie round in a circle :* orbis, or orbis terrā-rum, *the world.*

Orbo, āre, āvi, ātum, a. *to deprive ; to bereave of.*

Orcus, i, m. *Pluto, the god of the lower world ; the infernal regions.*

Ordīno, āre, āvi, ātum, a. *to order ; to ordain ; to arrange.*

Ordo, ĭnis, m. *order ; arrangement ; a row :* ordĭnes remō-rum, *banks of oars.*

Oriens, tis, m. (orior,) *the east ; the morning.*

Oriens, part. (orior.)

Orientalis, e, adj. *eastern.*

Origo, ĭnis, f. *source ; origin :* originem ducĕre, *to derive one's origin ;* from

Orior, oriri, ortus sum, dep. § 177 ; *to arise ; to begin ; to appear.*

Ornamentum, i, n. (orno,) *an ornament.*

Ornātus, ūs, m. *an ornament ;* from

Orno, āre, āvi, ātum, a. *to adorn ; to deck.*

Oro, āre, āvi, ātum, a. *to beg ; to entreat.*

Orōdes, is, m. *a king of Parthia, who took and destroyed Crassus.*

Orpheus, eï & eos, m. *a celebrated poet and musician of Thrace.*

Ortus, a, um, part. (orior,) *having arisen ; risen ; born ; begun.*

Ortus, ūs, m. *a rising ; east.*

Os, oris, n. *the mouth ; the face.*

Os, ossis, n. *a bone.*

Ossa, æ, m. *a high mountain in Thessaly.*

Ostendo, -tendĕre, -tendi, -tensum & tentum, a. (ob & tendo,) *to show ; to point out ; to exhibit.*

Ostia, æ, f. *a town, built by Ancus Marcius, at the mouth of the Tiber ;* from

Ostium, i, n. *a mouth of a river.*

Ostrea, æ, f. pl. ostrea, ōrum, n *an oyster.*

Otium, i, n. *leisure ; quiet ; ease ; idleness.*

Otos, i, m. *a son of Neptune, or of Aloeus.*

Ovis, is, f. *a sheep.*

Ovum, i, n. *an egg.*

P.

P., *an abbreviation of* Publius.

Pabūlum, i, n. (pasco,) *food ; fodder.*

Paciscor, pacisci, pactus sum, dep. *to make a compact ; to form a treaty ; to bargain ; to agree.*

Pactōlus, i, m. *a river of Lydia, famous for its golden sands.*

Pactum, i, n. (paciscor,) *an agreement ; a contract :* quæ pacto, *in what manner how.*

Pactus, a, um, part. (paciscor.)

Padus, i, m. *the largest river of Italy,* now *the Po.*

Pæne, or Pene, adv. *almost; nearly.*

Palea, æ, f. *chaff.*

Palma, æ, f. *the palm of the hand; a palm-tree.*

Palpĕbra, æ, f. *the eyelid :* pl. *the eyelashes.*

Palus, ŭdis, f. *a marsh ; a swamp; a lake.*

Paluster, palustris, palustre, adj. *marshy.*

Pan, Panis, m. *the god of shepherds.*

Pando, pandĕre, pansum & passum, a. *to open, to expand; to spread out*

Panionium, i, n. *a sacred place near mount Mycale in Ionia.*

Panis, is, m. *bread.*

Panthera, æ, f. *a panther.*

Papirius, i, m. *the name of several Romans.*

Papȳrus, d. g. & Papȳrum, i, n. *an Egyptian plant or reed, of which paper was made; the papyrus.*

Parátus, a, um, part. & adj. (ior, issimus,) (paro,) *prepared; ready.*

Parcæ, árum, f. pl. *the Fates.*

Parco, parcĕre, peperci *or* parsi, *to spare.*

Pardus, i, m. *a male panther ; a pard.*

Parens, tis, c. (pario,) *a parent; father ; mother creator ; author ; inventor.*

Pareo, ēre, ui, n. *to obey; to be subject to.*

Paries, ĕtis, m. *a wall.*

Pario, parĕre, pepĕri, partum, a. *to bear ; to bring forth ; to cause ; to produce ; to obtain ; to gain :* ovum, *to lay an egg.*

Paris, ĭdis *or* ĭdos, m. *a son of Priam, king of Troy, and the brother of Hector.*

Pariter, adv. *in like manner equally ; at the same time.*

Parnassus, i, m. *a mountain of Phocis, whose two summits were sacred to Apollo and Bacchus, and upon which the Muses were fabled to reside.*

Paro, āre, āvi, ātum, a. *to prepare ; to provide ; to procure ; to obtain ; to equip :* parāre insidias, *to lay plots against.*

Paropamisus, i, m. *a ridge of mountains in the north of India.*

Pars, tis, f. *a part ; a share ; a portion ; a region ; a party :* magnam partem, *for the most part :* in utrâque parte, *on each side :* magnâ ex parte, *in a great measure ; for the most part.*

Parsimonia, æ, f. (pasco,) *frugality.*

Parthus, i, m. *an inhabitant of Parthia ; a Parthian.*

Particŭla, æ, f. dim. (pars,) *a particle; a small part.*

Partiendus, a, um, part. (partior.)

Partim, adv. (pars,) *partly; in part.*

Partior, iri, itus sum, dep. (pars,) *to divide; to share.*

Partus, a, um, part. (pario.)

Partus, ûs, m. *a birth; offspring.*

Parum, adv. (minùs, minĭmè, § 194,) *little; too little.*

Parvŭlus, a, um, dim. adj. *small; very small;* from

Parvus, a, um, adj. (minor, minĭmus, § 125, 5,) *small or little; less; the least.*

Pasco, pascĕre, pavi, pastum, a. *to feed.*

Pascor, pasci, pastus sum, dep. *to feed; to graze; to feed upon.*

Passer, ĕris, m. *a sparrow.*

Passim, adv. *here and there; every where; in every direction.*

Passŭrus, a, um, part. (patior.)

Passus, a, um, part. (patior,) *having suffered.*

Passus, a, um, part. (pando,) *stretched out; hung up; dried:* uva passa, *a raisin.*

Passus, ûs, m. *a pace; a measure of 5 feet:* mille passuum, *a mile or 5000 feet.*

Pastor ôris, m. (pasco,) *a shepherd.*

Patefacio, facĕre, fēci, factum, a. (pateo & facio,) *to open;*

to disclose; to discover; to detect.

Patefīo, fiĕri, factus sum, irr. § 180, N.; *to be laid open or discovered.*

Patefactus, a, um, part. *opened, discovered.*

Patens, tis, part. & adj. *lying open; open; clear;* from

Pateo, ēre, ui, n. *to be open; to stand open; to extend.*

Pater, tris, m. *a father:* patres, *fathers; senators:* paterfamilias, patrisfamilias, § 91; *the master of a family; a housekeeper.*

Paternus, a, um, adj. *paternal.*

Patientia, æ, f. *patience; hardiness;* from

Patior, pati, passus sum, dep. *to suffer; to endure; to let; to allow.*

Patria, æ, f. (patrius,) *one's native country; one's birthplace.*

Patrimonium, i, n. (pater,) *patrimony; inheritance.*

Patrocinium, i, n. *patronage;* from

Patrŏnus, i, m. (pater,) *a patron; protector.*

Patruēlis, is, c. *a cousin (by the father's side.)*

Pauci, æ, a, adj. pl. *few; a few.*

Paulātim, adv. *gradually; little by little.*

Paulò, or Paullò, adv. *a little.*

Paulŭlùm, adv. *a little.*

Paullus, or Paulus, i, m. *a cog*

nōmen *or surname in the Æmilian tribe.*

Pauper, ĕris, adj. (ior, rĭmus,) *poor.*

Pauperies, ĕi, f. *poverty.*

Paupertas, ātis, f. *poverty; indigence.*

Paveo, pavēre, pavi, n. *to fear; to be afraid.*

Pavo, ōnis, c. *a peacock.*

Pax, pacis, f. *peace.*

Pecco, āre, āvi, ātum, n. *to sin; to commit a fault.*

Pecto, pectĕre, pexi & pexuī, pexum, a. *to comb; to dress.*

Pectus, ŏris, n. *the breast.*

Pecunia, æ, f. *money; a sum of money.*

Pecus, ŭdis, f. *a sheep; a beast.*

Pecus, ŏris, n. *cattle; a herd; a flock.*

Pedes, ĭtis, c. (pes,) *one on foot; a foot-soldier.*

Pelăgus, i, n. *the sea.*

Peleus, i, m. *a king of Thessaly, the son of Æacus, and father of Achilles.*

Pelias, æ, m. *a king of Thessaly, and son of Neptune.*

Peligni, ōrum, m. pl. *a people of Italy, whose country lay between the Aternus and the Sagrus.*

Pelion, i, n. *a lofty mountain in Thessaly.*

Pellicio, -licĕre, -lexi, -lectum, a. (per & lacio,) *to allure; to entice to invite.*

Pellis, is, f. *the skin.*

Pello, pellĕre, pepŭli, pulsum, a. *to drive away; to banish; to expel; to dispossess; to beat.*

Peloponnēsus, i, f. *a peninsula of Greece, now called the Morea.*

Pelusium, i, n. *a town of Egypt*

Pendens, tis, part. *hanging; impending.*

Pendeo, pendēre, pependi, pensum, n. *to hang.*

Pene, adv. *almost.*

Penetrāle, is, n. *the inner part of a house.*

Penĕtro, āre, āvi, ātum, (penītus,) a. *to penetrate; to enter.*

Penēus, i, m. *the principal river of Thessaly, flowing between Ossa and Olympus.*

Peninsŭla, æ, f. (pene & insŭla,) *a peninsula.*

Penna, æ, f. *a feather; a quill, a wing.*

Pensĭlis, e, adj. (pendeo,) *hanging; pendent.*

Penuria, æ, f. *want; scarcity.*

Peperci. *See Parco.*

Pepŭli. *See Pello.*

Pepĕri. *See Pario.*

Per, prep. *by; through; for, during; along.*

Pera, æ, f. *a wallet; a bag.*

Perăgro, āre, āvi, ātum, n. (per & ager,) *to travel through, to go through or over.*

Percontor & -cunctor, āri, ātus sum, dep. *to ask; to inquire.*

Percunctātus, a, um, part. (per-cunctor.)

l'ercussor, ŏris, m. *a murderer; an assassin; one who wounds;* from

Percutio,-cutĕre, cussi,-cussum, a. (per & quatio,) *to strike; to wound :* secŭri, *to behead.*

Perdītè, adv. *very; vehemently; exceedingly; desperately;* from

Perdītus, a, um, part. & adj. (perdo,) *ruined; lost; undone; desperate.*

Perdix, icis, f. *a partridge.*

Perdo, -dĕre, -dĭdi, -ditum, a. (per & do,) *to ruin; to lose; to destroy.*

Perdūco, -ducĕre, -duxi, -ductum, a. (per & duco,) *to lead to.*

Perductus, a, um, part. *brought; led; conducted.*

Perigrinatio, ōnis, f. *foreign travel; a residence in a foreign country.*

Peregrinus, a, um, adj. *foreign.*

Perennis, e, adj. (per & annus,) *continual; lasting; unceasing; everlasting; perennial.*

Pereo, -ire, -ii, -ĭtum, irr. n. *to perish; to be slain; to be lost.*

Perfidia, æ, f. *perfidy;* from

Perfĭdus, a, um, adj. (per & fides,) *perfidious.*

Pergămum, i, n., & -us, i, f., pl. -a, orum, n. *the citadel of Troy; also, a city of Mysia.*

situated upon the rive. Cu-cus. It was here that parchment was first made, which is hence called membrāna Per-gămi.

Pergo, pergĕre, perrexi, perrectum, n. (per & rego,) *to advance; to continue.*

Perīcles, is, m. *an eminent orator and statesman of Athens.*

Periculōsus, a, um, adj. *dangerous; perilous; hazardous;* from

Pericŭlum, & Periclum, i, n. *danger; peril.*

Peritūrus, a, um, part. (pereo.)

Perĭtus, a, um, adj. (ior, issĭmus,) *skilful; experienced.*

Permeo, āre, āvi, ātum, n. (per & meo,) *to go through; to flou through; to penetrate; to permeate.*

Permisceo, -miscĕre, -miscui, -mistum & -mixtum, a. (per & misceo,) *to mix; to mingle.*

Permistus, a, um, part. *mixed; mingled; confused.*

Permitto, -mittĕre, -misi, -missum, a. (per & mitto,) *to commit; to intrust; to permit; to allow; to give leave to; to grant.*

Permutatio, ōnis, f. *exchange; change;* from

Permūto, āre, āvi, ātum, a. (per & muto,) *to change; to ex change.*

Pernicies, ĕi, f. (pernéco,)*destruc-tion ; extermination.*

Pernicîosus, a, um, adj. (ior, issï-mus,) *pernicious ; hurtful.*

Perpendo, -pendĕre, -pendi, -pen-sum, a. (per & pendo,) *to ponder ; to weigh ; to consid-er.*

Perpĕram, adv. *wrong ; amiss ; rashly ; unjustly ; absurdly ; falsely.*

Perpetior, -pĕti, -pessus sum, dep. (per & patior,) *to bear ; to suffer ; to endure.*

Perpetuus, a, um, adj. *perpetual ; constant.*

Perrexi. *See* Pergo.

Persa, æ, m. *a Persian ; an in-habitant of Persia.*

Persecûtus, a, um, part. from

Persĕquor, -sĕqui, -secûtus sum, dep. (per.& sequor,) *to pur-sue ; to follow ; to continue ; to persevere in ; to perse-cute.*

Perseus, eï & eos, m. *the son of Jupiter and Danăe ; also, the last king of Macedon.*

Persĭcus, a, um, adj. *of Persia ; Persian.*

Perspicio, -spicĕre, -spexi, -spec-tum, a. (per & specio,) *to see through ; to discern ; to become acquainted with ; to discover.*

Persuadeo, -suadĕre, -suási, -suá-sum, a. (per & suadeo,) *to persuade.*

Perterreo, -terrĕre, -terrui, -terrï-tum, a. (per & terreo,) *to frighten greatly.*

Perterrïtus, a, um, part. *affright-ed ; discouraged.*

Pertinacĭter, adv. (iùs, issĭmè,) *obstinately ; constantly ; per-severingly.*

Pertĭnax, ácis, adj. (ior, issĭmus,) *obstinate ; wilful.*

Pertineo, -tinĕre, -tinui, n. (per & teneo,) *to extend ; to reach to.*

Pervenio, -venïre, -vĕni, -ventum, n. (per & venio,) *to come to ; to arrive at ; to reach.*

Pervenïtur, pass. imp. *one comes ; they come ; we come,* &c.

Pervius, a, um, adj. (per & via,) *pervious ; which may be pass-ed through ; passable.*

Pes, pedis, m. *a foot.*

Pessum, adv. *down ; under foot ; to the bottom.*

Pestilentia, æ, f. (pestĭlens,) *a pestilence ; a plague.*

Petens, tis, part. (peto.)

Petitio, ŏnis, f. *a petition ; a can-vassing or soliciting for an office ; from*

Peto, ĕre, ivi, ïtum, a. *to ask ; to request ; to attack ; to assail ; to go to ; to seek ; to go for ; to derive ; to bring.*

Petra, æ, f. *the metropolis of Arabia Petræa.*

Petræa, æ, f. (Arabia,) *Arabia Petræa, the northern part of Arabia, south of Palestine.*

Petulantia, æ, f. *petulance; inso-lence; mischievousness; wan-tonness.*

Phæax, ācis, m. *a Phæacian, or inhabitant of Phæacia,* now *Corfu. The Phæacians were famous for luxury.*

Paalēræ, ārum, f. pl. *the trappings of a horse; habiliments.*

Pharos, i, f. *a small island at the western mouth of the Nile, on which was a tower or light-house, esteemed one of the seven wonders of the world.*

Pharsālus, i, m. *a city of Thes-saly.*

Pharnāces, is, m. *a son of Mith-ridates, king of Pontus.*

Phasis, īdis & is, f. *a town and river of Colchis, on the east side of the Euxine.*

Phidias, æ, m. *a celebrated Athe-nian statuary.*

Philæni, ōrum, m. pl. *two Car-thaginian brothers, who suf-fered themselves to be buried alive, for the purpose of estab-lishing the controverted boun-dary of their country.*

Philippi, ōrum, m. pl. *a city of Macedon, on the confines of Thrace.*

Philippicus, a, um, adj. *belonging to Philippi.*

Philippides, æ, m. *a comic poet.*

Philippus, i, m. *Philip; the father of Alexander; also, the son of Demetrius.*

Philomēla, æ, f. *a nightingale.*

Philosophia, æ, f. *philosophy.*

Philosöphus, i, m. *a philosopher a lover of learning and wis-dom.*

Phineus, i, m. *a king of Arcadia, and priest of Apollo.*

Phocæi, ōrum, m. pl. *the Pho-cæans; inhabitants of Pho-cæa, a maritime city of Ionia.*

Phocis, īdis, f. *a country of Greece.*

Phœnīce, es, f. *Phœnicia, a mar-itime country of Syria, north of Palestine.*

Phœnix, īcis, m. *a Phœnician.*

Phryx, ygis, m. *a Phrygian; an inhabitant of Phrygia.*

Picentes, ium, m. pl. *the inhabit-ants of Picenum.*

Picēnum, i, n. *a country of Italy.*

Pictus, a, um, part. (pingo,) *painted; embroidered:* picta tabŭla, *a picture; a painting.*

Piětas, ātis, f. (pius,) *piety; filial duty.*

Pignus, ŏris, n. *a pledge; a pawn; security; assurance.*

Pila, æ, f. *a ball.*

Pileus, i, m. *a hat; a cap.*

Pilus, i, m. *the hair.*

Pindārus, i, m. *Pindar, a The-ban, the most eminent of the Greek lyric poets.*

Pingo, pingĕre, pinxi, pictum, a. *to paint; to depict; to deline ate; to draw; to represent in painting;* acu, *to embroider.*

Pinguis, e, adj. *fat; fertile; rich.*
inna, æ, f. *a fin.*

Piræeus, i, m. *the principal port
and arsenal of Athens.*

Pirata, æ, m. *a pirate.*

Piscator, oris, m. *a fisherman.*

Piscis, is, m. *a fish.*

Pisistratus, i, m. *an Athenian tyrant, distinguished for his eloquence.*

Pistrinum, i, n. *a mill.*

Pius, i, m. *an* agnomen, *or surname of Metellus.*

Pius, a, um, adj. *pious, dutiful,
or affectionate to parents.*

Placeo, ere, ui, itum, n. *to please:*
sibi, *to be vain* or *proud of; to
plume one's self.*

Placet, placuit, *or* placitum est,
imp. *it pleases; it is determined; it seems good to.*

Placidus, a, um, adj. (ior, issimus,)
*placid; quiet; still; tranquil;
mild; gentle.*

Plaga, æ, f. *a blow; a wound:*
plagæ, pl. *nets; toils.*

Plane, adv. *entirely; totally;
plainly.*

Planta, æ, f. *a plant.*

Platanus, i, f. *the plane-tree.*

Platea, æ, f. *a species of bird, the
spoonbill.*

Plato, onis, m. *an Athenian, one
of the most celebrated of the
Grecian philosophers.*

Plaustrum, i, n. *a cart; a wagon.*

Plebs, & Plebes, is, f. *the people; the common people; the
plebeians.*

Plecto, plectere, — plexum, a. *to
punish; to weave.*

Plerique, pleræque, pleraque,
adj. pl. *most; the most; many.*

Plerumque, adv. *commonly; generally; for the most part;
sometimes.*

Plinius, i, m. *Pliny; the name of
two distinguished Roman authors.*

Plotinus, i, m. *See* Catienus.

Plumbeus, a, um, adj. *of lead;
leaden;* from

Plumbum, i, n. *lead.*

Pluo, pluere, plui *or* pluvi, n. *to
rain.*

Plurimus, a, um, adj. (sup. of
multus,) *very much; most;
very many.*

Plus, uris, adj. (n. in sing., comp.
of multus, §§ 125, 5, & 110,)
more: pl. *many.*

Plus, adv. (comp. of multùm,)
more; longer.

Pluto, onis, m. *a son of Saturn,
and king of the infernal regions.*

Poculum, i, n. *a cup.*

Poëma, atis, n. *a poem.*

Pœna, æ, f. *a punishment.*

Pœnitet, ere, uit, imp. *it repents.*
pœnitet me, *I repent.*

Pœnus, a, um, adj. *belonging to
Carthage; Carthaginian:—*
subs. *a Carthaginian.*

Poëta, æ, m. *a poet.*

Pol, adv. *by Pollux; truly.*

Pollex, ĭcis, m. *the thumb; the great toe.*

Polliceor, ĕri, ītus sum, dep. *to promise.*

Pollicĭtus, a, um, part.

Pollux, ūcis, m. *a son of Leda, and twin brother of Castor.*

Polyxĕna, æ, f. *a daughter of Priam and Hecuba.*

Pomĭfer, ĕra, ĕrum, adj. (pomum & fero,) *bearing fruit:* pomĭf-ĕræ arbŏres, *fruit-trees.*

Pompa, æ, f. *a procession; pomp; parade.*

Pompĕiānus, a, um, adj. *belonging to Pompey.*

Pompeius, i, m. *Pompey; the name of a Roman gens, or clan, from which sprang many distinguished individuals:* (Cneius,) *a distinguished Roman, surnamed the Great.*

Pompilius, i, m. *See* Numa.

Pomum, i, n. *an apple; any edible fruit growing upon a tree.*

Pondus, ĕris, n. *a weight.*

Pono, ponĕre, posui, posĭtum, a. *to place; to put; to set.*

Pons, tis, m. *a bridge.*

Pontius, i, m. (Thelesĭnus,) *a general of the Samnites.*

Pontus, i, m. *a sea: by synec-dŏche, the Euxine or Black sea; also, the kingdom of Pontus, on the south of the Euxine.*

Poposci. *See* Posco.

Popŭlor, āri, ātus sum, dep. *to lay waste; to depopulate* from

Popŭlus, i, m. *the people; a nation; a tribe:* pl. *nations tribes.*

Porrectus, a, um, part. from

Porrĭgo, igĕre, exi, ectum, a. (porro & rego,) *to reach or spread out; to extend; to offer.*

Porsĕna, æ, m. *a king of Etruria.*

Porta, æ, f. *a gate.*

Portans, tis, part. (porto.)

Portendo, -tendĕre, -tendi, -tentum, a. (porro & tendo,) *to presage; to forebode; to portend; to betoken.*

Portĭcus, ūs, f. *a portico; a gallery; a porch.*

Porto, āre, āvi, ātum, a. *to carry; to bear.*

Portus, ūs, m. *a port; a harbor.*

Posco, poscĕre, poposci, a. *to demand; to earnestly request.*

Posĭtus, a, um, part. (pono,) *situated.*

Possessio, ōnis, f. *possession.*

Possessor, ōris, m. *a possessor, an occupant;* from

Possĭdeo, -sidĕre, -sēdi, -sessur, a. *to possess.*

Possum, posse, potui, irr. n. (potis & sum, § 154, R. 7,) *to be able; I can.*

Post, prep. *after:*—adv. *after, after that; afterwards.*

Postea, adv. *afterwards.*

Postĕra, ĕrum, adj. § 125, 4,(erior, rĕmus,) *succeeding; subsequent; next:* in postĕrum, (supply tempus,) *for the future:* postĕri, ŏrum, (§ 205, R. 7, (1); *posterity.*

Postis, is, m. *a post.*

Postquam, adv. *after; after that; since.*

Postrēmò & -ùm, adv. *at last; finally;* from

Postrēmus, a, um, adj. (sup. of postĕra, § 125, 4,) *the last:* ad postrēmum, *at last.*

Postùlo, áre, ávi, átum, a. (posco,) *to ask; to ask for; to demand.*

Postumius, i, m. *the name of a Roman gens or clan:* (Spurius,) *a consul defeated by the Samnites, at the Caudine Forks.*

Posui. *See* Pono.

Potens, tis, adj. (ior, issimus,) *powerful.*

Potentia, æ, f. *power; authority; government.*

Potesⁿᵃ, átis, f. (potis,) *power.*

Potio, ŏnis, f. (poto,) *a drink; a draught.*

Potior, īri, ītus sum, dep. *to get; to possess; to obtain; to enjoy; to gain possession of.*

Potissĭmùm, adv. (sup. of potiùs,) *principal'y; chiefly; especially.*

Potitus, a, um, part. (potior, *having obtained.*

Potiùs, adv. comp. (sup. potissĭmùm,) *rather.*

Poto, potáre, potávi, potátum o- potum, a. *to drink.*

Potuisse. *See* Possum.

Potus, ûs, m. *drink.*

Præ, prep. *before; for; in comparison of,* or *with.*

Præaltus, a, um, adj. *very high* or *lofty, very deep.*

Præbeo, ēre, ui, ĭtum, a. (præ & habeo,) *to offer; to supply; to give; to afford:* speciem, *to exhibit the appearance of:* usum, *to serve for.*

Præcēdens, tis, part. from

Præcēdo, -cedĕre, -cessi, -cessum, a. (præ & cedo,) *to precede; to go before.*

Præceptor, ŏris, m. (præcipio,) *a preceptor, master,* or *teacher.*

Præceptum, i, n. (præcipio,) *a precept; a doctrine; advice.*

Præcido, -cidĕre, -cīdi, -cīsum a. (præ & cædo,) *to cut off.*

Præcipio, -cipĕre, -cēpi, -ceptum, a. (præ & capio,) *to prescribe; to command.*

Præcipĭto, áre, ávi, átum, a. (præceps,) *to throw; to throw down; to precipitate.*

Præcipuè, adv. *especially; particularly;* from

Præcipuus, a, um, adj. *especial, distinguished; the chief; the principal.*

Præclārė, adv. *excellently*; *famously*; *gloriously*; from

Præclārus, a, um, adj. *famous.*

Præclŭdo, -cludère, -clúsi, -clúsum, a. (præ & claudo,) *to close*; *to stop*; *to shut up.*

Præco, ŏnis, m. *a herald.*

Præda, æ, f. *booty*; *the prey.*

Prædĭco, åre, àvi, åtum, a. (præ & dĭco,) *to praise*; *to declare*; *to assert*; *to affirm.*

Prædico, cĕre, xi, ctum, a. (præ & dico,) *to predict*; *to foretell.*

Prædictus, a, um, part. *foretold.*

Prædor, åri, åtus sum, dep. (præda,) *to plunder.*

Præfans, tis, part. from

Præfāri, fātus, def. § 183, 6; *to foretell*; *to announce*; *to predict.*

Præfĕro, -ferre, -tŭli, -låtum, irr. a. (præ & fero,) *to prefer*; *to bear before.*

Præfinio, ire, ivi, ĭtum, a. (præ & finio,) *to appoint*; *to determine.*

Præfinitus, a, um, part.

Prælåtus, a, um, part. (præfĕro.)

Prælians, tis, part. (prælior.)

Præliåtus, a, um, part. from

Prælior, åri, åtus sum, dep. *to give battle*; *to engage*; *to fight.*

Prælium, i, n. *a battle.*

Prænnium, i, n. *a reward*; *a prize.*

Præmitto -mittĕre, -misi, -mis-

sum, a. (præ & mitto,) *to send before.*

Præneste, is, n. *a city of Latium.*

Prænuntio, åre, àvi, åtum, a. (præ & nuntio,) *to announce*; *to tell beforehand*; *to signify*; *to give notice.*

Præpăro, åre, àvi, åtum, a. (præ & paro,) *to prepare*; *to make ready*; *to make.*

Præpŏno, -ponĕre, -posui, -posĭtum, a. (præ & pono,) *to set before*; *to value more*; *to place over*; *to prefer.*

Præsens, tis, adj. *present*; *imminent.*

Præsĕpe, is, n. *a manger*; *a crib.*

Præsidium, i, n. *a garrison*; *defence.*

Præstans, tis, part. & adj. (ior, issĭmus,) (præsto,) *excellent*; *distinguished.*

Præstantia, æ, f. *superiority*; *an advantage*; *a preëminence.*

Præsto, ståre, stĭti, n. & a. (præ & sto,) *to stand before*; *to perform*; *to pay*; *to grant*, *to give*; *to render*; *to execute*; *to cause*; *to excel*; *to be superior*; *to surpass:* se, *to show* or *prove one's self* præstat, imp. *it is better.*

Præsum, -esse, -fui, irr. n. (præ & sum,) *to be over*; *to preside over*; *to have the charge* or *command of*; *to rule over.*

Prætendo, -tendĕre, -tendi, -ten

.sum or tum, a. (præ & tendo,) *to hold before ; to stretch* or *extend before ; to be opposite to ; to pretend.*

Præter, prep. *besides ; except ; contrary to.*

Præterea, adv. (præter & ea,) *besides ; moreover.*

Prætereo, īre, ii, ĭtum, irr. a. § 182, 3, (præter & eo,) *to pass over* or *by; to go beyond ; to omit ; not to mention.*

Prætereundus, a, um, part. (prætereo.)

Præteriens, euntis, part. (prætereo.)

Præterĭtus, a, um, part. (prætereo,) *past.*

Præterquam, adv. *except ; besides :* præterquam si, *except in case.*

Prætorius, i, m. (vir,) *a man who has been a prætor; one of prætorian dignity.*

Pratum, i, n. *a meadow ; a pasture.*

Pravĭtas, ātis, f. *depravity ;* from

Pravus, a, um, adj. (ior, issĭmus,) *depraved ; bad.*

Precâtus, a, um, part. (precor.)

Preci, -em, -e, f. (prex not used, § 94,) *a prayer :* pl. preces.

Precor, āri, ātus sum, dep. *to pray ; to entreat.*

Premo, premĕre, pressi, pressum, a. *to press ; to grieve ; to urge.*

Pretiôsus, a, um, adj. (ior, issĭmus,) *precious ; valuable ; costly ;* from

Pretium, i, n. *a price ; a ransom a reward :* in pretio esse, *to be valued; to be in estimation.*

Priămus, i, m. *Priam, the last king of Troy.*

Pridie, adv. *the day before.*

Priēne, es, f. *a maritime town of Ionia.*

Primò & -ùm, adv. (sup. of priùs,) *first ; at first :* quum primùm, *as soon as.*

Primŏris, e, adj. *the first ; the foremost :* dentes, *the front teeth.*

Primus, a, um, num. adj. *the first.*

Princeps, ĭpis, adj. (primus & capio,) *the chief ; the first :* prinīces, *the princes the chiefs ; chief men.*

Principâtus, ûs, m. *a government ; principality.*

Priscus, i, m. *a cognōmen* or *surname of the elder Tarquin.*

Prior, us, adj. (sup. primus, § 126, 1,) *the former ; prior ; first.*

Priùs, adv. *before ; prior ; first.*

Priusquam, adv. *sooner than ; before that ; before.*

Privâtus, a, um, adj. (privo,) *private ; secret : —* subs. *a private man.*

Pro, prep. *for ; instead of.*

Probabĭlis, e, adj. (probo,) *probable.*

Proboscis, ĭdis, ·f. *proboscis; the trunk of an elephant.*

Procas, æ, m. *See* Silvius.

Procēdens, tis, part. from

Procēdo, -cedĕre, -cessi, -cessum, n. (pro & cedo,) *to proceed; to go forth; to go forward; to advance; to go out.*

Procerĭtas, ātis, f. *stature; height; tallness; length;* from

Procĕrus, a, um, adj. *tall; long.*

Proclāmo, āre, āvi, ātum, n. (pro & clamo,) *to cry out; to proclaim.*

Proconsul, ŭlis, m. (pro & consul,) *a proconsul.*

Procreo, āre, āvi, ātum, a. (pro & creo,) *to beget.*

Procul, adv. *far.*

Procūro, āre, āvi, ātum, a. (pro & curo,) *to take care of; to manage.*

Procurro, currĕre, curri & cucurri, cursum, n. (pro & curro,) *to run forward; to jut out; to extend.*

Prodigĭum, i, n. *a prodigy.*

Froditor, ŏris, m. (prodo,) *a traitor.*

Prodĭtus, a, um, part. from

Prodo, -dĕre, -dĭdi, -dĭtum, a. (pro & do,) *to betray; to relate; to discover; to disclose; to manifest.*

Prœlior, āri, ātus sum, dep. *ti fight;* from

Prœlium, i, n. *a battle.*

Profectus, a, um, part. (proficiscor.)

Proficiscens, tis, part. from

Proficiscor, icisci, ectus sum, dep. (pro & facio,) *to march; to travel; to depart; to go.*

Profiteor, -fitēri, -fessus sum, dep. (pro & fateor,) *to declare; to avow publicly; to profess:* sapientiam, *to profess wisdom; to profess to be a philosopher.*

Profugio, -fugĕre, -fūgi, -fugĭtum, n. (pro & fugio,) *to flee, to escape.*

Profŭgus, a, um, adj. *fleeing; escaping:*—subs. *a fugitive; an exile.*

Progredior, -grĕdi, -gressus sum, dep. (pro & gradior,) *to go forward; to proceed; to advance.*

Progressus, a, um, part. *having advanced.*

Prohibeo, ēre, ui, ĭtum, a. (pro & habeo,) *to prohibit; to hinder; to forbid.*

Prohibĭtus, a, um, part.

Projicio, -jicĕre, -jēci, -jectum, a. (pro & jacio,) *to throw away; to throw down; to throw.*

Prolābor, -lābi, -lapsus sum, dep. (pro & labor,) *to fall down; to fall forward.*

Prolapsus, a, um, part. *having fallen.*

Pro'āto. āre, āvi, ātum, a. (prof-ĕro,) *to enlarge; to extend; to amplify.*

Proles, is, f. *a race; offspring.*

Prometheus, i, m. *the son of Ia-pĕtus and Clymĕne.*

Promittens, tis, part. from

Promitto, -mittĕre, -mīsi, -mis-sum, a. (pro & mitto,) *to prom-ise; to offer.*

Promontorium, i, n. (pro & mons,) *a promontory; a headland; a cape.*

Promoveo, -movēre, -mōvi, -mō-tum, n. & a. (pro & moveo,) *to move forward; to enlarge.*

Pronus, a, um, adj. *inclined.*

Propāgo, āre, āvi, ātum, a. *to propagate; to prolong; to continue.*

Prope, adv. & prep. (propiùs, prox-īmè,) *near; near to; nigh.*

Propĕro, āre, āvi, ātum, n. *to has-ten.*

Propinquus, a, 'um, adj. (prope,) *near; related:* propinqui, subs. *relations; kinsmen.*

Propior, us, adj. comp. § 126, 1; (proxīmus, sup.) *nearer.*

Propiùs, adv. *nearer;* comp. of prope.

Propōno, -ponĕre, -posui, -posī-tum a. (pro & pono,) *to set before; to propose; to offer.*

Propōnor, -pōni, -positus sum, pass. *to be set before:* pro-posĭtum est mihi, *I intend or purpose.*

Propontis, ĭdis, f. *the sea of Mar-mŏra.*

Proposĭtus, a, um, part. *proposed; put.*

Propriè, adv. *peculiarly; partic-ularly; properly; strictly.*

Proprius, a, um, adj. *peculiar; proper; one's own; special.*

Propter, prep. *for; on account of.*

Propulso, āre, āvi, ātum, freq. (propello,) *to drive away; to ward off; to repel.*

Propylæum, i, n. *the porch of a temple; an entrance, the rows of columns leading to the A-cropŏlis at Athens.*

Prora, æ, f. *the prow of a ship.*

Proscribo, -scribĕre, -scripsi, -scriptum, a. (pro & scribo,) *to proscribe; to outlaw; to doom to death and confiscation of goods.*

Prosecūtus, a, um, part. *having accompanied.*

Prosĕquor, -sĕqui, -secūtus sum, dep. (pro & sequor,) *to accom-pany; to attend; to follow; to celebrate:* honorĭbus, *to heap* or *load with honors; to honor.*

Proserpĭna, æ, f. *the daughter of Ceres and Jupiter, and wife of Pluto.*

Prospectus, ûs, m. (prospicio,) *a prospect; a distant view.*

Prospĕrè, adv. (prosper,) *prosper-ously; successfully.*

Prosterno, -sternĕre, -strāvi,

-strātum, a. (pro & sterno,) to prostrate; to throw down.

Prostrātus, a, um, part. (proster-no.)

Prosum. prodesse, profui, irr. n. (pro & sum, § 154, R. 6,) to do good; to profit.

Protagŏras, æ, m. a Greek philosopher.

Protĕnus, adv. (pro & tenus,) immediately; directly.

Protĕro, -terĕre, -trivi, -tritum, ā. (pro & tero,) to trample upon; to tread down; to crush.

Protractus, a, um, part. from

Protrăho, -trahĕre, -traxi, -tractum, a. (pro & traho,) to protract; to prolong.

Proveniens, tis, part. from

Provenio, -venire, -vēni, -ventum, n. (pro & venio,) to come forth.

Provincia, æ, f. a province.

Provocatio, ōnis, f. a provocation; a challenge; from

Provŏco, āre, āvi, ātum, a. (pro & voco,) to call forth; to call out; to defy or challenge; to appeal.

Proxĭmè, adv. (sup. of prope,) nearest; very near; next to.

Proxĭmus, a, um, adj. (sup. of propior,) nearest; next.

Prudens, tis, adj. (ior, issĭmus,) prudent; wise; expert.

Prudentia, æ, f. prudence; knowledge.

Pseudophilippus, i, m. a false or pretended Philip, a name given to Andriscus.

Psittăcus, i, m. a parrot.

Psophidius, a, um, adj. of or belonging to Psophis; Psophidian.

Psophis, ĭdis, f. a city of Arcadia.

Ptolemæus, i, m. Ptolemy; the name of several Egyptian kings.

Publĭcè, adv. (publĭcus,) publicly; at the public expense; by public authority.

Publicŏla, æ, m. (popŭlus & colo,) a surname given to P. Valerius, on account of his love of popularity.

Publĭcus, a, um, adj. (popŭlus,) public: in publĭcum procēdens, going abroad or appearing in public:—subs. publĭcum, the public treasury.

Publius, i, m. the prænōmen of several Romans.

Pudibundus, a, um, adj. (pudeo,) ashamed.

Puer, ĕri, m. a boy; a servant.

Puerĭlis, e, adj. puerile; childish. ætas, boyhood; childhood.

Pueritia, æ, f. boyhood; childhood.

Pugna, æ, f. a battle.

Pugnans, tis, part. (pugno.)

Pugnātus, a, um, part. from

Pugno, āre, āvi, ātum, n. to fight: pugnātur, pass. imp. a battle is fought; they fight.

Pulcher, ra, rum, adj. (ior, rĭmus,) *fair; beautiful; glorious.*

Pulchritūdo, ĭnis, f. *fairness; beauty.*

Pullus, i, m. *the young of any animal.*

Pulsus, a, um, part. (pello.)

Pulvillus, i, m. (Horatius,) *a Roman consul in the first year of the republic.*

Punĭcus, a, um, adj. *Punic; belonging to Carthage; Carthaginian.*

Punio, ire, ivi, ītum, a. *to punish.*

Punītus, a, um, part.

Pupillus, i, m. *a pupil; a ward; an orphan.*

Puppis, is, f. *the stern of a ship.*

Purgo, āre, āvi, ātum, a. *to purge; to purify; to clear; to clean; to excuse.*

Purpŭra, æ f. *purple; the purple muscle.*

Purpurātus, a, um, adj. *clad in purple:* purpurāti, pl. *courtiers; nobles.*

Purpureus, a, um, adj. *purple.*

Purus, a, um, adj. *pure; clear.*

Pusillus, a, um, adj. *small; weak.*

Puteus, i, m. *a well.*

Puto, āre, āvi, ātum, a. *to think.*

Putresco, putrescĕre, putrui, inc. (putreo,) *to rot; to decay.*

Pydna, æ, f. *a town of Macedonia.*

Pygmæi, ōrum, m. *the Pygmies,* *a race of dwarfs, inhabiting a remote part of India or Ethiopia.*

Pyra, æ, f. *a funeral pile.*

Pyrămis, ĭdis, f. *a pyramid.*

Pyrenæus, i, m., & Pyrenæi, ōrum, m. pl. *Pyrenees, mountains dividing France and Spain.*

Pyrrhus, i, m. *a king of Epirus.*

Pythagŏras, æ, m. *a Grecian philosopher, born at Samos.*

Pythagorĕus, i, m. *a Pythagorean; a follower or disciple of Pythagoras.*

Pythia, æ, f. *the priestess of Apollo at Delphi.*

Pythias, æ, m. *a soldier of Philip king of Macedon.*

Q.

Q., or Qu., *an abbreviation of* Quintus. § 328.

Quadragesĭmus, a, um, num. adj. *the fortieth; from*

Quadraginta, num. adj. pl. ind *forty.*

Quadriennium, i, n. (quatuor & annus,) *the space of four years.*

Quadrīgæ, ārum, f. *a four-horse chariot; a team of four horses.*

Quadringentesĭmus, a, um, num. adj. *the four hundredth.*

Quadringenti, æ, a, num. adj. pl. *four hundred.*

Quadrūpes, pĕdis, adj. (quatuor

& pes,) *having four feet; four-footed*

Quærens, tis, part. from

Quæro, quærēre, quæsivi, quæsitum, a. *to ask; to seek for; to inquire; to search*: quærĭtur, *it is asked; the inquiry is made.*

Quæstio, ŏnis, f. *a question.*

Quæstor, ŏris, m. *a quæstor; a treasurer; an inferior military officer who attended the consuls.*

Quæstus, ûs, m. *gain; a trade.*

Qualis, e, adj. *of what kind; as; such as; what.*

Quàm, conj. & adv. *as; how:* after comparatives, *than.*

Quamdiu, *or* Quandiu, adv. *as long as.*

Quamquam, *or* Quanquam, conj. *though; although.*

Quamvis, conj. *although.*

Quando, adv. *when; since.*

Quantò, adv. *by how much; as.*

Quantopēre, adv. *how greatly; how much.*

Quantùm, adv. *how much; as much as.*

Quantus, a, um, adj. *how great; as great; how admirable; how striking.*

Quantuslibet, quantalĭbet, quantumlĭbet, adj. (quantus & libet,) *how great soever; ever so great.*

Quapropter, adv. *wherefore; why.*

Quare, adv. (quâ & re,) *where-*fore; *for which reason; whence; therefore.*

Quartus, a, um, num. adj. *the fourth.*

Quasi, adv. *as if; as.*

Quatriduum, i, n. (quatuor & dies,) *a space of four days.*

Quatuor, num. adj. pl. ind. *four*

Quatuordĕcim, num. adj. pl. ind. *fourteen.*

Que, enclitic conj. § 198, N. 1; *and; also.*

Queo, ire, ivi, itum, irr. § 182, R. 3, N; *to be able; I can.*

Quercus, ûs, f. *an oak.*

Queror, queri, questus sum, dep. *to complain.*

Questus, a, um, part. *complaining; having complained.*

Qui, quæ, quod, rel. pro. § 136; *who; which; what.*

Qui, quæ, quod, interrogative pro. *who? which? what?* § 137.

Qui, adv. *how; in what manner.*

Quia, conj. § 198, 7; *because.*

Quicunque, quæcunque, quodcunque, rel. pro. § 136; *whosoever; whatsoever; every one.*

Quidam, quædam, quoddam & quiddam, pro. § 138; *a certain one; a certain person or thing:* quidam homĭnes, *certain men.*

Quidem, adv. § 279, 3, (d.) *indeed; truly; at least.* See Ne.

Quin, conj. § 198, 8; *but: but that*

Quinctius, i, m. (Titus,) *a Ro-*
man general.

Quindĕcim, num. adj. pl. ind.
fifteen.

Quingentesĭmus, a, um, num.
adj. *the five hundredth.*

Quingenti, æ, a, num. adj. pl.
five hundred.

Quinquagēni, æ, a, num. adj. pl.
every fifty; fifty.

Quinquagesĭmus, a, um, num.
adj. *fiftieth.*

Quinquaginta, num. adj. pl. ind.
fifty.

Quinque, num. adj. pl. ind. *five.*

Quinquies, num. adv. *five times.*

Quinto, adv. *the fifth time.*

Quintus, a, um, num. adj. *the fifth.*

Quintus, *or* Quinctius, i, m. *a*
surname among the Romans.

Quis, quæ, quid, pro. *who? what?*
quid? *why?*

Quisnam, *or* Quinam, quænam,
quodnam *or* quidnam, pro.
§ 137; *who; what.*

Quisquam, quæquam, quidquam
or quicquam, pro. § 138, 3;
any one; any thing: nec
quisquam, *and no one.*

Quisque, quæque, quodque *or*
quidque, pro. *each; every;*
whosoever; whatsoever.

Quisquis, quidquid *or* quicquid,
rel. pro. § 136; *whoever;*
whatever.

Quivis, quævis, quodvis *or* quid-
vis, pro. *whosoever; whatso-*
ever; any one.

Quò, adv. *that; to the end that;*
whither: quò — eò, *for* quanto — tanto, *by how much; by*
so much; or the more — the
more.

Quòd, conj. *that; because.*

Quomĭnùs, adv. *that — not.*

Quomŏdo, adv. *how; by what*
means.

Quondam, adv. *formerly; once.*

Quoniam, conj. *since; because.*

Quoque, conj. *also.*

Quot, adj. ind. pl. *how many.*

Quotannis, adv. *annually; year-*
ly.

Quotidie, adv. (quot & dies,)
every day; daily.

Quoties, adv. *as often as; how*
often.

Quum, *or* Cùm, adv. *when;*
quum jam, *as soon as:*—conj.
since; although.

R.

Radius, i, m. *a staff; a ray; a rod.*

Radix, icis, f. *a root; the foot* or
base of a mountain.

Ramus, i, m. *a branch; a bough.*

Rana, æ, f. *a frog.*

Rapina, æ, f. *rapine; plunder;*
from

Rapio, rapĕre, rapui, raptum, a.
to rob; to seize; to plunder;
to hurry away.

Raptor, ōris, m. *one who seizes*
or takes away by violence; a
robber.

Raptŭrus, a, um, part. (rapio.)

Raptus, a, um, part. (rapio,) *seized ; robbed ; carried off.*

Rarĭtas, ātis, f. *rarity.*

Rarò, adv. *rarely ; seldom ;* from

Rarus, a, um, adj. *rare ; few.*

Ratio ōnis, f. (reor,) *a reason.*

Ratis, is, f. *a raft ; a ship ; a boat.*

Ratus, a, um, part. (reor,) *thinking ; having thought.*

Rebello, āre, āvi, ātum, n. (re & bello,) *to renew a war ; to rebel ; to revolt.*

Recēdo, -cedĕre, -cessi, -cessum, n. (re & cedo,) *to recede; to yield ; to retire ; to withdraw.*

Recens, tis, adj. *new ; recent ; fresh :*—adv. *recently ; lately ; newly :* recens nati, *new-born children.*

Receptus, a, um, part. (recipio.)

. Receptŭrus, a, um, part. (recipio.)

Recessus, ùs, m. (recēdo,) *a recess ; a corner.*

Recipio, -cipĕre, -cēpi, -ceptum, a. (re & capio,) *to receive ; to take ; to take back ; to recover :* anĭmam, *to come to one's self again ; to recover one's senses :* se, *to return.*

Recognosco, -noscĕre, -nóvi, -nĭtum. a. (re & cognosco,) *to recognize.*

Recolligo, -ligĕre, -lēgi, -lectum. a. (re, con, & lego,) *to gather up again to recollect ; to recover.*

Reconditus, a, um, part. from

Recondo, dĕre, dīdi, dītum, a. (re & condo,) *to hide ; to conceal.*

Recreātus, a, um, part. from

Recreo, āre, āvi, ātum, a. (re & creo,) *to restore ; to bring to life again.*

Rectè, adv. (iùs, issĭmè,) *right ; rightly ;* from

Rectus, a, um, adj. (ior, issĭmus,) (rego,) *right ; straight ; upright ; direct.*

Recuperātus, a, um, part. from

Recupĕro, āre, āvi, ātum, a. *to recover ; to regain.*

Redditŭrus, a, um, part. (reddo.)

Reddĭtus, a, um, part. from

Reddo, -dĕre, -dĭdi, -dĭtum, a. (re & do,) *to return ; to give ; to give back ; to make ; to render ; to restore ; to cause :* verba, *to repeat :* anĭmam, *to die :* voces, *to imitate.*

Redeo, -ire, -ii, -ĭtum, irr. n. (re & eo, § 182,) *to return ; to go back.*

Rediens, euntis, part. *returning.*

Redigo, -igĕre, -ēgi, -actum, a. (re & ago,) *to bring back ; to reduce :* in potestātem, *to bring into one's power*

Redimendus, a, um, part. from

Redĭmo, -imĕre, -ēmi, -emptum, a. (re & emo,) *to buy back ; to redeem ; to ransom.*

Reducendus, a, um, part. from

Redŭco, -ducĕre, -duxi, -ductum, a. (re & duco,) *to lead* or *bring back:* in gratiam, *to reconcile.*

Refĕrens, tis, part. *requiting; returning; referring;* from

Refĕro, -ferre, -tŭli, -lātum, irr. a. (re & fero,) *to bring back:* gratiam, *or* gratias, *to requite a favor; to show gratitude:* beneficium, *to requite a benefit:* victoriam, *to bring back victory,* i. e. *to return victorious:* imagĭnem, *to reflect the image; to resemble:* ad alĭquam rem, *to refer to; to reckon a part of.*

Refluens, tis, part. from

Refluo, -fluĕre, -fluxi, -fluxum, n. (re & fluo,) *to flow back.*

Refugio, -fugĕre, -fŭgi, -fugītum, n. (re & fugio,) *to fly back; to flee; to retreat.*

Regia, æ, f. (regius,) *a palace.*

Regina, æ, f. (rex,) *a queen.*

Regio, ōnis, f. (rego,) *a region; a district; a country.*

Regius, a, um, adj. (rex,) *royal; regal; the king's.*

Regnatūrus, a, um, part. from

Regno, āre, āvi, ātum, n. (regnum,) *to rule; to govern.*

Regnātur, pass. imp. *kingly government continues.*

Regnum, i, n. (rex,) *a kingdom; empire; dominion; reign; government; rule.*

Rego, regĕre, rexi, rectu̱ı̱, a. (rex,) *to rule.*

Regredior, -grĕdi, -gressus sum, dep. (re & gradior,) *to turn back; to return.*

Regréssus, a, um, part. *having returned.*

Regŭlus, i, m. *a distinguished Roman general in the first Punic war.*

Relātus, a, um, part. (refĕro.)

Relictūrus, a, um, part. (relinquo.)

Relictus, a, um, part. (relinquo.)

Religio, ōnis, f. (relĕgo,) *religion; sacredness; sanctity; reverence; religious rites.*

Relinquo, -linquĕre, -līqui, -lictum, a. (re & linquo,) *to leave; to desert; to quit; to abandon.*

Reliquiæ, ārum, f. pl. *the relics; the remains;* from

Relĭquus, a, um, adj. *the rest; the remainder; the other.*

Remaneo, -manēre, -mansi, -mansum, n. (re & maneo,) *to remain behind.*

Remedium, i. n. (re & medeor,) *a remedy.*

Remitto, -mittĕre, -mīsı, -missum, a. (re & mitto,) *to send back; to remit.*

Removeo, -movēre, -mōvi, -mōtum, a. (re & moveo,) *to remove.*

Remus, i, m. *an oar.*

Remus, i, m. *the twin brother of Romŭlus.*

Renovătus, a, um, part. from

Renóvo, āre, āvi, ātum, a. (re & novo,) *to make anew; to renew.*

Renuntio, āre, āvi, ātum, a. (re & nuntio,) *to inform; to report; to declare; to announce.*

Reor, reri, ratus sum, dep. *to believe; to think.*

Repăro, āre, āvi, ātum, a. (re & paro,) *to renew; to repair.*

Repentè, adv. *suddenly.*

Reperio, -perire, -pĕri, -pertum, a. (re & pario,) *to find; to discover; to invent.*

Repĕto, -petĕre, -petivi, -petītum, a. (re & peto,) *to demand back.*

Repleo, ēre, ēvi, ētum, a. (re & pleo,) *to fill; to fill up; to replenish.*

Repóno, -ponĕre, -posui, -posĭtum, a. (re & pono,) *to place again; to restore; to replace.*

Reporto, āre, āvi, ātum, a. (re & porto,) *to bring back; to gain or obtain.*

Repræsento, āre, āvi, ātum, a. *to represent; to paint; to depict.*

Repudio, āre, āvi, ātum, a. *to repudiate; to reject; to slight; to disregard:* uxórem, *to divorce.*

Requiro, -quirĕre, -quisĭvi, -quisĭtum, a. (re & quæro,) *to*

seek; *to demand; to require to need.*

Res, rei, f. *a thing; an affair a way; a kingdom; a government; a subject:* res gestæ, *actions; exploits:* res, res familiāris *or* domestĭca, *domestic affairs; property.*

Reservo, āre, āvi, ātum, a. (re & servo,) *to reserve; to keep for a future time.*

Resideo, -sidēre, -sēdi, n. (re & sedeo,) *to sit; to sit down; to remain.*

Resimus, a, um, adj. *bent back; crooked.*

Resisto, -sistĕre, -stĭti, -stĭtum, n. (re & sisto,) *to resist; to withstand.*

Resolvo, -solvĕre, -solvi, -solūtum, a. (re & solvo,) *to loosen; to unbind; to unloose; to dissolve; to untie.*

Respondeo, -spondēre, -spondi, -sponsum, n. (re & spondeo,) *to answer; to reply; to correspond·* respondētur, pass. imp. *it is answered,* or *the reply is made.*

Responsum, i, n. *an answer; a reply.*

Respublĭca, reipublĭcæ, f. §91; *the state; the government; the commonwealth.*

Respuo, -spuĕre, -spui, a. *to spit out; to reject.*

Restituo, -stituĕre, -stitui, -stitūtum, a. (re & statuo,) *to re-*

store; *to replace; to rebuild :* aciem, *to cause the army to rally.*

Retineo, -tinĕre, -tinui, -tentum, a. (re & teneo,) *to hold back; to retain; to detain; to hinder.*

Revērâ, adv. (res & verus,) *truly; in very deed; in reality; in good earnest.*

Reverentia, æ, f. *reverence.*

Reversus, a, um, part. *having returned.*

Reverto, -vertĕre, -verti, -versum, n. (re & verto,) *to turn back; to return.*

Revertor, -verti, -versus sum, dep. *to return.*

Reviresco, -virescĕre, -virui, inc. (revireo,) *to grow green again.*

Revŏco, āre, āvi, ātum, a. (re & voco,) *to recall; to call back.*

Revŏlo, āre, āvi, ātum, n. (re & volo,) *to fly back; to fly off again.*

Rex, regis, m. *a king;* also, *the name of a plebeian family at Rome.*

Rhadamanthus, i, m. *a lawgiver of Crete, and subsequently one of the three judges of the infernal regions.*

Rhæti, ōrum, m. pl. *the inhabitants of Rhætia, now the Grisons.*

Rhea, æ, f. (Silvia,) *the mother of Romulus and Remus.*

Rhenus, i m. *the river Rhine.*

Rhinocĕros, ōtis, m. *a rhinoceros.*

Rhipæus, a, um, adj. *Rhipæan* or *Riphæan :* montes, *mountains, which, according to the ancients, were found in the north of Scythia.*

Rhodănus, i, m. *the river Rhone.*

Rhodius, i, m. *an inhabitant of Rhodes; a Rhodian.*

Rhodŏpe, es, f. *a high mountain in the western part of Thrace.*

Rhodus, i; f. *Rhodes; an island in the Mediterranean sea.*

Rhœtēum, i, n. *a city and promontory of Troas.*

Rhyndăcus, i, m. *a river of Mysia.*

Ridens, tis, part. *smiling; laughing at;* from

Rideo, dēre, si, sum, n. & a. *to laugh; to laugh at; to mock; to deride.*

Rigeo, ēre, ui, n. *to be cold.*

Rigĭdus, a, um, adj. *severe.*

Rigo, āre, āvi, ātum, a. *to water; to irrigate; to bedew; to wet.*

Ripa, æ, f. *a bank.*

Risi. *See* Rideo.

Risus, ûs, m. *laughing; laughter.*

Rixor, āri, ātus sum, dep. *to quarrel.*

Robur, ŏris, n. *strength :* robur milĭtum, *the flower of the soldiers.*

Rogātus, a, um, part. *being asked;* from

Rogo, āre, āvi, ātum, a. *to ask;*

*to request; to beg; to en-
treat.*

Rogus, i, m. *a funeral pile.*

Roma, æ, f. *Rome, the chief city
of Italy, situated upon the Tiber.*

Romànus, a, um, adj. *Roman.*

Romànus, i, m. *a Roman.*

Romùlus, i, m. *the founder and
first king of Rome :* Romùlus
Silvius, *a king of Alba.*

Rostrum, i, n. *a beak; a bill; a
snout.*

Rota, æ, f. *a wheel.*

Rotundus, a, um, adj. *round.*

Ruber, rubra, rubrum, adj. (rior,
errìmus,) *red.*

Rudis, e, adj. (ior, issìmus,) *rude ;
uncultivated; new; uncivil-
ized.*

Ruina, æ, f. *a ruin; a downfall;
a fall.*

Rulliànus, i, m. *a Roman general, who commanded the cavalry in a war with the Samnites.*

Rumpo, rumpère, rupi, ruptum,
a. *to break; to break off; to
break down; to violate.*

Ruo, uère, ui, utum, n. *to run
headlong; to fall; to be ruined; to hasten down; to rush.*

Rupes, is, f. *a rock; a cliff.*

Ruptus, a, um, part. (rumpo,)
broken; violated.

Rursus, adv. *again.*

Rus, ruris, n. *the country; a
farm.*

Rustìcus, a, um, adj. *rustic, be
longing to the country.*

Rustìcus, i, m. *a countryman.*

Rutilius, i, m. *a Roman consul.*

S.

Sabìni, òrum, m. *the Sabines, a
people of Italy.*

Sacer, sacra, sacrum, adj. (comp.
not used; sup. errìmus,) *sacred; holy; divine; conse
crated.*

Sacerdos, òtis, c. *a priest; a
priestess.*

Sacra, òrum, n. pl. *religious service; sacrifice; sacred rites;
religious observances.*

Sacrifìcans, tis, part. (sacrifi
co,) *sacrificing; offering sac
rifices.*

Sacrificium, i, n. *a sacrifice,*
from

Sacrifìco, àre, àvi, àtum, a. (sacer & facio,) *to sacrifice.*

Sæpè, adv. (ìus, issìmè, § 194,)
often; frequently.

Sævio, ire, ii, ìtum, n. (sævus,)
to rage; to be cruel.

Sævìtas, àtis, f. *cruelty; severi-
ty; savageness; barbarity;*
from

Sævus, a, um, adj. *severe; cruel;
fierce; inhuman; violent.*

Saginàtus, a, um, part. from

Sagino, àre, àvi, àtum, a. *to fat
ten.*

Sagitta, æ, f. *an arrow.*

Saguntini, ōrum, m. pl. *the Saguntines; the inhabitants of Saguntum.*

Saguntum, i, n. *a town of Spain.*

Salio, salire, salui & salii, n. *to spring; to leap.*

Salsus, a, um, adj. (sal,) *salt; sharp.*

Salto, āre, āvi, ātum, n. freq. (salio,) *to dance.*

Salūber, -bris, -bre, adj. (brior, berrīmus,) *wholesome; salubrious; healthy.*

Salubrītas, ātis, f. *salubrity; healthfulness.*

Salum, i, n. *the sea.*

Salus, ūtis, f. (salvus,) *safety; salvation; health.*

Salūto, āre, āvi, ātum, a. *to salute; to call.*

Salvus, a, um, adj. *safe; preserved; unpunished.*

Samnites, ium, m. pl. *the Samnites, a people of Italy.*

Sanctus, a, um, adj. *holy; blameless.*

Sanguis, ĭnis, m. *blood.*

Sapiens, tis, adj. (ior, issĭmus,) *wise:*—subs. *a sage; a wise man.*

Sapientia, æ, f. *wisdom; philosophy.*

Sapio, ĕre, ui, n. *to be wise.*

Sarcĭna æ, f. *a pack; a bundle.*

Sardinia, æ, f. *a large island in the Mediterranean sea, west of Italy.*

Sarmătæ, ārum, m. *the Sarma-*

tians, a people inhabiting the north of Europe and Asia.

Sarpēdon, ŏnis, m. *a son of Jupiter and Europa.*

Satelles, ītis, m. *a satellite; a guard; a body-guard.*

Satiātus, a, um, part. from

Satio, āre, āvi, ātum, a. *to satiate; to satisfy.*

Satis, adj. & adv. *enough; sufficient; sufficiently; very; quite.*

Satur, ŭra, ŭrum, adj. *satiated; full.*

Saturnia, æ, f. *a name given to Italy; also, a citadel and town near Janiculum.*

Saturnus, i, m. *the father of Jupiter.*

Saucio, āre, āvi, ātum, a. *to wound.*

Saxum, i, n. *a rock; a stone.*

Scævŏla, æ, m. (Mucius,) *a brave Roman soldier.*

Scateo, ēre, n. *to be full; to abound.*

Scamander, dri, m. *a river of Troas, which flows from mount Ida into the Hellespont.*

Scaurus, i, m. *the surname of several Romans.*

Scelestus, a, um, adj. *wicked;* from

Scelus, ĕris, n. *wickedness; a crime;* by metonymy, § 324, 2, *a wicked person.*

Scena, æ, f. *a scene; a stage.*

Schŏneus, i, m. *a king of Ar-*

cadia, or *of Scyros, and father of Atalanta.*

Scheria, æ, f. *an ancient name of the island Corcўra,* or *Corfu.*

Scientia, æ, f. *knowledge;* from

Scio, ire, ivi, itum, a. *to know; to understand.*

Scipio, ŏnis, m. *a distinguished Roman family:* Scipiŏnes, *the Scipios.*

Scopŭlus, i, m. *a cliff; a rock.*

Scorpio, ŏnis, m. *a scorpion.*

Scotia, æ, f. *Scotland.*

Scriba, æ, m. *a writer; a secretary; a scribe;* from

Scribo, scribĕre, scripsi, scriptum, a. *to write:* scribĕre leges, *to prepare laws.*

Scriptor, ŏris, m. *a writer; an author.*

Scripturus, a, um, part. (scribo.)

Scriptus, a, um, part. (scribo.)

Scrūtor, ări, ătus sum, dep. *to search into; to trace out.*

Scutum, ı, n. *a shield.*

Scylla, æ, f. *the daughter of Nisus.*

Scyros, i, f. *an island in the Ægean sea.*

Scythes, æ, m. *an inhabitant of Scythia; a Scythian.*

Scythia, æ, f. *a vast country in the north of Europe and Asia.*

Scythĭcus, a, um, adj. *Scythian.*

Seco, secāre, secui, sectum, a. *to cut.*

Secēdo, -cedĕre, -cessi, cessum, n. (se & cedo,) *to secede; to step aside; to withdraw.*

Sectātus, a, um, part. *having followed* or *attended;* from

Sector, ări, ătus sum, dep. freq. (sequor, § 187, II., 1,) *to follow; to pursue; to accompany; to attend; to strive after.*

Secum, (se & cum, § 133, R. 4,) *with himself; with herself; with itself; with themselves.*

Secundus, a, um, adj. *the second; prosperous:* res secundæ, *prosperity.*

Secūris, is, f. *an axe.*

Secūtus, a, um, part. (sequor.)

Sed, conj. § 198, 9; *but.*

Sedĕcim, num. adj. ind. pl. (sex & decem,) *sixteen.*

Sedeo, sedēre, sedi, sessum, n. *to sit; to light upon.*

Sedes, is, f. *a seat; a residence; a settlement:* regni, *the seat of government.*

Seditio, ŏnis, f. *sedition; a rebellion; an insurrection.*

Sedŭlus, a, um, adj. *diligent.*

Seges, ĕtis, f. *a crop; a harvest.*

Segnis, e, adj. (ior, issĭmus,) *dull; slow; slothful; sluggish.*

Sejungo, -jungĕre, -junxi, -junctum, a. (se & jungo,) *to divide; to sever; to separate.*

Seleucia, æ, f. *a town of Syria near the Orontes.*

Semel, adv. *once:* plùs semel, *more than once.*

Semèle, es, f. *a daughter of Cadmus and Hermione, and mother of Bacchus.*

Semirămis, ĭdis, f. *a warlike queen of Assyria, and the wife of Ninus.*

Semper, adv. *always.*

Sempiternus, a, um, adj. *everlasting.*

Sempronius, i, m. *the name of a Roman* gens *or clan :* Sempronius Gracchus, *a Roman general.*

Sena, æ, f. *a town of Picĕnum.*

Senâtor, ōris, m. (senex,) *a senator.*

Senâtus, ûs & i, m. (senex,) *a senate.*

Senecta, æ, *or* Senectus, ûtis, f. (senex,) *old age.*

Senescens, tis, part. from

Senesco, senescĕre, senui, inc. *to grow old ; to wane.*

Senex, is, c. *an old man* or *woman :*—adj. *old :* (comp. senior.) § 126, 4.

Senónes, um, m. pl. *a people of Gaul.*

Sensi. *See* Sentio.

Sensus, ûs, m. (sentio,) *sense; feeling.*

Sententia, æ, f. *an opinion; a proposition; a sentiment;* from

Sentio, sentire, sensi, sensum, a. *to feel ; to perceive ; to be sensible of ; to observe ; to suppose.*

Separo, âre, âvi, âtum, a. se & paro,) *to separate ; to divide.*

Sepelio, sepelire, sepelivi, sepultum, a. *to bury ; to inter.*

Sepes, is, f. *a hedge ; a fence.*

Septem, num. adj. ind. pl. *seven.*

Septentrio, ōnis, m. *the Northern Bear ; the north.*

Septies, num. adv. *seven times.*

Septĭmus, a, um, num. adj. (septem,) *the seventh.*

Septingentesīmus, a, um, num. adj. *the seven hundredth.*

Septuagesīmus, a, um, num. adj. *the seventieth.*

Septuaginta, num. adj. ind. pl. *seventy.*

Sepulcrum, i, n. *a grave ; a sepulchre ; a tomb.*

Sepultûra, æ, f. *burial; interment.*

Sepultus, a, um, part. (sepelio,) *buried.*

Sequăna, æ, m. *the Seine, a river in France.*

Sequens, tis, part. from

Sequor, sequi, secûtus sum, dep. *to follow ; to pursue.*

Secûtus, a, um, part. (sequor.)

Serênus, a, um, adj. *serene; tranquil ; clear ; fair ; bright.*

Sergius, i, m. *the name of several Romans.*

Sermo, ōnis, m. *speech ; a discourse ; conversation.*

Serò. (seriùs,) adv. *late ; too late.*

Sero, serĕre, sevi, satum, a. *to sow ; to plant.*

Serpens, tis, c. (serpo,) *a serpent;
a snake.*

Sertorius, i, m. *a Roman general.*

Serus, a, um, adj. *late.*

Servilius, i, m. *the name of a
Roman family :* Servilius
Casca, *one of the murderers
of Cæsar.*

Servio, ire, ivi, itum, n. (servus,)
*to b. a slave; to serve, (as a
slave.)*

Servitium, i, n., *or* Servitus, utis,
f. (servus,) *slavery; bondage.*

Servius, i, m. (Tullius,) *the sixth
king of Rome.*

Servo, âre, âvi, âtum, a. *to preserve; to guard; to watch;
to keep.*

Servus, i, m. *a slave; a servant.*

Sese, pro. acc. & abl. § 133, R. 2;
himself; herself; themselves.

Sestertium, i, n. *a sestertium, or
a thousand sesterces.* § 327,(b)

Sestertius, i, m. *a sesterce, or
two and a half asses.* § 327, 3.

Sestos, i, *or* -us, i, f. *a town of
Thrace, on the shores of the
Hellespont, opposite to Aby-
dos.*

Seta, æ, f. *a bristle.*

Setinus, a, um, adj. *Setine; be-
longing to Setia, a city of
Campania, near the Pontine
Marshes, famous for its wine.*

Sex, num. adj. ind. pl. *six.*

Sexagesimus, a, um, num. adj.
the sixtieth.

Sexaginta, num. adj. ind. pl.
sixty.

Sexcentesimus, a, um, num. adj.
the six hundredth.

Sextus, a, um, num. adj. *the
sixth.*

Si, conj. *if; whether; to see
whether :* si quando, *if at any
time.*

Sic, adv. *so; thus; in such a
manner.*

Siccius, i, m. (Dentâtus,) *the name
of a brave Roman soldier.*

Siccus, a, um, adj. *dry :* siccum,
dry land.

Sicilia, æ, f. *Sicily, the largest
island in the Mediterranean.*

Siculus, a, um, adj. *Sicilian :*
fretum, *the straits of Messina.*

Sicut, & Sicuti, adv. (sic ut,) *as;
as if.*

Sidon, ônis, f. *a maritime city of
Phœnicia.*

Sidonius, a, um, adj. *belonging
to Sidon; Sidonian.*

Sidus, êris, n. *a star.*

Significo, are, âvi, âtum, a. (signum & facio,) *to designate;
to mark; to express; to signify; to give notice; to im-
ply or mean.*

Signum, i, n. *a sign; a token;
a statue; a standard; colors.*

Silens, tis, part. (sileo,) *silent;
keeping silence.*

Silentium, i, n. *silence.*

Silênus, i, m. *the foster-father
and instructor of Bacchus.*

Sileo, ĕre, ui, n. *to be silent; to conceal.*

Silva, *or* Sylva, æ, f. *a forest; a wood.*

Silvia, æ, f. (Rhea,) *the mother of Romulus.*

Silvius, i, m. *a son of Æneas, the second king of Alba:* Silvius Procas, *a king of Alba, the father of Numitor and Amulius.*

Simia, æ, f. *an ape.*

Simĭlis, e, adj. (ior, līmus,) *similar; like.*

Simĭlĭter, adv. *in like manner.*

Simplex, ĭcis, adj. (semel & plico,) *simple; artless; open; plain; single.*

Simŏis, entis, m. *a river of Troas, flowing into the Scamander.*

Simonĭdes, is, m. *a Greek poet, born in the island of Cea.*

Simul, adv. *at the same time; at once; together; as soon as:* simul — simul, *as soon as, or no sooner than.*

Simulācrum, i, n. (simŭlo,) *an image; a statue.*

Sin, conj. *but if.*

Sine, prep. *without.*

Singulāris, e, adj. *single; singular; distinguished; extraordinary:* certāmen singulāre, *a single combat.*

Singŭli, æ, a, num. adj. pl. *each; one by one; every:* singŭlis mensĭbus, *every month:* singŭlis singŭlas partes, *to each a share.*

Sinister, ra, rum, adj. *left.*

Sino, sĭnĕre, sivĭ, situm, a. *to permit.*

Sinus, ûs, m. *a bosom; a bay; a gulf.*

Siquis, siqua, siquod *or* siquid, pro. *if any one; if any thing.*

Siquando, adv. *if at any time; if ever.*

Sitio, īre, ii, n. & a. *to thirst; to be thirsty; to earnestly desire.*

Sitis, is, f. *thirst.*

Situs, a, um, adj. *placed; set; situated; permitted.*

Sive, conj. *or; or if; whether.*

Sobrius, a, um, adj. *sober; temperate.*

Socer, ĕri, m. *a father-in-law.*

Sociālis, e, adj. (socius,) *pertaining to allies; social; confederate.*

Sociĕtas, ātis, f. *society; alliance; intercourse; partnership;* from

Socius, i, m. *an ally; a companion.*

Socordia, æ, f. (socors,) *negligence; sloth.*

Socrătes, is, m. *the most eminent of the Athenian philosophers.*

Sol, sŏlis, m. *the sun.*

Solĕo, ĕre, ĭtus sum, n. pass. § 142, 2; *to be wont; to be accustomed:* solébat, *used.*

Solĭdus, a, um, adj. *whole; solid; entire.*

Solitūdo, ĭnis, f. (solus,) *a desert; a wilderness; a solitary place.*

Solītus, a, um, part. (soleo,) *accustomed; usual.*

Sollers, tis, adj. *ingenious; inventive; cunning; skilful; shrewd.*

Sollertia, æ, f. *sagacity; skill; shrewdness.*

Solon, ŏnis, m. *the lawgiver of the Athenians, and one of the seven wise men of Greece.*

Solstitium, i, n. (sol & sisto,) *the solstice, particularly the summer solstice, in distinction from* bruma, *the winter solstice; the longest day.*

Solum, i, n. *the earth; the soil; land.*

Solùm, adv. *alone; only;* from

Solus, a, um, adj. § 107; *alone.*

Solūtus, a, um, part. from

Solvo, solvĕre, solvi, solūtum, a. *to dissolve; to melt; to answer.*

Somnio, āre, āvi, ātum, n. *to dream;* from

Somnium, i, n. *a dream;* from

Somnus, i, m. *sleep.*

Sonĭtus, ûs, m. *a sound; a noise.*

Sono, āre, ui, ītum, n. *to sound; to resound;* from

Sonus, i, m. *a sound.*

Sorbeo, -ēre, -ui, *to suck in; to absorb.*

Soror, ŏris, f. *a sister.*

Sp., *an abbreviation of* Spurius.

Spargo, spargĕre, sparsi, sparsum, a. *to sprinkle; to strew; to scatter; to sow.*

Sparsi. See Spargo.

Sparsus, a, um, part.

Sparta, æ, f. *Sparta or Lacædæmon, the capital of Laconia.*

Spartăcus, i, m. *the name of o celebrated gladiator.*

Spartănus, i, m. *a Spartan.*

Sparti, ŏrum, m. pl. *a race of men, said to have sprung from the dragon's teeth which Cadmus sowed.*

Spartum, i, n. *Spanish broom, a plant of which ropes were made.*

Spatiōsus, a, um, adj. *large; spacious;* from

Spatium, i, n. *a space; room; distance.*

Species, ĕi, f. (specio,) *an appearance.*

Spectacŭlum, i, n. *a spectacle; a show;* from

Specto, āre, āvi, ātum, a. freq (specio,) *to behold; to see; to consider; to regard; to relate; to refer.*

Specus, ûs, m. f. & n. *a cave.*

Spelunca, æ, f. *a cave.*

Spero, āre, āvi, ātum, n. *to hope; to expect.*

Spes, ei, f. *hope; expectation; promise.*

Speusippus, i, m. *the nephew and successor of Plato.*

Sphinx, gis, f. *a Sphinx. The Egyptian Sphinx is represented as a monster, having a woman's head on the body of a lion.*

Spina, æ, f. *a thorn; a sting; a quill; a spine; a backbone.*

Spirĭtus, ûs, m. *a breath;* from

Spiro, āre, āvi, ātum, n. *to breathe.*

Splendeo, ēre, ui, n. *to shine; to be conspicuous.*

Splendĭdus, a, um, adj. *splendid; illustrious.*

Splendor, ōris, m. *brightness; splendor.*

Spolio, āre, āvi, ātum, a. *to despoil; to strip; to deprive;* from

Sponum, i, n. *spoils; booty.*

Spondeo, spondēre, spopondi, sponsum, a. *to promise; to engage.*

Sponsa, æ, f. *a bride.*

Spontis, gen., sponte, abl. sing., f. §.94; *of himself; of itself; of one's own accord; voluntarily; spontaneously.*

Spurius, i, m. *a prænōmen among the Romans.*

Squama, æ, f. *the scale of a fish.*

Stabŭlum, i, n. (sto,) *a stall; a stable.*

Stadium, i, n. *a stadium; a furlong; a measure of 125 paces; the race-ground.*

Stannum, i, n. *tin.*

Stans, stantis, part. (sto.)

Statim, adv. *immediately.*

Statio, ōnis, f. (sto,) *a station:* navium, *roadstead; an anchoring-place.*

Statua, æ, f. (statuo,) *a statue.*

Statuarius, i, m. *a statuary: a sculptor.*

Statuo, uĕre, ui, ūtum, a. *to determine; to resolve; to fix; to judge; to decide; to believe.*

Status, a, um, adj. *fixed; stated; appointed; certain.*

Statūtus, a, um, part. (statuo,) *placed; resolved; fixed; settled.*

Stella, æ, f. *a star.*

Sterĭlis, e, adj. *unfruitful; sterile; barren.*

Sterto, ĕre, ui, n. *to snore.*

Stipes, ĭtis, m. *a stake; the trunk of a tree.*

Stirps, is, f. *a root; a stock; a race; a family.*

Sto, stare, steti, statum, n. *to stand; to be stationary:* stare a partibus, *to favor the party.*

Stoïcus, i, m. *a Stoic, one of a sect of Grecian philosophers, whose founder was Zeno.*

Stolidĭtas, ātis, f. *stupidity;* from

Stolĭdus, a, um, adj. *foolish; silly; stupid.*

Strages, is, f. (sterno,) *an overthrow; slaughter.*

Strangŭlo, āre, āvi, ātum, a. *to strangle.*

Strenuè, adv. *bravely; actively; vigorously; strenuously;* from

Strenuus, a, um, adj. *bold; strenuous; brave; valiant.*

Strophădes, um, f. pl. *two small islands in the Ionian sea.*

Struo, struĕre, struxi, structum.

a. *to put together; to con-struct; to build:* insidias, *to prepare an ambuscade.*

Struthiocamêlus, i, m. *an ostrich.*

Strymon, ŏnis, m. *a river which was anciently the boundary be-tween Macedonia and Thrace.*

Studeo, êre, ui, n. *to favor; to study; to endeavor; to attend to; to pursue.*

Studiósè, adv. (studiósus,) *studi-ously; diligently.*

Studium, i, n. *zeal; study; dili-gence; eagerness.*

Stultitia, æ, f. *folly;* from

Stultus, a, um, adj. (ior, issĭmus,) *foolish:* stulti, *fools.*

Stupeo, êre, ui, n. *to be astonished at; to be amazed.*

Sturnus, i, m. *a starling.*

Suadendus, a, um, part. (suadeo.)

Suadens, tis, part. from

Suadeo, suadēre, suasi, suasum, a. & n. *to advise; to per-suade; to urge.*

Suavĭtas, àtis, f. (suavis,) *sweet-ness; grace; melody.*

Suavĭter, adv. *sweetly; agreea-bly.*

Sub, prep. *under; near to; near the time of; just before; at; in the time of.*

Subdùco, -ducĕre, -duxi, -duc-tum, a. (sub & duco,) *to with-draw; to take away; to with-hold.*

Subductus, a, um, part.

Subeo, ire, ivi & ii, ĭtum, irr. n.

(sub & eo, § 182,) *to go un-der; to submit to:* onus, *to take up* or *sustain a burden.*

Subĭgo, -igĕre, -ĕgi, -actum, a. (sub & ago,) *to subject; to subdue; to conquer.*

Subĭtò, adv. *suddenly;* from

Subĭtus, a, um, adj. (subeo,) *sud-den; unexpected.*

Sublàtus, a, um, part. (sustollo,) *taken away; lifted up.*

Sublimis, e, adj. *sublime; high in the air:* in sublime, *aloft.*

Sublimè, adv. *aloft; in the air.*

Submergo,-mergĕre,-mersi,-mer-sum, a. (sub & mergo,) *to over-whelm; to sink.*

Submergor, -mergi, -mersus sum, pass. *to be overwhelmed; to sink.*

Submersus, a, um, part.

Subridens, tis, part. *smiling at.*

Subrideo, -ridēre, -risi, -risum, n. (sub & rideo,) *to smile.*

Subsilio, -silire, -silui & -silii, n. (sub & salio,) *to leap; to jump.*

Substituo, -stituĕre, -stitui, -sti-tùtum, a. (sub & statuo,) *to put in one's place; to substi-tute.*

Subter, prep. *under.*

Subterraneus, a, um, adj. (sub & terra,) *subterranean.*

Subvenio, -venire, -vēni, -ven-tum, n. (sub & venio,) *to come to one's assistance; to succor to help.*

Subvŏlo, āre, āvi, ātum, n. (sub & volo,) *to fly up.*

Succēdo, -cedĕre, -cessi, -cessum, n. (sub & cedo,) *to succeed ; to follow.*

Successor, ōris, m. *a successor.*

Succus, i, m. *juice ; liquid ; sap.*

Suffĕro, sufferre, sustŭli, sublātum, irr. a. (sub & fero,) *to take away ; to undertake ; to bear.*

Suffetius, i, m. (Metius,) *an Alban general, put to death by Tullus Hostilius.*

Sufficio, -ficĕre, -fēci, -fectum, n. (sub & facio,) *to suffice ; to be sufficient.*

Suffodio, -fodĕre, -fōdi, -fossum, a. (sub & fodio,) *to dig under ; to undermine.*

Suffossus, a, um, part.

Suffragium, i, n. *suffrage ; vote ; a ballot ; choice.*

Sui, pro. gen. § 133; *of himself ; of herself ; of itself :* duæ sibi simīles, *like one another.*

Sulla, *or* Sylla, æ, m. *a distinguished Roman general.*

Sulpicius, i, m. (Gallus,) *a Roman, celebrated for his learning and eloquence, and for his skill in astrology.*

Sun, esse, fui, irr. n. § 153; *to be ; to exist ; to serve for :* terrōri esse, *to excite terror.*

Summus, a, um, adj. (*see* Supĕrus,) *the highest ; greatest ; perfect :* in summâ aquâ, *on the surface of the water.*

Sumo, sumĕre, sumpsi, sumptum, a. *to take.*

Sumptus, a, um, part.

Sumptus, ûs, m. *expense.*

Supellex, supellectīlis, f. *furniture ; household goods.*

Super, prep. *above ; upon.*

Superbè, adv. (iùs, issīmè,) *proudly ; haughtily.*

Superbia, æ, f. (superbus,) *pride ; haughtiness.*

Superbio, īre, īvi, ītum, n. *to be proud ; to be proud of ;* from

Superbus, a, um, adj. *proud ; a surname of Tarquin, the last king of Rome, the Proud.*

Superfluus, a, um, adj. (superfluo,) *superfluous.*

Superjăcio, -jacĕre, -jēci, -jactum, a. (super & jacio,) *to throw upon ; to shoot over.*

Superjacior, -jăci, -jactus sum, pass. *to be shot over.*

Supĕro, āre, āvi, ātum, a. (super,) *to surpass ; to conquer ; to excel ; to vanquish.*

Superstitiōsus, a, um, adj. *superstitious.*

Supersum, -esse, -fūi, irr. n. (super & sum,) *to remain ; to survive.*

Supĕrus, a, um, adj. (comp. superior ; sup. suprēmus *or* summus, § 125, 4,) *above high ; upper*

Supervacuus, a, um, adj. *super-fluous.*

Supervenio, -veníre, -věni, -ventum, n. (super & venio,) *to come upon; to come; to surprise suddenly.*

Supervŏlo, ăre, ăvi, ātum, n. (super & volo,) *to fly over.*

Suppěto, ěre, ivi, ĭtum, n. (sub & peto,) *to suffice; to remain; to serve; to be sufficient.*

Supplex, īcis, adj. *suppliant.*

Supplicium, i. n. *a punishment.*

Suppóno, -poněre, -posui, -posĭtum, a. (sub & pono,) *to put under; to substitute.*

Supra, prep. & adv. *above; before.*

Surěna, æ, m. *the title of a Parthian officer, next in authority to the king.*

Surgo, surgěre, surrexi, surrectum, n. *to rise*

Sus, uis, c. *swine; a hog.*

Suscipio, -cipěre, -cěpi, -ceptum, a. (sub & capio,) *to undertake; to take upon; to engage in; to receive.*

Suspectus, a, um, part. & adj. (suspicio,) *suspected; mistrusted.*

Suspendo, -penděre, -pendi, -pensum, a. (sub & pendo,) *to suspend; to hang; to hang up.*

Suspensus, a, um, part.

Suspicio, -spicěre, -spexi, -spectum, a. (sub & specio,) *to suspect.*

Suspĭcor, ări, ātus sum, dep. *to suspect; to surmise.*

Sustento, āre, āvi, ātum, freq. *to sustain; to support:* susertāre vitam, *to support one's self;* from

Sustineo, -tiněre, -tinui, -tentum, a. (sub & teneo,) *to bear; to carry; to sustain; to support.*

Sustollo, sustollěre, sustŭli, sublātum, a. *to take away; to lift up; to raise.*

Suus, a, um, pro. *his; hers; its; theirs.* § 139, R. 2.

Sylla. *See* Sulla.

Syllăba, æ, f. *a syllable.*

Sylva. *See* Silva.

Syphax, ăcis, m. *a king of Numidia.*

Syracûsæ, ărı m, f. pl. *Syracuse, a celebrated city of Sicily.*

Syria, æ, f. *a large country of Asia, at the eastern extremity of the Mediterranean sea.*

Syriăcus, a, um, adj. *Syrian; belonging to Syria.*

T.

T., *an abbreviation of* Titus.

Tabesco, tabescěre, tabui, inc. *to consume; to pine away.*

Tabŭla, æ, f. *a table; a tablet a picture; a painting:* plumbea tabŭla, *a plate or sheet of lead.*

Taceo, ěre, ui, ĭtum, n. *to be silent.*

Tactus, ûs, m. (tango,) *the touch.*

Tædet, tæduit, tæsum est *or* pertæsum est, imp. *to be weary of:* vitæ eos tædet, *they are weary of life.*

Tænärus, i, m., & um, i, n. *a promontory in Laconia,* now *cape Matapan.*

Talentum, i, n. *a talent; a sum variously estimated from* $860 *to* $1020.

Talis, e, adj. *such.*

Talpa, æ, c. *a mole.*

Tam, adv. *so; so much.*

Tamen, conj. *yet; notwithstanding; still; nevertheless.*

Tanäis, is, m. *a river between Europe and Asia,* now *the Don.*

Tanäquil, ïlis, f. *the wife of Tarquinius Priscus.*

Tandem, adv. *at length; at last; finally.*

Tango, tangĕre, tetĭgi, tactum, a. *to touch.*

Tanquam, *or* Tamquam, adv. *as; as well as; as if; like.*

Tantälus, i, m. *a son of Jupiter; the father of Pelops, and king of Phrygia.*

Tantò, adv. (tantus,) *so much.*

Tantopĕre, adv. (tantus & opus,) *so much; so greatly.*

Tantùm, adv. *only; so much;* from

Tantus, a, um, adj. *so great; such:* tanti, *of so much value:* tanti est, *it is worth the pains; it makes amends:* non est

tanti, *it is not best; it is not worth while.*

Tardè, adv. (iùs, issĭmè,) (tardus, *slowly.*

Tardĭtas, ātis, f. (tardus,) *slowness; dulness; heaviness.*

Tardo, āre, āvi, ātum, a. *to retard, to check; to stop;* from

Tardus, a, um, adj. *slow; dull.*

Tarentinus, a, um, adj. *Tarentine; of* or *belonging to Tarentum :* Tarentĭni, *Tarentines; the inhabitants of Tarentum.*

Tarentum, i, n. *a celebrated city in the south of Italy.*

Tarpëia, æ, f. *the daughter of Sp. Tarpeius: she betrayed the Roman citadel to the Sabines.*

Tarpëius, a, um, adj. *Tarpeian :* mons, *the Tarpeian* or *Capitoline mount.*

Tarquinii, ōrum, m. pl. *a city of Etruria, whence the family of Tarquin derived their name.*

Tarquinius, i, m. *Tarquin; the name of an illustrious Roman family, of which two, Priscus and Superbus, were kings :* Tarquinii, ōrum, pl. *the Tarquins.*

Tartärus, i, m., & -a, ōrum, pl. n. *Tartarus; the infernal regions.*

Taurĭca, æ, f. *a large peninsula of the Black sea,* now *called the Crimea* or *Taurida.*

Taurus, ῐ, m. *a high range of mountains in Asia.*

Taurus, i, m. *a bull.*

Taӯgĕtus, i, m., & -a, ŏrum, pl. n. *a mountain of Laconia, near Sparta.*

Tectum, i, n. *a roof; a house.*

Tectus, a, um, part. (tego,) *covered; defended.*

Teges, ĕtis, f. *a mat; a rug; a coverlet;* from

Tego, gĕre, xi, ctum, a. *to cover; to defend.*

Tegumentum, i, n. *a covering.*

Telum, i, n. *a weapon; a dart; an arrow.*

Temĕrĕ, adv. *at random; accidentally; rashly.*

Tempe, n. pl. indec. *a beautiful vale in Thessaly, through which the river Peneus flows.*

Temperies, iĕi, f. *temperateness; mildness; temperature.*

Tempestas, ātis, f. *a storm; a tempest.*

Templum, i, n. *a temple.*

Tempus, ŏris, n. *time; a season:* ad tempus, *at the time appointed:* ex tempŏre, *without premeditation.*

Temulentus, a, um, adj. *drunken; intoxicated.*

Tendo, tendĕre, tetendi, tensum, a. *to stretch; to stretch out; to extend; to go; to advance.*

Tenĕbræ, ārum, f. pl. *darkness.*

Teneo, tenēre, tenui, tentum, a. *to hold; to have; to keep; to possess; to know; to hold by a garrison:* portum, *to reach the harbor.*

Tentātus, a, um, part. from

Tento, āre, āvi, ātum, a. freq *to attempt; to try.*

Tentyrītæ, ārum, c. pl. *the inhabitants of Tentyra, a town and island in Upper Egypt.*

Tenuis, e, adj. *thin; light; rare.*

Tenus, prep. *up to; as far as.*

Tepesco, escĕre, ui, inc. (tepeo,) *to grow warm or cool; to become tepid.*

Ter, num. adv. *thrice.*

Terentius, i, m. *a Roman proper name.*

Tergum, i, n. *the back; the farther side:* a tergo, *from behind:* ad terga, *behind.*

Termino, āre, āvi, ātum, a. *to bound; to limit; to terminate.*

Termĭnus, i, m. *a boundary; a limit; an end; bounds.*

Terni, æ, a, num. adj. pl. *three by three; three.*

Terra, æ, f. *the earth; a country; the land:* omnes terræ, *the whole world.*

Terreo, ēre, ui, ĭtum, a. *to terrify; to scare; to frighten.*

Terrester, terrestris, terrestre, adj. *terrestrial:* anĭmal terrestre, *a land animal.*

Terribĭlis, e, adj. *terrible.*

Territo, āre, āvi, ātum, freq. (terreo,) *to terrify; to affright.*

Territorium, i, n. (terra,) *territory.*

Territus, a, um, part. (terreo.)

Terror, ŏris, m. *terror; consternation; fear.*

Tertius, a, um, num. adj. *the third.*

Tertiò, num. adv. *the third time.*

Testa, æ, f. *an earthen vessel; a shell.*

Testamentum, i, n. *a will; a testament.*

Testŭdo, ĭnis, f. *a tortoise.*

Tetĭgi. *See* Tango.

Teutŏnes, um, & Teutŏni, ŏrum, m. pl. *a nation who lived in the northern part of Germany, near the Cimbri.*

Texo, texĕre, texui, textum, a. *to weave; to plait; to form; to construct.*

Thalămus, i, m. *a bed-chamber; a dwelling.*

Thales, is & ētis, m. *a Milesian, one of the seven wise men of Greece.*

Thasus, i, f. *an island on the coast of Thrace.*

Theâtrum, i, n. *a theatre.*

Thebæ, ārum, f. pl. *Thebes, the capital of Bœotia.*

Thebănus, a, um, adj. *Theban; belonging to Thebes.*

Thelesinus, i, m. *a Roman proper name.*

Themistŏcles, is, m. *a celebrated Athenian general in the Persian war.*

Theodŏrus, i, m. *a philosopher of Cyrēnæ.*

Thermŏdon, ontis, m. *a river of Pontus.*

Theseus, i, m. *a king of Athens, and son of Ægeus, was one of the most celebrated heroes of antiquity.*

Thessalia, æ, f. *Thessaly; a country of Greece, south of Macedonia.*

Thessălus, a, um, adj. *belonging to Thessaly; Thessalian.*

Thestius, i, m. *the father of Althæa.*

Thetis, ĭdis & ĭdos, f. *one of the sea nymphs; the wife of Peleus, and mother of Achilles.*

Theutobŏchus, i, m. *a king of the Cimbri.*

Thracia, æ, f. *Thrace, a large country east of Macedonia.*

Thracius, a, um, adj. *belonging to Thrace; Thracian.*

Thrasybŭlus, i, m. *an Athenian general, celebrated for freeing his country from the thirty tyrants.*

Thus, thuris, n. *frankincense.*

Tibĕris, is, m. § 79; *the Tiber, a famous river of Italy.*

Tibi. *See* Tu.

Tibicen, ĭnis, m. *one who plays upon the flute; a piper.*

Ticinum, i, n. *a town of Cisalpine Gaul, where the Romans were defeated by Hannibal.*

Tigrānes, is, m. *a king of Armenia Major.*

Tigranocerta, ōrum, n. *a city of Armenia Major, founded by Tigrānes.*

Tigris, īdis, (*seldom* is,) f. *a tiger.*

Tigris, īdis & is, m. *a river in Asia.*

Timens, tis, part. from

Timeo, ēre, ui, n. & a. *to fear; to dread; to be afraid.*

Timĭdus, a, um, adj. *timid; cowardly.*

Timor, ōris, m. *fear.*

Tinnītus, ūs, m. *a tinkling.*

Tintinnabŭlum, i, n. *a bell.*

Titio, ōnis, m. *a brand; a firebrand.*

Titus, i, m. *a Roman* prænōmen.

Tolĕro, āre, āvi, ātum, a. *to bear; to endure; to admit of.*

Tollo, tollĕre, sustŭli, sublātum, a. *to raise; to pick up; to remove; to do away with.*

Tondeo, tondēre, totondi, tonsum, a. *to shave; to shear.*

Tonĭtru, u, n. *thunder.*

Tono, āre, ui, ĭtum, n. *to thunder:* tonat, *it thunders.*

Tormentum, i, n. (torqueo,) *an engine for throwing stones and darts.*

Torquātus, i, m. *a surname given to T. Manlius and his descendants.*

Torquis, is, d. *a collar; a chain.*

Tot, ind. adj. *so many.*

Totĭdem, ind. adj. *the same number; as many.*

Totus, a, um, adj. § 107; *whole entire; all.*

Trabs, is, f. *a beam.*

Tractātus, a, um, part. from

Tracto, āre, āvi, ātum, a. freq (traho,) *to treat; to handle.*

Tractus, ūs, m. (traho,) *a tract a country; a region.*

Tractus, a, um, part. (traho.)

Tradĭtus, a, um, part. from

Trado, -dĕre, -dĭdi, -dĭtum, a. (trans & do,) *to deliver; to give; to give up; to relate, to teach:* tradunt, *they report:* tradĭtur, *it is related; it is reported:* traduntur, *they are reported.*

Tragĭcus, a, um, adj. *tragic.*

Tragœdia, æ, f. *a tragedy.*

Traho, trahĕre, traxi, tractum, a. *to draw; to drag:* bellum, *to protract; to prolong:* liquĭdas aquas trahĕre, *to draw along clear waters; to flow with a clear stream.* •

Trajĭcio, -jicĕre, -jēci, -jectum, a. (trans & jacio,) *to convey over; to pass or cross over.*

Trames, ĭtis, m. (trameo,) *a path; a way.*

Trano, āre, āvi, ātum, n. (trans & no,) *to swim over.*

Tranquillus, a, um, adj. *tranquil; calm; serene.*

Trans, prep. *over; beyond; on the other side.*

Transactus, a, um, part. (transĭgo.)

Transeo, ire, ii, ītum, irr. n. (trans & eo,) *to pass* or *go over.*

Transfĕro, -ferre, -tŭli, -lātum, irr. a. (trans & fero,) *to transfer; to carry over:* se ad alĭquem, *to go over to.*

Transfigo, -figĕre, -fixi, -fixum, a. (trans & figo,) *to pierce; to run through; to stab.*

Transfūga, æ, c. *a deserter.*

Transgredior, -grĕdi, -gressus sum, dep. (trans & gradior,) *to go* or *pass over.*

Transĭgo, -igĕre, -ĕgi, -actum, a. (trans & ago,) *to transact; to finish; to spend.*

Transilio, -silire, -silui & -silivi, n. (trans & salio,) *to leap over.*

Transitūrus, a, um, part. (transeo,) *about to pass over; to pass on.*

Translātus, a, um, part. (transfĕro.)

Transmarīnus, a, um, adj. (trans & mare,) *beyond the sea; foreign; transmarine.*

Transno. *See* Trano.

Transvĕho, -vehĕre, -vexi, -vectum, a. (trans & veho,) *to carry over; to convey; to transport.*

Transvŏlo, āre, āvi, ātum, n. (trans & volo,) *to fly over.*

Trasimēnus, i, m. *a lake in Etruria, near which the consul Flaminius was defeated by Hannibal.*

Trebia, æ, f. *a river of Cisalpine Gaul, emptying into the Po.*

Trecenti, æ, a, num. adj. pl. *three hundred.*

Trecentesĭmus, a, um, num. adj. *the three hundredth.*

Tredĕcim, num. adj. pl. ind. *thirteen.*

Tres, tria, num. adj. pl. § 109; *three.*

Trevĭri, ōrum, m. pl. *a people of Belgium.*

Triangulāris, e, adj. (triangŭlum,) *triangular; three-cornered.*

Tribūnus, i, m. *a tribune.*

Tribuo, uĕre, ui, ūtum, a. *to attribute; to give; to grant; to bestow; to commit.*

Tribūtum, i, n. *a tribute; a tax; a contribution; an assessment.*

Tricesĭmus, a, um, num. adj. *the thirtieth.*

Triduum, i, n. *the space of three days:* per triduum, *for three days.*

Triennium, i, n. (tres & annus,) *the space of three years.*

Trigemĭni, ōrum, m. pl. *three brothers born at one birth.*

Triginta, num. adj. pl. ind. *thirty.*

Trinacria, æ, f. *one of the names of Sicily.*

Triptolēmus, i, m. *the son of Celeus, king of Eleusis.*

Tristitia, æ, f. *sorrow; grief.*

Triumphālis, e, adj. (triumphus,) *triumphal.*

Triumphans, tis, part. from

Triumpho, âre, âvi, âtum, n. *to triumph.*

Triumphus, i, m. *a triumph; a triumphal procession.*

Triumvir, vīri, m. (tres & vir,) *one of three joint public officers; a triumvir.*

Troas, ădis, f. *a country of Asia Minor, bordering upon the Hellespont.*

Trochĭlus, i, m. *a wren.*

Troglodȳtæ, ârum, c. pl. *Troglodytes, a people of Ethiopia, who dwell in caves.*

Troja, æ, f. *Troy, the capital of Troas.*

Trojânus, a, um, adj. *Trojan.*

Trucĭdo, âre, âvi, âtum, a. *to slay; to murder; to massacre.*

Trux, ucis, adj. *savage; cruel; fierce; stern; grim.*

Tu, subs. pro. *thou;* § 133.

Tuba, æ, f. *a trumpet.*

Tuber, ĕris, n. *a bunch; a tumor; a protuberance.*

Tubĭcen, ĭnis, m. (tuba & cano,) *a trumpeter.*

Tueor, tuêri, tuĭtus sum, dep. *to defend; to protect.*

Tugurium, i, n. *a hut; a shed.*

Tuli.   See Fero.

Tullia, æ, f. *the daughter of Servius Tullius.*

Tullius, i, m. *a Roman.*

Tullus, i, m. (Hostilius,) *the third Roman king.*

Tum, adv. *then; and; so; also:*

tum — tum, *as well — as; both — and:* tum demum, *then first.*

Tumultus, ûs, m. *a noise; a tumult.*

Tumŭlus, i, m. *a mound; a tomb.*

Tunc, adv. *then.*

Tunĭca, æ, f. *a tunic; a close woollen garment, worn under the toga.*

Turbâtus, a, um, part. *disturbed; confused; troubled;* from

Turbo, âre, âvi, âtum, a. (turba,) *to disturb; to trouble.*

Turma, æ, f. *a troop; a company.*

Turpis, e, adj. *base; disgraceful.*

Turpitûdo, ĭnis, f. *baseness; ugliness.*

Turris, is, f. *a tower.*

Tuscia, æ, f. *a country of Italy the same as Etruria.*

Tuscŭlum, i, n. *a city of Latium.*

Tuscus, a, um, adj. *Tuscan; belonging to Tuscany; Etrurian.*

Tutor, ôris, m. *a guardian; a tutor.*

Tutus, a, um, adj. (ior, issĭmus,) *safe.*

Tuus, a, um, adj. pro. § 139; (tu,) *thy; thine.*

Tyrannis, ĭdis & ĭdos, f. *tyranny; arbitrary power.*

Tyrannus, i, m. *a tyrant; a usurper; a king.*

Tyrius, a, um, adj. *Tyrian:* Tyrii, *Tyrians; inhabitants of Tyre.*

Tyrrhēnus, a, um, adj. *Tyrrhenian* or *Tuscan; belonging to Tuscany.*

Tyrus, i, f. *a celebrated maritime city of Phœnicia.*

U.

Uber, ĕris, n. *an udder; a teat.*

Ubertas, ātis, f. *fertility; fruitfulness.*

Ubi, adv. *where; when; as soon as.*

Ubīque, adv. *every where.*

Ulcisor, ulcisci, ultus sum, dep. *to take revenge; to avenge.*

Ullus, a, um, adj. § 107; *any; any one.*

Ulterior, us, (ultīmus,) § 126, 1; *further.*

Ulteriùs, adv. *farther; beyond; longer.*

Ultīmus, a, um, adj. (sup. of ulterior,) *the last.*

Ultra, prep. *beyond; more than:* —adv. *besides; moreover; further.*

Ultus, a, um, part. (ulciscor,) *having avenged.*

Ulysses, is, m. *a distinguished king of Ithaca.*

Umbra, æ, f. *a shade; a shadow.*

Umbro, āre, āvi, ātum, a. *to shade; to darken.*

Unâ, adv. (unus,) *together.*

Unde, ac. r. *whence; from which.*

Undĕcim, num. adj. pl. ind. *eleven.*

Undenona esīmus, a, um, num adj. *the eighty-ninth.*

Undequinquaginta, num. adj. pl. ind. *forty-nine.*

Undetricesīmus, a, um, num. adj *twenty-ninth.* [*nineteenth.*

Undevicesīmus, a, um, num. adj.

Undeviginti, num. adj. *nineteen.*

Undīque, adv. *on all sides.*

Unguis, is, m. *a claw; a talon; a nail.*

Ungŭla, æ, f. *a claw; a talon; a hoof:* binis ungŭlis, *cloven-footed.*

Unīcus, a, um, adj. *one alone; sole; only.*

Unio, ōnis, m. *a pearl.*

Universus, a, um, adj. (unus & versus,) *whole; universal; all.*

Unquam, adv. *ever:* nec unquam, *and never.*

Unus, a, um, num. adj. § 107; *one; only; alone.*

Unusquisque, unaquæque, unumquodque, adj. *each one; each;* § 138, 4.

Urbs, is, f. *a city; the chief city; Rome.*

Uro, urēre, ussi, ustum, a. *to burn.*

Ursus, i, m. *a bear.*

Usque, adv. *even; as far as; till; until.*

Usus, a, um, part. (utor.)

Usus, ûs, m. *use; custom; profit; advantage.*

Ut, conj. *that; in order that; so that;* adv. *as.*

Utcunque, adv. *howsoever; somewhat; in some degree.*

Uter, tra, trum, adj. § 107; *which? which of the two?*

Uterque, trăque, trumque, adj. § 107; *both; each; each of the two.*

Utĭlis, e, adj. (utor,) *useful.*

Utĭca, æ, f. *a maritime city of Africa, near Carthage.*

Utor, uti, usus sum, dep. *to use; to make use of.*

Utrınque, adv. *on both sides.*

Utrùm, adv. *whether.*

Uva, æ, f. *a grape; a bunch of grapes :* passa, *a raisin.*

Uxor, ŏris, f. *a wife.*

V.

Vaco, āre, āvi, ātum, n. *to be free from.*

Vacuus, a, um, adj. *empty; unoccupied; vacant; free; exempt :* vacuus viător, *the destitute traveller.*

Vadŏsus, a, um, adj. *fordable; shallow; from*

Vadum, i, n. *a ford; a shallow.*

Vagans, tis, part. (vagor.)

Vagĭna, æ f. *a scabbard; a sheath.*

Vagitus, ûs, m. *weeping; crying.*

Vagor, āri, ātus sum, dep. *to wander about; to stray.*

Valeo, ēre, ui, n. *to be strong; to avail; to be distinguished; to be eminent :* multum valēre,

to be very powerful : vale, *farewell.*

Valerıus, i, m. *a Roman proper name.*

Vallis, is, f. *a valley; a vale.*

Variĕtas, ātis, f. (varius,) *variety; change.*

Vario, āre, āvi, ātum, a. *to change, to vary; from*

Varius, a, um, adj. *various; diverse.*

Varro, ŏnis, m. (Marcus,) *a very learned Roman, some of whose works are still extant :* P. Terentius, *a consul, who was defeated by Hannibal.*

Vasto, āre, āvi, ātum, a. *to lay waste; to ravage; from*

Vastus, a, um, adj. *wide; vast; great.*

Vates, is, m. *a poet; a bard.*

Ve, conj. (enclitic, § 198, R. 2,) *or.*

Vecordia, æ, f. *madness; folly.*

Vectus, a, um, part. (veho.)

Vehĕmens, tis, adj. (ior, issĭmus,) *vehement; immoderate.*

Vehementer, adv. (iùs, issĭmè,) *vehemently; greatly; very; much; violently.*

Veho, vehĕre, vexi, vectum, a. *to bear; to carry; to convey.*

Veiens, tis, & Veientānus, i, m. *an inhabitant of Veii.*

Veii, ŏrum, m. pl. *a city of Tuscany, memorable for the defeat of the Fabian family.*

Vel, conj. § 198, 2; *or; also*

even : vel lecta, *even when read :* vel — vel, *either — or.*

Vello, vellĕre, velli *or* vulsi, vulsum, a. *to pluck.*

Vellus, ĕris, n. *a fleece.*

Velox, ŏcis, adj. (ior, issĭmus,) *swift ; rapid ; active.*

Velum, i, n. *a sail.*

Velut, & Velūti, adv. (vel & ut,) *as ; as if.*

Venālis, e, adj. *venal ; mercenary.*

Venans, tis, part. (venor.)

Venatĭcus, a, um, adj. *belonging to the chase :* canis, *a hound.*

Venātor, ŏris, m. (venor,) *a huntsman.*

Vendĭto, āre, āvi, ātum, freq. *to sell ;* from

Vendo, vendĕre, vendĭdi, vendĭtum, a. (venum & do,) *to sell.*

Venenātus, a, um, adj. *poisoned ; poisonous ;* from

Venēnum, i, n. *poison.*

Veneo, ire, ii, irr. n. § 142, 3 ; *to be exposed for sale ; to be sold.*

Venētus, i. m., *or* Brigantinus, *a lake between Germany and Switzerland, called the Boden sea, or lake of Constance.*

Venio, venire, veni, ventum, n. *to come ; to advance.*

Venor, āri, ātus sum, dep. *to hunt.*

Venter, tris, m. *the belly ; the stomach.*

Ventus, i, m. *a wind.*

Venus, ĕris, f. *the goddess of love and beauty.*

Ver, veris, n. *the spring.*

Verber, ĕris, n. *a whip ; a rod ; a blow ; a stripe.*

Verbĕro, āre, āvi, ātum, a. *to strike.*

Verbum, i, n. *a word.*

Verè, adv. (verus,) *truly.*

Vereor, ēri, ĭtus sum, dep. *to fear ; to be concerned for.*

Vergo, vergĕre, versi, n. *to tend to ; to incline ; to verge towards ; to bend ; to look.*

Verisimĭlis, e, adj. (verum & simĭlis,) *probable.*

Verĭtus, a, um, part. (vereor.)

Verò, conj. § 279, 3, (verus,) *but :* —adv. *indeed ; truly.*

Verŏna, æ, f. *Verona, a city in the north of Italy.*

Versātus, a, um, part. from

Versor, āri, ātus sum, dep. freq. (verto,) *to turn ; to revolve ; to dwell ; to live ; to reside.*

Versus, a, um, part. (vertor.)

Versùs, prep. *towards.*

Vertex, ĭcis, m. *the top ; the summit ; the crown of the head.*

Verto, tĕre, ti, sum, a. *to turn ; to change.*

Veru, u, n. § 87 ; *a spit.*

Verùm, conj. *but ; but yet ;* from

Verus, a, um, adj. *true.*

Vescor, i, dep. *to live upon ; to feed upon ; to eat ; to subsist upon.*

Vespĕri, *or* -è, adv. *at evening.*

tam vespĕri, *so late at even-ing.*

Vesta, æ, f. *a goddess, the mother of Saturn.*

Vestālis, is, f. (virgo,) *a Vestal virgin, a priestess consecrated to the service of Vesta.*

Vestibŭlum, i, n. *the porch; the vestibule.*

Vestigium, i, n. *a footstep; a vestige; a trace; a mark; a track.*

Vestio, ire, ivi, itum, a. *to clothe;* from

Vestis, is, f. *a garment; clothes.*

Vesŭlus, i, m. *a high mountain of Liguria, and a part of the Cottian Alps.*

Veterānus, a, um, adj. (vetus,) *old; a veteran.*

Veto, āre, ui, itum, a. *to forbid; to prohibit.*

Veturia, æ, f. *the mother of Coriolanus.*

Veturius, i, m. (Titus,) *a Roman consul, who was defeated by the Samnites at the Caudine Forks.*

Vetus, ĕris, adj. *ancient; old:* vetĕres, *the ancients.*

Vetustas, ātis, f. *antiquity; age.*

Vetustus, a, um, adj. *old; ancient.*

Vexi. *See Veho.*

Via, æ, f. *a way; a course; a path; a journey.*

Viātor, ōris, m. *a traveller.*

Vicēni, æ a, num. adj. pl. *every twenty, twenty.*

Vicesĭmus, a, um, num. adj. *the twentieth.*

Vici. *See Vinco.*

Vicies, num. adv. *twenty times.*

Vicinĭtas, ātis, f. *the neighborhood; vicinity;* from

Vicinus, a, um, adj. *near; neighboring.*

Vicinus, i, m. *a neighbor.*

Vicis, gen. f. § 94; *change; reverse; a place; a turn:* in vicem, *in turn; in place of; instead.*

Victĭma, æ, f. *a victim; a sacrifice.*

Victor, ōris, m. (vinco,) *a victor; a conqueror:*—adj. *victorious.*

Victoria, æ, f. *a victory.*

Victūrus, a, um, part. (from vivo.)

Victus, a, um, part. (vinco.)

Vicus, i, m. *a village.*

Video, vidēre, vidi, visum, a. *to see; to behold.*

Videor, vidēri, visus sum, pass. *to be seen; to seem; to appear.*

Viduus, a, um, adj. *bereaved; widowed:* mulier vidua, *a widow.*

Vigil, ĭlis, m. *a watchman.*

Vigĭlans, tis, adj. (ior, issĭmus,) *watchful; vigilant.*

Vigilia, æ, f. *a watching:*—pl *the watch.*

Viginti, num. adj. pl. ind. *twenty.*

Vilis, e, adj. *vile; bad; mean.*

Villa, æ, f. *a country-house; a country seat; a villa.*

Villĭcus, i, m. *an overseer of an estate; a steward.*

Villus, i, m. *long hair; coarse hair.*

Vincio, vincīre, vinxi, vinctum, a. *to bind.*

Vinco, vincĕre, vici, victum, a. *to conquer; to vanquish; to surpass.*

Vinctus, a, um, part. (vincio.)

Vincŭlum, i, n. *a chain :* in vincŭla conjicĕre, *to throw into prison.*

Vindex, ĭcis, c. *an avenger; a protector; a defender; an asserter;* from

Vindĭco, āre, āvi, ātum, a. *to claim; to avenge.*

Vindicta, æ, f. *vengeance; punishment.*

Vinum, i, n. *wine.*

Viŏla, æ, f. *a violet.*

Viŏlo, āre, āvi, ātum, a. *to violate; to pollute; to corrupt.*

Vir, viri, m. *a man.*

Vireo, ĕre, ui, n. *to be green; to be verdant; to flourish.*

Vires. *See* Vis.

Virga, æ, f. *a rod; a small staff; a switch.*

Virgĭlius, i, m. *Virgil, a very celebrated Latin poet.*

Virginia, æ, f. *the daughter of Virginius.*

Virginius, i, m. *the name of a distinguished Roman centurion.*

Virgo, ĭnis, f. *a virgin; a girl; a maid.*

Virgŭla, æ, f. (dĭm. from v̄rga, *a small rod.*

Viriāthus, i, m. *a Lusitanian general, who was originally a shepherd, and afterwards a leader of robbers.*

Viridomārus, i, m. *a king of the Gauls, slain by Marcellus.*

Virtus, ūtis, f. (vir,) *virtue; merit, excellence; power; valor, faculty.*

Vis, vis, f. § 85; *power; strength; force :* vis homĭnum, *a multitude of men :* vim facĕre, *to do violence :*—pl. vīres, ium, *power; strength.*

Viscus, ĕris, n. *an entrail :* viscĕra, pl. *the bowels; the flesh.*

Vistŭla, æ, f. *a river of Prussia, which still bears the same name, and which was anciently the eastern boundary of Germany.*

Visurgis, is, m. *the Weser, a large river of Germany.*

Visus, a, um, part. (video.)

Visus, ūs, m. *the sight.*

Vita, æ, f. *life.*

Vitandus, a, um, part. (vito.)

Vitĭfer, ĕra, ĕrum, adj. (vitis & fero,) *vine-bearing.*

Vitis, is, f. *a vine.*

Vitium, i, n. *a crime.*

Vito, āre, āvi, ātum, a. *to shun; to avoid.*

Vitupĕro, āre, āvi, ātum, a. *to find fault with; to blame.*

Vivĭdus, a, um, adj. *lively; vivid* from

Vivo, vivĕre, vixi, victum, n. *to live: to fare; to live upon.*

Vivus, a, um, adj. *living; alive.*

Vix, adv. *scarcely.*

Vixi. See Vivo.

Voco, āre, āvi, ātum, a. (vox,) *to call; to invite; to name.*

Volo, āre, ι vi, ātum, n. *to fly.*

Volo, velle, volui, irr. a. § 178, 1; *to wish; to desire; to be willing.*

Volsci, ōrum, m. pl. *a people of Latium.*

Volŭcer, -cris, -cre, adj. *winged :* —subs. *a bird.*

Volumnia, æ, f. *the wife of Coriolānus.*

Voluntas, ātis, f. (volo,) *the will.*

Voluptas, ātis, f. (volŭpe,) *pleasure; sensual pleasure.*

Volutātus, a, um, part. from

Voluto, āre, āvi, ātum, a. freq. (volvo,) *to roll.*

Volvo, vĕre, vi, ūtum, a. *to roll; to turn.*

Votum, i, n. (voveo,) *a wish; a vow.*

Vox, vocis, f. *a voice; a word; an expression; an exclamation.*

Vulcānus, i, m. *Vulcan, the god of fire, the son of Jupiter and Juno.*

Vulgus, i, m. or n. *the common people; the populace; the vulgar.*

Vulnerātus, a, um, part. from

Vulnĕro, āre, āvi, ātum, a. *to wound;* from

Vulnus, ĕris, n. *a wound.*

Vulpecŭla, æ, f. dim. (vulpes,) *a little fox.*

Vulpes, is, f. *a fox.*

Vultur, ŭris, m. *a vulture.*

Vultus, ūs, m. *the countenance; the look.*

X.

Xanthippe, es, f. *the wife of Socrates.*

Xanthippus, i, m. *a Lacedæmonian general, who was sent to assist the Carthaginians, in the first Punic war.*

Xenocrătes, is, m. *a philosopher of Chalcēdon, the successor of Speusippus in the* Academīa.

Xerxes, is, m. *a celebrated king of Persia.*

Z.

Zama, æ, f. *a city of Africa.*

Zeno, ōnis, m. *a philosopher of Citium, a town of Cyprus, and founder of the sect of the Stoics.*

Zetes, is, m. *a son of Boreas.*

Zona, æ, f. *a girdle; a zone.*

Zone, es, f. *a city and promontory in the western part of Thrace, opposite to the island of Thasus.*

NOTES AND REFERENCES

FIRST LATIN BOOK.

BY means of the following Notes, the Reader can be used in connection with Andrews' First Latin Book. The same letters which originally, by means of notes at the foot of the page, referred to the sections of Andrews and Stoddard's Grammar, may now be taken as referring also to these Notes, and through these to the First Latin Book.

In preparing these Notes, while regard has constantly been had to the editor's former mode of commenting simply by reference to the Grammar, occasional explanations have been added, for the sake of the younger classes. In some instances, when special reasons seemed to render it expedient, the reference to the First Latin Book relates to a different principle from the corresponding one to the Grammar, and sometimes, though rarely, a reference to the Grammar is here left with no corresponding note. In addition, however, to the original notes, numerous references will be found in the following pages, to principles contained in the First Latin Book; and as in such cases the text contains no letter of reference, the word or phrase to be explained is cited in the notes.

What is the rule for the agreement of a verb? Less. 90, 2. PAGE What is a sentence? L. 83, 1. Of what does a simple 7. sentence or proposition consist? L. 83, 3. What is the subject of a sentence? L. 83, 4. What is the predicate? L. 83, 5. The grammatical subject? L. 84, 2. The grammatical predicate? L. 84, 3. How many moods have Latin verbs? L. 47, 1. How do the several moods represent an action? L. 47, 2. What is an active verb? L. 46, 3. What are the terminations of the active voice, indicative mood, present tense, in each conjugation? L. 52. • L. 5, 1; and L. 17, 2. ɩ L. 5, 1; and L. 9, 1; and L. 10, 1. When are the nominatives *ego, tu, nos,*

23

and *vos* omitted ? L. 51, R. 4. *c* L. 15, 1 and 2. *d* L. 5, II. *arbor*, L. 12, 1, and L. B., or.

8. *a* L. 5, 1.; and L. 12, 2. *b* L. 12, 1 and 2. *c* L. 9, 1; and L. 11. *d* L. 7, 3; and L. 25; and L. 26, Exc. 1. *sol*, L. F. *e* L. 18, 2 and 4. *f* L. 15, 1; and L. 17, 1; and N. *g* L. 5, N. 3. *h* L. 15, 1, 2, and 3. How does the imperfect tense represent an action ? L. 47, 7. What are the terminations of the active voice, indicative mood, imperfect tense, in each conjugation ? L. 52, p. 75. *i* L. 62, 2. *j* L. 8. How does the future tense represent an action ? L. 47, 8. What are the terminations of the active voice, indicative mood, future tense, in each conjugation ? L. 52, p. 75. *Deus*, L. 9, Ex. 4. *k* L. 12, 1; and L. 15, 2. *l* L. 12, 2, 3, and L. B. or. How does the perfect tense represent an action ? L. 47, 9. What are the terminations of the active voice, indicative mood, perfect tense ? L. 54. *i* See Ref. *i*, above, and L. 63. *m* L. 48, 6; and L. 49. *n* See Ref. *g*, above. How does the pluperfect tense represent an action ? L. 47, 10. What are the terminations of the active voice, indicative mood, pluperfect tense ? L. 54, p. 78. How does the future perfect tense represent an action ? L. 47, 11. What are the terminations of the active voice, indicative mood, future perfect tense ? L. 54, p. 78.

9. How do the several moods represent an action ? L. 47, 2. What are the terminations of the active voice, subjunctive mood, present tense, in each conjugation ? L. 56. How is the subjunctive used in independent sentences ? L. 57, 2.—*Note*. The first six sentences in the subj. pres. are to be taken independently. The first and fifth can be translated as hortatory, by *let*; the remainder as denoting wishes or requests, by *may*; as, " may fortune favor." *a* L. F. What are the terminations of the active voice, subjunctive mood, imperfect tense, in each conjugation ? L. 56, p. 80. *b* L. 77. *c* L. 5, II. What are the terminations of the active voice, subjunctive mood, perfect tense ? L. 58. *d* L. 9, 1 and 2. What are the terminations of the active voice, subjunctive mood, pluperfect tense ? L. 58. *e* L. 64. *f* L. 76. How do the several moods represent an action ? L. 47, 2. *g* L. 126, 1. Define the passive voice. L. 46, 9. What is frequently omitted, or left indefinite, with the active voice ? With the passive voice ? L. 46, N. 4. What are the terminations of the passive voice, indicative mood, present tense, in each conjugation ? L. 66.

*L. 15, 1; and L. 17, 2. *L. 12, 1; and L. 13. *L. 8, 1 anc **10 8.** *L. 18, 2 and 3; L. 23, II., and R. 2. What are the terminations of the passive voice, indicative mood, imperfect tense, in each conjugation? L. 66. *L. 9, 1; and L. 11. What are the terminations of the passive voice, indicative mood, future tense, in each conjugation? L. 66. *L. 26, 1 and 3. What are the terminations of the passive voice, indicative mood, perfect tense? —pluperfect tense?—future-perfect tense? L. 68. What are the terminations of the passive voice, subjunctive mood, present tense?—imperfect tense? L. 70—perfect tense?—pluperfect tense? L. 72. What are the terminations of the passive voice, imperative mood, in each conjugation? L. 74. *L. 126, 1. *L. 13, and L. C, o.

What is the rule for the predicate-nominative? L. 92, 1. *L. 11. B, os, and L. C, os. *L. 79. *L. 5, I. and N. 1. *L. 15, 1; and 16, 1. *L. 5, N. 3; and L. 17, 2. What is the rule for the agreement of adjectives? L. 91, 1. What is the logical subject of a proposition? L. 85, 1—the logical predicate? L. 85, 1. *L. 37; and L. 28, 2; and L. 17, 2. *L. 15, 1; and L. 17, 1, and N. *Nom. plur. neut. *vetĕra;* Gen. plur *vetĕrum,* L. 37, Exc. p. 57. *L. 29, N. 2. *L. 32, 1. *How is this adjective used? L. 91, N. 1.

*L. 90, 3. *L. 91, 2. *L. 40, 3. *L. 121, 6, (b.) *L. 88, 1, 12. and R. 2. *L. 14, 1 and 2. *L. 18, 2; L. 20, 2. *Is this noun the subject of the sentence, or is it the predicate? L. 83, 4 and 5. *L. 91, 4. *Bipĕdes,* "two footed," *i. e.,* on "two feet." It is a predicate adjective following the verb of motion *ingrediuntur,* L. 92, 2, and R. 1, (a.) *L. 90, N. 2. *L. 32, 1, and R. 3. *L. 82, 3–5: What do these adverbs modify? What is the rule for the object of an active verb in the active voice? L. 96, 1. *L. 27, and Exc. *L. 9, 1; and L. 11, 1. *L. 81, 2, 3 and 4. *L. F, Excs. in gender and in declension—us. *See preceding note. *L. G, I., 2. *L. 12, 1, and R. *L. B, or. *L. C, ex. *L. 45, R. 2.

*L. C, es. *What is omitted before *vinum* and *littĕras?* *L. 13 32, 1. *L. 45, R. 2. *L. 88, 1, and R. 1. *Novi,* and other tenses of *nosco,* derived from the 2d root, are used like the same tenses of *odi* and *memĭni;* L. 81, 4. *L. 18, 2 and 3. *L. 9. *L. 15, 1; and L. 17, 2. *L. J, 9. What is the rule for nouns in apposition? L. 89, 1. *L. 40, 3. *L. 39, 6, and N. 2. *L. 116, 4. *L. 18, 2; L. 20, 2. *L. 109. *L. 116, 5. *L. 5, II.

PAGE

. L. 15, 1, and L. 17, 1, and N. L. 118, 2. L. 117, N. 1.
. L. 35. L. 24, 8. What is the rule for the genitive after
nouns? L. 100. L. 92.

14. *Infinita*, L. 92, 2. L. 15, 1 and 5. *Antiquissimus*, L. 39, N. 2.
L. 90, R. 2. *Non benignus*, " a not kind," *i. e.*, " an unkind."
L. 92. What verb is here omitted? L. 90, N. 3. What is
the rule for the genitive after adjectives? L. 104—after partitives? L. 103. L. 126, 2. L. 18, 2 and 4. L. 24, 6. Su-
perlatives followed by a partitive genitive are used like nouns,
agreeing in gender and number, though not in case, with the
genitives following them; as *stultissima animalium*, i. e., *stultissima animalia*. What is the rule for the dative after adjectives
and verbs? L. 109. L. 96, 1. L. 45, 2.

15. L. 88, 2. L. 9, 1; and L. 11. L. 32, 1. L. 15, 1; and
L. 13. L. 90, R. 2. L. 97, 1. L. 40, 2. L. 113 and N
. L. 21, *summa*, L. 40, 3 and 39, N. 2. L. 39, 6. L. 99. L
114. See *ne quidem*, in Dict., under *ne*. L. 91, N. 1
What is a preposition? L. 82, 7—the rule for the accusative
after prepositions? L. 97, 1. L. 91, 4. L. 12, 1, and L. 14, 4.
To find the nom. sing. of *culices* make use of L. 22, I., of R. 3,
and R. 2. L. 91, 5. L. 10, R. 2. *Mitis* is sometimes followed
by a dative; here it takes *erga* with the accusative. L. 109, R. 5.

16. L. 97, 3. L. 22, I., R. 1. L. 47, N. 2; and L. 96, N. 2.
What is the rule for *in* and *sub*? L. 97, 3. L. 88, 2. L. 15,
1; and L. 16, 2. L. 75, 2. L. 82, (1.) L. 8, 5. L. 126,
2; and L. 57, 2. What is the rule for the ablative after prepositions? L. 99. L. 117, N. 1. L. 32, 1 and 3.

17. L. 144, N. L. 12, 1. L. 117, N. 2. *Primus* is translated as if it were *primùm* limiting *duxit*, " first led." L.
91, 9. *Esse*, "exist," L. 95, N. 5. L. 17, 1, and N. *Possum*
is sometimes followed by the accusative of a neuter adjective or
pronoun, *nihil*, &c., where in English we supply *do* or the like;
as, *nihil potest*, "can do nothing." *Dulce*, L. 91, 7. L. 95, 4.
What is the rule for nouns denoting the *cause, manner*, &c.? L.
117, 1—for *utor*, &c.?—for verbs signifying *to rejoice, glory* or
confide in, &c.? L. 116, 4—for verbs which in English are followed by *with*? L. 117, 2—for verbs signifying to *abound*, &c.?
L. 117, 3—for the ablative of *price* and *time*? L. 118, 1 and 2—
for a genitive or ablative of *property, character* or *quality*? L.
101. L. 110, 1. L. 89. L. 12, 1; and L. 22, I., and R. 1.
L. B, er.

*L. 39, N. 2. ᵇ L. 5, II. ᶜ L. 9. ᵈ L. 44, N. *L. 7, 3; and **18**
L. 25, 1. ᶠ L. 12, 1. *Prioribus*, sc. *pedibus*, "their fore feet." ᵍ L.
79, N. ʰ Sing. *locus, m.;* plur. commonly *loca, n.* ᶦ L. 103, 1.
ᵏ L. 101. Upon what may the infinitive depend? L. 95, 5.
After what classes of verbs is the infinitive used without a subject? L. 95, N. 5. After what classes of verbs does the infinitive with a subject accusative follow? L. 95, N. 4.

What is the object of *cupio*? L. 95, 5; and L. 96, R. 2. *L. **19.**
18, 2 and 3: to find the nom. sing., see L. 23, II., and R. 2. ᵇ L.
76. *L. J, 5. *Tibĕrim*, L. G, I., 1. ᵈ L. 47, N. 2. *L. 99, R. 2.
ᶠ L. 126, 2. ᵍ L. 92, 2. ʰ L. 81, Exc. ᶦ L. 111. ʲ L. 117, 1.
What is the rule for the infinitive as a subject? L. 95, 4. ᵏ L.
90, 5. ᶦ L. 91, 7.

*L. 109. With what does *turpius* agree? ᵇ *Suos* being used **20.**
without reference to a definite person, is to be translated "one's."
What are gerunds? L. 47, 17. By what cases are gerunds followed? L. 123, 2. How are gerunds governed? L. 123, 3.
What rule is to be given for the genitive of gerunds? L. 100.
ᶜ L. 117, 1. ᵈ L. 17, 2: to find the nom. sing. see L. 22, I., and
R. 2. ᵉ A predicate adjective. ᶠ L. 117, 1. *Nova*, L. 91, 5. ᵍ L.
109, and L. 91, 4, "to one ignorant of reading." ʰ From *ineo*.
ᶦ Instead of *urbem delendi, cives trucidandi, nomen Romānum exstinguendi*. L. 123, 4. What is the rule for the dative of gerunds
and gerundives? L. 109. ʲ L. 47, N. 2. ᵏ *Et—et*, see *et* in Dict.
What is the rule for the accusative of gerunds and gerundives?
L. 97. *Ad discendum*. L. 123, 5.

ᵃ For what is *ædificandam* used? L. 123, 4. What is the rule **21**
for the ablative of gerunds and gerundives? Answer. Either L.
99, or L. 117, 1, according as a preposition is or is not expressed.
ᵇ This adverb modifies the gerund on account of the gerund having the nature of a verb. L. 88: see also L. 123, 1. *Lacedæmonii,
ōrum*, subst. *m.*, the Lacedemonians. ᶜ "Were accustomed to
exercise." L. 47, N. 2. What is a compound sentence? L. 93,
1. How may the members of a compound sentence be connected? L. 93, 8. What is the rule for copulative and disjunctive conjunctions? L. 88, II. ᵈ L. 92, 1. *L. 82, 8, (4.) What
is the object of *accipĕre*? L. 96, 1. ᶠ What is the subject of
præstat? L. 95, 4; and L. 81, 8 and 9.

ᵃ A conjunction placed before each of two or more connected **22.**
words, gives peculiar emphasis to each. ᵇ L. 15, 1; and L. 17,
R. What is the root of *nox*? How is the nom. sing. formed?

In translating *nox erat*, supply *it* before the verb, and let the noun
follow the verb, " it was night." L. 22, l., R. 1 and 2. *c* L. 90, 3.
d To what class of conjunctions does this belong? L. 82, (3.)
e L. 131, N. *f* L. 109, R. 2: the dative after a verb is often thus
used in Latin, where the English idiom requires a possessive
case or a possessive adjective pronoun; as, *mihi in mentem
revŏco*, "I recall to my mind." *g* On what verb does the dependent clause *crocodīlum crescĕre* depend? L. 95, N. 4. Why is *crocodīlum* in the accusative? L. 95, 3. What is to be supplied in
English before the subject of the infinitive? L. 95, N. 1. *h* L.
128, II. *i* L. 95, 1. *Autem, enim* and *vero* occupy the second
or third place in their clause. *k* L. 98. *l* What are the two constructions which may follow the comparative degree? *Ans.* A
dependent clause connected by *quàm*, or an ablative. When is
the comparative degree followed by an ablative? L. 119, 1.
When *quàm* is expressed, what case follows it? L. 119, 2.
m What words are to be supplied? *n* What is the positive of
this adjective?—its root? How are the comparative and superlative formed? L. 39, 6.

23. *a* L. 36, 2. *b* What is to be supplied before this genitive? *c* In
what case is *feræ*, and why? L. 109. Why is *homini* in the
dative? *d* L. 1 and 9. *e* What is the rule for the construction
of relatives? L. 94, 2. *f* L. 78. *g* L. 15, 1; L. 17, 2; and L. 22,
I. and 2. *h* L. 18, 2. *i* L. 117, 1. *j* L. 116, 4. *k Is*, though often
following *qui*, is commonly to be translated before it: *bona*,
"good things;" *mala*, "evil things" L. 91, 5. *l* L. 79. *m* L.
104, and R 1. *n* L. F, us. *o* L. 133, 1.

24. What mood follows *cùm?* L. 132, 2. How is the subjunctive after adverbs of time to be translated? L. 132, R. 1. *c* L.
117, 2. *c* L. 116, 4. *d* L. 15, 1 and 2. *e* See Ref. *e*, p. 17. *f* L
117, 1. *g* L. 81, 6–12. *h* L. 89, 1. For what purpose is *rex Macedoniæ* added? L. 89, R. *i* L. 110. What is the rule for the
mood in a clause denoting a purpose, object or result? L. 133, l.
j L. 134, 3. *k* L. 5, II., and L. 97, 3. *l* Give the rules for forming
its nom. sing. L. 22, I., and R. 1 and 3. *m* Rule for its nom.
sing. *n Ne-quidem*, "not even," see Dict. *o* L. H, 1. *p* L. 97, 4.
q Dico, duco and *facio*, like *fero*, p. 104, commonly lose *e* in the
2nd pers. sing. of the imperative active, and become *dic, duc, fac*.
L. 129, p. 171. *r* L. 106, 1. *s* L. 109. *t* L. 128, I.

25. *a* "*Him*," i. e., Alexander. *b* The subj. imperfect after the perfect indefinite, L. 135, 2. *c* L. 116, 4. *d* L. 34, and L. 2, 5, (*b*).

ᵉL. 135, 1. ƒL. 88, I., R. 1. ᵉ L. 133, 1 and 6. ʰL. 123, 3; and
L. 117, 1. ᶦL. 135, 1. ʲL. 108, 2, and R. 1. ᵏL. 95, N. 6. ᶦL.
135, 2. In what mood is the verb of an indirect question? L.129, 1.
When is a question indirect? L. 129, N. How is the subj jnc-
tive in indirect questions translated? L. 129, 2. ᵐL. 36, 3.
What is to be supplied? ⁿ Its subjects are the preceding clauses,
L. 90, 5, and L. 91, 7. What is the rule for the infinitive with the
accusative? L. 95, 3. What word is to be supplied in English
before the subject of the infinitive? L. 95, N. 1. ᵒ L. 117, N. 1.

ᵃ L. 117, N. 1. ᵇ Supply *esse*, which is often omitted in the **26.**
compound forms of the infinitive. ᶜ L. 95, 3. ᵈL. 90, 5, and L.
91, 7. ᵉ L. 97, 1. ƒ What preceding thing does the pronoun *id*
here indicate? See L. 41, 1. ᵍL. 8, 5. What is the rule for
the agreement of participles? L. 91, 1. By what cases are they
followed? L. 121, 9. What is said of the time denoted by the
present, perfect, and future active participles? L. 121, N. 3.
ʰ L. 117, 1. ᶦL. 96, 2.

ᵃ See Ref. *e*, p. 17. ᵇL. 108, 1. ᶜ A Greek accusative, L. G. **27.**
II., 1; see also L. D, is. ᵈL. 98. ᵉL. 111, and N. 1. ƒL. 121,
9, and L. 96, N. 2. ᵍL. 89, R., "when a boy." ʰL. 117, 1. ᶦOn
what does this infinitive depend? ʲL. 91, 4. ᵏL. 110, 1; and L.
91, 4. ᶦL. 116, 4. *Congregantur;* the passive voice is here
used like what is called in Greek the middle voice, or like the
active voice with *se.* ᵐ "In that," or, "in the thing," L. 91, 5.
ⁿ What does this adverb modify? ᵒ 105, 1. ᵖL. 108, R. 2.

Saliāti, L. 122, 2. ᵃL. 110. ᵇ97, 4. ᶜ *Transitūri,* "when **28.**
about to pass over," L. 121, 4; and L. 122, 2—*laudātus*, "when
praised." L. 121, 5; and L. 122, 2. ᵈL. 117, N. 1. ᵉ "Upon
those which go before (them)," L. 122, 3; and L.111. ƒL. H, 1.
ᵍ L. 116, 5. ʰL. 92—*Bucephălon*, a Greek noun, L. 11, 2 and 3;
also L. 92, 1, and L. 121, 9. ᶦL. 111, N. 2—*heres*, L. 92, 1, and
L. 121, 9. ʲL. 109, R. 1. ᵏL. 133, 1. ᶦL. 88, 2.

ᵃ L. 108, R. 1. ᵇL. 111. ᶜ L. 101. ᵈ L. 123, and L. 109. ᵉ L. **29.**
133, 1, and L. 134, 1 and 3. ƒ L. 123, 4 and 5. ᵍ L. 113, and N.
ʰ L. 91, 4. What is the rule for the ablative absolute? L. 120.
Senescente Lunâ, L. 120, N. 2: the same note is applicable to the
other ablatives marked (*). ᶦL. 97, 3. ʲL. 108, 2. ᵏL. 103, N.
2. ᶦL. 120, R. 1. ᵐL. 108, 1.

Aculeo amisso, L. 120, N. 3. ᵃ L. 117, 1. *Convolvuntur*, in a **30**
middle or reflexive sense, for *se convolvunt.* See note on *congregantur*, p. 27. ᵇL. 45, 4. ᶜL. 133, 1, and N. 1

FABLES.

31. *Metu,* "through fear," or, "influenced by fear." L. 117, 1; L. 133, 1 and 2. ᵇ L. 97, 3. ᶜ L. 118, 2. ᵈ L. 128, R. ᵉ L. 91, 4. ᶠ L. 95, 3. ᵍ L. 121, 6 (*b*). ʰ L. 95, N. 4. ⁱ L. 117, 1. ʲ *Exoravit* here takes an acc. of the person and a subj. clause with *ut,* denoting the thing, L. 96, 3, and N. 6. ᵏ L. 120, "That having gnawed the nets, he would set him at liberty;" or, "that he would gnaw the nets and set him at liberty," L. 120, N. 3; or, "to gnaw the nets and," &c., L. 133, 2. *Liberatus.* L. 121, 5, (*a*). ⁱ L. 88, 2. ᵐ What is the object of this verb? L. 96, R. 2. ⁿ L. 95, N. 5. ᵒ L. 129, 1 and 2. ᵖ L. 112, 1. ᵍ L. 122, 3.

32. ᵃ L. 109. ᵇ L. 127, R. ᶜ L. 90, R. 2. ᵈ L. 90, R. 2. ᵉ L. 45, R. 2. ᶠ L. 94, 1 and 2. ᵍ L. 91, 4. ʰ L. 133, 1 and 2. ⁱ L. 91, 5. ʲ L. 88, 2. ᵏ L. 88, 1., R. 2. ˡ L. 47, N. 2. ᵐ L. 89, 1. ⁿ L. 128, 1. ᵒ *Autem, enim* and *vero* commonly occupy the second place in a clause. *Bona* is in the acc., the subject of *conferri,* L. 95, 3. ᵖ The subject of *oportuit* is, *omnia bona in unum conferri,* L. 95, 4: see also L. 81, 6, 8, and 9. ᵍ L. 97, 3. ʳ L. 120, and N. 2. In translating a participle, its time must conform to that of the verb with which it is connected; as, *adveniente domino grues avŏlant,* "when the owner *comes,* the cranes *fly* off;" *adveniente domino grues avolābant,* "when the owner *came,* the cranes *flew* off," &c. ˢ L. 117, 1. ᵗ L. 47, N. 2.

33. ᵃ L. 121, 9. *Relinquis,* L. 50, R. 4 and 5. ᵇ L. 113. ᶜ L. 91, 5. For the case of *tutis,* see L. 111. ᵈ *Dulcia tutis præponĕre* is the subject of *est.* ᵉ L. 82, (4), and L. 50, R. 3. ᶠ The adverb is often separated from the word which it modifies by the oblique case of a noun modifying the same word. ᵍ L. 117, 1. ʰ L. 50, R. 4. ⁱ L. 116, 4. ʲ L. 111. ᵏ ˡ L. 107, 2, and N. ᵐ "Was accustomed to lie," or, "kept lying," L. 47, N. 2. ⁿ L. 24, 3. ᵒ L. 117, 1. ᵖ L. 103, 1, and L. 1, 6. ᵍ L. 42, 1. ʳ L. 116, 4. ˢ L. 133, 1, and 134, 1. ᵗ The subjunctive denoting a result after *quem,* L. 133, 1, and L. 134, 2 and 3. ᵘ L. 111. ᵛ L. 132, 2. ʷ L. 134, 3.

34. ᵃ L. 117, 1. ᵇ L. 121, 9. ᶜ *Quidem* follows an emphatic word. ᵈ L. 88, 1., 1. ᵉ L. 110, 4. ᶠ L. 79, N. ᵍ L. 97, 4. ʰ L. 47, N. 2. ⁱ L. 29, N. 2. ʲ L. 9, Exc. 3. ᵏ L. 126, 3. ˡ L. 110, 1. ᵐ L. 47, 11. ⁿ L. 95, 3. ᵒ L. 88, 2. ᵖ L. 95, N. 4. ᵍ L. 40, 3. ʳ When a noun is limited by another noun and by an adjective,

the adjective usually stands first. * L. 120. ‡ L. 117, N 1.
* L. 103, 3. * L. 129, 1 and 2. * L. 117, 2 ‡ L. 131, 1. ‡ L.
119, N. 3.

* L. 91, 4. ‡ L. 117, 1. ‡ L. 95, 5. ‡ L. 95, N. 4. * Supply *id* 35.
before *quod*, "that which," or "what." ‡ L. 111. ‡ "Had seen
it first," the comparative is used when only two are spoken of.
L. 39, 4. ‡ L. 128, II., 1 and N. ‡ L. 82, 7, (1.) ‡ L. 116, 4.
‡ *Peto* has various constructions, it is here construed with the *acc.*
of the thing and the *abl.* of the person with *a ;* see L. 96, 3, and
N. 6. ‡ L. 98. ‡ "Not even *our* bodies ;" see note (*c*), p. 34. ‡ L.
110, 1. ‡ L. 131, 1, and (*a*.)

Spectātur has for its subject the clause, *quid fiat.* L. 90, 5. * L. 36.
129, 1 and 2. ‡ L. 120, and N. 3. ‡ L. 94, N. 2. ‡ L. 132, 2.
* L. 131, 1, and (*a*) and (*b*.) ‡ "These fellows." L. 42, N. 2.
‡ L. 103, 1. ‡ See note (*c*), p. 32. ‡ *Epŭlor* takes either the *acc.* or
the *abl.* L. 116, 5. ‡ L. 133, 1 and 2. ‡ L. 128, R. ‡ L. 134, 3.
* L. 132. ‡ L. 91, 5; and L. 95, 3. ‡ L. 95, N. 4. ‡ L. 95, N.
5. ‡ L. 117, N. 1. ‡ L. 126, 3. ‡ *Neque*, "and not," is properly
both an adverb and a conjunction. ‡ L. 127, R. ‡ L. 123, 3; and
L. 100. ‡ L. 91, 4. ‡ L. 121, 6, (*b*); and L. 95, N. 4. ‡ *Eos,
qui*, "those who," or "such as." ‡ L. 123, 3 and 5. ‡ L. 133, 1,
and L. 134, 1, 2 and 3.

* *Reducĕre* depends on *condĭtæ.* L. 95, N. 5. ‡ L. 96, R. 2. 37
* *Inter se*, "between themselves," or "with each other." *Facĕrent.* L. 134, 1. ‡ L. 120, and N. 2. ‡ L. 95, 3, and N. 4. ‡ L.
91, 4; and L. 111. ‡ L. 96, R. 2. ‡ L. 131, 1. ‡ L. 95, N. 4.
The subject of *fore* is the clause following, beginning with *ut.*
‡ The distributives denote the number of eggs expected *each day,*
L. 38, 4. ‡ L. 132, 2, and R. 1. ‡ L. 91, N. 1. ‡ L. 117, 1. *Conspicāta—discēdens.* Both these participles may be translated by
the English present participle, but the Latin words mark the
time more accurately, as the past participle denotes an act prior
to that of the verb with which it is connected, L. 121, N. 3,
conspicāta, "having seen," or "after she had seen," L. 122, 1 and
6; while the present participle denotes an act coëxistent with
that of the verb in the clause—*discēdens*, "departing," or "while
departing," or "as she was departing." L. 122, 1, 2 and 5. * *Nec*
" and—not." * *Repertas*, "if found." L. 122, 2 and 6. This
participle supplies the place of a conditional clause, which would
have been in the subjunctive, according to L. 131, 1. * L. 131,
(*a*). ‡ L. 95, 3.

38. ᵃ L. 128, II., 1, and N. 2. ᵇ L. 121, ₵ (b.) ᶜ L. 109. ᵈ L. 123, 1. ᵉ L. 91, 5. ᶠ L. 110. ᵍ L. 111. ʰ For that in this way, or by this means, they, &c. ⁱ The verb of *saying* on which an infinitive with the accusative depends, is often implied in some preceding verb. Here it is implied in *placuit*. ʲ "The inquiry was made," its subject is the following clause. L. 81, 7, 8, 11 and 12. ᵏ L. 123, 3; and L. 97, 3. ˡ L. 22, I., and R. 2. ᵐ L. 88, 2. ⁿ L. 95, 5. ᵒ L. 133, 1 and 2. ᵖ L. 116, 5. ᵠ L. 131, 1, and N. ʳ L. 92, 1. ˢ L. 115. ᵗ What is the object of *ignorāre?* L. 96, R. 2. ᵘ L. 95, N. 4.

39. ᵃ L. 97, 2. ᵇ L. 110. What is the subject of *licet?* L. 81, 8. ᶜ L. 99, R. 2. ᵈ L. 133, 3. ᵉ L. 116, 4. ᶠ Sc. *esse.* ᵍ L. 111, N. 2. ʰ L. 115. ⁱ L. 97, 5. ʲ L. 109, R. 1. ᵏ L. 106, 1. ˡ L. 133, 1; and L. 134, 2. ᵐ L. 133, 1 and 2. ⁿ For what does this pronoun stand? L. 41, 1. ᵒ L. 92, 1. ‡ The subject is *quod caput, &c.,* for which the pronoun *it* is prefixed to the verb in English.

40. ᵃ L. 117, 1. ᵇ The ablative of place without *in.* L. 108, R. 2. ᶜ L. 91, 6. ᵈ L. 21. ᵉ L. 111. ᶠ L. 129, 1 and 2. ᵍ L. 96, N. 5. ʰ L. 133, 1; and L. 134, N. 1: see note (ʰ), p. 41, ʲ L. 132, 2. ᵏ L. 120, and N. 1; and L. 121, 7. ˡ L. 117, N. 1, and L 121, 9. ᵐ L. 99, R. 1. ⁿ "As to happen is usual or common," *i. e.,* "as often happens," L. 81, 8. ᵒ L. 95, N. 4. ᵖ See L. 120, N. 2. ᵠ L. 133, 1 and 2. ʳ What is the antecedent of *quod?* L. 94, N. 2.

41. ᵃ L. 96, 3, and N. 6. ᵇ L. 117, 4. † In English the order of the subject- and predicate-nominatives in questions and exclamations is reversed. ᵈ L. 129, 1. The question is denoted by *quăm.* L. 125, 1. ᵉ The reflexive is used because it stands for *asinus,* the subject of the leading clause. L. 127, IV. ᵈ L. 133, 1 and 2. ᵉ L. 128, II. 1. ᶠ L. 111, N. I. ᵍ L. 115. ʰ A relative clause, containing a reason for something preceding, takes a subjunctive, which is translated by the indicative or a gerundive, "who was unwilling," "because I was unwilling," or, "in being unwilling." ⁱ L. 117, 1. ʲ L. 95, 5. ᵏ What is the antecedent of *quo?* ⁱ L. 101, R. 3. ᵐ L. 104, R. 2. *Prima nocte,* L. 91, 8.

42. ᵃ *Sese,* the same as *se,* L. 127, IV. ᵇ L. 133, 1 and 2. ᶜ "That she," L. 95, 3, and N. 1. ᵈ L. 96, 1. ᵉ L. 109. ᶠ L. 119, 3. ᵍ L. 96, 3, and N. 6. ʰ *Se,* "her," *i. e.,* the tortoise. ⁱ L. 133, 1 and 2. *Arreptam,* translate according to L. 122, 8. ʲ L. 45, R. 2. ᵏ L. 117, 1. ˡ L. 111. *Se enim,* L. 127, IV. *Perdat,* L. 133,

1, and N. 1. ⁎ L. 127, N. 1. *Explēre*, L. 127, I. ⁕ L. 131, 1, and (*a*.) ⁑ L. 91, 5. ⸸ L. 47, 10. ⸰ L. 120. ⁕ L. 108, 2, and R. ⁕ L. 98. ⸰ L. 103, 1 and 2. ⁕ *Et—et*, " both— and." ᵈ L. 99, **43.** 2. ⁕ L. 121, 9. ⸍ L. 117, 4. ⸶ L. 133, 1 and 2. ⸰ L. 120. ⸰ L. 129, 1 and 2. ⸽ ᵏ L. 107, 2. ⸰ L. 81, 6, *pœnitet*, &c., have no subject expressed, and in general none can be supplied. ⁓ Supply *aliquem* or *hominem* after *acquiro.* ⁕ L. 91, 4. ⁑ L. 103, 1. ⸸ The historical present, L. 47, N. 4, and L. 135, N. What is the accusative of the thing after *interrŏgat*, L. 96, N. 6. ¶ What is to be supplied with *proram?* ⸰ L. 132, 2. ⸰ L. 49, R. 2. ⸰ L. 29, N. 2. ⁕ *Multo major*, " much larger," L. 119, 3. ⸰ L. 119, 1.

⁕ L. 88, 2, and R. 2. ⸰ L. 133, 1. ⁕ L. 81, 6, 8 and 9.—*Vera* **44.** *memŏras*, literally, " you say true things," *i. e.*, " what you say is true," or more concisely, " that is true." ⸰ L. 109.—*Audita voce*, " when I hear," L. 120, N. 2 and 3. ⸰ L. I, Gen. pl. 2. ⸰ L. 117, 1. ⸍ A predicate adjective, L. 92, 2. ⸶ L. 24, 7. ⸰ *Quid?* " what!" An accusative depending upon an active verb or preposition understood. ⸰ *Esse* and *fuisse* in compound infinitives are often understood. ⸰ L. 129, 1 and 2. ⸰ *Si moriendum sit*, supply *mihi*⸸ L. 112, 2 and Rem. (*a*) and (*c*), " if I must die :" as *moriendum sit* is impersonal, see also L. 81, 7 and 10, and N. ⸰ L. 119, 3. ⁓ *Præclarius* agrees with the clause, *meo cruŏre aspergi*, &c., which also is the subject of the impersonal verb *erit*, L. 91, 7, and L. 81, 8 and 9. ⁑ Depending on *præclarius*, L. 109. ⸰ L. 95, 3, and N. 1. ⁑ L. 94, 2, and N. ⸸ L. 111. ⸰ L. 95, N. 4. ⸰ L. 131. ⸰ L. 49, R. 2. *Adoritur*, L. 47, N. 4.

⸰ L. 24, 7. ⸰ L. 131, 1 and (*a*). ᵈ L. 109. ⸰ See N. (⸰), p. 32. **45.** *Arreptum devorāvit*, L. 122, 8. ⸍ L. 121, 6, (*b*.) ⸶ L. 109. *Ovis*, supply *et*, L. 88, II., R. 3. ⸰ L. 120. ⸰ " For itself," the reflexive referring to *labor;* L. 45, R. 2. ⸍ L. 133, 1, and L. 134, 1 and 3.

⸰ as the antecedent of *qui*, is usually placed after it. ⸰ *Is sciat*, " let him know," L. 126, 2, and L. 57, 2. ⁓ L. 95, N. 4; see N. (⸰) on p. 44. ⁑ L. 109. ⸰ L. 134, N. 2; *quæ*, " who," or, " what one." ⁑ L. 117, N. 1. ⸸ When the noun depending on a preposition is limited by a genitive or an adjective, the preposition commonly stands first. ⸰ ⸰ L. 134, 1 and 3. ⸰ L. 131. N.

⸰ The historical perfect, L. 47, N. 3. ⸰ *Datūrus esset*, " proposed **46.** to give," L. 128, II., 1; and L. 121, 4, (*b*.) ⸰ L. 118, 2. *Quæ quum*, " when they," L. 94, 5. ᵈ The perfect infinitive, connected with a verb in a past tense, has the meaning of a pluperfect; " had taken a wife," *i. e.*, " was married," L. 95, 1. ⸰ L. 119, 1.

f L. 115.—*Nonne*, L. 53, 4; and L. 125, 2 and 4, and N. 2. *g* L. 81, 3 and 4. *h* L. 129, 1 and 2. *i* L. 47, 11. *j* L. 21. *k* Instead of *refugiëbant*, L. 90, N. 1, (*b*). *m* L. 121, 4, (*b*). *n* L. 117, N. 1. *Pœnituit*, L. 107, 2. *o* L. 117, 1.

47. *a* "To him," L. 109. *b* *Iis—ante ocŭlos*, literally, "for them before the eyes," *i. e.*, like *ante eorum oculos*, "before their eyes," L. 109, Rem. 2. *c* *Ponëret* denotes the purpose for which he related the fable, L. 133, 1 and 2. *d* The indirect quotation or *oratio obliqua* depending on *dixit*, begins at *lupos*, L. 127, 3 and I.—*Se esse impugnatūros*, "that they, the wolves," L. 127, IV. The agreement of the wolves constitutes a second *oratio obliqua* within the first, depending on *pactos esse*, a verb of saying, L. 95, N. 4.—*Dederentur*, L. 131, 1.—*Placuisse*. The second *oratio obliqua* ends with *dederentur*, and *placuisse* together with *dilaniasse*, like *pactos esse*, depends on *dixit*. *f* L. 117, 4. *g* L. 88, 2. *h* L. 120.— *Oves pascens*, L. 122, 2, 3 and 5.—*Lupos* depends on the verb of saying *fingens*, L. 127, 3 and I.—*Aggressos esse*, "had attacked," L. 127, N. 2.—*Fingens*, L. 122, 1. *i* L. 121, 9. *j* See N. (*m*) on p. 46. *k* L. 117, N. 2. *i* L. 110. *m* L. B, ex. *n* *Ludëre* depends on *existimantes*, L. 95, N. 4. *o* L. 122, 1, *preces*, L. B, ex. *p* L. 103, 1. *q* L. 117, 1. *r* L. 94, 3 and 5. *s* L. 111, N. 2.

48. *a* *Gratŭlor* is sometimes construed with the dative of the person and the accusative of the thing in respect to which the congratulation is given, "to congratulate one upon," or, "on account of something." *b* L. 128, II., 1. *c* L. 126, 2 and 3. *d* The English order is, *eos pullos quos.—Dominus*, sc. *meus*, L. 91, 6.—*Raptos*, "having seized," see L. 120, N. 3. *e* L. 121, 6, (*a*). *f* L. 123, 6. *g* L. 90, 3; and L. 86, 2.—*Illam*, "it." *h* L. 95, N. 4.—*Ponëret*, L. 132, Rem. 1.—*Correptum*, translate according to L. 120, N. 3. *i* L. 123, 3.—*Astutior*, sc. *asino*. *j* L. 111. *k* L. 129, 1 and 2. *l* L. 129, 3. *i* L. 95, N. 5. *m* *Nequeo* is conjugated like *eo*, L. 80. *n* L. 115, 3.

49. *a* L. 123, 3, and L. 104.—*Adspĭcit*, &c., L. 47, N. 4. *b* *Salo*, "in the sea," L. 108, R. 2. *c* *Qui voluĕrim*, literally, "who wished;" the relative clause denotes the reason of the declaration, *næ jure plector*, and the passage may be translated, "I am rightly punished for wishing, or, because I wished, though I was born in the sea," &c.—*Salo—solo:* here is the play upon words, called *paronomasia.—Suus*, "his own." *d* *Unusquisque* has a double declension, see L. 45, N. 2. *e* *Quem præterire sine periulo* is the subject of *licet*, L. 81, 8. *f* L. 127, 3, 1., III. and IV. *g* *Eum*,

"him," *i. e.*, the bull. ᴬ Supply *esse;* "would fly off." L. 95, N.
3. ⁱ Supply *dixit* or *respondet*, L. 127, N. 1.—*Considentem*, "when
you lighted," L. 122, 5. † Supply *unam* sc. *peram*, "the one filled,"
&c.—*Propriis*, "own," *i. e.*, in connection with the preceding
nobis, "our own."—*Vitiis*, L. 117, 2.—*Dare*, "to give," *post tergum dare*, "to place behind the back."—*Aliènis*, sc. *vitiis*, "with
the faults of others."—*Hac re*, "on this account, for this reason."—
Alii simul, the order is, *simul alii*.

MYTHOLOGY.

·ᵉ L. 89, I., and R.—Give the rules for forming the nominative **50.**
singular of *Agenóris, dracónem, Martis, fontis, custódem, prolem*
and *uxóre;* see L. 22 and L. 23. ᵇ L. 117, N. 2. ᶜ "All who had
come," L. 134, 1; or "all such as had come," L. 134, 2, and N.
1. ᵈ L. 132, 2 and Rem. ᵉ L. 89, 2. ᶠ L. 101, and Rem. 3.
ᵃ L. 118, 2. ⁱ L. 98. *Annórum novem*, lit. "of nine years," *i. e.*,
"nine years old," L. 101, and R. 1. The rule for forming the nom.
sing. of *Apollinis*. ᴶ L. 47, N. 2. ᵏ L. 91, 2, and N. 2.

ᵃ L. 108, 1. ᵇ L. 97, 2 and 3. ᶜ L. 117, N. 1; and L. C, os. **51.**
ᵈ L. 117, 1. ᵉ L. 117, N. 2.· ᶠ L. 119, N. 3. ᵍ L. 92, and (*b*). ᵃ A
Greek accusative, L. G, II., 1. ⁱ L. 127, 3 and IV. ᴶ L. 133, 1.
ᵏ L. 110, 1. ˡ L. 114. ᵐ L. 127, II. ⁿ L. 90. 3. The English idiom
requires the singular number. ᵒ L. 99, R. 4.

ᵃ L. 111. ᵇ L. 96, 3, and N. 6. ᶜ L. 133, 1 and 2. ᵈᵉ L. **52.**
120, and N. 3. † Literally "which having been seen," L. 120,
N. 1; i. e., "at sight of which," L. 120, N. 2. ᶠ L. 117, N. 2,
quum, L. 132, R. 2, *pariunt*, "lay," an active verb used absolutely,
i. e., without its case. ᵍ L. 27, Exc. *Alcyonéos*, L. 96, N. 5.
ᵃ L. 9, Exc. 4. ⁱ L. 134, 1. ᴶ *Quæ*, i. e., *ea, quæ*, "those things
which." As antecedent *is* is often omitted, L. 94, 7.—*Communi-
cábat*, "used to tell," or "was wont to tell," L. 47, N. 2. ᵏ *Dicitur*,
sc. *ille*. ˡ "Attempts to take," L. 121, 4. ᵐ *Ei super caput*, "over
his head," L. 109, Rem. 2.

ᵃ L. 111. ᵇ L. 110, 1. ᶜ L. 133, 2. ᵈ L. 127, N. 1. ᵉ L. 109. **53.**
ᶠ L. 127, II. ᵍ See N. (ᵒ), p. 32. ᵃ The object of *dare*. ⁱ L. 127,
I., III. and IV. ᴶ *Dare*, "to give," or, "that he would give," because the verb of saying is in the perfect indefinite. See on the

connection of tenses, L. 135, remembering that the infinitive in
Latin often corresponds with the indicative, or potential in English, L. 95, N. 3. *k* L. 120, N. 3. *l* L. 108, 2. *m* L. 111, N. 2.
* *Agamemnŏne duce*, literally, "Agamemnon being the commander," *i. e.*, "under the command of Agamemnon;" L. 120,
Rem. 1.—*Quum sciret;* L. 132, R. 2.—*Periturum esse*, "would
perish," the leading verb *sciret*, being in the imperfect, see L. 135,
and N. (*j*) above. *p* L. 117, 1. *q* "That he was concealed," L. 127,
N. 2. *r* L. 103, 1. * Possessive adjectives often supply the place
of the genitive of the corresponding noun ; as, *regius* for *regis*.

54. * L. 95, N. 4.—*Quæ dum*, "while they," L. 94, 5.—*Audito*, L.
120, N. 3. *b* L. 95. 3. *c* The predicate accusative after *esse*, L.
92, R. 2.—*Intellectum est;* its subject is the preceding infinitive
clause, for which *it* is supplied in English. *d* The adjective separated from its noun by a genitive limiting the same noun. *e* **L.**
108, 1. *f* See N. (*o*), p. 32. *g* L. 109.—*Sacram ;* an adjective
usually follows its noun when any thing depends upon it. *h* The
comparative to be translated by the positive with *too*, L. 119, N.
3. *i* Sc. *illi.* *j* L. 127, 3 and I.—*Non posse*, "could not ;" the imperfect depending on the perfect indefinite, L. 135. *k* L. 95, N.
5. *l* L. 108, 2; so *Argos* above. *m* L. 111. *n* Supply *eam* before
sacerdōtem, L. 96, 2.— *Trojâ eversâ*, "after the destruction of Troy,"
L. 120, N. 2. *o* L. 108, Rem. *p* L. 133, 1 and 2, and N. 1. *Promētheus*, a trisyllable. *q* L. 91, 9. *r* L. 129, 1.

55. *a* L. 111. *b* L. 133, 1 and 2. *Quantum—tantum.* *Tantum* is a
demonstrative adjective to which the relative adjective *quantus*
relates. The same is to be remarked of *talis* and *qualis.* As in
the case of *is* and *qui*, the relative word is usually placed first.
c The imperfect denoting repeated, that is, eager action, "earnestly
requested." *d* L. 127, I. *e* L. 133, 1 and 2. *f* L. 129, 1. *g* L.
133, 1 and 2.—*Quo facto, quod quum*, and *qui quum*, see L. 94, 5.
h *Mittĕre*, "putting," L. 95, N. 6. *i* L. 109. *j* L. 121, N. 3. *k* Sc.
esse. *l* L. 127, II.

56. *a* L. 109, R. 6. *b* L. 101. *c* L. 133, 1 and 2. *d* L. 117, N. 2.
e L. 111, N. 2 and 1. *f* L. 117, 1. *g* L. 42, N. 2. *h* L. 108, 2.—
Conditiōne addita, L. 120, N. 3. † L. 120. *i* L. 128, II. *j Cadmus
nomine*, "Cadmus by name," *i. e.*, "named Cadmus," L. 117, 5.
k L. 108, 2. *l* L. 133, 3. *m* L. 47, 7. *n* L. 122, 2.

57. *a* L. 94, 5. *b* L. 117, 1. * Why in the subjunctive, and by what
mood to be translated ? *Quicquid* or *quidquid.* This pronoun,
like the English *whoever* and *whatever*, seems often to include both

antecedent and relative. *L. 128, II. 1. *d* L. 133, 1 and 2.—*Gavisus est*, L. 79, N. *e* L. 116, 5. *f* L. 95, 3, and N 4.—*Ipsi*, L. 109. *g* L. 119, 1. *h* L. 90, Rem. 2. *i* The present *petit* is used for the perfect indefinite, L. 47, N. 4; and hence is followed by the imperfect, L. 135, 2, N. *j* L. 95, 3. *k* Sc. *ea*, " it." *l* L. 101, Rem. 3. *m* " Was wont" or " used," L. 47, N. 2. *n* L. 117, N. 1. *o* L. 95, N. 4.

a The preposition usually precedes the adjective, but particular **58** phrases are excepted. *b* L. 81, 13; what is the subject represented by *it* before *prædictum fuit?* *c* L. 95, 4. *d* L. 128, II., 1. *e* L. 117, 1. *f* L. 135, 2. *g* L. 111—*dormienti*, L. 122, 2. *h* L. 132, 2 and Rem.—*Cirim*, L. G. II., 2. *i* L. 96, 2. *j* L. 131, (*d*). *Raptum* sc. *piscem*, " having seized it," L. 120, N. 3. *k* L. 119, N. 3. *Venantes*, L. 122, 2. *l* What is to be supplied? *m* L. 117, 4.

a A dissyllable. *b* The genitive plural of other participles in **59** *rus* is seldom used, but *venturōrum* is found in Ovid, Met. 15, 835. *c* Repeated past action, L. 47, N. 2. *d* L. 111. *e* Pronounced *Har-py'yas* *f* *Ab ore ei*, i. e., *ab ore ejus*, " from his mouth," L. 109, R. 2, and L. 111, N. 2. *g* L. 96, 3. *h* L. 135, 2. *i* L. 127, III. and IV. *j* L. 127, I. *k* L. 117, 4. *Habuisse*, L. 127, N. 2. *Strophădas*, L. I, Acc. Plur. 2.

ANECDOTES OF EMINENT PERSONS.

a L. 96, Rem. 1, and L. 124, 3. In the active voice it would **60.** be (*Aliquis*) *Thalen* (Greek acc.) *interrogāvit, an facta etc.*, and the accusative of the person is changed to the nominative in the passive, L. 124, 2. *b* *Latet* takes an accusative of the person from whom any thing is concealed. *b* L. 129, 1 and 2. *c* *Ne cogitāta quidem*, " not even their thoughts." *d* From *neminem* to the end the words are in the *oratio obliqua*. See L. 127. *e* *f* L. 127, II.— *Pythagŏræ*, L. 8, 5. *f* L. 134, 3.—*Autem*, see N. (*o*), p. 32. *g* L. 133, 1 and 2. *h* " That he had said (so)." Hence our phrase, " a mere *ipse dixit*." *i* L. 103, N. 2.—*Priēnen*, L. 8, 5.—*Expugnātum et eversam*, L. 122, 3 and 6. *k* L. 133, 1 and 2, and N.

a L. 120, N. 3. *b* *Vacuus* is construed with the *gen.*, or the *abl.* **61.** with or without *ab*. In construction, with *vacuum* supply *hominem*; in translating, nothing is to be supplied; " than, free from every care, to devote," &c. *c Dare* is connected by *quàm* to *esse*. *d Scientiæ augendæ* depends on *causâ*, L. 100, "for the purpose of enlarging (his) knowledge," L. 123, 4. *e* L. 131, 1. *f* L. 42, N. 2. † L. 81, 8. *g* L. 111. *h* L. 135, 2. *i* The imperfect denoting customary action, L. 47, N. 2. *j* L. 133, N. 1. *k Nihil* in the accusative without a preposition, used for *non*, "nothing changed," or, "in no respect changed," L. 97, 5. ‡ L. 119, N. 3.

62. *a* L. 133, 4. *b* L. 110, 1. *c* L. 133, 1 and 2. *d* L. 123, 3; and L. 100. *e* L. 117, 1.—*Videbâtur*, L. 128, II., 2. *f* L. 79, N. *g* See N. (°), p. 32 *h* L. 129, 1 and 2. *i* L. 128, II., 1. *j* L. 108, 2, and Rem. *k* L. 108, 1, and Rem. *l* L. 111. *m* L. 88, 2. *n* ° L. 107, 2 and Rem.—*Repræsentâbat*, see N. (*i*), p. 61. *s* L. 117, N. 1.

63. *a* L. 109. *b* L. 117, 5. *c* See N. (*r*), p. 34. *d* L. 129, 1 and 2. *e* L. 134, 4. *f* L. 116, 3, and N. *g* L. 103, 1. *h* Infinitives and oblique cases of nouns generally stand before the words on which they depend. *i* L. 128, II., 1. *j* What is the verb of saying on which this subject accusative depends? *k* L. 98. *l* L. 91, 9. *m* L. 118, 1.—*Venâlem*, L. 96, N. 5. *n* L. 92, 1

64. *a* L. 111. *b* L. 44, N. *c* L. 132, 2 and Rem. *d* L. 103, 1. *e* Present participles with *homo, homines*, or the like understood, sometimes supply the place of a noun ending in *tor*, and denoting the *agent*, "the (persons) sacrificing," *i. e.*, "the sacrificers." *f* A Greek accusative, L. 24, 2; and L. G, II., 3. *g* L. 116, 5.— *Thebas*, L. J, 9. *h* L. 110, 1. *i* L. 133, 1 and 2. *j* L. 132, 2 and Rem. *k* L. 117, 5. *l* L. 81, 12.

65. *a* L. 131, 1. *b* L. 103, 2. *c* L. 91. 5. *d* L. 96, 3, and N. 6 *e* L. 111, N. 2. *f* L. 133, 1. *g* L. 110, 1. *h* L. 108, 1. *i* L. 130, and 129, 1.—*Appellandus sis*, L. 121, 6, (*b*). *j* L. 92, 1. *k* "To one who inquired," L. 122, 3. *l Te victôrem renuntiâri*, L. 92, Rem. 2.

66. *a* Sc. *esse*, L. 121, 6 (*b*). *b* L. 95, 5. *c* L. 111. *d* L. 129, 1 and 2. *e* L. 120. *f* L. 101, Rem. 3. *h* L. 99, 4. *i Ne* precedes and *quidem* follows the emphatic word. *j* "Of one about to plunder," L. 91, 4. *k* L. 133, 1.

67. *a* L. 126, 2. *b* See note on *quantum—tantum*, p. 55. *c* L. 133, 1.—*Monentibus eum quibusdam*, "when certain persons cautioned him." L. 124, 5. *d* L. 133, 1 and 2. *e Alienâtus* is usually followed by the *abl.* with a preposition, but here takes a dative. *f* L. 128, II., 1. *g* See N. (*h*), p. 44. *h* L. 131, 1 and (*a*).—*Pythiam vocâtum*, "having called Pythias," L. 120, N. 3.—*Acceptâ*

PAGE

difficultāte, "when he had learned the embarrassment," &c ᴸ
122, 5 and 6. ⁱ L. 117, 2. ʲ L. 119, 1. ˡ L. 95, N. 5. ᵐ L. 95,
N. 4. ⁿ A predicate adjective, L. 92, 2. ᵒ L. 117, 1. ᵖ L. 105,
3. ⁱ L. 109.—*Verbis*, L. 117, 1. ˢ " For which," L. 97, 5.—*Contigit*, what is its subject? ᵗ *Fore* is used impersonally, its subject
being the remaining words in the period, L. 81, 8 and 9.—*Dignus*, L. 92, 2. ᵘ L. 116, 2.

. *Puer*, "while a boy," L. 89, R. ᵃ L. 115. ᵇ L. 116, 4. ᶜ L. 68.
109. ᵈ L. 134, 3. ᵉ L. 110, 1. ᶠ *Asiā debellātā*, " after his conquest of Asia," L. 120, N. 2. ᵍ L. 97, 1. ʰ L. 117, 2. ⁱ L. 88,
2.—*Quo audīto*, "when Alexander heard this," L. 120, N. 2, or
N. 3. ʲ L. 133, 1 and 2. ᵏ L. 126, 1. ˡ L. 104. ᵐ L. 126, 2.
ⁿ L. 106, Rem. 4. ᵒ L. 106, Rem. 2. ᵖ L. 108, R. 1.

ᵃ L. 117, 2.—*Ab ejus nomine*, " after his name."—*Propositis*, L. 69.
120, N. 3. ᵇ L. 134, 3.—*Tottus*. L. 2, Exc.—*Senex* "when old."
ᶜ L. 117, 4. ᵈ L. 108, 1. ᵉ L. 96, 3.—*Factum est*, impersonal:
what is its subject? *Pompeio*, pronounced, *Pom-pē'yo*. ᶠ L. 133,
1 and 2. ᵍ L. 103, 1. ʰ L. 116, 2.—*Arcessitos*, L. 120, N. 3, or
L. 122, 8. ⁱ L. 134, 3. ʲ L. 103, N. 2.—*Defecisset*, L. 131, 1 and
(a). ᵏ L. 119, 3. ˡ L. 121, 4, (b).

ᵃ L. 117, 3. ᵇ L. 89, 3. ᶜ *Per medios ignes*, " through the midst 70.
of the fires," L. 91, 8.—*Cum periculo*, " at the risk." ᵈ L. 128, II.,
1. ᵉ L. 111. ᶠ L. 95, 4. ᵍ " That it afforded him," &c. L. 114, and
N. 1 : *esse* being used impersonally, its subject is the clause *quàd
patria*, &c., L. 81, 8. ʰ " His," L. 127, IV. ⁱ " Than he," L.
119, 1.—What is the object of *didicĕrat?* L. 96, Rem. 2. ʲ L.
103, 1. ᵏ L. 117, 2.—*Inspectante populo*, "in view of the people,"
L. 120, N. 2. ˡ L. 132, 1. ᵐ L. 121, 6, (b).

ᵃ L. 111. ᵇ *Instandum esse* is used impersonally; supply *nobis*, 71
&c., " that we ought to pursue," L. 112, 2, and Rems. (a) and (c),
and L. 121, 6, (b). ᶜ *Cedo* takes the ablative of a place with *de*,
ex, or without a preposition, L. 108, R. 2. ᵈ L. 131, 1 and (a).—
Corintho captā, " by the capture of Corinth," L. 120, N. 2. ᵉ L.
117, 2. ᶠ L. 103, N. 2.—*Eo defuncto*, " after his death," L. 120,
N. 2.—*Non esset unde*, " there was no property from which." ᵍ L.
134, 4. † L. 128, 2. ʰ L. 95, N. 4. ⁱ L. 99, Rem. 4. ʲ L. 81, N.
2.—*Acceptis—recuperāto*, L. 120, N. 3.—*Ad suos*, L. 91, N. 4. ᵏ L
109.—*Jussas*, " ordered five cohorts," &c., *misit*, " and sent them,"
L. 122, 8. ˡ L. 123 5.—*Receptum iri*, " should be taken back," L.
95, N. 3: the future inf. passive, consists of the former supine
and *iri*, the present inf. pass. of *eo*, to go, L. 74, N. 2.

PAGE

72. *L. 89, (k).* **¹** L. 105, 4.—*Cæsos,* "after they had been beaten," L. 122, 5 and 6: or, " to be beaten," L. 122, 8. *L. G, I., 3, and L. H, 3. *L. 101. ƒ What is the subject of *accĭdit?* L. 81, 8 and 9. *L. 108, R. 2. ʰ L. 117, 2. ʲ The accusative is the usual construction, according to L. 96, Rem. 4: the ablative here appears to depend on the preposition *in* understood. ʰ L. 117, 2.

73. *L. 96, Rem. 3. ¹ L. 38, 8.—*Carpetanōrum,* L. 103, 1. *L. 109. ᵈ L. 133, 1 and 2. *L. 128, I. ƒ L. 97, 4.

ROMAN HISTORY.

74. *L. 91, 9. ¹ L. 96, 3.—*Sub hoc rege,* "in his reign."—*Hinc,* i. e., *ex Trojâ.* *L. 117, N. 2. ᵈ L. 110.—*Ei benignè recepto,* "received him kindly (and)." L. 122, 8. *L. 96, 2.

75. *Lit. "until Rome founded," i. e., "until the founding of Rome." L. 121, 5, (b). ¹ L. 108, 1. *L. 119, 1. ᵈ "Used to say." L. 47, N. 2. *Sc. *est.* ƒ L. 89, 3. *L. 103, 1. ʰ *Minor natu,* lit., "less or inferior in respect of birth," i. e., "born later, younger," L. 117, 5. ¹ L. 129, 1 and 2. ʲ L. 128, I.—*Rheam Silviam—Vestālem virgĭnem,* L. 96, 2. ʲ L. 110, 1.—*Geminos filios, Romŭlum et Remum,* L. 89, 3. ¹ L. 91, 5, and L. 94, N. 2. ᵐ L. 121, 6, (a).

76. *L. 129, 1 and 2. ¹ L. 97, 4. *L. 109. ᵈ In construction *venissent* follows *rapuěrunt,* L. 135, 2. *ƒ L. 133, 1 and 2. *The reflexive referring, as usual, to the leading subject. ʰ L. 128, II., 1. ¹ L. 97, 2 and 3, *et ea,* "these also." ʲ L. 91, 8, *raptæ,* see § 9.

77. *See Dict. under *cùm.* ¹ L. 121, 9. *Ortam,* "which had arisen," L. 122, 3. ᵈ L. 111.—*Quo elapso,* "after this had passed," or, "at the expiration of this," L. 94, 5; and L. 120, N. 2. *L. 108, 1. ƒ *Quidem* following the emphatic word. *Repeated past action. ʰ L. 96, N. 4. ¹ L. 117, N. 2. ʲ L. 117, 5. ʲ L. 109.

78. *L. 111, N. 2. ¹ L. 104. *L. 111. ᵈ *Gentium* limits *senatōres* understood. *A* or *ab* denotes the *doer,* (L. 99, N.) *per* signifies "by means of," "at the instigation of," L. 97, N. ƒ L. 116, 3. *L. 110, 1.

79. *L. 97, 4. ¹ L. 132.—*Sed benè,* &c. The adversative *sed* (L. 82, (3.)) is opposed to the fraudulent manner of obtaining the

crown implied in the preceding *sic.—Cum his,* " including those."
* L. 111. *d* L. 108, 2, and Rem.—*Prima salutāvit,* " first saluted,"
i. e., " was the first to salute," L. 91, 9. *e* " As king," L. 96, 2.
f L. 103, 1. *g* " Herself." *h In,* " for." *i* L. 110, 1.—*Ei* " against
him."

a L. 108, 1. *b Regnātum est,* " the kingdom continued," or, " the 80.
regal government lasted," L. 81, 12. *c* L. 131, 1. *d* " After the
banishment of the kings," *i. e.,* of Tarquin and his sons, L. 120,
N. 2. *e* L. 111, N. 2. *f* L. 133, 1 and 2.—*Qui quum,* " and when
he," L. 94, 5. *g* L. 132, 1. *h* L. 101, and Rem. 2.

a L. 117, 1.—*Terrēret,* " was trying to terrify." The imperfect 81.
tense not unfrequently denotes an attempt to perform an action,
L. 47. N. 2. *c* Supply *suam,* L. 91, 6. *d* L. 111. *e* L. 132, 1. *f* L.
49, Rem. 2. *g* " After the banishment of the kings," L. 121, 5,
(*b*). *h* L. 108, 1. *i* L. 128, II., 1.—*Eam,* " them," referring to
plebem, a collective noun, L. 5, 4. L. 133, 1 and 2.—*Iis* refers to
plebem, but instead of agreeing with it, like the preceding *eam,*
is put in the plural referring to the individuals which the noun
denotes. See L. 91, 3.—*Alia,* L. 91, 5. *j* L. 133, 1. *k* L. 121, 9,
and L. 92, 1 and (*b*). *l* L. 89, 1. *m* L. 99, Rem. 4.—*Ad quintum
milliarium urbis,* lit., " to the fifth milestone from the city."

a Quo facto, lit., " this having been done," L. 94, 5; or, " having 82.
done this," L. 120, N. 3: it may also be translated, " because he
had done this," L. 122, 5 and 6; *i. e.,* " for doing this," or finally,
" for this." *a* L. 88, 2. *b* " Under the command of Fabius," L.
120, Rem., and N. 2. *c* L. 116, 4. *d* L. 122, 3. *e Ille,* " *the celebrated* Q. Fabius Maximus, who," &c., L. 42, N. 2. *f* See *alter*
in Dict.—*Ab urbe conditâ,* see N. (*f*), p. 81. *g* L. 133, 1 and 2.
h L. 111, N. 2.—*Manibus post tergum vinctis,* " after tying his
hands," &c., L. 120, N. 2 and 3.

a L. 108, 2. *b* L. 122, 6, (*a*). *c* L. 133, 1 and 2.—*Urbem,* sc. *suam.* 83.
d L. 114. *e* L. 128, II., 1. *f* Supply *est* from below. *g* L. 49,
Rem. 2. *h In eo,* see *is* in Dict. *i Præsidium* which is used as a
collective noun takes in its own clause a verb in the singular,
but in the following clauses the verbs are in the plural, L. 90, 4.
j L. 38, 3. *k* L. 108, R. 2. *l* L. 101. *m* L. 117, 4. *n* L. 117, 2.

a L. 117, 5. *b* Depending on *sedit,* L. 109, but to be translated 84.
as if it were *ejus,* L. 109, R. 2. *c* L. 117, 1. *d* This verb with its
clause is the subject of *factum est.* *e* L. 109. *f* L. 110. *g* L. 117,
N. 1. *h* L. 105, 4. *i* L. 95, 3. *k* Supply *esse;* for the translation
see L 121, 6, (*b*). *l* L. 129, 1 and 2. *m* L. 121, 6, (*b*).

85. *a* L. 111.—*Fecissent*, L. 128, II., 1 and N. 2. *b* L. 96, 3. *c* L. 128, I. *d* L. 38, 8. *e* A conditional sentence, in which the condition is implied in *ego cum talibus viris*, " if I had such men;" and the conclusion, " I could with them," &c., is fully expressed, L. 131, 1, and (*a*). *f* L. 123, 4.

86. *a* L. 131, 1. *b* L. 117, 1. *c* L. 127, I. *d* See *alter* in Dict. *e* Supply *esse*.

87. *a* L. 120, R. and N. 2. *b* L. H, 1. *c* L. 103, 1.—*Perditis*, " having lost," or " after losing," L. 120, N. 3; L. 122, 6; *i. e.*, " with the loss." *d* L. 96, 3, and N. 6. *e* L. 110. *f* L 118. *g* L. 127, II. *h* L. 133, 1 and 2. *i* L. 127, N. 1. *j* L. 106, 1 and R. 1.

88. *a* L. 103. *b* L. 99, R. 4. *c* As a verb, *parata fuisse* has, for its logical subject, *millia* with its connected words; as a noun, the same verb with its clause is the subject of the impersonal *traditum est*, L. 95, 2, 3 and 4. *d* L. 118, 2. *e* L. 81, 10, 11 and 12.

89. *a* Per, " by means of." *b* L. 98. *c* The infinitive and oblique cases usually stand before the words on which they depend. *d* L. 133, 1 and 2. *e* *Mando* in the active voice takes the acc. and the dat.; hence in the passive it retains the dative, L. 124, 4; *mandaretur* is used impersonally, and in English the subject is the dative *Hannibali*, L. 81, N. 2.—*Fratre—relicto*, " leaving his brother," L. 120, N. 3. *f* L. 111, N. 1.—*Commisso—accepto*, L. 120, N. 3.—*Superat*, the historical present, used instead of the historical perfect. So *vincitur*, above.

90. *a* See N. (*c*), p. 88. *b* L. 104. *c* L. 92. *d* The antecedent of *quod* is the clause *servi manumissi*, &c., " which thing was never done before," L. 94, N. 2. *e* L. 110. *f* L. 96, R. 2.—*A senatu*, L. 81, 12.—*Potuissent*, L. 128, I. *h* L. 133, 1 and 2. *i* L. 133, and 7.

91. *a* L. 103, 1.—*Recepta*, L. 120, N. 3. *b* L. A, 11. *c* L. A, Exc. 2. *d* " When a boy." So *juvenis* below, L. 89, R. *e* Partitive adjectives commonly agree in gender with the individuals, of which the genitive plural depending on them consists, and in respect to their case, they are to be parsed like nouns: hence *multos* is in the masculine gender, agreeing in this respect with *juvenum*, and in the accusative after *deterruit*. *h* L. 95, 5, and N. 5.—*Aurum* sc. *suum*. *i* " Their."

92. *a* Used like *plusquam*. *b* L. 118, R. 2. *c* What is to be supplied ? *d* L. 117, 1. *e* L. 133, 1 and 2.

93. *a* ' As a hostage ' L. 89, R. *b* L. 89, 1. *d* Sc *est*. *e* L. 103, 1.

f Cum is often used with the ablative of manner, when accompanied by an adjective.

a L. 101. *b* L. 108, R. 2. *c Alter* for *secundus*. *d* " From the building of the city," L. 121, 5, (*b*). *f* " Though defended," L. 122, 2. **94.**

a L. 89, 1. *b* L. 91, N. 4. † L. 81, 3. **95.**

Coss., L. 120, R. and N. 2. *a* L. 128, II., 1. *b* L. 110, 1. *c* L. 108, 1. *d* L. 133, 4. *e* L. 92, 1. **96.**

a L. 81, 10, 11 and 12. *b* L. 112, N. 2. *c* See *cùm* in Dict. *d* L. 117, N. 2. *e Id quod*, "the thing which:" *id* stands for the idea contained in the clause *jus civitâtis*, &c. *f* L. 133, 1 and 2,—*Relictâ*, L. 120, N. 3. **97.**

a L. 103, N. 2.—*Eversa*, L. 120, N. 3. *b* L. 117, 2. *c* L. 121, 5, (*b*). *d* L. 120, N. 2. *f* L. 96, 2. *g* L. 120, N. 3. *h* L. 108, 2. **98.**

a L. 111.—*Ipse*, sc. *Lucullus.*—*Eum*, sc. *Mithridâtem.*—*Consumptum* can be translated passively, as agreeing with *Mithridâtem*, the object of the verb, or actively with *Lucullus*, its subject. *b* L. 102, 2. *c* L. 118, 2. *d* " Under the command of," L. 120, R. and N. 2. *e* L. 108, 1. *f* L. 119, 2. *g* L. 100, R. 2. **99.**

a L, 109, R. 1. *b* L. 134, 1 and 3. *c* L. 108, R. 2. *d* L. 101. *e* L. 98. *f* " He, the former," L. 42, 1 and 2. *g* L. 46, R. 2. *h* " To him," *i. e.*, to Pompey. *i* L. 105, 4. *k* L. 117, 2. *l* L. 128, II., 1. **100.**

b L. 99, R. 4. *c* L. 117, 1, and L. 123, 3. *d* L. 118, 2. **101.**

Quem, sc. *consulâtum*. *a* The imperfect, denoting that which was proposed, or on the point of being done, L. 47, N. 2. *b* " It was opposed," L. 81, 9. *c* L. 101. *d* L. 81, 10, 11 and 12. **102.**

Insolentiùs, L. 119, N. 3. *a* L. 81, 10, 11 and 12.—*Interfecto Cæsâre*, L. 122, 6. *b* L. 110, 1. *c* L. 109, R. 1. *d* L. 121, 4. *e* L. 101. **103.**

a L. 91, N. 3, and L. 122, 8. *b Ipse*, in such sentences, may agree either with the subject or the case depending on the verb, according as either is intended to be emphatic. **104.**

ANCIENT GEOGRAPHY.

PAGE

105. *ᵃ* L. 89, 3. *ᵇ* " Aʃ boundaries," L. 96, N. 4. *ᶜ* A Greek ᵃᶜcusative.

106. *ᵃ* L. 132, 2. *ᵇ* L. H, 2. *ᶜᵈ* L. 117, 3 and 5. *ᵉ* L. 111. *ᶠ* "You would believe," or, "one would think." *ᵍ* L. 104. *ʰ* L. 116, 5.

107. *Qui, quæ se,* &c., i. e., *ea, quæ.* *ᵃ* L. 109, R. 5. *ᵇ Quanto—tanto,* L. 119, 3. *ᶜ* L. 109, R. 4. *ᵈ* L. 91, 4. *ᵉ* Supply the preposition *a.* *ᶠ* L. 111. *ᵍ* L. 109, and L. 123, 3 and 4. *ʰ* L. H, 1. *ⁱ* L. 98. *ʲ* L. 97, 4.

108. *ᵃ* L. 117, 1, and L. 123, 3. *ᵇ* L. 100, and L. 123, 3. *ᶜ* L. 109, R. 5. *ᵈ Morāri* is the subject of *esse* understood, L. 95, 4 ; and *periculōsum* agrees with *morāri,* L. 91, 7. *ᵉ* L. 109. *ᶠ* L. 110, 1. *ᵍ* L. 103, N. 2. *ʰ* L. 98.

109. *Probabile est.* The two preceding infinitive clauses are the subject of this predicate, L. 95, 4, and L. 91, 7. *ᵃ* "The reign of Clauʊius," L. 120, N. 2. *ᵇ* L. 117, 5. *ᶜ* L. 119, 1. *ᵈ* L. 116, 5. *ᵉ* L. 117, 2. *ᶠ* L. 119, 3. *ᵍ* In such expressions the comparative is to be translated by the positive degree, "than it is wide," *i. e.,* "its length far exceeds its breadth." *ⁱ* L. 109. *ʲ* "And there is clearly no other," &c.

110. *ᵃ* L. 134, 4. *ᵇ* " Of that kind." *Genus* with *id, hoc, quod,* &c , is put in the accusative without a preposition. *ᶜ* L. 111. *ᵈ* L. 90, N. 3. *ᵉ* L. 117, 3. *ᶠ* L. 132, 2.

111. *ᵃ* L. 117, 5.—What is the logical subject of *verisimile est?* *ᵇ* L. 111, N. 2. *ᶜ* L. 109.—*Jactum fuĕrit,* L. 127, II.

112. *ᵃ* L. 129, 1 and 2.—What is the logical subject of *appāret?* *ᵇ* L. 108, R. 2. *ᵈ* L. 110, 1. *ᵉ* L. 90, N. 3. *ᶠ* L. 103, 2. *ᵍ* L. 117, 5. *ʰ* L. 104. *ⁱ* L. 42, 1. *ʲ* L. 111, N. 2.

113. *ᵃ Significāsse* depends on *fama est,* which is equivalent to a verb of saying, L. 95, 1. *ᵇ* Like the old English expression, "at what time," for, "at the time when," or, "in which." *ᶜ* L. 108, 1. *ᵈ* L. 134, 3. *ᵉ* L. 117, 5. *ᶠ* "By means of which." *ᵍ* See note (*ᵇ*), page 104.

114. *ᵃ* What is the subject? L. 32, 1. *ᶜ* L. 109.—*Viderētur,* L. 134, 3. *ᵈ* L. 90, N. 3. *ᵉ* L. 81, 10, 11 and 12. *ᶠ* L. 117, 5. *ᵍ* L. 129, 1 and 2. *ʰ* L. 108, 2.

115. *Col æret,* sc. *ea,* i. e., *Peloponnēsus.* *ᵃ* L. 91, 8. *ᵇ* L. 11, 2 ar. 3. *ᵉ* " Which they call ;" both the subject of *appellant* and its object are to be supplied. *Opibus—copiis*, L. 117, 5. *c* "As colonists," L. 96, N. 4. *Ebŏre*, L. 22, R. 4 and (*d*). *Facta*, sc. *est*, L. 90, N. 3. *d* L. 123, 4 and 5. *e* L. 81, 10, 11 and 12. *Res gestas suas numĕrat*, " their memorable occurrences," which they reckoned by Olympiads, or periods of four years, the time which intervened between the celebration of the Olympic games. *f* L. 90, 3 and R. 2. *g* L. 117, 5. *Pluresque;* the English idiom requires that *que* should here be translated "or." *h* The comparative and superlative of *prope*, viz., *propiùs* and *proximè*, are followed by either the accusative or the dative. *i* " They say."

a L. 103, 1. *b* L. 111. *c* L. 95, 4, and L. 81, 8. *d* L. 134, 4. **116.** *Aristotĕlem*, L. 127, I. *e* L. 127, II. *f* L. 126, 2.

Vino, L. 117, 5. *Nominibus—moribus;* why in the ablative? **117.** *a* L. 109, R. 5. *Contendo*, with the *acc. id*, signifies, "to strive eagerly for this." *Mercēde datâ*, L. 121, 5, (*b*). *c Cùm—tum*, see *cùm* in Dict. *Rerum—copiâ;* the genitive separated by a relative clause from the noun which it limits. *d* L. 117, 5. *Herûs*, L. C, o. *Post Trojam dirūtam*, L. 121, 5, (*b*). *Zone*, sc., *nomen habet*.

a L. 91, 8. *b* L. 117, 2. *c* L. 134, 4. *d* L. 119, 3. *e Quis* **118.** after the particles, *si, ne, neu, ubi, nisi, num, quo, quanto* and *quum*, signifies " some one," or, " any one." *f* L. 116, 5. *g* L. 119, 1. *h* L. 91, N. 4. *Maxima fluminum*, L. 103, 1; the adjective on which a partitive genitive depends, commonly, as here, agrees in gender with the following genitive, rather than with the noun or nouns which it limits, unless it follows the latter. *i* " We have spoken," L. 81, 11 and 12.

a L. 123, 9. *b* L. 24, 2. *c* See N. (*), p. 115. *c* L. 117, 3. **119.** *d* L. 118, 2. *Sine*, " free from, exempt from." *e f* L. 107, 2 and N. *Beatissimum*, L. 96, 2, and N. 5. *Locis*, L. 117, 4. *Eōus*, sc. *Oceănus*. *Asiæ nomine*, &c. In English the relative clause often separates the principal subject from its predicate. *g* L. 97, N. *Stadia*, L. 98.

a L. 109. *b* L. 101. *c Homines* is often to be supplied with **120.** verbs of *saying*, &c., and to be translated " people, men," &c., or simply, " they." *d* L. 131, (*d*). *Asia propria dictæ*, i. e., of Asia Minor. *e* "Clearly, unquestionably." *f* A noun is often annexed to a relative for the purpose of explaining its antecedent. *g* L. 111. *h* L. 101, R. 1. *Numĕro*, L. 117, 5. *Altitudine*, L. 101; a genitive (*sexaginta pedum*) supplies the

PAGE

place of the adjective in limiting *altitudīne :* see Andrews and Stoddard's Lat. Gr. § 211, R. 6, (1).

121. *L. 90, N. 3. *L. 109. *L. 104. *L. 116, 4. *Issici,* se. *sinûs,* "the Issic gulf" *L. 101. *Sc. *se,* L. 96, N. 3. *L. 133, 1. *L. 81, 10 and 11. *Those who are entering, L. 91, 4.

122. *L. 91, 4, and 122, 3. *L. 90, N. 3. *L. 45, R. 2. *Cum terra conjuncta,* "joined to the mainland." *L. 81, 10 and 11. *L. 133, 1, and L. 134, 1 and N. 1. *L. 116, 5. *Primus e Romānis,* L. 103, N. 2. *Bactriānæ,* sc. *camēli.* In this passage from the 8th book of Pliny, *camēlus* is feminine, but in the best authors it is always masculine. *Tubēra,* L. B, er. *L. 117, 3. *L. G, I., 2.

123. *Bibant,* L. 132, 1. *L. 98: so above, *quatriduo.* *"A hundred each,"* L. 38, 4. *L. 117, 2. *L. 119, 3. *L. 97, 4. *This genitive limits *ambitu.* *See note on *altitudīne,* p. 120. *L. 89, 1. *L. 103, 1. *L. 95, 4. *L. 119, 1. *L. 91, 7.

124. *L. 99, R. 4. *L. 117, 2. *L. 91, 3. *L. 90, 4. *Nefas,* sc. *esse,* the predicate of the two preceding infinitive clauses taken as subjects. *L. 116, 5. *Arēnis,* L. 111. *L. 119, N. 3. *Natu,* L. 117, 5.

125. *Transitūri,* L. 122, 2, and L. 121, 4, (a). *L. 103, N. 2. *L. 103, 1. *L. 81, 4. *Crura,* L. F, Exc. in Decl. us. *L. 113: so above, *dentibus.* *"They cover."* *Navigāre* is sometimes used actively, in the sense of *sailing over,* when it is followed by *oceānum, æquor,* &c.; the expression here used by Pliny, *insūlas navigāre,* appears to be peculiar, and to signify, to sail or carry on navigation among the islands. *Id* stands for the idea in the preceding clause and hence is neuter, L. 91, 7.

126. *Centēna.* Why is the distributive number used? *Omnium,* L. 103, 1. *Sibi similes,* "like each other." *L. 111. *L. 95, 4. *Uniōnes,* L. D, io. *Arābas,* L. I, acc. plur. 2. *L. 104, and R. 3. *L. I, gen. plur. 6. *"This thing, this fact,"* *i. e.,* its fertility, L. 91, 7.

127. *Usu,* L. 117, 3. *L. 110, 4. *L. 101. *The place of the adjective with the limiting noun is supplied by a genitive, see note on *altitudīne,* p. 120. *L. 118, 2. *Memphin,* L. G, I., 1.

128. *Pedum quindĕcim millium.* This is wholly erroneous. The slant height of the largest pyramid is variously estimated, from 600 to 800 feet. *Centum duos,* supply *et. Peaum centum,* etc.,

L. 101, R. 1. *L. 117, 2, see N. (*), p. 129. *L. 90, N. 3. *L. 123, 5. *L. 81, 10 and 11. *L. 123, 2. *Pergămi*. Parchment was sometimes called *charta Pergamēna*, because invented at Pergămus; in this sentence, *Pergămi* does not depend on *membrānas*, but is the genitive of place, L. 108, 1.

*L. 95, 4 and 1. *Mersum*, L. 122, 4, or 8. *Supply thus: **129.** [*Apim*] *altĕrum* [*thalămum*] *intrâsse lætum est; in altĕro* [*ille*] *dira portendit*, "To have entered the one is, &c., [by being] in the other he," &c. *Canunt*, L. 90, 4. *L. 103, 1. *L. 117, 2; with the names of materials *of* is used rather than *with*.

Alia ejusmŏdi signa maris—effūsi. Two genitives depend on **130.** *signa:—maris effūsi*, "of the sea having extended." *L. 90, R. 2. *L. 81, 8. *Convenissent*, L. 128, I. *L. 127, II.

Potus est lac—cibus caro; which are the subject-nominatives? **131.** *in specŭbus*, L. 26, 4. *L. 113. *Ipse* in such sentences is put in the nominative or in the accusative, according as the subject or the object is emphatic. See N. (*), p. 104. *The preterite tenses of *nosco* are used like the same tenses of *odi* and *memini*, L. 81, 4. *L. 111.

Vicĕnûm for *vicenôrum*, see L. 11, R. 4. **132.**

EXERCISES.

THE following are given merely as examples of exercises in orthography and etymology, and can be varied by the teacher at his pleasure. Their object is to secure a perfect knowledge of all those parts of the grammar which relate to the forms of words and their division into syllables. These exercises can be easily imitated by the student who commences with the larger grammar.

I. 1. Write down the nominative singular of all nouns and adjectives of the first declension, found on the eleventh page of the Reader.

(a) If any of these nouns are excepted in gender or declension, write opposite to them a reference to the passage in the F.rst Latin Book, if such can be found, where the exception is mentioned: thus,

Eurōpa,	culpa,	terra,
peninsŭla,	tua,	rotunda,
poēta, *m.* L. 5, I.	mora,	amicitia,
inertia,	nulla, L. 32, 1 and 2,	vera,
insania,	via,	sempīterna.
sylva,	parva,	

(*b*) Mark the quantity of the penult in each word, making use for this purpose of the general rules of quantity in Lesson 3, and of the dictionary, when no rule can be found.

(*c*) Mark the accented syllable in each word according to Lesson 2, 4 and 5.

(*d*) Divide each word into syllables, according to Lesson 2, 1; and Lesson A; putting a point between the syllables, and repeating from memory the rule for the division of each syllable. Thus e. g. say, " Eurōpa has three syllables, because " (here repeat Less. 2, 1) " It is thus divided, *Eu-ro'-pa;* for *p* must be joined to the last vowel, because " (here repeat Less. A, 1.); and *r* must be joined to the penult, because," (repeat Less. A, 3.)

2. Prepare a similar exercise on each of the following pages to page 30.

II. 1. Write down the nominative singular of all nouns and adjectives of the second declension found on page 11, marking the gender of each, and referring for exceptions in gender or declension to the First Latin Book, thus:

vitium, *n.*	annus, *m.*
electus, *m.* L. 91, 1.	dirum, *n.* L. 91, 1.
Quintius, *m.* L. 9, Exc. 3.	bellum, *n.*
Fabius, *m.* L. 9, Exc. 3.	

2. Finish this exercise like the preceding one according to (*b*), (*c*) and (*d*).

3. Prepare a similar exercise on each of the following pages to page 30.

III. Write down the nominative singular of all nouns and adjectives of the third declension found on page 11.

(*a*) Mark the gender of each noun and the rule or exception on which its gender or genitive depends, thus:

os, *n.* L. B, os : L. C, os.
lapis, *m.* L. D, is : L. E, is.
homo, *c.* L. 5, N. 3 : L. C, o.
ebriĕtas, *f.* L. 15, 1 : L. 16, 1.
dux, *c.* L. 5, N. 3 : L. 17, 2.
fugax, *m.* L. 91,1 : L. 28, 2 : L. 37, 2.
vetus, *f.* L. 91,1. L. 37, 1 & 2 : abl. sing. *e*, L. 37, Exc.

irreparabĭle, *n.* L. 91, 1 : L. 35.
tempus, *n.* L. 18, 2, and 4.
glaciālis, *f.* L. 91, 1 : L. 35.
hiems, *f.* L. 15,1 : L. 17,1 and N.
brevis, *f.* See glaciālis.
voluptas, *f.* See ebriĕtas.

(*b*) Write the root of each of the preceding wcrds, and from the root form the nominative singular by Lessons 22 and 23, giving the same rules for the adjectives as for the nouns, thus :

Lapid, by L. 22, I., (which repeat) becomes *lapids*, by Remark 1, (which repeat) it becomes *lapis*.

Fugac, by L. 22, I., becomes *fugacs*, i. e., by Remark 2, *fugax*.

(*c*) Mark the quantity and the accented syllable of each of these nouns and adjectives, and divide them into syllables according to the modes pointed out in the first exercise (*b*), (*c*) and (*d*).

2. Prepare a similar exercise on each of the following pages to p. 30.

IV. Write the nouns of the 4th and 5th declensions, found on the 11th, 12th and 13th pages, and prepare them in all respects as directed in the first and second exercises.

2. Do the same with each three of the succeeding pages to page 30.

V. 1. Write the first person singular, in the indicative mood present tense, of each verb on the 11th page, separating the four conjugations and also the irregular verbs; thus,

1. salūto, 2. —— 3. elĭgo, 4. venio. *irr.* sum, L. 62.
   sto,   fugio, L. 74, N. 1.   fio. L. 79.
   paro.   cresco,
                     labor, dep. L. 75.

2. Repeat from memory the *principal parts* of each, as set down in the Dictionary.

3. Repeat all the *roots* of each verb; thus, *salut, salūtav salūtat :—st, stet, stat, &c.*

4. Do the same with each of the following pages to page 30.

VI. 1. Write in separate columns, according to their kind, all the particles found on pages 12, 13 and 14.

Conjunctions.	*Adverbs.*		*Prepositions.*
et, L. 82, (1).	semper,	diu,	a, L. 99.
-que, L. 82, (1) & (4).	non,	quotannis,	inter, L. 97, 1.
atque, L. 82, (1).	interdum,	minime, L. 82, 3 & 4.	
neque, L. 82, (1).	citiùs, L. 82, 3 & 4.	bene,	
	serius, L. 82, 3 & 4.	longè,	
	nunquam,	quàm,	
	diligentissìme, L. 82, 3 and 4.		

Do the same with each three pages following, to page 30

Lightning Source UK Ltd.
Milton Keynes UK
UKHW020739261118
332983UK00008B/417/P